Revisiting Minjung

perspectives on CONTEMPORARY KOREA

SERIES EDITORS: NOJIN KWAK AND YOUNGJU RYU

Perspectives on Contemporary Korea is devoted to scholarship that advances the understanding of critical issues in contemporary Korean society, culture, politics, and economy. The series is sponsored by The Nam Center for Korean Studies at the University of Michigan.

Hallyu 2.0: The Korean Wave in the Age of Social Media
  Sangjoon Lee and Abé Mark Nornes, editors

Smartland Korea: Mobile Communication, Culture, and Society
  Dal Yong Jin

Transgression in Korea: Beyond Resistance and Control
  Juhn Y. Ahn, editor

Cultures of Yusin: South Korea in the 1970s
  Youngju Ryu, editor

Entrepreneurial Seoulite: Culture and Subjectivity in Hongdae, Seoul
  Mihye Cho

Revisiting Minjung: New Perspectives on the Cultural History of 1980s South Korea
  Sunyoung Park, editor

Revisiting Minjung

New Perspectives on the Cultural History of 1980s South Korea

Edited by Sunyoung Park

UNIVERSITY OF MICHIGAN PRESS
Ann Arbor

Copyright © 2019 by Sunyoung Park
All rights reserved

This book may not be reproduced, in whole or in part, including illustrations, in any form (beyond that copying permitted by Sections 107 and 108 of the U.S. Copyright Law and except by reviewers for the public press), without written permission from the publisher.

Published in the United States of America by the
University of Michigan Press
Manufactured in the United States of America
Printed on acid-free paper
First published March 2019

A CIP catalog record for this book is available from the British Library.

Library of Congress Cataloging-in-Publication Data

Names: Park, Sunyoung, 1971– editor.
Title: Revisiting minjung : new perspectives on the cultural history of 1980s South Korea / edited by Sunyoung Park.
Description: Ann Arbor : University of Michigan Press, 2019. | Series: Perspectives on contemporary Korea | Includes bibliographical references and index. |
Identifiers: LCCN 2018052339 (print) | LCCN 2019001119 (ebook) | ISBN 9780472125159 (E-book) | ISBN 9780472074129 (hardcover : alk. paper) | ISBN 9780472054121 (pbk. : alk. paper)
Subjects: LCSH: Korea (South)—Civilization—20th century. | Populism—Korea (South)—History—20th century. | Social movements—Korea (South)
Classification: LCC DS922.27 (ebook) | LCC DS922.27 .R48 2019 (print) | DDC 951.9504/4—dc23
LC record available at https://lccn.loc.gov/2018052339

This work was supported by the Academy of Korean Studies (KSPS) Grant funded by the Korean Government (MOE) (AKS-2011-BAA-2102).

Cover: "Tide of Candles," by Lim Ok-Sang. Courtesy of the artist.

Contents

Acknowledgments   vii

Introduction   1
   Sunyoung Park

Part I. The 1980s in Korean History and Memory

1. Social Memories of the 1980s: Unpacking the Regime of Discontinuity   17
   Namhee Lee

2. The Irrepressibility of Teleology: The 1980s as Historiography   46
   Kyung Moon Hwang

Part II. Transnationalism

3. In Search of Alternative Modernity: The 1980s in South Korean Intellectual History   65
   Jae-Yong Kim

4. Political Travel at Cold War's End: International Student Exchanges between Australia and the Two Koreas   85
   Ruth Barraclough

5. Exhibiting Minjung Art Abroad: Tokyo, New York, and Pyongyang in the Twilight of the Cold War   103
   Sohl Lee

Part III. New Labor Culture

6. Where Have All the "Shouting Stones" Gone? South Korean Workers' Literary Clubs and Labor Literature, 1970s–1990s   129
    Jung-Hwan Cheon

7. Indie before Indie: Minjung Song in the History of South Korean Popular Music   149
    Chang Nam Kim

Part IV. Intersectional Feminism

8. Bright Constellation: The Rise and Significance of Women's Liberation Literature in 1980s South Korea   169
    Hye-Ryoung Lee

9. Queering the Dreams of a Third-World Brotherhood: Black Women in Early 1980s South Korean Literature and Film   195
    Kyunghee Eo

Part V. Popular Culture

10. Between Progression and Regression: Ero Film as Cinema of Retreat   223
    Yun-Jong Lee

11. Reciprocal Assets: Science Fiction and Democratization in 1980s South Korea   247
    Sunyoung Park

Afterword   275
    Jin-kyung Lee

Contributors   289

Index   293

Digital materials related to this title can be found on the Fulcrum platform vis the following citable URL: https://doi.org/10.3998/mpub.10027900

Acknowledgments

This book is the fruit of more than four years of collaborative research and conference activity among a group of scholars based in Korea, Australia, and the United States. An initial conference was held at Sungkyunkwan University, South Korea, in November 2013, focusing on 1980s labor literature and its relation to the process of democratization. It was followed by a panel on Korea's proletarian culture at the annual meeting of the Association for Asian Studies in Philadelphia (May 2014) and by a second Sungkyunkwan conference on 1980s cultural history (November 2014). Finally, a two-day workshop called New Perspectives on the Cultural History of 1980s South Korea took place in November 2015 at the University of Southern California in Los Angeles. It was there that the essays appearing here were first presented and then subjected to commentary and communal discussion. One of the highlights of the meetings was the participation of scholars who personally lived through the political and cultural activism during the 1980s in South Korea. As their essays show, the testimonial contribution of writers such as Ruth Barraclough, Chang Nam Kim, and Jae-Yong Kim plays an important role in providing an experiential basis to a more nuanced account of the decade.

Chapters 3, 6, 7, and 8 have been translated from the Korean by Sunyoung Park. Three of these chapters rely on materials that have previously appeared in Korean: Jung-Hwan Cheon's essay in chapter 6 is an abridged version of "Kŭ mantŏn 'oech'inŭn tolmaengi'dŭl ŭn ŏdiro kassŭlkka: 1980-90-yŏndae Han'guk nodongja munhakhoe wa nodongja munhak," in *Yŏksa pip'yŏng* 106 (2014): 173–205; Chang Nam Kim's study in chapter 7 is an updated version of "Minjung kayo ŭi taejung ŭmaksajŏk ŭiŭi," in *Minjok munhwa nonch'ong* 35 (2007): 55–81; and Hye-Ryoung Lee's essay in chapter 8 has appeared in an earlier version as "Pinnanŭn sŏngjwadŭl: 1980-yŏndae, yŏsŏng haebang munhak ŭi t'ansaeng," in *Sanghŏ hakpo* 47 (2016): 411–57. All three essays have been substantially revised and updated for their inclusion in this volume.

Several institutions deserve thanks for their financial and organizational support of the meetings and workshops. They include the Korea Foundation via the Northeast Asia Council of the Association for Asian Studies, the Academy of East Asian Studies at Sungkyunkwan University, and multiple departments and centers at the University of Southern California, including the Center for Feminist Research, the Department of East Asian Languages and Cultures, the Department of History, the East Asian Studies Center, the Korean Heritage Library, the Korean Studies Institute, and the School of Cinematic Arts.

Also important were the contributions of many individuals at various stages of the book's production. Alice Echols, Viet Nguyen, and Akira Lippit all generously supported the November 2015 workshop at USC. Also contributing in different capacities to this group project were Joy Kim and Sun-Yoon Lee, the Korean studies librarians at USC, and the administrators of USC's East Asian Languages and Cultures Department, Brianna Correa and Christine Shaw. At the University of Michigan, Nojin Kwak and Youngju Ryu have encouraged and supported the project, while Christopher Dreyer has been always reliable and patient in his role as the acquisitions editor for Asian Studies at the University of Michigan Press. The contributors to this volume are also grateful to two anonymous reviewers at the press for their detailed feedback. Many thanks are also owed to the volume's copyeditors, Katie Van Heest at Tweed Academic Editing and John Raymond for the University of Michigan Press. Last but not least, artist Lim Ok-Sang graciously allowed the use on the cover of his celebrated painting, *Kwangjang e, sŏ* (Tide of candles; 2017).

All Korean names and words that appear in this volume are transliterated according to the McCune-Reischauer romanization system. An exception is made for the names of historical and cultural figures (presidents, writers, film makers, and other artists) that are already known in different English spellings, in which case the existing transliteration is used. In the notes, English names are given by the family name, but Korean names are written out in full at their first mention to avoid confusion, except for when they are listed as a coauthor or coeditor along with an English name. Also, in the reference lists, the indication of the publication venue is omitted from the books that were published in Seoul—the majority of Korean references.

Introduction

Sunyoung Park

Globally marked by the end of the Cold War, the 1980s was the decade that transformed South Korea from a long-standing military dictatorship into a vibrant civil democracy. The ruling order established by Park Chung Hee in 1961 finally came to an end on June 29, 1987, when Roh Tae Woo, then the presidential candidate of the ruling party, announced a series of conciliatory measures under the pressure of citizens demonstrating on the streets. Included in his announcement were the adoption of general presidential elections, the release of political prisoners, and the expansion of freedom of speech. In winning these concessions, the dissident forces known as the *minjung*—a broad alliance of laborers, students, intellectuals, religious activists, and oppositional politicians—decisively claimed a central role for civil society in Korean politics and public affairs. Their victory was as much political as it was cultural, and it came on the heels of an intense process of ideological legitimation that was rooted in the activism of the early 1970s. By the late 1980s, what would come to be known as *minjung* culture had become ascendant in ways that rendered its political implementation almost inevitable.[1]

The term *minjung* (the people) was first popularized in the 1920s by Sin Ch'aeho, an anarchist-nationalist revolutionary and scholar who pioneered modern historiography in colonial Korea.[2] The term, however, gained its contemporary activist currency only in the 1980s, when it started to be used by dissident intellectuals as an alternative to the more narrow and theoretical concept of "proletariat." To this day, *minjung* connotes in Korean public discourse the counterhegemonic masses and, in Namhee Lee's words, "those who are oppressed in the sociopolitical system but who are capable of rising up against it."[3] A competing term, *simin* (citizen), was introduced even earlier, in the late nineteenth century, along with Western republicanism and in the context of the national reform movement of late Chosŏn Korea (1392–1910). Lacking the revolutionary echo of the French concept of *citoyen*, however, the term languished on the margins of public discourse until the early 1990s, when a constellation of civic associations and nongovernmental organizations came into being in the wake of democratization. In adopting the term *simin*, the members of these organizations strived to distinguish their own social activism from that of the minjung movement, often in critique of the minjung's alleged ethnonationalist and Marxist excesses.

Their later fortunes aside, the paradigms of minjung politics and culture played a defining role in the 1980s. The decade started with a military coup d'état led by General Chun Doo Hwan on December 12, 1979, in the aftermath of President Park Chung Hee's assassination on October 26. The coup was met with nationwide demonstrations invoking democracy, and tensions came to a head in the provincial city of Kwangju on May 18, 1980. There, the military deployed special forces in brutal combat that left hundreds of civilians dead and thousands more injured.[4] In order to dampen public reaction to the bloodshed, the regime implemented a series of oppressive measures of "purification" (*sunhwa*) and "purge" (*sukchŏng*), including the establishment of the notorious Samchŏng Re-education Camp (1980–81) to which tens of thousands of citizens were consigned. Censorship was intensified, journalists were forcibly laid off, and opposition leaders were imprisoned. These measures temporarily succeeded in restoring the status quo, but in the long run they also served to galvanize the resistance. In current historiography, almost forty years after the events, the massacre in Kwangju and its ghastly aftermath are widely regarded as the decisive, unleashing moments of South Korea's democratization. The progressive movement had certainly been building momentum well before Kwangju, and during the 1970s it had made strides in the vindication of the rights of dissident intellectuals and labor union workers. It was only after 1980, however, that prodemocracy forces grew into a mass movement around which the whole nation could eventually come together.[5]

What was set in motion in 1980 came to its fulfillment in 1987 through another fateful chain of events. In January of that year, a university student and activist named Pak Chongchŏl was tortured and killed during an interrogation in the Seoul offices of the Agency of National Security Planning. The subsequent efforts to keep the death secret backfired when the event was leaked to the press, setting up a mediatic clamor that would go unabated for weeks. Soon demonstrations against the regime, which had already become quite common, started getting bigger and more focused on the demand for democratization. The public's indignation grew even stronger on April 13, 1987, when Chun Doo Hwan rejected the opposition party's legislative proposal for popular (as opposed to indirect) election of the president. Finally, on June 5, another student, Yi Hanyŏl, was killed by riot police during a demonstration at Yonsei University. What followed were three weeks of historic demonstrations in major Korean cities, culminating on June 10 in the gathering of 1.5 million people in front of City Hall in Seoul. Chun reacted by ordering the deployment of the army, but he was immediately forced to take a step back by the opposition of the United States.[6] On June 29 the regime buckled, and presidential candidate Roh Tae Woo announced the release of political prisoners as well as the concession of constitutional and electoral reform.

Laying the groundwork for political developments had been a broader context of protest and unrest at multiple levels of South Korean society. The year 1985 had witnessed the so-called Kuro Solidarity Strike, in which about 2,500 workers at factories in the Kuro district laid down their tools for an unprecedented general strike that lasted six days. The strikers were joined by students and prodemocracy groups, as workers' struggles represented in many ways a twin cause to that of democratization. In June 1986, a female student-turned-labor activist named Kwon Insuk publicly denounced the sexual molestation that she had suffered while in the custody of the police. The ensuing scandal and trial gave momentum to the rising feminist movement, and February 1987 saw the formation of the Korean Union of Women's Associations (Han'guk yŏsŏng tanch'e yŏnhap). Earlier mobilizations had taken place among farmers, who in 1984 rose up in Chŏlla Province against government neglect and market liberalization, as well as among the urban poor who around that time resisted the authorities' cynical plans of "urban beautification." Between 1983 and 1986, a protest campaign was sustained by the squatters and low-rent dwellers of the Seoul district of Moktong. They eventually had to leave, but once again, the violence and bullying employed by the government further tarnished its image in the eyes of the South Korean public.[7]

What would come to be known as "minjung culture" was in many ways a response to the extraordinary challenges of this era. In taking to the streets to protest dictatorship, labor exploitation, gender violence, and police abuse, South Korean citizens were symbolically designating themselves—the people—as the rightful subjects of their country's history. The demand for people's sovereignty came in this way to be constitutive of minjung activism, and it also became the common thematic thread among cultural texts across the fields of literature, poetry, film, theater, and more.[8] From Cho Chŏngnae's epic novel *The Taebaek Mountains* (*T'aebaek sanmaek*; 1983–89) and Pak Nohae's poems in *Dawn of Labor* (*Nodong ŭi saebyŏk*; 1984) to Pak Kwangsu's cinematic satire *Chilsu and Mansu* (*Ch'ilsu wa Mansu*; 1988), the most representative works of minjung culture engaged in a wide-ranging remapping of the national past and present. Against the slowly crumbling order of an oppressive regime, these and other works gave ordinary South Koreans a glimpse of an alternate reality that was finally in reach via a process of historical reappropriation.

In the years immediately following democratization in 1987, some of the products of 1980s minjung culture achieved national prominence as reference points for the whole of South Korea's progressive movement. Ironically, in this process of canonization, works that once symbolized change and political urgency became established and celebrated as monuments to the country's epochal turn to democracy. Not surprisingly, minjung culture also became a field of contention and a polemical target for the conservative reaction led by New Right intellectuals. In other words, the culture of the 1980s remarkably became even more political—and politicized—in the following decades. Minjung writers, filmmakers, and artists found themselves invested with the role of guardians of the memory of 1980s activism, and with it they often became the supposed carriers of the democratizing spirit. Today still, recollection of the 1980s in South Korea is often associated with controversy, historical recrimination, and the inescapability of politics. It is a testament to the centrality of the 1980s that contemporary Koreans are in this way still trapped by, if not in, that decade. And it speaks to the relevance of minjung culture that, as time goes by and historians get to work, looking back has become ever more interesting, urgent, and complicated.

Revisiting minjung culture today means, first and foremost, bringing new themes, new subjectivities, and new theoretical perspectives to the study of one of the most crucial eras in South Korean history. The decade of the 1980s is nowadays rightly celebrated in Korea as a momentous turning point, a time when a collective effort by ordinary citizens finally brought forth democratization. It is precisely because of its topical political importance, however, that scholarly treatments of the decade have tended to emphasize narratives of upheaval and liberation to the detriment of other complexities and contradictions. On the one hand, the frequent focus on political events has marginalized alternative themes such as economic development, social change, and the flourishing of culture amid the introduction of new media and technology. On the other hand, the centering of minjung intellectuals as the agents of democratization has led to a neglect of the contributions of other groups such as workers, women, everyday citizens, and artists outside the intellectual mainstream. The result has been a frequent bracketing of the 1980s as an ideologically saturated time of crisis in Korean history, an anomalous era whose social and cultural atmosphere holds little relevance to the subsequent decades of globalization and postdemocracy. Promoted in varying degrees by both disillusioned minjung intellectuals and conservatives, this "regime of discontinuity" has discouraged the study of 1980s culture and, in the process, it has turned the decade into a blind spot in contemporary Korean cultural studies.[9]

Each in its own way, the essays collected in this book aim at promoting an appreciation and an evaluation of the diversity of social, intellectual, and artistic formations that made up the rich ecosystem of 1980s South Korean culture. The volume as a whole strives for an expansion and reinterpretation of its subject matter by doing three main things. First, it embeds cultural history within a historiographical framework that highlights the discontinuous and heavily teleological narratives that affect today's memory of the 1980s. Second, it deploys the new theoretical lenses of transnationalism, new labor culture, intersectional feminism, and popular culture to reveal alternative narratives and hitherto unexplored aspects of the decade. Third, it combines a multitheoretical approach with an interdisciplinary one, drawing critical insights from fields as diverse as cultural history, social history, literature, film, art, music, gender studies, and historiography. While pursuing these directions of research, the essays presented here also trace the continuities, transformations, and ruptures between the culture of the 1970s and that of the 1980s, the 1980s and the 1990s, and beyond. They thus display the diversity of 1980s South Korean culture along with its living relevance. Far from being an anomalous and now faded era of activism that is disjointed from globalization and contemporary life, the minjung era was a time of vibrant political and cultural energy that enabled the flourishing of democratic culture and society on the Korean Peninsula.[10]

The volume articulates its intervention in Korean cultural history in five main parts. Part I provides an analytical and historiographical foundation by examining the current location of minjung and 1980s culture in both the official and popular memory of the era. In chapter 1, Namhee Lee takes interest in the displacement and reification of the minjung movement in post-1980s social memories. In examining the imposition of a "regime of discontinuity" between the 1980s and the rest of Korean history, Lee offers a wide-ranging analysis of conservative cultural politics as a reaction to the values of the democratization movement. Central elements of this regime, she observes, were the perpetuation of Cold War enmity toward North Korea, the quasi-hagiographic recuperation of the figure of Park Chung Hee, and the ideologically motivated attempt at introducing alternative, revisionist textbooks that purportedly render a "more objective" account of Korean history. As Lee argues, behind the creation and sustenance of this powerful ideological formation are cultural gatekeepers such as writers, political commentators, and journalists affiliated with a powerful circle of conservative media. Propped up by them, the regime of discontinuity induces a form of social amnesia that has long marginalized the 1980s within South Korean political as well as cultural debates.

Keeping the focus on the historiographical memory of the 1980s, Kyung Moon Hwang offers in chapter 2 an analysis of retrospective accounts of 1980s South Korea in both English and Korean scholarship. As Hwang shows, contemporary left-leaning historians tend to project a pessimistic view of democratization as a time of missed social and political opportunities, in an assessment that is very much influenced by current debates about inequality at multiple levels of Korean society. By contrast, conservative scholars have rather leaned toward a triumphalist representation of the era as a culmination of the advancement of neoliberal values and capitalism in South Korea. Commenting on this polarized historiographical scenario, Hwang details the ways in which both camps are in effect projecting alternative teleological frameworks in their analysis of salient events from the decade. This breach of historical methodology, however, may be understandable, Hwang suggests, given South Korea's charged political atmosphere and the ongoing significance of the 1980s in public memory.

Taken together, chapters 1 and 2 provide the context for a revisionary look at culture in 1980s South Korea. Part II then opens up to cultural history by contesting the ethnonationalist characterization of the minjung movement and by bringing to light the transnational circulation of ideas and people that made the movement possible. In chapter 3, Jae-Yong Kim traces the evolution of progressive thought in Korea with special attention to the transnational connections that in many ways shaped it. As Kim shows, early and mid-twentieth-century Korean intellectuals hoped in vain that either the United States or the Soviet Union would steer away from the imperialist politics that had characterized Europe since the nineteenth century. In their frustrated quest for an alternative anti-imperialist modernity, many South Korean intellectuals turned in the 1980s toward the discourse of Third World literature and the politics of nonalignment that came from Africa, Asia, and Latin America. Kim argues, in a spirit that is at once personal and generational, that Third World discourse has provided South Koreans with a promising avenue of ideological regeneration ever since its introduction by minjung intellectuals in the early 1980s.

Kim's essay offers a rare assessment of international influences over minjung ideology, and in this it finds an important echo in Ruth Barraclough's contribution in chapter 4. Hers too is a cultural-historical reflection interestingly filtered through the lens of autobiography and recollection.[11] Centered around her own political travel to South Korea in the summer of 1989, Barraclough's essay opens a window onto the hitherto little publicized networks of travel and communication among Christian leftist organizations in Australia, South Korea, North Korea, and elsewhere. Barraclough mobilizes concepts such as "cosmopolitanism from below" and "horizontal solidarity" to characterize the often clandestine international activism of this era of early globalization at Cold War's end, bringing to bear as well the experience of British youth's travels to apartheid South Africa and the extraordinary event of the International Youth Festival in Pyongyang, North Korea, in August 1989. As her essay makes clear, student exchanges such as these had a deeply symbolic function in the cultural politics of their time. Barraclough reports, among other things, about the scandal that followed upon the appearance of Lim Sukyung, a South Korean female student activist, at the Pyongyang festival in 1989.

Expanding the volume's reflection on 1980s culture in a transnational perspective, Sohl Lee offers in chapter 5 a rare account and assessment of the exhibitions of minjung art that took place in Japan, the United States, and North Korea between 1986 and 1989. In a refreshing revision of previous domestic-centered narratives, Lee's essay shows how the art of the democratization movement was from the start characterized by a strong international vocation, as artists and activists themselves saw exposure to foreign audiences as an important cultural and political tactic. The essay reconstructs vividly the debates that surrounded the exhibitions in Tokyo, New York, and Pyongyang, and in the process it provides insights into global and globalizing artistic debates at the end of the Cold War. As Lee argues, the international encounters of and with minjung art were often marked by misunderstandings and the difficulties of cultural translation. They were also moments of growth for the democratization movement as a whole, however, and through these exhibitions the works themselves took on new meanings that reverberated powerfully on the domestic as well as the international scenes.

Part III moves on to two contributions that, following recent trends in South Korean cultural criticism, may be fittingly brought under the label of "new labor culture." Both scholars featured here are active in the ongoing recuperation of worker-centered culture in South Korea. In chapter 6, Jung-Hwan Cheon excavates the archives of factories and workers' associations to produce a groundbreaking survey of literature written by laborers between the 1970s and the 1990s. As Cheon argues, the period in question was marked by an epochal alliance between industrial workers and college student activists, which led to a movement for proletarian literacy that considerably affected the Korean cultural world. A proliferation of workers' reading groups, writing workshops, night schools, and literary festivals meant that many laborers gained access to the world of literature even when they had received but scarce formal education in their childhood. Cheon's outline takes readers through the historical stages of the literary movement, starting with its autonomous beginnings within 1970s labor organizations, through the peak of collaboration of laborers and students in the 1980s, and ending with the rapid dispersion of the activist spirit in the postdemocratization era.

An analogous tale of artistic appropriation, this time focused on activist music, is provided by Chang Nam Kim in chapter 7. As Kim argues, workers' strikes and student gatherings in the late 1970s were the social locus for the formation of a thriving scene of minjung activist song. Kim thus surveys the evolution of this genre within the broader context of the history of popular music in South Korea. As he shows, the assumed opposition between the two genres is belied by a side-by-side comparison of their contextual as well as musical features—from their similar business models, to their shared audiences, and on to the common trove of rhythms and melodies from which they both drew. According to Kim, we should see minjung song as an integral part of the history of mainstream popular music, indeed a very important one. In the terse negotiation of cultural freedom that accompanied South Korea's democratization process, Kim shows, minjung singers were the first to challenge state censorship and, relatedly, they were the first to introduce socially critical lyrics to the thematic palette of popular music.

Women were an active social group in 1980s South Korea, yet their contributions to the decade's cultural landscape remain little acknowledged today. Part IV reexamines women's cultural agency and their accomplishments in the decade through the analytical lens of intersectional feminism.[12] Hye-Ryoung Lee offers in chapter 8 a comprehensive, extended overview of women's social and cultural activism during the 1980s, a time she sees as marking a "rebirth" of South Korean women's literature. As Lee writes, women writers, intellectuals, students, and workers reshaped the then traditionally gendered institution of women's literature (yŏryu munhak) into the more activist form of "female liberation literature" (yŏsŏng haebang munhak). Through a close reading of Pak Wansŏ's "An Episode from Bygone Days" (Chŏmun nal ŭi saphwa), Lee shows how this harrowing tale of battered housewives successfully recasts the issue of domestic violence from a private family affair into a human rights concern. It is an example of the increased political awareness of 1980s women's cultural production, and with it an attestation of intersectionality in the vivid description of the protagonist's investment in the male-dominated process of democratization.

Moving from women's agency to their representation, chapter 9 offers a penetrating analysis of 1980s African American and South Asian female characters across genres as diverse as the Vietnam War novel, camptown prostitution literature, and erotic film. As Kyunghee Eo shows, the period's minjung theorization of a Third World anticolonial alliance was often at odds with an ethnonationalist masculinist ethos that saw Third World women as, essentially, exotic sexual commodities. Paradoxically, Eo reveals, a more respectful and empowering representation of different races, genders, and sexualities was to be found in popular culture rather than in high literature and academia. The chapter thus features among others a pathbreaking analysis of two black female characters—a lesbian G.I. and a badass nightclub hostess—whose striking diversity epitomizes otherness as much as it attests to a desire to disrupt rigid racist, patriarchal, and heteronormative assumptions within 1980s South Korean culture.

In a volume devoted to revisiting minjung culture, a look at its assumed historical foil—mainstream popular culture—is bound to yield some surprises. Indeed, as the essays in Part V show, activist resistant culture and "conformist" popular culture were never as separate as was believed to be the case. In chapter 10 Yun-Jong Lee offers a revisionary reading of a historically dismissed chapter of 1980s Korean popular culture: the erotic ("ero") cinema that achieved considerable success from the early decade through the mid-1990s. Locating the ero films in the lineage of the international soft-porn trend as well as 1970s hostess films, Lee proposes to reconceptualize ero film as "a cinema of retreat." Through her overview of the genre's history and themes, she shows how these erotic fantasies, which were also the survival strategy of a politically censored film industry, reflected a socially widespread desire of withdrawal from the dehumanizing experience of South Korea's militarized modernization. Seen in this light, the ero cinema of the 1980s acquires a symptomatic significance as part of the same cultural and political environment that expressed minjung culture. Short of being a conformist opposite of social engagement, Lee suggestively argues, this subculture of sexual spectacles may be more fittingly read as an individualist stance that equally resists the authoritarian encroachment upon both men and women's lives.

Part V closes with a contribution by Sunyoung Park, whose essay in chapter 11 probes the hitherto unexplored relation between the pop-cultural genre of science fiction and the political process of democratization in 1980s South Korea. Focusing her analysis on one of the decade's classic science fictional works—Bok Geo-il's novel *In Search of an Epitaph* (*Pimyŏng ŭl ch'ajasŏ*; 1987)—Park envisions 1980s science fiction in South Korea at once as an active reappropriation of a Western (especially Anglo-American) genre and as an autochthonous creation that responded to local tradition and conditions. As she argues, Bok's novel is especially interesting when read against the background of the period's minjung politics and culture, of whose ethos and values it can be seen as a speculative fictional representation. As much as Bok's book upheld the ideals of the democratization movement, Park suggests, it can also be said that it was the time's intense political activism that lent gravitas and urgency to the genre of science fiction, which had until then commanded little respect from literati and general readers alike.

In her afterword to the volume, Jin-kyung Lee broadens our focus on the 1980s by placing the decade in the context of what she identifies as "the 1960s–1980s authoritarian era." She thus proceeds to offer a fascinating rereading of the ideological dynamics of these decades. The linkage between the state and the ethnonation (*minjok*) during the early authoritarian era, Lee argues, profoundly influenced the *minjok*/minjung dissident movement, which positioned itself against state nationalism and yet retained the emphasis on the ethnonation. The minjung thus created a new intellectual hegemony that rendered invisible categories and social formations such as class, race, gender, immigrant labor, and more. An operation of literary recanonization, Lee concludes, should take its cue from these elisions and exclusions in order to forge a path forward for progressive cultural politics now and in the future.

On November 12, 2016, hundreds of thousands of South Koreans gathered in central Seoul to demand the resignation of President Park Geun

Hye, who had come to power three years earlier partly due to the enduring aura of her father Park Chung Hee. The assembly represented the largest demonstration in South Korean history since the epoch-making turn of June 1987.[13] As one news website commented, the event and the subsequent months-long protests reminded South Koreans as well as international observers of that profound platitude: that history sometimes does repeat itself.[14] Beyond attesting to the continuing relevance of the political experience of the 1980s, the recent demonstrations speak volumes to the way in which a culture of democratization has taken root in South Korea. Hagen Koo once noted that the strength of South Korean democracy lies not "in the multiplicity of independent civic organizations or in the existence of powerful social classes but in a stubborn and resistant political culture and a latent mobilizational capacity of civil society."[15] Neither such enduring counterculture nor a mass mobilization is, or ever was, possible without internal conflicts and tensions in which old and new ideas ceaselessly confront each other. If the authors of this volume have a collective aspiration, it is not to pass any definitive judgment on the 1980s. Rather, the aspiration is to explore and open up new avenues of research in the study of one of the most significant decades of modern Korean history, in the process contributing what little we can to the ongoing struggle for democracy and the continual rejuvenation of South Korean democratic culture.

NOTES

1. For the historical account of the 1980s democratization movement, see Namhee Lee, *The Making of Minjung*; Wells, ed., *South Korea's Minjung Movement*; and Minjuhwa undong kinyŏm sahŏphoe, *Han'guk minjuhwa undongsa 3*.
2. For the terminological origin of *minjung*, see also Em, "*Minjok* as a Modern and Democratic Construct."
3. Lee, *The Making of Minjung*, 5. A key moment in the 1980s repurposing of the term came in April 1984 with the founding of the Council of the Minjung Cultural Movement (Minjung munhwa undong hyŏbŭihoe) by a group of dissident intellectuals across the fields of religion, literature, film, drama, and fine arts.
4. Gi-Wook Shin and Kyung Moon Hwang, eds., *Contentious Kwangju*, xvii.
5. For the history of 1970s social and cultural movements, see Barraclough, *Factory Girl Literature*; Paul Chang, *Protest Dialectics*; Hwasook Nam, *Building Ships, Building a Nation*; and Youngju Ryu, *Writers of the Winter Republic*. For scholarship in English about the uprising in Kwangju and its repression, see Shin and Hwang, eds., *Contentious Kwangju*. It is worth noting that the heavily censored events in Kwangju found *perforce* little cultural representation in the early 1980s. That began to change in 1985 with the publication of the (immediately banned) book *Kwangju Diary: Beyond Death and the Darkness of Age* (Chugŭm ŭl nŏmŏ, sidae ŭi ŏdum ŭl nŏmŏ), edited by the Chŏnnam

sahoe undong hyŏbŭihoe (Council of Social Movements in the South Chŏlla Province). For the representations of Kwangju in Korean popular music, literature, and film, see Chŏng Yuha, *Kŭraedo uri nŭn norae handa*; Kang Jin-ho, "5.18 kwa hyŏndae sosŏl"; and Kyung Hyun Kim, "Post-Trauma and Historical Remembrance in *A Single Spark and A Petal*," in *The Remasculinization of Korean Cinema*, 107–35.

6. For the U.S. responses to the 1980s Korean democratization movement, see Adesnik and Kim, "South Korea: The Puzzle of Two Transitions," 283–85.

7. Key documents of the 1980s social movements are available in English translation in Namhee Lee and Kim Won, eds., *The South Korean Democratization Movement*. Workers' struggles are recounted in Lee, *The Making of Minjung*, as well as Hagen Koo, *Korean Workers*. The women's movement is addressed in Louie, *Minjung Feminism*. For farmers' protests, see Abelmann, *Echoes of the Past*. For urban redeployment disputes, see Porteux and Kim, "Public Orders and Private Coercion." See also Seungsook Moon, *Militarized Modernity and Gendered Citizenship in South Korea*, chapter 4.

8. For the role of the *maddanggŭk* (folk theater) in the minjung movement, see Lee, *The Making of Minjung*, 187–212, and Chungmoo Choi, "The Minjung Culture Movement." For the minjung literature and film movements, see Hyun-moo Choi, "Contemporary Korean Literature," and Nam Lee, "Repatriation and the History of Korean Documentary Filmmaking."

9. Illustrative of the effects of this discursive discontinuity is the near absence of the 1980s from *The Korean Popular Culture Reader* (2014), edited by Kyung Hyun Kim and Youngmin Choe, a volume that otherwise offers an impressive coverage of popular culture in modern Korea through the decades. Within the field of social science, by contrast, a spotlight on the 1980s has been shone by many of the contributors to *South Korean Social Movements* (2011), edited by Gi-Wook Shin and Paul Y. Chang.

10. In reconsidering the location of 1980s culture in established historical narratives, this volume shares its orientation with recent studies in South Korean scholarship on the subject. See, for instance, Cheon Jung-hwan, "1980-yŏndae munhak, munhwasa yŏn'gu," and Kim Chŏnghan et al., *Sŭp'och'ŭ konghwaguk kwa yangnyŏm t'ongdak*.

11. The partly autobiographical form of Kim's and Barraclough's essays is also offered as a contribution to current debates, as scholars in South Korea have been engaged in the recuperation of the 1980s through both personal and collective memory rather than through the more official registers of national history. See Kim Won, *Memories about the Forgotten* (*Ich'ŏjin kŏttŭl e taehan kiŏk*, 1999, repr. 2011) and Kim Kwiok and Yun Ch'ungno, *Experiences and Memories of the 1980s Democratization Movement* (*1980-yŏndae minjuhwa undong ch'amyŏja ŭi kyŏnghŏm kwa kiŏk*, 2007).

12. See Crenshaw, "Demarginalizing the Intersection of Race and Sex." In Crenshaw's theorization, intersectional feminism is a form of feminism in which the stances of race, class, gender, sexual orientation, and more are compounded as at times conflictual but interrelated facets of women's identities. The concept applies relevantly if retroactively to the women's liberation movement of 1980s Korea, in which identity as a woman was inescapably joined with that of a citizen demanding her rights as well as that of a subject in a neocolonial historical predicament.

13. Choe Sang-Hun, "Protest against South Korean President Estimated to Be Largest Yet," *New York Times*, November 26, 2016.

14. "2016-yŏn 11-wŏl minjung ch'ong kwŏlgi."

15. Hagen Koo, "The State, *Minjung*, and the Working Class," 149.

REFERENCES

"2016-yŏn 11-wŏl minjung ch'ong kwŏlgi" [General popular uprisings of November 2016]. *Namu Wiki*. Accessed December 8, 2016. https://namu.wiki/w/2016년11월 민중 총궐기

Abelmann, Nancy. *Echoes of the Past, Epics of Dissent: A South Korean Social Movement*. Berkeley: University of California Press, 1996.

Adesnik, A. David, and Sunhyuk Kim. "South Korea: The Puzzle of Two Transitions." In *Transitions to Democracy: A Comparative Perspective*, edited by Kathryn Stoner-Weiss and Michael McFaul, 266–89. Baltimore: Johns Hopkins University Press, 2013.

Barraclough, Ruth. *Factory Girl Literature: Sexuality, Violence, and Representation in Industrializing Korea*. Berkeley: University of California Press, 2012.

Chang, Paul Y. *Protest Dialectics: State Repression and South Korea's Democracy Movement, 1970–1979*. Stanford: Stanford University Press, 2015.

Cheon Jung-hwan. "1980-yŏndae munhak, munhwasa yŏn'gu rŭl wihan siron" [A proposal for the study of 1980s literature and cultural history]. *Minjok munhwaksa yŏn'gu* 56 (2014): 389–416.

Choi, Chungmoo. "The Minjung Culture Movement and the Construction of Popular Culture in Korea." In *South Korea's Minjung Movement*, edited by Kenneth M. Wells, 105–18.

Choi, Hyun-moo. "Contemporary Korean Literature: From Victimization to Minjung Nationalism." Translated by Carolyn So. In *South Korea's Minjung Movement*, edited by Kenneth M. Wells, 167–78.

Chŏng Yuha. *Kŭraedo uri nŭn norae handa: Minjung kayo wa 5-wŏl undong iyagi* [Still we sign: Minjung songs and the May movement]. Hanul, 2017.

Chŏnnam sahoe undong hyŏbŭihoe, ed. *Chugŭm ŭl nŏmŏ, sidae ŭi ŏdum ŭl nŏmŏ* [Kwangju diary: Beyond death, beyond the darkness of the age]. P'ulbit, 1985.

Crenshaw, Kimberlé. "Demarginalizing the Intersection of Race and Sex: a Black Feminist Critique of Antidiscrimination Doctrine, Feminist Theory and Antiracist Politics." In "Feminism in the Law: Theory, Practice and Criticism." Special issue, *Chicago Legal Forum* (1989): 139–67.

Em, Henry. "*Minjok* as a Modern and Democratic Construct: Sin Ch'aeho's Historiography." In *Colonial Modernity in Korea*, edited by Gi-Wook Shin and Michael Robinson, 336–61. Cambridge: Harvard University Press, 2001.

Kang Jin-ho. "5.18 kwa hyŏndae sosŏl" [5.18 and contemporary Korean novels]. *Hyŏndae sosŏl yŏn'gu* 64 (2016): 5–33.

Kim Chŏnghan et al., *Sŭp'och'ŭ konghwaguk kwa yangnyŏm t'ongdak* [Sports republic and friend chicken]. Ch'angjak kwa pip'yŏng. 2016.

Kim Kwiok and Yun Ch'ungno. *1980-yŏndae minjuhwa undong ch'amyŏja ŭi kyŏnghŏm kwa kiŏk* [Experiences and memories of the 1980s democratization movement]. Minjuhwa undong kinyŏm saŏphoe, 2007.

Kim, Kyung Hyun. *The Remasculinization of Korean Cinema*. Durham: Duke University Press, 2004.

Kim, Kyung Hyun, and Youngmin Choe, eds. *The Korean Popular Culture Reader*. Durham: Duke University Press, 2014.

Kim Won. *Ich'ŏjin kŏttŭl e taehan kiŏk* [Memories about the forgotten]. Imaejin, 2011 [1999].

Koo, Hagen. *Korean Workers: The Culture and Politics of Class Formation*. Ithaca: Cornell University Press, 2001.

Koo, Hagen. "The State, *Minjung*, and the Working Class in South Korea." In *State and Society in Contemporary Korea*, edited by Hagen Koo, 131–62. Ithaca: Cornell University Press, 1993.

Lee, Nam. "Repatriation and the History of Korean Documentary Filmmaking." *Asian Cinema* 16, no. 1 (2005): 16–27.

Lee, Namhee. "From *Minjung* to *Simin*: The Discursive Shift in Korean Social Movements." In *South Korean Social Movements: From Democracy to Civil Society*, edited by Gi-Wook Shin and Paul Y. Chang, 41–57. New York: Routledge, 2011.

Lee, Namhee. *The Making of Minjung: Democracy and the Politics of Representation in South Korea*. Ithaca: Cornell University Press, 2007.

Lee, Namhee, and Kim Won, eds. *The South Korean Democratization Movement: A Sourcebook*. Sŏngnam: Academy of Korean Studies Press, 2016.

Louie, Miriam Ching Yoon. "*Minjung* Feminism: Korean Women's Movement for Class and Gender Liberation." *Women's Studies International Forum* 18, no. 4 (1995): 417–43.

Minjuhwa undong kinyŏm sahŏphoe Han'guk minjujŭi yŏn'guso [Korean democracy foundation research institute], ed. *Han'guk minjuhwa undongsa 3: Sŏul ŭi pom put'ŏ munmin chŏngbu surip kkaji* [History of Korean democracy: From the spring of Seoul to the establishment of a civil government]. Tolbegae, 2010.

Moon, Seungsook. *Militarized Modernity and Gendered Citizenship in South Korea*. Durham: Duke University Press, 2005.

Nam, Hwasook B. *Building Ships, Building a Nation: Korea's Democratic Unionism under Park Chung Hee*. Seattle: University of Washington Press, 2002.

Porteux, Jonson N., and Sunil Kim. "Public Orders and Private Coercion: Urban Development and Democratization in South Korea." *Journal of East Asian Studies* 16 (2016): 371–90.

Ryu, Youngju, ed. *Cultures of Yusin: South Korea in the 1970s*. Ann Arbor: University of Michigan Press, 2018.

Ryu, Youngju. *Writers of the Winter Republic: Literature and Resistance in Park Chung Hee's Korea*. Honolulu: University of Hawai'i Press, 2015.

Shin, Gi-Wook, and Paul Y. Chang, eds. *South Korean Social Movements: From Democracy to Civil Society*. New York: Routledge, 2011.

Shin, Gi-Wook, and Kyung Moon Hwang, eds. *Contentious Kwangju: The May 18th Uprising in Korea's Past and Present*. New York: Rowman & Littlefield, 2003.

Wells, Kenneth M., ed. *South Korea's Minjung Movement: The Culture and Politics of Dissidence*. Honolulu: University of Hawai'i Press, 1996.

PART I

The 1980s in Korean History and Memory

1

Social Memories of the 1980s

Unpacking the Regime of Discontinuity

Namhee Lee

The *minjung* movement of the 1980s, now almost three decades old, has become defined by its subsequent representations. It is true that there is still no dominant official history, nor an active attempt to assign it a definitive and objective meaning; there might even be a sentiment, at least among historians, that the movement is not sufficiently distant to be summoned up as an object of history, one open to historical inquiry and research. Yet at the same time there has been a proliferation of memories from the previous authoritarian regimes, giving rise to a particular contour of the social memory of its constitutive counterpart, the minjung movement of the 1980s.

The proliferation of, and preoccupation with, memory of an earlier period in the popular culture—and the subsequent reorientation of history as part of a turn to the right in South Korea—constitute what Pierre Nora calls, in a different context, the "regime of discontinuity";[1] that is, scholars, social commentators, and cultural gatekeepers claimed that South Korea had entered a new era and was in the midst of a break with the past.

The regime of discontinuity has multiple levels of historical reference, but for the purposes of this chapter I discuss only three of the most salient ones. The first is obviously South Korea's transition to democracy in the late 1980s and early 1990s: both the civilian government and civil society emphasized the rupture from the previous authoritarian system and the dawning of a new era. A less obvious but perhaps more pervasive kind of regime of discontinuity was the articulation—both explicit and implicit—

that the 1990s represented a rupture from the 1980s. This was the proliferation of a discourse that, through a few ready-made and schematic representations of the 1980s, reduced the decade to an object of either "sentimental remorse or ruthless liquidation." At its core, the discourse of rupture—whether it was to celebrate the transition from the "era of deficiency" to the "era of desires and pleasures,"[2] or, to borrow Ko Misuk's felicitous phrase, "the unbearable lightness of being, freed from the shackles of the [excess of the] ideologies"[3] of the previous era, or something else—was a break from the 1980s and all that it represented.

The third level of discontinuity was the rise of the New Right and, more specifically, the controversy surrounding history textbooks, which became a major intellectual crisis in South Korea—what one might call civil war among intellectuals. Propelled by the unhinging of the Cold War structure and reforms ushered in by the Kim Dae Jung and Roh Moo Hyun governments, the articulation of the rupture from the past also was characterized by what I call a discourse of triumphalism. What are some of the social and political conditions that gave rise to the regime of discontinuity, and how is this being narrated? What are the broad intellectual patterns of this narration, and what contours of social memory of the 1980s minjung movement might emerge from this narration? What might be some of the historical and political implications of the construction of memory in contemporary South Korea? This chapter makes a preliminary foray into exploring these questions by examining the statements, literary works, and historical narratives published by various groups: academics; former movement activists, such as ex-*chusap'a* (*chuch'e sasangp'a*) leaders; cultural gatekeepers, such as novelists; and the mainstream media. My analysis of the construction of social memory is situated in the context of the persistence of the Cold War regime in Korea as well as the global context of rewriting histories of revolutions in the last three decades or so.

The dichotomous representation of the 1980s and the 1990s—with its attendant discourse about paradigm shifts such as from *minjung* (common people) to *simin* (citizen), from the collective to the individual, and from the political to the cultural, all within the context of the worldwide transition to neoliberalism—articulates the double historical displacement of the 1980s: an inability or unwillingness, or even a refusal, to evaluate the decade in its entirety, all of its achievements and failures, as well as the consequent "ossification" of the 1980s.[4] The discourse of the rupture by the New Right is also mostly practiced and functions as a form of social amnesia—the loss of memory propelled by the social and economic dynamic of the society—in the contemporary political, economic, and social constellation. Furthermore, while the proliferation of memory may indicate the fragmentation of history or the decline of the hegemony of the past—"the loss of a single explanatory principle" in Pierre Nora's words—the reconfiguration of memory is bound up with triumphalist discourse and tends to comply with the tendencies of the present and stands as an articulation of contemporary configurations of power.

Persistence of the Cold War Regime

One of the primary constraining social and political conditions in post-1987 South Korea and the enabling factor for the regime of discontinuity is the continuing geopolitics of the Cold War regime. Despite the claim of a total break from the past, the country still maintains the National Security Law (NSL), a most draconian law whose indiscriminate application became one of the principal mechanisms through which the previous authoritarian—and the present, supposedly more liberal—regimes controlled and disciplined society.[5] Throughout the authoritarian era, the democratization movement had vociferously and persistently called for the abolishment of the NSL; since 1987, there has also been widespread agreement on the part of the Korean public on the need to repeal the NSL. That even the governments of Kim Dae Jung and Roh Moo Hyun, widely considered to have been mandated with liberal agendas, could not overturn the NSL speaks volumes about the entrenched power of conservative forces in South Korea.

As late as 2003, the possession and quoting of Karl Marx's *Capital* was a violation of the NSL in South Korea.[6] But a large international conference with superstar intellectuals on communism and Marxism taking place in Seoul a decade later was not. In September 2013, well-known leftist thinkers such as French philosopher Alain Badiou and Slovenian psychoanalytic philosopher Slavoj Žižek were among the participants who discussed leftist philosophy, politics, and art, with Badiou giving a keynote address on the topic. Befitting the image of hypermodern and ever-globalizing South Korea, the conference venue was a military-bunker-cum-art-space called Platoon Kunsthalle, located in Kangnam, "the zone of gaudy consumerism made famous by [the pop musician] Psy."[7] In his closing remarks at the conference, Žižek asked: "It may appear crazy to talk about communism here in South Korea. Is the divided Korea not the clearest imaginable, almost clinical, case of where we stand today *after the end of the Cold War*?"[8] While Žižek's stay in Korea was brief, as befitting a visiting scholar (a "Global Eminent Scholar" at Kyung Hee University), most of the conference attendees were, and still are, living with the reality of unending Cold War Korea. After all, Kangnam is only thirty-five miles away from the DMZ (Demilitarized Zone), the boundary between South Korea and its nemesis to the north.

Not only is the Cold War not over in Korea but, as events surrounding the Korean Peninsula remind us on a daily basis, and as anthropologist Heonik Kwon points out in his book *The Other Cold War*, the Cold War was not cold at all for the vast majority of people outside North America and Europe. This is particularly true in such places as Korea and Vietnam, where the landscapes of war memorials and mass graves are constant reminders of the hot wars that were fought during the Cold War period. Memories of the wars are also seared into the minds of the generations who had to live through them, and these memories remain with the subsequent generations who were affected by the bipolar allegiances the hot wars required.

Yet, as Žižek's comment reminds us, for many in North America and Europe, the Cold War effectively ended in 1989. Moreover, the period of political tension ended with the definitive victory of liberal capitalism over communism, foreclosing multiple assessments of its impact. Again, I quote Heonik Kwon: "When we say the cold war is over, whose cold war and which dimension of the cold war do we refer to? Did the cold war end the same way everywhere, or was the 'struggle for the world' the same everywhere?"[9] As Kwon reminds us, the Cold War never existed in the singular, as much of the postcolonial world experienced it as brutal civil wars and vicious forms of political violence, leading to some forty million casualties throughout the world.

At the turn of the century, the persistence of the Cold War regime in South Korea is manifested in part in the rise of *chongbuk chwap'a*, a term commonly translated as "pro-North leftists." This term denotes not only suspected agents of North Korea but also anyone seen as advocating on behalf of, paying respect to, or willing to work with the North. As Jamie Doucette and Se-Woong Koo note, the way in which *chongbuk* has been coupled with *chwap'a* as a compound term in contemporary conservative discourse "attempts to erase the distinction between what were originally two different concepts, such that in the current political climate the left become synonymous with *chongbuk*, and vice versa."[10] With the continuing geopolitics of the Cold War and the unfinished Korean War, however, the discourse of *chongbuk chwap'a* is most insidious in its amorphousness, as was the case with the anticommunism of South Korea. *Chongbuk chwap'a* has neither a specific target nor a clear geographic boundary; anyone anywhere could be its potential target, as in the case of Shin Eun-mi, a Korean American author.[11]

Much as the politics of anticommunism was borne out of the unrelenting competition with North Korea and the state-building process of eliminating dissent, the politics of *chongbuk chwap'a* initially functioned to discredit groups or individuals associated with the previous governments of Kim Dae Jung and Roh Moo Hyun.[12] Through his "Sunshine Policy" of engaging North Korea through economic assistance and cooperation, Kim had tried to overcome the Cold War politics and promote national reconciliation. His successor, Roh, continued with the Sunshine Policy and carried out reforms that aimed for greater socioeconomic equality and to balance out historically lopsided development patterns. He also took a more independent position vis-à-vis the United States. All of these stances made him emblematic of the aspirations and concern of the "386 generation."[13]

The rise of the politics of *chongbuk chwap'a* and the New Right were in part due to conservative forces' recognition of their loss of any monopoly on state power, which they had held from the inception of the Republic of Korea. This dynamic was in part a generational conflict between those whose life trajectories paralleled the rising fortunes of South Korea from the ashes of the Korean War and those who came of age during the democratic transformation of the 1980s, who tended to be more progressive on political, social, and economic issues, more reconciliatory to North Korea, and more independent-minded regarding South Korea's relations with the United States. On the other hand, these developments were part of a triumphal discourse that gave primacy to economic development over redistributive justice, that prioritized gaining personal wealth over a collective future, and, most seriously, that involved a willful ordering of the disappearance of North Korea, whose divergent trajectory from South Korea symbolized the North's failure as a civilization, which then justified its anticipated demise.

Among the politicians and intellectuals associated with the conservative bloc as well as those who call themselves the New Right, post-1987 reform politics, especially that of the governments of Kim Dae Jung and Roh Moo Hyun, are considered to belong to a period of leftist aberration—what they call the "lost ten years." Given that the conservatives had dominated state power for most of the post-1945 period, including the immediate post-1987 period, the successive loss of the two presidencies to the leftists was indeed a big shock and a rude awakening. The New Right's project of cleansing the state of the leftist legacy of previous reform governments was not, however, simply a lament of defeatism or despair. It was also the triumphalist cry of neoliberalism. I return to this point later in the chapter.

The "Failure" of Revolutions

The rise of the New Right in South Korea, and its attendant discourse of triumphalism, must be situated within the broader cultural framework of the shift from authoritarianism to parliamentary democracy and the breakdown of socialism, within which the New Right was first articulated. South Korea's transition from an authoritarian dictatorship to a parliamentary democracy in the late 1980s occurred concurrently with the breakdown of the socialism that existed in Eastern Europe. The worldwide transformation heralded a concomitant demise of the left and Marxist social theory and of political Marxism, which has also resulted in questioning the premises of modernity and in the rise of postmodernity. As I write elsewhere,[14] postmodernity—defined more specifically here as "social philosophy"—has posed a "formidable challenge" to social movements and theorists alike.[15] This was especially so given the centrality of socialism and liberalism in modern political and social thought—socialism was successful in terms of intellectual attraction and public support during the twentieth century. Sociologist Jeffrey Alexander finds in the "demoralization and uncertainty of the left in the aftermath of late 1960s and early 70s euphoria" a possible source for the attraction toward postmodernity. That is, postmodern theory might have been seen by many of the former leftists who embraced postmodernity "as an attempt to redress the problem of meaning created by the experienced failure of 'the sixties.'"[16]

This "problem of meaning" created by the failure of the sixties has also been fed on the discourse of that "failure"—the academic community's discrediting of revolutionary experiences and revolutionary discourse worldwide. Beginning from François Furet's revisionist work on the French Revolution to a German sociologist's claim that "nothing happened in France in 1968," as well as the charge of "excess" in the Chinese Cultural Revolution (a charge that tends to apply to the Chinese Revolution as a whole), the discourse of failure has had profound consequences in the appraisal of modernity, whose history is inseparable from the history of revolutions. This discourse of failure, as historian Arif Dirlik argues, not only "calls into question one of the founding moments of modernity," but also "cast[s] doubt on all revolutions, regardless of political orientation, and the aspirations and visions that endowed revolutionary change with meaning."[17] One of the unintended consequences is to "deprive revolution of its social legitimation—its claim, in other words, that it was a product of social forces and gave voice to the aspirations of the oppressed in society. Revolution appears now as a political act that may even have gone against deepest social aspirations."[18]

In fact, a strong "anti-1968" discourse, as well as systematic repression of its memory by the establishment, has been on the rise as a whole. In France, Germany, and the United States, the vision of 1968 is associated with moral stagnation and social decline and is seen as responsible for the many social ills that beset contemporary societies. The upheavals of 1968 are seen to have triggered a spiral of decline, "marking the descent from the moral certainties of the post-war period to a new phase of moral turpitude, permissiveness and social violence."[19] In the United States, the conservatives' lament that all of society's problems—"identity politics, political correctness, the collapse of the nuclear family, a perversion of sexual mores, a decline in civility, and disregard for the law"[20]—began in the sixties conveniently forgets that institutional racism and social injustice gave rise to the civil rights movement and antiwar movement, which were as vital a part of the sixties as the countercultural movements that conservatives so passionately denounce.

The political establishment has tried to appropriate the memories of 1968 in order to serve vested political interests.[21] The Republican Party in the United States has portrayed all Democratic presidential candidates since 1984 as children of the sixties unfit to hold public office because their liberal viewpoints would only do more harm to the country.[22] During the 2007 presidential election in France, candidate Nicolas Sarkozy launched a fierce attack on the "moral and intellectual permissiveness" of May 1968: he accused the heirs of that historical moment of being responsible for all French ills—"the demise of tradition, the undermining of authority and even the making of an 'unethical capitalism.'"[23]

In academia as well, in the triumphalist neoliberal climate of the early 1990s, following the breakdown of the Soviet Union and "actually existing socialism," there was a surge of recharged anti-Bolshevism. A strictly political reading of 1917 became reinstated in academic writings as well: according to this reading, Bolshevism may have been an opportunistic product of the mass disorder of the First World War, but the later violence of Soviet history came only from the dictatorial utopianism of Bolshevik ideology, "always already inscribed in the very idea of trying to make a revolution in the first place—that is, in the illusory belief of revolutionaries that society was available for the remaking."[24]

François Furet's 1978 book, *Interpreting the French Revolution* (*Penser la Révolution française*), was a product of this thinking—that is, interpreting the French Revolution in the shadow of the Soviet gulag. This book offered an analysis of Jacobinism in light of totalitarianism and an implicit accounting of the extremist postwar politics of French intellectuals. For this reason, among others, the book resonated with contemporary political debates and, according to Michael Scott Christofferson, played an important role in the collapse of the post-1945 French intellectual left.[25] Similar thinking also informed the revisionist scholarship of the New Right in West Germany in the well-known instance of the Historians' Dispute of the 1980s. In the case of Ernest Nolte, the French Revolution serves as "a dress rehearsal for Lenin's Red Terror which was a dress rehearsal for the Holocaust and the Holocaust itself as a defensive response to 'Asiatic terror.'"[26]

Here in these narratives, as historian Geoff Eley has explained, revolutions have nothing positive to offer: "revolutions are treated as exclusively destructive and damaging events, as dysfunctions, as breakdowns, as outbreaks of irrationality, as misguided popular explosions, as mendacious conspiracies of the power-hungry."[27] But, according to Eley, this view of revolutions stems from looking at revolutions as primarily "political events," ignoring the scholarship accumulated since the 1970s in social history, which looks at the ideas motivating or situating actors as produced by discursive environments. Eley also notes that this animus against revolutions is actually a reversion to a much older tradition of thought. Prior to the emergence of social history in the 1960s and 1970s, much of the historical treatment of revolution was "an expression of the ruthlessness of the revolutionaries in a wider narrative of irrationalism and excess, which belittled the motives and agency of the ordinary participants."[28] The new historiography of social protest and collective action challenged this, much of it focused around the French Revolution. Historians such as George Rudé, Eric Hobsbawm, Charles Tilly, and E. P. Thompson "transformed perceptions of food riots, machine-breaking, urban crowds, popular uprising, and all manners of collective actions, so that it became possible to see popular violence accompanying or precipitating revolutionary crises as rationally based, socially explicable and morally legitimate."[29]

In South Korea's post-minjung era, the previous era's collectivity encapsulated in the slogans of *minjok*, *minju*, and *minjung* (nation, democracy, and minjung) became nullified by the advance of capitalism and the subsequent diversification in class structure, as well as the democratic transition, giving rise to new forms of identities, consciousness, and desires. As Manuel Castells notes, in a postideological period of widespread fading away of major social movements and ephemeral cultural expressions, "identity is becoming the main, and sometimes the only, source of meaning.... People increasingly organize their meaning not around what they do but on the basis of what they are, or believe they are."[30] If contradictions in society during the previous era were harbingers of radical change, with various social movements acting as carriers of a different future, the demise of such movements and the restructuring of economy by the 1990s worldwide has shattered fundamentally the belief in the future. As Perry Anderson pessimistically noted in 2007, there seems to be a deep world-cultural acceptance that there is no real alternative, notwithstanding some "sputtering contestatory efforts."[31]

Post-1987 democratic consolidations have been ambivalent enough to cast doubt on the real achievement of the democratization movement. The disappointment with the less than satisfactory reforms of Kim Young Sam's civilian government had increasingly led South Koreans, particularly the middle class, to brush "democracy" aside as a socially irrelevant or threadbare term in the post-1987 era. In 1997, a series of economic downturns beset the country and culminated in what is known as the IMF crisis, an experience many South Koreans considered the second toughest since the Korean War. Meanwhile North Korea plummeted into a series of both political and economic crises and had become a pariah of the world, infamously castigated by U.S. president George W. Bush in 2002 as part of the "axis of evil," along with Iran and Iraq. All of these had the effect of reducing the terms of public debate to a series of simple binary markers: authoritarianism versus democracy, for example, and economic development and prosperity versus economic downturn and social chaos.[32] Under these circumstances, memory of the former authoritarian leader Park Chung Hee has become reconstructed, rendering him a nationalist hero—a phenomenon known as "Park Chung Hee syndrome," which shares an intellectual and political basis with the New Right that has emerged following the syndrome.

Park Chung Hee Syndrome

"Park Chung Hee syndrome" refers to a phenomenon beginning in 1997 of ordinary Koreans professing their positive reappraisal of and admiration for the former authoritarian leader who had ruled South Korea with an iron fist for nearly two decades. The syndrome began quite humorously and innocuously at first, as university students chose Park as the leader they most wished to clone, which was initially seen as more of an expression of their dissatisfaction with the then Kim Young Sam government than a positive evaluation of Park Chung Hee per se. But numerous newspaper surveys and polls indicated that a sustained and a positive reappraisal of the former leader was emerging in society, which the mass media promptly dubbed "Park Chung Hee syndrome."[33]

The syndrome was clearly a case of what Richard Slotkin calls a "complex system of historical associations," "where history, memory and politics intersect and compete with contemporary debates over national identity or public policy over how to remember the past for the sake of the present and future."[34] The questions of what Park represents for contemporary South Korea, his conflicting legacies, and the various meanings attributed to his rule have become all the more salient and controversial for South Korea since the early 1990s, especially since the economic crisis of 1997 and later his daughter's presidency of the country (starting in 2012). What was at stake in the ensuing public debate about the syndrome were questions such as the following: How have Park's authoritarianism and the accompanying economic development been remembered in the context of the subsequent disappointment with the democratic reforms that also accompanied drastic measures to restructure the economy? How do memories of the Yusin period (1972–79) shape responses to rebuilding democracy? How have these memories, both sociological and psychological (collective and individual), been reshaped into social change in the broadest sense, as well as into political changes?

Philosophers of historiography such as Hayden White, Paul Ricoeur, and Reinhart Koselleck have argued to the effect that the "historical event is not that which happens but that which is narrated."[35] They remind us not only of the inadequacies of historical narration in general but also of the critical importance of social and political contingencies in the practice of historical writing and obtaining historical knowledge. According to them, representations of the past are "only realized through social and personal perspectives, standpoints, and positions that both constrain and create meaning—the trinity of place, time, and person gives birth to shifting and multiple historical perspectives."[36]

In the same vein, theorists of social memory tend to see it as "political technology." That is, social memory is culturally reproduced, with the crucial roles played by the above-mentioned trinity: agents of memory, collective practices of recollection, and creation of spaces where such memory is articulated and conveyed. Paul Connerton in particular emphasizes the social aspect of memory by highlighting the intention of, and the mediation by, social actors; for him, it is "performance practices that can intervene in the meaning systems of the present."[37] As Allen Feldman notes, both philosophers of history and theorists of cultural memory view social and political conditions as critical, as providing either constraint or possibility for the social capacity to narrate the past.[38]

Mass media was the most critical agent of memory involved in Park Chung Hee syndrome. As with most public debates of critical issues in South Korea, as well as those in other parts of the world, mass media (especially conservative channels that had been openly hostile to Kim Young Sam government's reform movement at the time) played a central and deliberate role in shaping the content and form of the debate and thereby reconstructing the public's social memory. Critics of the syndrome had pointed out that numerous public opinion polls and surveys conducted by the mass media, which had begun prior to the full-fledged appearance of the syndrome in the spring of 1997, in fact contributed to and constituted the syndrome.

Mass Media as Historiographical Apparatus

There are of course multiple ways and various media useful in producing and narrating the past; many of them have increasingly become what Allen Feldman calls "historiographical apparatus," which can certainly function as "a prosthetic"[39] for professional historians' history. However, during the height of Park Chung Hee syndrome, the mass media certainly constituted two elements of the previously mentioned trinity: agents of memory and spaces where such memory is articulated and conveyed. Indeed, the mass media was the most assiduous student of the Gramscian call for a "war of position"—a "culture war," as it were.[40]

By the late 1990s the conservative newspapers especially became the main medium through which revisionist views of Park Chung Hee were voiced and propagated. These newspapers became the main theater on which the regime of discontinuity played. The ultraconservative *Chosun Ilbo* (*Korea Daily*) serialized Park's biography by Cho Kapche, a well-known journalist and the editor-in-chief of the paper. Cho also made it clear that he was clearly critical of what the transition in post-1987 brought: "The process of democratization in the last ten years was a process of pursuing regional interest, individual interest, partisan interest in the name of democracy, freedom, equality, and human rights, thereby destroying national and public interest."[41] *Joongang Ilbo* (*Central Daily*)—which, along with *Chosun Ilbo* and *Dong-A Ilbo* (*East Asia Daily*) form the troika of conservatism known as Cho-Joong-Dong—also serialized the memoir of Kim Chŏngnyŏm, who had served in the Park Chung Hee government for ten years in the capacities of minister of finance and secretary-general of the Blue House.[42] These personal reminiscences, memoirs, and biographies led an effective campaign of revisionist history for Park's era, to promote what they called "a new era in South Korea's history."

In these retellings, Park Chung Hee emerges not only as an able statesman who accomplished two of the most urgent tasks faced by postcolonial Korea, industrialization and modernization; he is also presented as a revolutionary figure possessing the highest degree of integrity—"an incarnation of justice"—as well as a figure of tragedy. Most importantly, Park emerges as a fervent nationalist who—while embodying the Korean people's *han*, the long-accumulated suffering—devoted his life to "sublimate his plebian but uncompromising spirit for the nationalist cause." His death at the hands of a trusted assistant is also seen as revolutionary martyrdom.

Unlike previous appraisals of Park Chung Hee, which focused on his accomplishments as a statesman and a president, the accounts of the new publications elevate Park almost to a superhuman. Cho Kapche's serialization of his long-awaited biography of Park, *Spit on My Grave* (*Nae mudŏm e ch'im ŭl paet'ŏra*), is an exemplary case. Cho's interest in Park began with his publication of *The Posthumous Work* (*Yugo*) in 1987 and *Park Chung Hee* in 1992. As noted by political scientist Chŏn Chaeho, Cho's assessment of Park Chung Hee gradually became more hagiographic over the years. In *The Posthumous Work*, for example, Cho considers Park a "Confucian pragmatist," an important historical figure whose achievement "will remain in our history in thick Gothic font."[43] But Park also "lacked philosophical strength to sustain himself when he found himself alone and suffered from nihilistic sentiments."[44] In the 1997 biography, however, Cho's accolades for Park had no limit: he is framed a "superhuman who held his spirit high," a "first-rate thinker," "a bashful hero," a "superhuman with much tears," a "plebian everyman," an "indigenous Korean," and finally a "revolutionary who sublimated the nation's suffering with his personal energy for modernization."[45] As philosopher Hong Yun'gi notes, Cho effectively reorganizes South Korea's modern history into a Hegelian trajectory: the nation's history is the manifestation of the infusion of both the will of the individual Park and of national destiny.[46]

Fig. 1.1. The statue of Park Chung Hee located in Park's hometown of Kumi, North Kyŏngsang Province. Courtesy of OhmyNews.

Whatever the intention of the author, Cho's biography functions as Friedrich Nietzsche's "monumental" history. Nietzsche's warning to historians was that they tend to present historiography as a scientifically ordered analysis of history, thereby obscuring its actual value-driven and selective nature. It is dangerous, he admonished, to believe that historians are not subject to, and condemned to repeat, the errors of their ancestors: "Monumental history is the cloak under which their hatred of present power and greatness masquerades as an extreme admiration of the past. The real meaning of this way of viewing history is disguised as its opposite; whether they wish it or no, they are acting as though their motto were 'Let the dead bury the living.'"[47] Well-known novelists of the 1990s have also searched in the past for more ideal and more appealing alternatives to the present, as individuals were increasingly becoming dispossessed of a sense of one's place in history. Literary critic Han Mansu points out that the best sellers of the 1990s were mostly past oriented, noting that this phenomenon contrasts with the 1980s, when the majority of novels that received attention were oriented toward the future.[48]

In fact, along with Cho's biography, it was the literary works that were loosely based on the life of Park that performed "monumental" history in the 1990s. Yi In-hwa's *A Man's Road* (*In'gan ŭi kil*), published in 1997, is the very first literary representation of Park Chung Hee and his era. Yi's portrayal of Park as a great statesman and a nationalist hero, someone who had transcended his individuality for the higher call of historical responsibility for the nation, recalls Cho Kapche's conflation of Park as the Hegelian manifestation of supreme spirit.

In what a literary critic dubbed a "courageous" move—given the intellectual community's less than friendly sentiment toward Park, at least in the beginning phase of the syndrome—Yi unabashedly relies on myth to emphasize Park's greatness. In the novel, Park's father has a dream, before his wife becomes pregnant with Park, that a red dragon baby jumps out of his body. The dragon here is implied as Yu the Great, a legendary ruler in ancient China, and the chapter in which this dream is told is entitled "Reappearance of Yu the Great" (*Taeuhyŏnsin*), with the implication that Park Chung Hee is a reincarnation of Yu the Great.[49] Park's mother is also endowed with the unusual gift of being able to communicate with spirits. As soon as she becomes pregnant with Park, however, all the spirits stay away. Even more dramatically, everywhere she goes, the spirits who have resided in those places run away![50]

During numerous interviews with news media, Yi has repeatedly said how he had given all of himself to the task of writing this novel. If he were asked by God after his death what he has done in his life, he would reply that he wrote this novel. This monomania was in part due to his faith and confidence that Park was a worthy object of his devotion as a true great man.[51] Yi said, "when an individual endowed with a genius shows a way and becomes a role model, many will choose and follow his path"; "that way might be the only ingredient for the progress of humankind."[52]

Born in 1966, Yi In-hwa belongs to the much-discussed—and also much maligned—386 generation that led the democratization movement in the 1980s. Yi's portrayal of Park as someone "who possessed the wisdom and foresight to intuit what the era demanded and led [the nation] to fulfill the [people's] aspirations despite the tribulations"[53] is therefore one of the first cases of a "counter-" memory to his own generation. Yi In-hwa stated that he wanted to write "national literature" (*kungmin munhak*) of the same caliber as Shiba Ryōtarō's *Ryōma Goes His Way*.[54] Much as Sakamoto Ryōma's life—he was a key figure in the movement to overthrow the Tokugawa shogunate—is juxtaposed with the nation-building process of Meiji Japan in *Ryōma Goes His Way*, Yi juxtaposes Park Chung Hee's individual life history with the task of building the Republic of Korea.[55] In another interview, Yi said that when he started to think about writing a novel about the nation-state (*kungmin kukka*), he could come up only with the name of Park Chung Hee, not of notions of "freedom or democracy or such things."[56]

Yi In-hwa's choice to reconstruct Park Chung Hee's life for a *kungmin munhak*, recounting the history of this period from the vantage point of someone who has been regarded by many as either singlehandedly responsible for South Korea's modernization and industrialization or for its deeply rooted authoritarianism, performs (however inadvertently) a number of historical displacements. Yi's foregrounding of Park's achievement necessarily accompanies the backgrounding of not only the "dark side of the miracle"—many of the negative side effects of the quick-paced industrialization—but also the Korean people's participation in the process and their many sacrifices. More specifically, as the achievement of South Korea is all laid upon Park's own mythic qualities, the crucial historical context, such as the Cold War liberalism that arranged for South Korea to exchange its military dependency on the United States for economic aid and political support, recedes into the background. Furthermore, the three-decades-long democratization movement in which many of Yi's own peers participated and sacrificed themselves also recedes into the background.

In fact, a set of novels captured the South Korean public's imagination and spawned public debate over Park's legacy, directly or indirectly, while also signaling a move to the right that was taking place among South Korea's cultural gatekeepers—its well-known novelists and public commentators. In all of these cases, the mass media, especially the previously mentioned troika of conservative newspapers, played a critical role in promoting the authors by sponsoring well-known personalities to write book reviews, carrying extensive interviews with the authors, featuring the authors on talk shows, and other initiatives. Yi In-hwa's novel in particular received an inordinate amount of attention from the mass media at the time of its publication, as the author emerged as a poster child, as it were, of the revisionist assessment of Park Chung Hee. In 1993, when Yi In-hwa published *Everlasting Empire* (*Yŏngwŏnhan cheguk*), a novel set in the eighteenth century, it was none other than Yi Mun-yol, a well-known novelist and conservative commentator, who wrote a glowing review in *Chosun Ilbo*, declaring that the novel had elevated to an epic "confrontation of differing worldviews and visions" what previously had been treated mainly as a factional fighting among literati groups (*tangjaeng*).[57]

Kim Chinmyŏng's *The Rose of Sharon Has Blossomed* (*Mugunghwa kkoch'i p'iŏssŭmnida*) was published in July 1993; three million copies were reportedly sold within the first year of its publication, the highest number of any title in the history of South Korea at the time. Its plot involves a U.S.-based ethnic Korean nuclear physicist who returns to South Korea—thereby giving up the prospect of receiving a Nobel Prize—to help Park Chung Hee realize his quest for nuclear development. As in Yi's *A Man's Road*, Park Chung Hee here cuts a heroic figure, as one for whom national interest is of supreme importance. Park's pursuit of nuclear weapons is depicted as a nationalist quest as well, showing Park's steadfast determination despite having to juggle between the two superpowers and withstanding frequent meddling by the United States. Park Chung Hee is also portrayed as singularly responsible for the economic development of South Korea, since many of the institutions and infrastructure laid out during the earlier period of his rule—the Five-Year Economic Plans, the New Village Movements, construction of the Kyungbu Expressway, and so forth—were attributed to his genius and unparalleled determination to bring prosperity to the country.[58]

Kim Chŏnghyŏn's *Father* (*Abŏji*), published in 1996, is a "portrait of fathers who are tired and abandoned"[59]—abandoned presumably by the brash generation of the 1980s, who rebelled against the authoritarian and oppressive regime. *Father* sold a million copies within six months of its publication. Literary critics by and large dismissed the novel as yet another problematic case of fanning nostalgia for patriarchy.[60] In the spring of 1997, Yi Mun-yol published *Choice* (*Sŏnt'aek*), which is also set in the Chosŏn period and has a *yangban* (aristocrat) woman as a main protagonist, creating a storm of controversy over what critics called its implicit nostalgia for the Confucian patriarchal order.[61]

Bok Geo-il is another well-known novelist and conservative commentator on a par with Yi in terms of his literary success and his influence. In 2001, he published "A Collection of Maxims from Jupiter" (*Moksŏng chamŏnjip*), a medium-length science fiction story set on an imaginary planet in the future, sometime between 2600 and 2900. The collection in the title refers to the records of important people of this planet, which was destroyed in a collision with a comet. The planet's leader, an obvious reference to the former president Kim Dae Jung, is described as "having served too long as an opposition party's leader to be a president of the country . . . he has pursued the Sunshine policy unreasonably; but the policy was so unrealistic and ended in a complete failure, leaving only the deep scar of a divided public opinion."[62] As one blogger-cum-literary critic points out, this novel should be treated more like a political pamphlet put out by the likes of the Center for Free Enterprise, a probusiness think tank, than the bona fide science fiction for which Bok Geo-il is deservedly respected and famous.[63]

It is the collusion among cultural gatekeepers such as Yi Mun-yol and Bok Geo-il and the mass media, and the privilege associated with their status as distinguished authors, that gave them the public platform that might not have been otherwise available. Both Yi and Bok protest that they are mere novelists, with no real influence in society, and yet as Kang Chunman perceptively points out, it is precisely their status among the privileged ranks of cultural producers that allows them to play the role of powerbrokers.[64] In fact, Yi Mun-yol wielded his powerful position as a celebrity figure and novelist to enact his political vendetta against the Kim Dae Jung government. In 1999, at the time of the Kim government's investigation of *Chosun Ilbo* for tax evasion, Yi published a novel that was a blatant and loud protest of the investigation, calling the individuals associated with the government "dogs" and those who called for press reform "Red Guards."[65] Incidentally, Bok Geo-il's previously mentioned "Collection" was also a jab at the government investigation of *Chosun Ilbo*'s tax evasion. Given what one may call "Cho-Joong-Dong and Literary Complex" and Yi's particularly cozy relationship with *Chosun Ilbo*, his plea that the public view his novel "only as a literary work" and nothing more seems less than genuine. In fact, his demand for the public's indulgence of authors' literary imagination and creativity is what culture critic Kang Chunman has characterized as "privilegism of culture" (*munhwa t'ŭkkwŏnjuŭi*): "it is the kind of social sentiment that takes for granted that those who work in the cultural sphere can intervene in societal issues without taking any accountability, in the belief that they do not enjoy as much political power or earn as much as those who work in the political and economic sphere."[66]

According to Kang, under the appearance of Yi's "cultured-ness" (*kyoyang*), much of his anti-intellectualism and epistemic violence go unnoticed.[67] Yi is known for an arresting writing style and a dazzling display of erudition, especially with his references to classical writings. In the 1980s, someone of Yi's ilk who put literary skills to political use would have been castigated as "minjung-oriented" (read: political); many of the minjung writers were open and honest about their commitment—no minjung authors would have insisted that they were merely or purely novelists. Yi and Bok, on the other hand, hide their sloganeering under the veneer of "pure literature" with the institutional support of the troika of Cho-Joong-Dong.

The Discourse of Triumphalism

In the rise of the New Right, as in the case of the previously discussed Park Chung Hee syndrome, conservative media has played a critical, perhaps central, role. The term "New Right" itself was coined by the media and later adopted by the proponents themselves. Beginning in November 2004, *Dong-A Ilbo* carried extensive coverage on the emergence of the New Right, and in February 2005 a special report on the New Right was serialized. Around this time, various organizations that openly identified as New Right began to appear, beginning with the Liberty Union (Chayujuŭi yŏndae) in November 2005. Some similar groups had existed prior to 2005, but the organization of the Liberty Union heralded a new current of South Korea's social movement.

The South Korean New Right consists not of skinheads in jackboots but of politicians, journalists, novelists, professors, lawyers, and historians. Its champions include former politicians such as Sin Chiho, well-known historians such as An Pyŏngjik and Yi Yŏnghun, Christian leaders such as Kim Chinhong, and journalists and editors of newspapers such as Cho Kapche and Ch'oe Hongje. New Right groups also have an array of publication outlets: for example, a quarterly, *Sidae Chŏngsin* (*Geist*); a web magazine, *Polizen*; and an Internet newspaper, the *New Daily*.

A flurry of memoirs by former *undonggwŏn* (activist) intellectuals started with Sin Chiho's "Are You Still Dreaming of Revolution?" (*Tangsin ŭn ajikto hyŏngmyŏng ŭl kkumkkunŭn'ga*) and "Confession" (*Kobaek*), both published in 1992. From the late 1990s and early 2000s, the increase in the number of polemical and scholarly works and publication outlets attests to the sea change in the relationship between politics and intellectual legitimacy and the consequent urgency of efforts to comprehend or, in many cases, explain away discredited past political identities. To maintain that the legitimacy of the previous paradigm of the minjung movement and all the attendant historiography had been broken and that one had been "vaccinated" from Marxism or leftist ideas became a source of political legitimacy in a Korean intellectual community haunted by North Korea's dysfunctional state. Historian An Pyŏngjik, columnist Yu Kŭnil (of *Chosun Ilbo*), politician Sin Chiho, the "founder" of 1980s *chusap'a* (followers of North Korea's *chuch'e sasang*) Kim Yŏnghwan, and a fellow former *chusap'a* by the name of Hong Chinp'yo all burnished their political credentials by having each been a *undonggwŏn*, having overcome the lures of *chuch'e sasang*, and having awakened to the reality of North Korea. The case of former radical social movement leaders undergoing a Damascene conversion is not unique to South Korea, as I have mentioned with respect to French intellectuals. In Japan as well, some of the present-day leading neoconservative ideologues were student leaders in the radical Zenkyoto movement of the early 1970s.[68]

Most of the sixty or so founding members of the Liberty Union were former *undonggwŏn*, activists in various social movements: Sin Chiho had been a labor activist, Hong Chinp'yo a reunification movement activist, and Ch'oe Hongjae a president of the Student Association of Korea University, a position that until about the mid-1990s was usually occupied by an *undonggwŏn*. The inaugural statement calls for the liberalism of Korean society for its future: "The *geist* of the twenty-first century is not the authoritarianism of industrialization forces, nor the minjungism of some democratization forces; it is the twenty-first century style liberalism that, true to the reality of Korea, would fully realize globalization (*segyehwa*), informatization (*chŏngbohwa*), and liberalization."[69]

Scholars of the New Right have organized the New Right Textbook Forum and have written alternative textbooks to remove what they considered "distorted" as a representation of the Korean past and to proffer a more positive view of Korean history. In their 2010 publication, *Alternative Textbook: Modern and Contemporary Korean History* (*Han'guk kŭnhyŏndaesa: Taean kyogwasŏ*), the conservatives took issue with the current history books of modern and contemporary Korea. They took issue particularly with what they consider to be a negative portrayal of modern Korean history in textbooks used in middle and high schools:

> Surely there have been ups and downs (*kulgok*) and pain [in our history].... But the Republic of Korea can be proud of its accomplishing "the mission impossible."... But these textbooks... do not contain what [a textbook] should naturally contain: The image of ourselves as having done our best to establish, defend, and nurture our country; the portrait of ourselves as having shed blood and tears to improve the quality of our lives. [In these textbooks] there are only accounts of dictatorship and oppression, and pitiful (*ch'amdamhan*) contradictions of capitalism. For how long should the future generation of the Republic of Korea wear a scarlet letter?[70]

As with histories of other parts of the global world, modern Korean history encompasses both excruciating pain and violence, on the one hand,

and wealth, progress, and phenomenal success, on the other. The seeming incommensurability of simultaneous industrialization, wealth, consumption, and the destruction of the war, utter poverty, and hunger—not to mention the continuous confrontation between North and South (the outcome of both the global Cold War structure as well as the internal political struggle centered on conflicting visions for a postcolonial Korea)—is a challenge for scholarship. Neither of these contradictory images alone typifies twentieth-century Korean history, which holds both trajectories in a single generation. This paradox raises high the political, emotional, and intellectual stakes of interpreting post-1945 Korean history.

The textbook controversy is in large part related to these high stakes. With the division of Korea happening simultaneously with its liberation from Japan, the real meaning of liberation was stripped, and two separate states were established. The unrelenting drive for economic development, aided by anticommunist state ideology and draconian authoritarian rule, inspired an oppositional movement known as the minjung movement. This also accompanied a process of reinterpreting post-1945 history "in terms of powerful binaries": "genuine nationalism vs mindless anticommunism, and *minjung-* (people-) oriented democracy vs mere formal democracy."[71] The state violence unleashed during the Kwangju Uprising in 1980 further propelled historians to search for the origins of the country's plight; these historians set as their task to overcome the "structure of division" and to bring about reunification, by emphasizing or validating efforts that were seen as doing away with the division system.

With the democratic transition in South Korea, the collapse of the Soviet Union and the downward spiral of North Korea, and the liberal governments of Kim Dae Jung and Roh Moo Hyun, the New Right began to challenge this historiography as leftist, nationalist, and in collusion with the ruling regime. They accused it of not only discouraging more "objective" scholarship but also of polluting the minds of the younger generation with a distorted historical perspective that invited self-doubt and self-torment. The New Right's task is therefore to bring "balance" to the previous historical understanding of colonial and postcolonial history, setting the record straight regarding what it considers the leftist-nationalist narratives of anti-Japanese resistance of the colonial period and the privileging of antiauthoritarian struggles in the postliberation period, all of which is seen as undermining or delegitimizing the Republic of Korea.[72] Coupled with South Korea's unprecedented economic development of the 1970s and 1980s, and its all-out push for neoliberal globalization after the IMF crisis of 1997, the New Right became the voice of triumphalism, justifying and further demanding economic growth through the market, as an extension of Park Chung Hee's economic development.[73]

Historian Owen Miller calls the *Alternative Textbook* a form of "neoliberal historiography" that revises the historical assessment of imperialism and authoritarianism "in order to reinvigorate the fortunes of the South Korean Right."[74] In their attempt to uphold the legitimacy of the Republic of Korea and its market-oriented economy, the authors of the *Alternative Textbook* go so far as to argue that colonial rule also helped to develop the "social capacity" that Koreans needed to establish a modern nation-state.[75] They believe that the market economy was created by Park Chung Hee's "modernizing revolution" and was modeled on earlier colonial development; the dictatorship and all other violations of human and civil rights under his regime thus become an unavoidable—and possibly even small—price to pay in South Korea's inexorable march toward a modern market economy, which is ultimately seen by many on the right as the highest form of human civilization.[76]

The New Right's critique of leftist nationalist historiography in South Korea has the appearance of responding to the predicament faced by historiography in contemporary society's uncertainty with the role of history for charting its future.[77] Postcolonial theory in particular has offered trenchant critiques of nation and class, the central categories of modern historiography, as totalizing and undemocratic. In fact, some of the New Right scholars, such as economic historian Yi Yŏnghun, have embraced postcolonial scholarship for its "recentering" the "individual" as a category of historical analysis.[78] In reality, however, the New Right historians have pushed out the nation only to bring back the state in its place. As many scholars in Korea have pointed out, some of the most conspicuous aspects of the New Right scholarship's historical narratives are the *centrality* of the South Korean state and the consequent marginalization—and eventual disappearance—of North Korea.[79] Some notable examples of this include the hagiographical treatment of Syngman Rhee, who is praised unproblematically for his role in the founding of the Republic of Korea, overlooking his flagrant disregard of liberal democratic principles and his oppressive policies, and the similarly sanctifying image of Park Chung Hee as a mythical figure who is responsible for the "revolution of modernization," without due acknowledgement of the political and epistemic violence committed in the process of state building and modernization.[80]

Conclusions

I have characterized as the regime of discontinuity the narrative strategies that articulate the 1980s in such a way that its historical meanings and significances are displaced and its multifacetedness is compressed to serve contemporary needs and political considerations. Such historical displacement does not provide a new perspective to guide Korean society for the future. As historian Jörn Rüsen argues, proffering counter or alternative images from a bygone era provides, much like Nietzsche's monumental history, "only a negative orientation to one's own present." They may assuage momentarily the pervasive sense of loss of meaning in contemporary society, but they do not help eliminate or overcome it. Rather, these historiographical images provide an appearance of the alternative, masking the serious sense of loss of direction experienced in contemporary society, obscuring the depth and shape of the present predicament.[81]

I conclude this chapter by reflecting upon West Germany's Historians' Dispute in the late 1980s. Similar to the South Korean textbook controversy, the historiographical issues involved in the debate were less about what happened than about how to evaluate or contextualize what had taken place. At the center of the debate also lay the ancient topos of history as "teacher": that is, "we learn from history only if it tells us something positive, something worth imitating."[82] The belief that historical knowledge and traditions nourish a national political self-understanding also led to the charge of "self-flagellation" when scholars proposed a reflective preoccupation with the past, including its dark aspects; the right was concerned that such a historical pedagogy would have a destabilizing effect; instead of making people aware of a disturbing past, Germans should seek to mobilize pasts that can be endorsed.[83]

An active and passionate participant of the Dispute, philosopher Jürgen Habermas called for a way to engage critically with the repressed or negative elements of the past so as to make possible their *critical* appropriation for contemporary society. Habermas proposed that societies learn not only from positive experience but also from negative ones, and even from disappointments, which they then seek to avoid in the future: "We learn historically chiefly from the way historical events challenge us, showing us that traditions fail, and that we and the convictions that heretofore guided our actions have gone aground on the problems that must be solved."[84] Furthermore, one's personal identity or national identity does not passively derive from infusion by some mystical history; rather, identity is the result of accepting responsibility, of accepting historical choices, not just faits accomplis.⁸⁵ The South Korean New Right's argument that only a positive image of history would give a historical lesson—hence, its lamentation about young generations wearing a scarlet letter—is not tenable, nor is it productive. To learn from history, Habermas urges, is not to push unsolved problems aside or repress them but to remain open to critical experiences, so that one "can perceive historical events as counterevidence, as proofs of shattered expectations."⁸⁶ The authoritarian regimes of Syngman Rhee and Park Chung Hee, contra the New Right's effort to sanitize their brutal legacy, offer examples of such counterevidence in South Korea.

NOTES

1. Nora, "Between Memory and History," 17. Nora's project was very much initiated by what he perceived to be an overall decline in the importance of the French nation and in the capacity of its national culture to sustain what he called "realms of memory," the array of rituals, sites, ideas, and traditions that had long been part of the nation's collective past.
2. Pak Yŏnggyun, "Minjung undong kwa panchabonjŏk chuch'e," 14.
3. Ko Misuk, *Pip'yŏng kigye*, 158–59.
4. Ibid., 159.
5. See Namhee Lee, *The Making of Minjung*, 70–108.
6. Eperjesi, "Communists Meet Gangnam Style." In 2003, two Konkuk University students were arrested for the violation of the NSL for their possession and quoting of sections of Karl Marx's *Capital*, Louis Althusser's *For Marx*, and George Katsiaficas's *The Imagination of the New Left* in a pamphlet they wrote and distributed in a neighborhood slated for demolition.
7. Ibid.
8. Ibid., emphasis added.
9. Heonik Kwon, *The Other Cold War*, 6.
10. Doucette and Koo, "Distorting Democracy," 3.
11. In December 2014, Shin Eun-mi, author of a travelogue of North Korea, was accused of *chongbuk chwap'a* by a group of online and offline grassroots organizations, allegedly for making "supportive comments" about North Korea in her book and in a series of public forums. The South Korean government deported her to the United States, after having detained and interrogated her for twenty-one days, and barred her from entering South Korea for five years. See Hyun Lee, "A Korean American Housewife Confronts South Korea's National Security Law."
12. The trajectory the discourse of *chongbuk chwap'a* is more complicated than rendered here, as it first originated within the left-leaning political party to denounce fellow members who were seen as intransigent followers of North Korea's *chuch'e sasang*. Here my focus is exclusively on the discourse articulated at a societal level and its function in the society.
13. "386 generation," coined in the 1990s, refers to those who were in their thirties at the time, went to college in the 1980s, and were born in the 1960s.

14. Namhee Lee, "From *Minjung* to *Simin*," 51–57.
15. Therborn, "After Dialectics," 70.
16. Ibid., 71.
17. Dirlik, *Postmodernity's Histories*, 46.
18. Ibid.
19. Waters, "1968 in Memory and Place," 15.
20. Krystal, "The Long Goodbye: Notes on a Never-Ending Decade," 84.
21. Waters, "1968 in Memory and Place," 15.
22. Cullen, "Review of *Happy Days and Wonder Years*."
23. Marlière, "Sarkozysm as an Ideological Theme Park," 382.
24. Christofferson, "An Antitotalitarian History of the French Revolution," 557.
25. Ibid.
26. Heilbrunn, "Germany's New Right," 85.
27. Eley, "What Produces Democracy?," 178.
28. Ibid., 179.
29. Ibid.
30. Castells, *Information Age*, 3, quoted in Dirlik, *Postmodernity's Histories*, 51.
31. Anderson, "Jottings on the Conjuncture," 9.
32. For example, Sin Chiho, one of the rising stars of the right, laments in his otherwise evenhanded 2014 book that all economic policies pursued by the liberal governments of Kim Dae Jung and Roh Moo Hyun brought about contemporary economic mayhem.
33. See Han'guk chŏngch'i yŏn'guhoe, *Pak Chŏnghŭi rŭl nŏmŏsŏ*.
34. Slotkin, *Gunfighter Nation*, 5–6.
35. Feldman, "Political Terror and the Technologies of Memory," 61.
36. Ibid.
37. Connerton, *How Societies Remember*, quoted in Feldman, "Political Terror," 61.
38. Feldman, "Political Terror," 61.
39. Ibid., 63.
40. Gramsci, *Prison Notebooks*, 3:168.
41. Cho Kapche, *Nae mudŏm e ch'im ŭl paet'ŏra*, 13, quoted in Chŏn Chaeho, "Pak Chŏnghŭi robut'ŏ yŏksa rŭl kuch'ul haja," 45.
42. Kim Chŏngnyŏm, *Ch'oebin'guk esŏ sŏnjin'guk muntŏk kkaji*. Kim had already published his memoir in 1991, which focuses on his role in the economic development; his second volume is titled *Ah, Park Chung Hee* and was published as a book in 1998 after having been serialized in *Joongang Daily*. The revised edition came out in 2006.
43. Quoted in Chŏn Chaeho, "Pak Chŏnghŭi robut'ŏ yŏksa rŭl kuch'ul haja," 44.
44. Ibid.
45. Ibid.
46. Hong Yun'gi, "Tagŭkjŏk hyŏndaesŏng," 76.
47. Nietzsche, *The Use and Abuse of History*, 17.
48. Han Mansu, "90-yŏndae pesŭt'ŭsellŏ sosŏl," 200.
49. Ha Chŏngil, "P'asijŭm ŭi sinhwa," 67–68.
50. Ibid., 68.
51. Ibid., 67.
52. Quoted in ibid., 70–71.

53. Yi In-hwa, "In'gan ŭi kil e nat'anan kŭndaesŏng munje," 276, quoted in Yi Ch'unghun, "'Yŏngung' ŭi chŏngch'ihak," 255.
54. In the interview Yi mentions the title as *The Grand Dream* (*Taemang*) rather than *Ryōma Goes His Way*. In Korean translation, *The Grand Dream* comprises three volumes, originally written by three Japanese novelists, that detail political, economic, cultural, and military dimensions of Japan's nation-building process from the time of Tokugawa to the Russo-Japanese War. Only the third volume is attributed to Shiba Ryōtarō. *Ryōma Goes His Way* (*Ryōma ka kanda*) is a novel based on Sakamoto Ryōma, which was first serialized in the newspaper *Sankei* from 1962 to 1966 before being published as a book.
55. Son Chŏngsu, "In'gan ŭi kil, chakka ŭi kil," 134.
56. Kang Yŏnghŭi, "In'gan ui kil ro Pak Chŏnghŭi puhwal," 80.
57. Sŏl Chun'gyu, "Somunnan chanch'i," 425–26.
58. See Kim Chinmyŏng, *Mugunghwa kkoch'i p'iŏssŭmnida*, 1994.
59. "Chich'igo pŏrimbadŭn abŏjidŭl ŭi chahwasang."
60. See, among others, Han Mansu, "90-yŏndae pesŭt'ŭsellŏ sosŏl."
61. See, among others, Ko Misuk, *Pip'yŏng kigye*.
62. Bok Geo-il, "Moksŏng chamŏnjip," 234, 238, quoted in Kang Chunman, "Pok Kŏil ŭi sosŏl," 185.
63. alt.SF: an alternative SF fanzine, "Pyŏnmyŏng ŭl ch'ajasŏ—Pok Kŏil non."
64. Kang Chunman, "Yi Munyŏl ŭl almyŏn."
65. Yi Mun-yol, "Sultanji wa chanŭl kkŭrŏdanggimyŏ," 50; see also Kim Tongmin, "Tasi Yi Munyŏl e taehayŏ."
66. Kang Chunman, "Yi munyŏl ŭl almyŏn," 137.
67. Ibid., 138.
68. Koschmann, *Revolution and Subjectivity in Postwar Japan*, 247.
69. Ibid.
70. Quoted in Chŏng Haegu, "Nyurait'ŭ undong ŭi yŏksa insik," 223–24.
71. Em, "Historians and Historical Writing in Modern Korea," 670.
72. Ibid., 673.
73. Chŏng Haegu, "Nyurait'ŭ undong ŭi yŏksa insik," 219–20.
74. Miller, "The Idea of Stagnation in Korean Historiography," 10.
75. Ibid.
76. Kim Yŏnghwan, interview with author.
77. See, among others, Rüsen, "Historical Enlightenment in the Light of Postmodernism."
78. Em, "Historians and Historical Writing," 674.
79. Yun Haedong, "Nyurait'ŭ undong kwa yŏksa," 238–39.
80. See, among others, Yun Haedong, "Nurait'ŭ undongkwa yŏksa."
81. Rüsen, "Historical Enlightenment in the Light of Postmodernism," 117–20.
82. Habermas, *A Berlin Republic*, 11.
83. Ibid.
84. Ibid., 44.
85. Maier, *The Unmasterable Past*, 136.
86. Habermas, *A Berlin Republic*, 13.

REFERENCES

Anderson, Perry. "Jottings on the Conjuncture." *New Left Review* 48 (2007): 5–37.
Bok Geo-il. "Moksŏng chamŏnjip" [A collection of maxims from Jupiter]. *Munye chung'ang* 96 (Winter 2001): 226–79.
Castells, Manuel. *Information Age: Economy, Society, and Culture*. Vol. 1 of *The Rise of the Network Society*. Malden, MA: Blackwell, 1997.
"Chich'igo pŏrimbadŭn abŏjidŭl ŭi chahwasang: 1997-yŏn ŭi hwajejak Kim Chŏnghyŏn ŭi *Abŏji*." *Webzine Taesan Munhwa*, fall 2006, http://daesan.or.kr/webzine_read.html?uid=1195&ho=18
Cho Kapche. *Nae mudŏm e ch'im ŭl paet'ŏra: Cho Kapche kija ka ssŭnŭn kŭndaehwa hyŏngmyŏngga Pak Chŏnghŭi ŭi pijanghan saengae* [Spit on my grave: The tragic life of Park Chung Hee, the revolutionary of modernization, written by reporter Cho Kapche]. 8 vols. Chosun Ilbosa, 1998–2001.
Chŏn Chaeho. "Pak Chŏnghŭi robut'ŏ yŏksa rŭl kuch'ul haja" [Let's rescue history from Park Chung Hee]. *Chŏngch'i pip'yŏng* 7 (2000): 35–58.
Chŏng Haegu. "Nyurait'ŭ undong ŭi yŏksa insik e taehan pip'anjŏk kŏmt'o" [Critical review of historical consciousness of the New Right movement]. *Yŏksa pip'yŏng* 76, no. 8 (2006): 215–37.
Christofferson, Michael Scott. "An Antitotalitarian History of the French Revolution: François Furet's *Penser la Révolution française*." *French Historical Studies* 22, no. 4 (1999): 557–611.
Connerton, Paul. *How Societies Remember*. Cambridge: Cambridge University Press, 1989.
Cullen, David. Review of *Happy Days and Wonder Years: The Fifties and the Sixties in Contemporary Cultural Politics*, by Daniel Marcus. H-Net, August 2005, https://networks.h-net.org/node/19474/reviews/19994/cullen-marcus-happy-days-and-wonder-years-fifties-and-sixties
Dirlik, Arif. *Postmodernity's Histories: The Past as Legacy and Project*. Lanham, MD: Rowman & Littlefield, 2000.
Doucette, Jamie, and Se-Woong Koo. "Distorting Democracy: Politics by Public Security in Contemporary South Korea." *Asia-Pacific Journal* 11, issue 48, no. 4 (December 2, 2013).
Eley, Geoff. "What Produces Democracy? Revolutionary Crises, Popular Politics and Democratic Gains in Twentieth-Century Europe." In *History and Revolution: Refuting Revisionism*, edited by Mike Haynes and Jim Wolfreys, 172–201. New York: Verso, 2007.
Em, Henry. "Historians and Historical Writing in Modern Korea." In *Oxford History of Historical Writing*, edited by Daniel Woolf and Axel Schneider, 5:659–77. Oxford: Oxford University Press, 2011.
Eperjesi, John R. "Communists Meet Gangnam Style: Alain Badiou and Slavoj Žižek in South Korea." *Huffington Post*, October 8, 2013, http://www.huffingtonpost.com/john-r-eperjesi/communists-meet-gangnam-style_b_4047098.html
Feldman, Allen. "Political Terror and the Technologies of Memory: Excuse, Sacrifice, Commodification, and Actuarial Moralities." *Radical History Review* 85 (Winter 2003): 58–73.

Furet, François. *Penser la Révolution française* [Interpreting the French Revolution]. Translated by Elborg Forster. Cambridge: Cambridge University Press, 1981.
Gramsci, Antonio. *Prison Notebooks*. Vol. 3. Translated by J. A. Buttigieg. New York: Columbia University Press, 2007.
Habermas, Jürgen. *A Berlin Republic: Writings on Germany*. Translated by Steven Rendall. Lincoln: University of Nebraska Press, 1997.
Ha Chŏngil. "P'asijŭm ŭi sinhwa, tansŏnjŏk kŭndaegwan ŭi yŏksŏl—Kin'gŭp chindan 2. Sidaech'agojŏk kukka chisangjuŭija, Yi Inhwa" [Myth of fascism, an irony of the unilateral modern perspective—Emergency diagnosis 2. Yi In-hwa the anachronistic worshipper of a state]. *Silch'ŏn Munhak* 8 (1997): 65–77.
Han'guk chŏngch'i yŏn'guhoe. *Pak Chŏnghŭi rŭl nŏmŏsŏ* [Overcoming Park Chung Hee]. P'urŭnsup, 1998.
Han Mansu. "90-yŏndae pesŭt'ŭ sellŏ sosŏl, kŭ segyegwan kwa oraksŏng" [Best sellers of the 1990s, the worldview, and its entertainment quality]. *Han'guk munhak yŏn'gu* 20, no. 3 (1998): 189–211.
Heilbrunn, Jacob. "Germany's New Right." *Foreign Affairs* 75, no. 6 (1996): 80–98.
Hong Yun'gi. "Tagŭkchŏk hyŏndaesŏng maengnak sok ŭi miwan ŭi p'asisŭm kwa misŏngsuk simin sahŏe" [Incomplete fascism and immature civil society in the context of multipolar modernity]. *Sahoe wa ch'ŏrhak* 2, no. 10 (2001): 57–103.
Kang Chunman. "Pok Kŏil ŭi sosŏl e sosŏl ro taphanda" [I respond with a novel to the novel of Bok Geo-il]. *Inmul kwa sasang* 47, no. 3 (2002): 184–202.
Kang Chunman. "Yi Munyŏl ŭl almyŏn Han'guk sahoe ŭi 'munbŏp' i poinda" [To figure out Yi Mun-yol is to figure out how Korean society operates]. *Inmul kwa sasang* 47, no. 3 (2002): 130–54.
Kang Yŏnghŭi. "In'gan ui kil ro Pak Chŏnghŭi puhwal ŭi kippal ŭl tŭn Yi Inhwa" [Yi Inhwa, with his novel *A Man's Road*, has raised high a banner to call for revival of Park Chung Hee]. *Sahoe p'yongnon kil* 97, no. 6 (1997): 78–87.
Kim Chinmyŏng. *Mugunghwa kkoch'i p'iŏssŭmnida* [The rose of Sharon has blossomed]. Haenaem, 1994.
Kim Chŏnghyŏn. *Abŏji* [Father]. Munidang, 1996.
Kim Chŏng'in. "Sŏnt'aek (Yi Munyŏl 1997) kwa na" [*Choice* (Yi Mun-yol 1997) and me]. *Han'guk yŏksa yŏn'guhŏe hŏebo* 31, no. 1 (1998): 31–34.
Kim Chŏngnyŏm. *Ch'oebin'guk esŏ sŏnjin'guk muntŏk kkaji: Han'guk kyŏngje chŏngch'aek 30-yŏnsa* [From a poor country to the gate of the developed country: A thirty-year history of South Korean economic planning]. Raendŏm Hausŭ, 2006.
Kim Tongmin. "Tasi Yi Munyŏl e taehayŏ" [Again, on Yi Mun-yol]. *Hwanghae munhwa* 33 (Winter 2001): 390–96.
Kim Yŏnghwan. Interview with author. Seoul, South Korea. July 28, 2005.
Ko Misuk. *Pip'yŏng kigye* [The machine of critics]. Somyŏng ch'ulp'an, 2000.
Koschmann, J. Victor. *Revolution and Subjectivity in Postwar Japan*. Chicago: University of Chicago Press, 1996.
Krystal, Arthur. "The Long Goodbye: Notes on a Never-Ending Decade." Review of *The Sixties Unplugged: A Kaleidoscopic History of a Disorderly Decade*, by Gerard J. DeGroot, 81–88. *Harper's Magazine*, October 2008.
Kwon, Heonik. *The Other Cold War*. New York: Columbia University Press, 2010.
Kyogwasŏ p'orŏm. *Han'guk kŭnhyŏndaesa: Taean kyogwasŏ* [Alternative textbook for Korean modern history]. Kip'arang, 2010.

Lee, Hyun. "A Korean American Housewife Confronts South Korea's National Security Law." *Asia-Pacific Journal* 3, issue 4, no. 3 (January 26, 2015).

Lee, Namhee. "From Minjung to Simin: The Discursive Shift in Korean Democratic Movements." In *South Korean Social Movements: From Democracy to Civil Society*, edited by Gi-Wook Shin and Paul Y. Chang, 51–57. New York: Routledge, 2011.

Lee, Namhee. *The Making of Minjung: Democracy and the Politics of Representation in South Korea*. Ithaca: Cornell University Press, 2007.

Maier, Charles S. *The Unmasterable Past: History, Holocaust, and German National Identity*. Cambridge: Harvard University Press, 1997.

Marlière, Philippe. "Sarkozysm as an Ideological Theme Park: Nicolas Sarkozy and Right-Wing Political Thought." *Modern & Contemporary France* 17, no. 4 (2009): 375–90.

Miller, Owen. "The Idea of Stagnation in Korean Historiography: From Kukuda Tokuzo to the New Right." *Korean Histories* 2, no. 1 (2010): 1–12.

Nietzsche, Friedrich. *The Use and Abuse of History*. Translated by Adrian Collins. 1949. Reprint. Indianapolis: Bobbs-Merrill, 1957.

Nora, Pierre. "Between Memory and History: Les Lieux de Mémoire." *Representations* 26 (Spring 1989): 7–25.

Pak Yŏnggyun. "Minjung undong kwa panjabonjŏk chuch'e" [Minjung movement and anticapitalistic subjectivity]. *Ch'ŏrhak yŏn'gu* 102, no. 5 (2007): 13–36.

Park Chung Hee. *Minjok ŭi chŏryŏk* [Underlying strength of the Korean nation]. Kwangmyŏng ch'ulp'ansa, 1971.

"Pyŏnmyŏng ŭl ch'ajasŏ—Pok Kŏil non" [To look for an explanation—on Bok Geo-il]. *alt.SF: An Alternative SF Fanzine*, February 1, 2011, https://altsf.wordpress.com/2011/02/01/sp04/

Rüsen, Jörn. "Historical Enlightenment in the Light of Postmodernism: History in the Age of the 'New Unintelligibility.'" Translated by Bill Templer. *History and Memory* 1, no. 2 (1989): 109–31.

Sin Chiho. *Kogae sugin Taehan Min'guk* [Republic of Korea: Its head is lowered]. 21-segi puksŭ, 2014.

Sin Sŭnghŭi. "*Sŏnt'aek* kwa 'Ingmyŏng ŭi sŏm' e nat'anan Yi Munyŏl ŭi yŏsŏnggwan kyumyŏng" [Examining Yi Mun-yol's perspective on women in Choice and "Unnamed Island"]. *Asia munhwa yŏn'gu* 40, no. 12 (2014): 55–85.

Slotkin, Richard. *Gunfighter Nation: The Myth of the Frontier in Twentieth-Century America*. New York: Maxwell Macmillan International, 1992.

Sŏl Chun'gyu. "Somunnan chanch'i ŭi mŏgŭlgŏri: 'Segyegwan ŭi taerip'?" [The food is not worth the rumor: "Confrontation of world views?"]. *Ch'angjak kwa pip'yŏng* 21, no. 4 (1993): 425–28.

Son Chŏngsu. "In'gan ŭi kil, chakka ŭi kil—Yi Inhwa ron" [A man's road, an author's road—On Yi In-hwa]. *Chakka segye* 15, no. 4 (2003): 117–37.

Therborn, Göran. "After Dialectics." *New Left Review* 43 (January–February 2007): 63–114.

Ventresca, Robert A. "Mussolini's Ghost: Italy's Duce in History and Memory." *History and Memory* 18, no. 1 (2006): 86–119.

Waters, Sarah. "1968 in Memory and Place." Introduction to *Memories of 1968: International Perspectives*, edited by Ingo Cornils and Sarah Waters, 1–22. New York: Peter Lang, 2010.

Yi Ch'unghun. "'Yŏngung' ŭi chŏngch'ihak—Pak Chŏnghŭi kukkajuŭijŏk t'onghap tae minjujŏk sahoe t'onghap" [Politics of 'heroes'—Park Chung Hee's state-oriented integration versus democratic social integration]. *Chŏngch'i pip'yŏng* 3 (1997): 251–61.

Yi In-hwa. *In'gan ŭi kil* [A man's road]. Sallim, 1997–1998.

Yi In-hwa. "*In'gan ŭi kil* e nat'anan kŭndaesŏng munje" [On the issue of modernity in *A Man's Road*]. *Sangsang* 5, no. 3 (1997): 258–76.

Yi Mun-yol. *Sŏnt'aek* [Choice]. Minŭmsa, 1997.

Yi Mun-yol. "Sultanji wa chan ŭl kkŭrŏdanggimyŏ" [Drawing near a wine jug and glass]. *Hyŏndae munhak* 47, no. 10 (October 2001): 32–55.

Yun Haedong. "Nyurait'ŭ undong kwa yŏksa insik–'piyŏksajŏk yŏksa'" [Ahistorical history: The New Right movement and its historical perspective]. *Minjok munhwa nonch'ong* 51, no. 8 (2012): 227–63.

2

The Irrepressibility of Teleology

The 1980s as Historiography

Kyung Moon Hwang

As a representation of South Korea's tumultuous transitions, the 1980s remains a focal point of intense historical study and debate, shaped by the circumstances of today as much as of the past. Historians are trained to remain wary of teleology, the goal-oriented view that frames and interprets events in accordance with what came afterward, as if historical phenomena can and should be explained mostly through their apparent contributions to the resulting end. Teleology is not considered as fallacious as the notion of "post hoc ergo propter hoc" ("after this, thus caused by this"), but historical investigation is supposed to treat the people and circumstances of the past as a result of what preceded them, which in turn formed the unique set of conditions that produced the moment in question, irrespective of what came thereafter. These lofty lessons, however, frequently become overridden by a contradictory impulse: the historian's ingrained desire to contextualize the significance of what she studies, particularly if the larger stakes reflect urgent or contentious contemporary issues.

So it should come as little surprise that the 1980s in South Korea continues to be viewed teleologically, both within the decade and following it. This is because, in either case, the decade seems dominated by one moment, the 1987 democratization, the long-term impact and cause of which are vigorously debated. Its historiographical gravity continues to be formidable, bending the light shone on the entire period and beyond; even the solemn voices of social critics and historians who see 1987 as ultimately a failure are forced to focus on this event, if only to downgrade its significance. Like all historic transitions, the 1987 democratization has remained a fruitful source of reinterpretation in light of what has occurred subsequently, but this revisitation has colored also the perspectives on what happened in the 1980s before 1987, and, indeed, on the decade's relationship to preceding eras.

As with modern Korean history in general, there remains a fairly clear ideological division in the historiography of the 1980s, even with significant variations within the left or right camp and interventions by scholars outside South Korea who are less keen to draw connections to recent political developments. Actually, compared to most other periods, events, or major figures of modern Korean history, the polemical range regarding the 1980s has been relatively narrow. Almost all observers seem to agree that the establishment of electoral democracy was a good thing (at least initially), that the Chun dictatorship was a bad thing, that the industrialization of the preceding decades shaped society in a way that contributed to democratization, and that geopolitical forces and concerns played a major role in the outcome. Just as importantly, most seem to view the 1980s as a major step in a gradual, stage-by-stage linear progression that reached a climax, a (false) peak, or even the end of modern Korea's historical development.

Within these generally accepted parameters, however, have emerged major differences of prioritization and interpretation—about who or what were the contributing factors, about their relative significance, and even about the nature and impact of the major event that kicked off the decade and seemed to foreshadow, if not directly lay the basis for, 1987: the 1980 Kwangju Uprising. Through a survey of this historiography in the Korean and English-language scholarship, this chapter locates the teleological pulls of the 1980s and explores their implications by dividing the overview thematically, first by examining the political narratives of the decade, and then by considering accounts that frame the events in socioeconomic and geopolitical terms. While competing camps employ both thematic approaches, the balance between the two is struck differently between left-leaning and right-leaning historical views, a reflection of opposing perspectives on that decade's contributions to what came afterward, as well as to broader understandings of modern Korean history.

The 1980s as Political History

For progressive Korean historians, most of whom are also left-nationalist, in this larger scheme of things the 1980s before democratization represented the darkness before dawn, with the long night having begun in the 1960s or the 1940s, if not the 1890s. South Korea's external relations, economic and industrial development, and other historical factors contributed to this situation, but most of all it was the country's *political* trajectory that was responsible for this descent. And the nadir came in the opening year of the 1980s with the Kwangju Uprising, which encapsulated the repressive and bloody path to power initiated by Chun Doo Hwan's coup of December 1979, a process that had permanently stripped Chun of any legitimacy. The rest of the decade until the 1987 breakthrough, then, is taken as a constant struggle for rectification of the crimes committed in the half-year period beginning with the coup, as well as the path toward fulfillment, driven by the indignation over Kwangju, of the longing for democracy and social justice that had been trampled upon in the spring of 1980.

The prevailing leftist characterization of the politics of the 1980–87 period, likewise, reinforces the picture of a brutal regime struggling to gain a semblance of order and acceptance by maintaining the "Yusin" approach to rule from the 1970s. In essentially following the Park Chung Hee playbook, Chun's Fifth Republic constitution differed little from that of Yusin. Furthermore, the indirect and rigged methods by which this constitution was ratified and Chun was "elected" president in the summer of 1980 continued the "gymnasium elections" (*ch'eyukkwan sŏn'gŏ*) that Park had deployed to stay in power. Furthermore, Chun's deep ties to Park and the dominant TK (Taegu-Kyŏngsang) military group dating back to the early 1960s, his professed admiration for Park's method of rule, and his pronouncements upon seizing power of being driven by a grand sense of responsibility—a throwback to Park's justifications following his own coup of 1961—all indicated that Chun's regime would essentially continue the Yusin system. Despite the growing and vociferous resistance put up by a wide range of social actors, and the electoral successes of the opposition parties in the mid-1980s that took advantage of the small allowance for democratic challenges to the ruling clique, Chun continued to disregard this pressure to liberalize Korean politics. Indeed he tightened the authoritarian screws under the banner of "protecting the [Fifth Republic] constitution" (*hohŏn*), as seen in the harsh crackdown on student and labor actions, the surveillance and torture operations of the secret police, and the "Samchŏng Re-Education Centers," which purported to round up gangsters but in fact nabbed student and worker activists.[1] Only after the extraordinary gathering of millions in the streets of the major cities in June 1987, in response to the regime's pronouncement that the indirect presidential election system would continue—which in turn stood as the explosive culmination of developments, from the formation of a majority opposition party through the national assembly elections of 1986 to the death through torture of student leader Pak Chongchŏl—did Chun and Roh, Chun's handpicked successor and partner in the "TK twosome" since 1979, agree to a direct presidential election in 1987 as part of a new constitutional system, the Sixth Republic. This "June Declaration" of 1987 was, from this view, a sign of the ruling system's unavoidable surrender to the forces of democratization that had been building for decades,[2] and particularly in response to the 1979–80 half-year period that led to Kwangju. It was as if everything that had happened in the chronic struggle between democratization and dictatorship led ultimately, if not inevitably, to this breakthrough moment.

In a bitter or bemusing irony, depending on one's perspective, the 1987 presidential election produced in the winner, Roh Tae Woo, the same person bound for this post in the Fifth Republic, and who thereafter seemed to sustain military autocracy in all but name. For the progressive historical camp, the explanation for this fiasco had to go beyond the most self-evident one, which was that Kim Dae Jung and Kim Young Sam, the two politicians who had stood at the forefront of opposition to the military dictatorship, both insisted on running and hence split the majority, anti-TK vote. No, the real problem, particularly given the conservative turn that Kim Young Sam would take in the early 1990s, lay in the mismanaged, undemocratic means by which the 1987 transition had taken place. As political historian Choi Jang Jip, among the most vocal and conspicuous of the activist progressive scholars, put it in the opening years of the new century, South Korean political culture, despite formal democratization, failed to democratize. He attributed this to the botched birth of formal democracy in 1987 through the construction of the Sixth Republic's constitution, a process that he deemed nothing more than a "game among elites" that excluded the movement activists behind the democratization as well as their primary issues of greater access and equality.[3] As a result, in Choi's view, the 1987 "transition" brought no fundamental change, as the political sphere did not expand beyond its conservative, Cold War, and anticommunist core to include a wider range of socioeconomic sectors and concerns.

A decade later, in the early 2010s, this sense of 1987 having led not to a true transformation but rather to another form of conservative entrenchment and undemocratic politics seems only to have deepened among leftist historians, one of the most forcefully representative voices of whom was the late An Pyŏnguk.[4] In wondering why 1987 did not succeed in implementing a completely democratic order, An suggested that the blame lay not in the transition itself but in the failures of the administrations that subsequently came to power. Like most other historians of the antidictatorship struggle, An perceived the accomplishments of the 1980s within the larger progression of people-centered movements throughout the modern era. The democratization struggle, then, stood on the shoulders of the anti-imperialist and anticolonial independence campaigns beginning with the Tonghak Uprisings of 1894 and the March First Movement of 1919, of the failed revolutionary efforts in the south in the "liberation space" of 1945–50, then of the resistance against the Syngman Rhee and Park Chung Hee dictatorships. Throughout this process, An believed, the masses stood at the forefront of major change, and the democratization of the 1980s was no different. The problem was that, ironically, the 1987 breakthrough produced not only Roh Tae Woo, but more importantly, the consolidation of establishment forces in 1990 when Kim Young Sam joined hands, literally, with Roh in forming a new conservative party as a vehicle for his presidential ambitions. This moment halted the momentum of democratization, solidified political regression, and laid the foundation of neoliberalism as the pervasive ideological framework thereafter, which strengthened the abusive hold on Korean society of big capital, a force that gripped even the administrations of progressive presidents Kim Dae Jung and Roh Moo Hyun at the turn of the twenty-first century.

This view of the democratization as a long-term failure squarely reflects alarm over the electorate's conservative turn during and after Roh Moo Hyun's presidency (2003–8), but scholars like An Pyŏnguk have even questioned whether the entire effort of the 1980s that led to 1987 was itself of questionable value. Beyond maintaining the students' and intellectuals' spiritual fortitude, for example, was there really any practical impact of major debates within the *undonggwŏn* (movement circles) of the 1980s over the stage and character of South Korea's "social composition" (*sahoe kusŏngch'e*), since it appears that the *minjung* (the people) movement might have homogenized the differing voices that needed to be heard?[5] If so, how successfully could it have been in spreading a forward-looking democratic culture and priorities of social justice, given that a true democracy characterized by a protection of human rights, greater economic equality, the dissipation of anticommunism, and progress toward national reunification failed to gain hold once into the 1990s and beyond? Or rather, as An notes, did these priorities become overwhelmed by mostly geopolitical developments, particularly the fall of Soviet-led communism around the world, that accelerated the embrace and domination of neoliberalism? In any case, the primacy of the masses is viewed as having been discarded at some point following the democratic transition, with the middle classes in particular becoming satisfied with procedural democracy and overwhelmed by the neoliberal turn, and thereby abandoning the cause, as it were, particularly when it came to the unfinished business of addressing the needs of the working class.[6] In such a scenario, the 1980s can be considered the high point of the historical arc of modern Korea that bent toward a particular set of political and social ends, with the laboring core of the common people always at the center.

A similar kind of retrospective that sees the 1980s as the culmination of major trends appears also in the English-language scholarship on the minjung movement led by students and intellectuals, the most thorough of which is Namhee Lee's *The Making of Minjung*. Unlike much of the scholarship, however, Lee's book looks backward from the 1980s far more than forward in order to situate the movement's historical significance, demonstrating how the students' and intellectuals' discursive representations of the masses arose from the antiregime efforts of the 1960s and especially the anti-Yusin struggles of the 1970s, and then became crystallized, theorized, and mobilized following the events of the spring of 1980.[7] Lee makes clear that the minjung movement, in its various forms, acted as democratization's primary force, without which it would be difficult to properly assess or understand this signal moment, and hence it reflected in essence the path from Kwangju to June 1987. But understandably, Lee also looks ahead to the dissolution of the minjung phenomenon in the 1990s, offering insights on how and why it might have lost its purpose following the democratization breakthrough. And here, she seems to indicate that internal structural impediments might have played the greatest role: the movement could not overcome the inherent tension between, on the one hand, a purported collectivity centered on the masses, and on the other, the indispensability of intellectuals and students who somehow had to join and guide the working classes while remaining cautiously peripheral. With the passage of time, this *undonggwŏn* corps of movement activists, known generally as the "3-8-6" generation,[8] moved on to the next stage of their lives, in a fitting allegory, as both national and geopolitical developments rendered their efforts less urgent. Democratization, in other words, brought not only a great sense of achievement but also a sense of deflation. Once this goal was reached (somewhat) in the 1980s, the accomplishments of the minjung struggle and their meaning entered another realm of retrospection and introspection that may or may not have had much to do with the actual historical experience of the 1980s.

From the perspective of the right and the New Right historical scholarship, such a view is considered a defeatist distortion of the true significance of democratization, with some of the more conservative observers even reaching into the time-tested rhetoric of red-baiting to claim that this leftist "failure" narrative is nothing more than a blind following of the North Korean stance (*chongbuk*).[9] But both the extremist and more mainstream conservative perspectives draw from the same reservoir of nationalist teleology to explain the significance of the 1987 democratization. This can be seen, for example, in the 2007 publication by the Kyogwasŏ Porŏm association of the "Alternative Modern Korean History" textbook in opposition to what was considered the prevailing leftist orthodoxy.[10] Here it is made clear that the modern experience should be considered a long-term project—beginning, as with the progressive-nationalist narrative, in the late nineteenth century—of establishing "liberal democracy," a process that had to overcome the traditional hierarchies of society and polity, colonial domination, and then, despite good intentions, the incapacity of the 1948 founding of the Republic of Korea to implant a durable democratic order. But due substantially to the economic development beginning in the 1960s amid, admittedly, the autocracy of the Park and Chun years, South Koreans finally achieved in 1987 the proper end to their modern historical struggle.

Beyond noting vaguely that democracy takes a long time to achieve, explaining why and how this breakthrough took four decades following South Korea's foundation presents an explanatory conundrum, and the solution seems to be to acknowledge the excesses of the dictatorship era through the somewhat detached manner of a journalistic chronicle, while forwarding the sense of continuing advancement in more comprehensive terms. But despite the avowedly critical stance toward the Chun regime and recognition of the flaws of the Sixth Republic—regionalism and personality-based party politics, for example—the conservative view of the 1980s has been pervasively triumphalist, lauding the buildup toward the great achievement of 1987, which is said to have eventually introduced a slew of reforms and breakthroughs: the retreat of the military from politics, the peaceful transfer of presidential power (even to the opposition, in 1997), the introduction of local autonomy, and the general liberalization of the political culture that tolerated and even encouraged a plurality of voices and interests. In stark contrast, then, to the left's historiographical tone of regret and unfinished business, given what are seen as setbacks in the decades following procedural democratization, the right sees democratization as having been emphatically accomplished in the 1980s, with the succeeding period constituting little more than further refinements of this great achievement. Thus a major facet of modern Korean history, in this right-nationalist sense of political development, came to an end in 1987—a view largely shared, whether intentionally or not, by some U.S.-based historians.[11]

Socioeconomic and Geopolitical Framework

While right-leaning narratives treat South Korea's pre-1987 political development, especially of the 1980s, broadly as a contributing cause behind the democratization, they also tend to view domestic politics as having proceeded almost on a separate path from the course of other social sectors, particularly the economy. The emphasis, rather, turns to industrialization and geopolitical factors as having played a greater role in establishing the foundation upon which the political breakthrough could emerge. As noted above, there is little effort to deny the damage from the Chun dictatorship, but the strong implication is that such hardship, extending back to the Yusin period and beyond, was the necessary price to pay in order to strengthen the economic and resultant social trajectories of growth that made 1987 possible. And informed by an unmistakable anticommunism, this narrative also stresses international circumstances, particularly concerning South Korea's neighbor to the north.

All of these strains—South Korean triumphalism, anticommunism, economism, positivism, and the teleology of democratization—come together most strikingly, perhaps, in the work of Yi Yŏnghun, the name most associated with the New Right historiography that emerged in the 2000s. Interestingly, Yi does not come from conventional historical training, but rather cut his research teeth as an economic historian. This difference is crucial, for he is also somewhat of an unwitting neo-Marxist in his staunch materialism and stage-ism. And unlike many others on the right, he is not necessarily a nationalist, or at least not an ethnic Korean nationalist. He is, if anything, a South Korean nationalist who bemoans his compatriots' lack of patriotism and proper historical understanding (for which he faults the leftist orthodoxy), but importantly he does not premise his historical valuations on the attainment or attainability of north-south unification. Rather he is more interested in prioritizing the accomplishment of a liberal democratic, economically advanced Republic of Korea, which he believes largely took place in 1987. Hence his survey *History of South Korea: Steps toward the Making of a Country, 1948–1987*

(2013), which interestingly includes a section on North Korea, stops in the late 1980s, and shows the progress of history taking a gradual, step-by-step path toward its goal. The fact that this happened only in the southern half of the peninsula is less important to him than that it happened at all. If South Korea became an "advanced country" (sŏnjin'guk) as a counterpart to what took place in the north, so be it. It all ultimately resulted in the common good, and everything that preceded the 1980s breakthrough, including even the Korean War, contributed inexorably, in a Hegelian way, to the march of freedom. Indeed, all the military actions and institutions of the South Korean regime, such as participation in the Vietnam War and, presumably, the anticommunist regimentation of society, preserved this path toward the proper end. To Yi, the leftist framing of South Korean history as that of dependency within a neocolonial order is absurd; given the Cold War, this was South Korea's unavoidable means of avoiding communization.

This bring us to another major feature of the New Right, its pro-Americanism. In fact this trait extends to the embrace of those views, which oddly share fundamental traits with Marxism, that once prevailed in American academia, such as modernization theory and positivist materialism—namely, the notion that the liberalization of politics and society is built upon the liberalization, or capitalist development, of the economy. And in echoing journalistic American narratives of the 1987 democratization,[12] which not surprisingly stress the American role, the New Right tends to view South Korea as a comprehensive beneficiary of the American-led postwar order in East Asia, as if the United States had been a caretaker ensuring that South Korea would follow the proper course of history, under American protection and assistance, toward the great achievement of industrialization plus (or preceding) liberal democracy, the two great pillars of modern development. Even the dark years under Chun can be rationalized in this way: Ronald Reagan's invitation to Chun to visit the White House in early 1981 made possible the granting of the 1988 Olympics to Seoul, the successful staging of which confirmed, according to Yi Yŏnghun, that South Korea had finally become a "legitimate country" (nara-daun nara).[13] This narrative also places South Korean history, again in ironically following classic Marxism, within a universalist direction of historical development. In this case, the path was laid by the great victory of U.S.-led liberalism and capitalism in the Cold War struggle. And in South Korea, America's triumph made possible the confident emergence of South Korea, now strengthened through democratization, onto the world stage through Roh Tae Woo's new approach to inter-Korean relations and outreach to the communist bloc, encapsulated in the so-called "Nordpolitik" policy, at the turn of the 1990s.

Perhaps nothing better epitomizes the left-right historiographical split regarding the 1980s than the perceptual gap regarding the United States, particularly the nature of its contribution to South Korean democratization. If the right sees America as a fount of liberal ideals (both political and economic) and anticommunist protection that provided the necessary economic, cultural, and geopolitical conditions for democratization,[14] the left sees the United States as having exerted the opposite effect of prompting, through American complicity in the Kwangju massacre and indeed through its leading, domineering role in the neoliberal makeover of South Korea since the 1980s—a sobering reconsideration of not only that decade, but of South Korea's history as a whole. A product of Korean historiography that emerged in the 1970s and 1980s that began to openly question received understanding—a movement that ironically gained a major push from American scholars such as Bruce Cumings as well—Korean students and intellectuals began to systematize and reassess the entire past relationship with America. Not only was the United States, as the globe's supreme imperialist power, responsible for national division, but America nurtured and protected anticommunist dictatorships like South Korea's in the pursuit of Cold War interests,[15] and the baneful effects converged in Kwangju through the U.S. commanders' refusal to prevent South Korean troops under American control from brutally suppressing the civil unrest in Kwangju. The fierce effort among students and laborers to rectify Kwangju for the remainder of the decade until 1987, then, was fueled considerably by the accompanying passions to overturn America's comprehensive hold on South Korea.

For progressive scholars, therefore, Kwangju both encapsulated and exploded the comprehensive structural tensions from the dictatorship period, and accelerated them toward the 1987 breakthrough, which resulted from the intolerability of continuing dictatorship for the rising middle class and white collar workers, now including legions of former students raised in the democratization struggle.[16] Seungsook Moon, for example, finds the militarized, indeed gendered regimentation of the populace in the pursuit of anticommunist developmentalism from the 1960s to the 1980s as eventually making South Koreans, and women in particular, aware of their economic marginalization in service to the patriarchal visions of industrialization and domesticity. Both the working and middle classes thus came to recognize that democratization constituted the sole means by which they could assert their citizenship in the nation-state.

Such a view therefore constituted a counterhegemonic reaction against the statist model of modernization but also reflected broader developments in civil society, including the formation of numerous civic groups, that drove the agitation in the 1980s.[17] Even the repressive Chun regime had to account for this rapidly changing atmosphere by eventually rescinding some social restrictions, from curfews to the dress code, that had only served to accentuate the gap between social and political reality.[18] From this perspective, then, the inexorable social forces of the 1980s, in marshaling the manifold yearnings for fundamental change and translating them into political action, brought to fruition the democratic transition that Kwangju had attempted in the beginning of the decade.

Conservative accounts, too, acknowledge social development as the basic cause, but the view from the right credits less the potency of democratic resistance during the dictatorship years than the breakneck pace of industrialization over the same period. This set the economic foundations of material plenitude necessary for forming a critical mass of urban, middle-class citizens who recognized that South Korea could no longer be considered an "advanced country" while continuing to be ruled by a military dictatorship. Again one finds here the right's (and New Right's) remarkable appropriation of Marxist historical frameworks, including even the centrality of class consciousness, now fused with a globalist explanation that sees the 1986 "people's revolution" in the Philippines, a matured Cold War American diplomacy, and the anticipation of the 1988 Olympics all having supplemented the core dynamic of social change following economic growth. This geopolitical materialist orientation appears pointedly in accentuating the impact of the "three lows" (*samjŏ hohwang*) that bolstered the South Korean economy in 1987: low interest rates, low oil prices, and the low dollar (in relation to the yen), which combined to further render this particular moment in South Korean history the one that would enable the great transition to democracy.[19]

The point is that socioeconomic and geopolitical factors, more than the political resistance, made 1987 possible. Whereas the left sees the dictatorship period, encapsulated in Kwangju, as having been characterized by intensifying pressure until it burst open into mass demonstrations that forced the regime's surrender, the right views authoritarian rule as the necessary trial of hardship and sacrifice, within the Cold War order of American protection against communism, so that a true democracy could be realized, at its proper time. And whereas the left finds in industrialization an instrument and ruse of the corrupt political and military autocracy for exploiting and suppressing workers, which further heightened the fervor for social liberation, the right considers the country's economic growth trajectory as having shielded South Korea from the social instability and communist agitation that would have jeopardized or at least delayed the steady path toward a substantive and sustainable liberal democratic order. In focusing on economic causes, then, the teleological pull here comes not only from the post-1980s era but also from 1987 itself as the culmination of the social and economic development of South Korea, and of modern Korea as a whole. In assessing the 1980s before democratization, progressives highlight the growing popular resistance to the Chun regime's continuation of Yusin patterns, which repressed labor actions and wages while doubling down on the collusion with both big business and American strategic interests. This dynamic both intensified labor's contributions to pressuring the regime leading up to June 1987 and accounted for the explosion of labor unrest in the immediate months thereafter.

As noted above, however, to progressives the political liberalization and even the Great Labor Struggle of the summer of 1987 failed to halt the concentration of economic power and might even have facilitated it. Such an understanding takes us to the prevailing leftist economic view of the 1980s, which frames the decade within the longer history of capitalist domination and class antagonism in South Korea in order to demonstrate how electoral democratization actually contributed to the neoliberal turn thereafter. Although devoid of an explicit orientation toward a particular historical goal, this view is clearly conscious of South Korea's current circumstances, particularly by establishing the structural connection between economic disparities and political power, and thereby finding that the South Korean economic development has followed the internal logic of longstanding dependence on the American-led global order. Hence this narrative squares unmistakably with progressive understandings of the 1980s as a missed opportunity to escape comprehensively the broader, mostly baneful impact of American domination in South Korean history.

According to a systematic analysis recently put forth by Chi Chu-hyŏng, for example, through the influence of American-trained economic bureaucrats, led by Kim Chaeik, officials in the Chun administration began to formulate policies that prioritized the opening of import markets, liberalization of the finance sector, and the stabilization of the currency.[20] Opposition from certain economic sectors and officials, and the sudden death of Kim and other officials in the Burma bombing of 1983, temporarily halted this momentum, but according to Chi, the ascendant formulation for how to transition away from the developmentalist model of the Park years laid the groundwork for neoliberalism's revival in the 1990s.

Most significantly, by the time of the financial crisis of 1997, the foundation had been laid by the steady influence of bureaucrats ready to embrace the prescription pushed by the IMF (International Monetary Fund), which to Chi was first and foremost an instrument of international financial interests, particularly Wall Street, that demanded fiscal austerity and a loosening of import duties and internal Korean markets, especially in the financial sector. Because of these Korean officials' central role in the negotiations, the IMF bailout of the South Korean government facilitated the process by which the political autocracy of the predemocratization period was replaced by a plutocracy in the hands of the *chaebol* conglomerates and the financial industry. Their subsequent dominance, according to progressive scholars, produced the ever-widening economic polarization of South Korean society up to the present day.

Conservatives, needless to say, proffer a more salutary explanation: the country's gradual integration into the global economy, at levels appropriate to South Korea's stage of material development, not only enabled democratization but also eventually brought forth the end of the developmental state beginning in the 1980s. The difficult adjustments to this transition culminated in the struggles of the IMF period, which compelled further structural reforms, particularly in forcing major enterprises to become more efficient in the new century's turn toward the postindustrial economy. But in general terms the continuing concentration of economic power in the hands of the major conglomerates is viewed with much less concern, given the larger benefits of further incorporation into the world trading system, however dependent on American domination this was. Though not expressed in so many words, the idea is that the growth of Samsung and Hyundai as major players in global markets facilitated the emergence and further consolidation of a democratic South Korea, almost as if the political conditions of the country had to catch up to its economic standing.

Conclusion

From the economistic and internationalist perspective of conservative scholars, then, the 1987 breakthrough and the 1980s decade as a whole represented the almost inevitable outcome of the development of grand forces that had been transforming the country for decades. Democratization was the capstone of South Korea's progress toward realizing its destiny, a necessary and affirmative signal that the great project of modern nation-state building had reached its end, although this process still required fine-tuning in the ensuing decades up to the present day. Most remarkable about this formulation is that anticommunist conservatives have forwarded such a transparently materialist, indeed Marxist explanation of a linear, stage-based historical process, albeit one heading toward an idealized end of a national quest for freedom.

Left-leaning narratives have also defied methodological expectations: spurred by a view that indexes historical progress and social rectitude by the core measurement of economic justice and national (unified) independence as much as political liberalization, progressive perspectives find the 1980s, particularly 1987, an incomplete achievement at best and a noble failure at worst, despite the extraordinary advances by popular forces in raising mass consciousness sufficiently to bring down the four-decade-old system of political dictatorship. Indeed the shortcomings in further disseminating this consciousness, in a way that would have transposed it onto political and social challenges following the 1980s, account for much of the disappointment at what that decade could have become, but ultimately did not. The more recent growing consensus among progressives—that the 1980s failed to redirect the larger trajectory of not only political but also economic history, in the sense of preventing the path of capitalist domination in South Korea from taking the neoliberal turn—thus continues to view the decade in terms of its causal impact on later periods as much as on its standing as the product of prior historical development.

Of course there are many variations in perspectives that cross this basic divide, but all sides continue to frame the 1980s in understandably teleological terms, whether in light of what came afterward or within the decade itself, with the 1987 breakthrough serving as the moment through which to view the preceding years of the 1980s, indeed the country's past as a whole. Naturally this preoccupation with finding direct connections to what followed constrains due consideration of that period's significance and particularities, the classic problem of teleology. As this volume's chapters demonstrate, the 1980s produced a rich cultural and social tapestry that reflected both contemporary circumstances and prior historical development, regardless of how these features may have contributed either to the succeeding periods or to particular meta-narratives of the country's past. But otherwise, perhaps the overwhelmingly teleological view of the 1980s can be forgiven, for it is a sign less of a faulty historical approach than of the extraordinary standing, still today, of that decade in South Korean and modern Korean history.

NOTES

1. Yŏksahak yŏn'guso, *Hamkke ponŭn Han'guk kŭnhyŏndaesa*, 425. A representative summary of the left-nationalist view concerning this and other matters can be found in this general history book.
2. No Yongp'il, *Han'guk kŭnhyŏndaesa tamnon*, 297–301.
3. Choi Jang Jip, *Minjuhwa ihu ŭi minjujuŭi*, 113.
4. An Pyŏnguk, "Minjuhwa undong e taehan p'yŏngga wa insik ŭi chŏnhwan ŭl wihayŏ."
5. Ibid., 36–38. Prompted by thoughts on South Korea's place within the American-dominated global order, these "theories of social composition" were competing leftist positions premised on stage-based Marxist frameworks of historical development. They were known by their respective English acronyms, such as NL (National Liberation) or PD (People's Democracy).
6. Han Honggu, *Chigŭm i sun'gan ŭi yŏksa*, 153–57.
7. See Namhee Lee, *The Making of Minjung*, and also Paul Chang, *Protest Dialectics*.
8. The "3-8-6 generation," which borrowed the name of Intel's microprocessor chip, was a common term circulating in the 1990s in reference to those who at the time were in their thirties, attended university in the 1980s, and were born in the 1960s. By the opening decade of the twenty-first century, they had entered the established orders of politics, academia, and civil society.
9. See, for example, Pak Sŏkhŭng, *Chegukchuŭi ch'imnyak kwa kongsanhwa kŭkpok*. For more on the New Right's place in modern Korean historiography, including its intriguing yet "tenuous" appropriation of postcolonial methodology in challenging nationalist binaries, see Em, *The Great Enterprise*, 155–58.
10. Kyogwasŏ porŭm, *Taean kyogwasŏ*, 14–17 and 217–47.
11. See, for example, the accounts of South Korean democratization's significance in Cumings, *Korea's Place in the Sun*, 391–403; and Kyung Moon Hwang, *A History of Korea*, chapters 23, 24, and 26.
12. See, for example, Oberdorfer, *The Two Koreas*.
13. Yi Yŏnghun, *Taehan min'guk yŏksa: Nara mandŭlgi paljach'wi, 1948–1987*, 44.
14. See also Brazinsky, *Nation Building in South Korea: Koreans, Americans, and the Making of a Democracy*.
15. Yŏksahak yŏn'guso, *Hamkke ponŭn Han'guk kŭnhyŏndaesa*, 415.
16. No Yongp'il, *Han'guk kŭnhyŏndaesa tamnon*, 283–92.
17. Seungsook Moon, *Militarized Modernity and Gendered Citizenship in South Korea*, especially chapter 4. As suggested in the book's title, Moon calls this transition in the populace's status as one from "dutiful nationals" to citizens integrated into the "discourse of democratization." She finds, however, that this process of citizenship formation was markedly gendered, a consequence of the dualistic mobilization of the population according to sex in the predemocratic era.
18. Yŏksahak yŏn'guso, *Hamkke ponŭn Han'guk kŭnhyŏndaesa*, 426.
19. Kyogwasŏ porŭm, *Taean kyogwasŏ*, 222–23.
20. Chi Chuhyŏng, *Han'guk sinjayujuŭi ŭi kiwŏn kwa hyŏngsŏng*, especially chapters 4 and 9. After having begun his official career in 1974, Kim Chaeik became Chun's senior secretary for economic affairs (*kyŏngje susŏk pisŏgwan*) in the fall of 1980.

REFERENCES

An Pyŏnguk, "Minjuhwa undong e taehan p'yŏngga wa insik ŭi chŏnhwan ŭl wihayŏ" [For the sake of changing the assessment and perception of the democratization movement]. In *Han'guk minjuhwa undong ŭi sŏnggyŏk kwa nolli* [Character and logic of the South Korean democratization movement], edited by An Pyŏng-uk, 19–44. Sŏin, 2010.

Brazinsky, Gregg A. *Nation Building in South Korea: Koreans, Americans, and the Making of a Democracy*. Chapel Hill: University of North Carolina Press, 2009.

Chang, Paul. *Protest Dialectics: State Repression and South Korea's Democracy Movement, 1970–1979*. Stanford: Stanford University Press, 2015.

Chi Chuhyŏng, *Han'guk sinjayujuŭi ŭi kiwŏn kwa hyŏngsŏng* [Origins and development of neoliberalism in South Korea]. Ch'aek sesang, 2011.

Choi Jang Jip. *Minjuhwa ihu ŭi minjujuŭi: Han'guk minjujuŭi ŭi posujŏk kiwŏn kwa wigi* [Democracy after democratization: The conservative origins and crisis of South Korean democracy]. Humanisŭtŭ, 2002.

Cumings, Bruce. *Korea's Place in the Sun—A Modern History*. Rev. ed. New York: W. W. Norton, 2005.

Em, Henry. *The Great Enterprise: Sovereignty and Historiography in Modern Korea*. Durham: Duke University Press, 2013.

Han Honggu. *Chigŭm i sungan ŭi yŏksa* [History as it stands at this moment]. Han'gyŏrye ch'ulp'an, 2010.

Hwang, Kyung Moon. *A History of Korea: An Episodic Narrative*. 2nd ed. London: Palgrave Macmillan, 2016.

Kyogwasŏ porŭm. *Taean kyogwasŏ: Han'guk kŭnhyŏndaesa* [Modern Korean history: An alternative textbook]. Kip'arang, 2008.

Lee, Namhee. *The Making of Minjung: Democracy and the Politics of Representation in South Korea*. Ithaca: Cornell University Press, 2007.

Moon, Seungsook. *Militarized Modernity and Gendered Citizenship in South Korea*. Durham: Duke University Press, 2005.

No Yongp'il. *Han'guk kŭnhyŏndaesa tamnon* [Discourse on modern Korean history]. Han'guk sahak, 2007.

Oberdorfer, Don. *The Two Koreas: A Contemporary History*. New York: Basic Books, 1999.

Pak Sŏkhŭng. *Chegukchuŭi ch'imnyak kwa kongsanhwa kŭkpok hago sŏnjin'guk e chiniphan Han'guk kŭnhyŏndaesa ŭi chaengjŏm yŏn'gu* [Debates on the history of modern Korea, which overcame imperialist invasion and communization to become an advanced country]. Kukhak charyowŏn, 2013.

Yi Yŏnghun. *Taehan min'guk yŏksa: Nara mandŭlgi paljach'wi, 1948–1987* [History of South Korea: Steps toward the making of a country, 1948–1987]. Kip'arang, 2013.

Yŏksahak yŏn'guso. *Hamkke ponŭn Han'guk kŭnhyŏndaesa* [Examining together Korea's modern history]. Sŏhae munjip, 2004.

PART II

Transnationalism

3

In Search of Alternative Modernity

The 1980s in South Korean Intellectual History

Jae-Yong Kim

I have been invited to write an essay that details my journey as a literary critic who played a role in the development of the *minjung* (people's) nationalist scholarship of 1980s South Korea. I welcome the opportunity, but I would like to slightly shift the focus of my contribution in order to reflect on a more general intellectual journey, one that involves not just myself but, I believe, the majority of Korean progressive intellectuals of the twentieth century. What we have collectively and intergenerationally been searching for, I will suggest, is an alternative to the colonial and imperialist modernity that has hegemonized history in a Western-dominated world over the last two centuries. As my narrative will make clear, the 1980s and the minjung movement played a special role in that search, and it is from that perspective that their legacy should be recounted and evaluated in today's cultural discourses in Korea as well as abroad.

On the 1980s Discourse of National Literature (*Minjok munhak*)

The 1980s were a time of unprecedented intellectual flourishing for Korean writers. Never before, going back at least to the 1948 division of the two Koreas, had such a diversity of ideas been advanced in the South Korean public sphere. The inclusion of socialist and leftist influences in the decade's debates particularly distinguished the 1980s discourse of national literature from that of the 1970s, which had remained largely within the confines of official state nationalism. To that effect, during the 1980s the very idea of "national literature" (*minjok munhak*) came, rather, to be parsed as *national-popular* literature (*minjung munhak*), in a deliberate effort to differentiate it from its 1970s precedent.

The decade's renewed understanding of Korean literature drew much of its inspiration from the leftist cultural debates of postliberation Korea in the 1950s, which became accessible to the South Korean public in the 1980s through the opening of old archives as well as the discovery of new ones. Right after Korea's liberation from Japan in 1945, the former socialist members of the KAPF (Korea Artista Proleta Federatio; 1925–35) began recasting their previous commitment to proletarian literature into a commitment to what they now called "national literature." In leading the efforts, critics Im Hwa and An Hamgwang insisted on distinguishing their new ideal from the "nationalist" (*minjokchuŭi*) literature of the right wing.[1] Underlying these critics' new emphasis on the "national" was their renewed awareness of other colonies, mostly in Asia and Africa, that had just been liberated like Korea or still remained under imperial rule.

Korean intellectuals had acquired an enhanced awareness of the non-Western parts of the world during the late colonial years, when they had been forced to renounce their support for proletarian internationalism. It may be tempting to interpret their advocacy of national literature as a symptom of their conversion from socialism to nationalism, yet that would not explain their insistence on distinguishing two kinds of national literature. More plausibly, these intellectuals adjusted their previous socialist internationalism into a more concrete, more nuanced, and more globalized internationalism that paid greater attention to the non-Western world.

In spite of this recalibration, a certain Sovietcentric bias persisted in the postliberation leftist discourse of national literature, and it was that bias that arguably hampered a genuine overcoming of the ethos and worldview of colonial modernity. Recognizing this fact, some leftist critics made an attempt at decentering the Soviet experience by turning to modern Chinese literature as a new and alternative model for the postcolonial rebirth of Korean literature. The presence of such argument suggests that Korean leftists were then giving priority to the colonial issue over that of universal socialism. These writers, however, stopped short of directly questioning the legitimacy of the Soviet Union as the center of the international socialist alliance. After all, following Lenin's writing of *Imperial-*

ism, the Highest Stage of Capitalism (1916), the Soviet Union had paid much attention to anti-imperialist struggles in Asian and African colonies. There were early signs, however, that the Soviet Union regarded its Third-World allies not as their equal revolutionary partners but rather as inferior substitutes for its more desirable European allies. The Soviets' support for anticolonial struggle appeared at times to be less a matter of principle than of strategic need. The full realization of such insight was, however, beyond the epistemological horizon of postwar Korean leftists.

It was not until the 1980s that intellectuals could resume the postliberation effort to envision an alternative to Korea's colonial modernity in the southern half of the Korean Peninsula. Emerging out of the decade's struggle was a shared aspiration for an alternative modernity that would be anti-imperialist in character. As we said, these aspirations can be traced back to the early twentieth century, but they could congeal into a pursuable vision, albeit with its own internal disputes and uncertainties, only during the 1980s.

Imperial Modernity as a Monster of History

To grasp the substance of the idea of alternative anti-imperialist modernity as a novel geopolitical paradigm in 1980s South Korea, we shall first clarify its antithesis, namely, the imperial and colonial modernity of the late nineteenth to twentieth centuries. A colonial consciousness inevitably questions the West-centered view of modernity, as it calls for a reinterpretation of modernity that encompasses its global, and not just Western, experience.

The history of European modernity may be divided into three periods at large. The first is the Renaissance, which is the time when Europe broke out of the medieval social and cultural order by rediscovering and reinterpreting the cultural heritage of ancient Greece. Europe then became "Hellenistic." The second period is the Enlightenment, or the time when Europe cultivated its "culture of reason," helped in no small measure by the immense wealth from the new American continents and also by the intellectual inspirations from China and India. Seventeenth-century Jesuit literature on Asia—from Matteo Ricci's *De Christiana expeditione apud Sinas* (On the Christian expedition to China; 1615) to Philippe Couplet's *Confucius sinarum philosophus* (Confucius: A Chinese philosopher; 1687)—did not quite reach its purpose of helping the missionaries Christianize the Chinese. It did provide, however, important intellectual stimuli to the development of Europe's age of light.² Voltaire, for instance, was inspired by this literature, and in his turn he influenced figures such as Johann Wolfgang von Goethe and Victor Hugo.

The third and last period of modernity is the one Europe entered in the 1840s, when industrial capitalism fueled a drive for global imperialism that quickly led to Europe's establishing colonial dominions across the entire world. The European mind now reimagined the world with itself at the center, thereby turning most other continents into "peripheries," and it projected upon them an image as backward regions in need of salvation through the glory of European civilization. My label of "imperial modernity" refers specifically to this last stage of European modernity.

The global advancement of imperial modernity that began in the late nineteenth century had one of its pivotal moments in the partition of Africa at the 1884 Berlin Conference. With the increasing development of industrial capitalism, European empires recognized then the need to negotiate their competing economic interests in order to prevent military conflicts. They succeeded in defusing immediate tensions for the time being, but the peace established at the conference did not last long and was soon undermined by the expansion of the colonial race well beyond the territories of Africa. Imperialistically motivated conflicts broke out around this time in both the Balkans and in East Asia. In the East, Russia and Japan fought the Russo-Japanese War in 1904 on account of Russia's seeking access to the maritime trade route for the growing demand of its commercial capitalism. For its part, Japan, which had triumphed in the recent Sino-Japanese War (1894), was determined to secure East Asia as a market for its manufactured goods and as a source of natural resources. The war went far beyond the two directly involved countries. France and Germany formed an alliance in support of Russia against Japan, while Britain and the United States sided with Japan, all for their own interests in the region. The war quickly assumed a global significance, and Korea found itself in the awkward position of standing by while witnessing a conflict for the dominion over its own territory. Eventually, the Russo-Japanese War did not evolve into a full-blown world war, which is what would happen in the Balkan Peninsula ten years later. One of the preeminent intellectuals of early twentieth-century Korea, Sin Ch'aeho, was correct when he predicted that the Korean and Balkan Peninsulas were essentially two powder kegs for imperialist world wars.³

The worldwide expansion of imperial modernity forced intellectuals of non-Western countries to formulate their own response to the changing world order. At first, European modernity was widely regarded by them as an object of admiration and emulation. They strove to learn about "civilization" by traveling to Western cities, studying overseas, and translating Western books. Indeed, many people of a non-Western origin at this time reexamined their own cultures from Western perspectives and were persuaded of their "uncivilized" condition. Yet, following the Berlin Conference, when European empires cast off the mantle of reason and divided Africa into colonial territories, those outside the West began to reconsider European modernity as the ultimate ideal for humanity, doubting whether it could at any time offer *them* a path to genuine liberation. In this context, the Russo-Japanese War gave further momentum to this search for alternative paths to modernization. Intellectuals such as Rabindranath Tagore and Jamāl al-Dīn al-Afghānī in Asia, José Martí and José Carlos Mariátegui in Latin America, and Edward Wilmut Blyden and W. E. B. Du Bois of the African diaspora began to reconceive themselves not as the subjects of imperial tutelage in modern civilization but rather as the agents of a modernization that should be conceived and practiced in an anti-imperialist key.

Korean intellectuals were an integral part of this worldwide search for an alternative modernity. In 1905, Korea became a protectorate of Japan as a direct consequence of the Russo-Japanese War. Even among those who embraced European modernity as a historical inevitability, the absolute desirability of a Western-style path to modernization began then to seem questionable. Sin Ch'aeho, for instance, wrote a short story titled "A Dream of the Future of the Earth" (Chigusŏng miraemong; 1919), in which he set up an imaginary dialogue between two Asian intellectuals, an Indian and a Korean.[4] Both characters in the story criticized the evils of imperial modernity and urged colonial intellectuals and the masses to rise up in resistance. Sin's forceful anti-imperialist stance contrasted with that of Yi Injik, who, as one of the earliest writers of Western-style novels, had more of an investment in the West's reputed civilizational power. Even when he grew critical of imperial modernity, Yi keenly subscribed to Japan's call for a pan-Asianist communion of all East Asian people.[5] By contrast, Sin regarded pan-Asianism as a deceitful ethnocentrist doctrine that tried to establish artificial commonalities among people of East Asian descent. Another Korean intellectual, Pyŏn Yŏngman, wrote articles such as *Three Monsters of the World* (*Segye sam koemul*; 1908)—where the three monsters were militarism, capitalism, and colonialism—and *Imperialism: The Great Tragedy of the Twentieth Century* (*Isip-segi tae ch'amgŭk chegukchuŭi*; 1908), in which he observed that European nationalism turned into imperialism after the Industrial Revolution and that, as a consequence, the erstwhile civilization was now fast degenerating into barbarian practices.⁶ At this stage, these writers did not offer any concrete vision for an alternative to Western modernity. They did perform an exacting negative critique, however, and in the process they displayed a stirring desire for overcoming colonial modernity.

The quest for alternative modernity continued to be a topic of interest to Korean writers and intellectuals throughout the first half of the twentieth century. There existed internal divisions and variations, but it is safe to say, in the face of difference, that most thinkers of the era aspired to a path of historical progress that was alternative to the one upheld by imperial conquerors. All these strivings, however, came to be severely constrained and suppressed after the Korean War. It was only during the 1980s that intellectuals were again able to openly consider a new and alternative future for their own communities and for the world. They could do so only after they took on one of the most powerful regulatory ideals of postwar South Korea, namely, the master narrative of Pax Americana.

Demystifying Pax Americana

Koreans first came face to face with American imperialism in the early years of the twentieth century. Until then, the United States had been seen as a country whose nature differed from that of European empires such as Britain, France, and Germany. Korea's sovereign, King Kojong, and some intellectuals even expected the United States to intervene in their favor amid the imperial powers' competition over the Korean Peninsula. The Philippine-American War, however, changed all that. Unbeknownst to the Koreans, in 1905 William Howard Taft, the U.S. secretary of war, and Katsura Tarō, Japan's prime minister, exchanged mutual approval of their countries' claims on, respectively, the Philippines and Korea. Some intellectuals immediately sensed a growing imperialist tenor in the American attitude toward the Philippines. Pyŏn Yŏngman, for instance, commented as follows:

> For the United States of America to have adopted an imperialist policy is the most surprising development in recent world affairs. The country had so far honored a principle of non-intervention, but now it has joined the colonial race for greedy territorial expansion. Such change of policy has been accomplished at a rather revolutionary speed. If a few American officials have objected to

this transformation, apparently a far greater number have accused the critics of being unpatriotic, and they have enthusiastically supported the country's imperial advances into Hawaii and the Philippines.[7]

Ever since the "transformation" lamented by Pyŏn, the Korean view of America continued to waver along with the United States' shifting stances in major historical events, such as President Wilson's speech on people's right to self-determination in 1918, the Treaty of Versailles in 1919, and the Washington Naval Conference in 1922. A few decades later, Korea gained its independence as a direct consequence of America's victory over Japan in the Pacific War. Koreans at that point mostly welcomed the Americans as liberators of their nation. Very soon, however, some intellectuals started to get suspicious of American self-interest. In his dystopian novel *Dawn* (*Hyop'ung*; 1948), for example, leftist-nationalist writer Yŏm Sangsŏp had no qualms in portraying the United States as Japan's replacement in being the new imperial master of Korea.[8]

A military government soon took over South Korea, and under it any critical perception of the United States was suppressed. It then became taboo to question the status of America as an ideal nation, lest one be branded a communist. South Korea experienced a brief democratic spell in 1960, following a successful regime change in the wake of the April 19 student uprising. Some anti-U.S. voices arose then, but they were rapidly quashed by soon-to-be president Pak Chung Hee's military coup in 1961. Even the experience of the Vietnam War, to which South Korea sent over 300,000 troops (second only to the United States), did not substantially affect the muted support of South Koreans for America and its influence on the peninsula.

Against this historical background, the popular uprising that took place in 1980 in the provincial city of Kwangju marked a sea change in Koreans' views of America. Koreans expected Americans to intervene to prevent the government's violent suppression of citizen protestors, but the United States virtually acquiesced to the ensuing massacre by not intervening.[9] Koreans knew then that American officials would do anything to maintain and promote their perceived interests in South Korea. The magic spell of Pax Americana, along with the belief in the fundamental goodness of U.S. oversight of the world order, was finally broken.

Korean intellectuals then began to recontextualize the American-Korean relationship within the global history of imperialism. A representative example of this is the evolution in the works of Hyŏn Kiyŏng, a writer whose life's work was devoted to raising awareness about the 1948 uprisings on Cheju Island. Ever since his debut in the mid-1970s, Hyŏn consistently wrote about this historical incident, in which the U.S. Army was aided by South Korean government forces in the mass killing of local partisans and civilians. The American role in this tragic chapter of Korean history, however, was not recorded in Hyŏn's works during the 1970s, and it was only faintly hinted at in "Asphalt" (Asŭp'alt'ŭ; 1983).[10] The writer eventually turned around in his later work "A Sacred Life" (Kŏrukhan saengae; 1991), which tells the story of a fierce Cheju *haenyŏ* (a female fishing diver) who managed to survive the Pacific War and the division of the two Koreas only to be killed by the American military police during the uprisings of 1948.[11] In the story, the woman is sacrificed because her husband is a socialist sympathizer, an ideology that he came to espouse in his opposition to Japanese imperialism. This story was remarkable for, among other things, its suggestion that American neoimperialism and anticommunism could be even worse than the Japanese occupation that Koreans had hated so much. Such a view had until that moment been rarely represented in South Korean literature or public discourse.

Another literary work that was in many ways emblematic of the 1980s was Cho Chŏngnae's *The Taebaek Mountains* (*T'aebaek sanmaek*; 1989).[12] A quintessential product of the decade's cultural activism, the novel recounts the forgotten stories of the South Korean partisans who sympathized with North Korea during the Korean War. These *ppalch'isan*, as they came to be known, had been long demonized by the anticommunist regime of South Korea. In rescuing their legacy, Cho portrayed these fighters as ordinary Koreans who, at the height of a confounding historical time, tried to do what was best for their country. And he cast American-backed President Syngman Rhee in the role of the unpatriotic pawn. Cho's novel became a best seller in the 1980s because many of its readers were experiencing the tyranny of anticommunism as a state doctrine. For its critique of the Cold War political order, the novel was a standout in the anti-imperialist pedigree of Korean literature.

The recalibration of the U.S.-Korean relationship during the Cold War also led to South Korean intellectuals' reconsideration of North Korea. Going beyond the previous dismissive caricatures of the North, many in the country began to question the role of the United States in the division of the Korean Peninsula and its political consequences. Through this process, some came to assume a more friendly position toward Northerners as South Koreans' brethren in suffering, while others renewed their criticism of the North for the autocratic ways of Kim Ilsung and his *Chuch'e* doctrine.¹³ In spite of such diverging stances, a widespread attitude among progressive intellectuals was that of disapproving of the North Korean regime and its social order all the while withholding open criticism of it. A near consensus was that the United States put pressures on North Korea, thereby stoking military tensions on the peninsula, in order to maintain and motivate its political hegemony in the East Asian region. This attitude of muted criticism has since gained broad popularity in South Korean society, and it informs the views of many South Koreans toward the North today. Such position may seem to some to be too conciliatory and even self-contradictory, but it has an important precedent in, among others, writer Gabriel García Márquez' position on Cuba. Famously, the Colombian Nobel laureate refused to publicly disparage Castro's regime despite his critical view of it, lest his voice should be used as a chorus for the United States' condemnation of the Cuban Revolution.

In the year 2000, on the twentieth anniversary of the uprisings in Kwangju, activist Mun Pusik recalled in a commemorative speech how "the experience of 1980 in Kwangju broke the spell of Americanism for Koreans."¹⁴ The disillusionment cleared the way for Koreans like me to resume our pursuit of an alternative modernity. But there were more spells waiting to be broken, and among them was the Sovietcentric vision of an international socialist alliance that could point the way to the future of Third World countries.

Overcoming Sovietcentrism and Its Vision of the Third World

King Kojong of Korea may have felt friendly toward Russia when he took refuge at its embassy between 1896 and 1897, after the Japanese had orchestrated the brutal assassination of his royal consort, Queen Min. Yet Russia's imperial ambitions over Korea soon became evident, which led King Kojong to assume the title of emperor, in 1897, in the vain hope of keeping his country independent from all other imperial powers. Once Russia turned into the Soviet Union in 1922, however, Koreans' attitudes toward the country shifted to a positive mood. The northern neighbor emerged then as a new shiny socialist state, and the Korean intellectuals who had felt betrayed by the Western powers came to stake their hopes in the USSR. Kim Kyusik, for instance, had gone to Paris in 1919 to represent the Shanghai-based Korean Provisional Government at the Versailles Peace Conference. Kim was turned away at the entrance, which sent him packing to take part in the Congress of the Peoples of the East in Baku, Azerbaijan, in September 1920.

Throughout the colonial era (1910–45), Koreans looked toward the Soviet Union as a possible center for the global effort to overcome imperial modernity. But they also regarded the USSR with suspicion for its own Eurocentrism. Both Sin Ch'aeho and Yŏm Sangsŏp, for instance, maintained a critical distance from the Soviet Union in spite of their sympathies for socialism. Their skepticism was validated when Soviet troops moved to occupy Manchuria and the northern part of the Korean Peninsula in 1945 and exhibited their sense of superiority and their ignorance of local culture to the people of newly occupied territories. Writer Han Sŏrya's short story "Hat" (Moja; 1946), which narrated a soldier's violence against the locals, exemplifies well the Koreans' reaction to the Soviet occupation.[15] Here, too, in spite of being a committed socialist, Han distanced himself immediately from the Soviet Union and its actions in Korea.

After the Korean War, in which the Soviet Union provided aid for North Korea, any positive views of the USSR became anathema in South Korea. Enmity was the only feeling that could be officially or unofficially expressed in reference to the country. The Cold War vilification of the USSR, however, began to be questioned in the 1980s. A process of rediscovery of Soviet history and its relevance to modern Korea initially stirred some excitement among intellectuals, who typically felt euphoric and defiant in breaking a decades-old taboo. A perhaps uncritical and romanticized view of the Soviet Union thus prevailed for a while among South Korean intellectuals. The discourse of labor liberation literature (*nodong haebang munhak*) blossomed and achieved its maximum influence then, and it was then that the Soviet Union came to be seen by Korean activist intellectuals as the global base for international labor activism.[16]

The influence of the Soviet Union ran much deeper in 1980s Korean intellectual discourse than might at first appear to be the case. A perfect example of this would be the rise of the so-called discourse of Third World literature, that is, the critical formation that tried to look at Korean literature through the lens of and in synergy with the cultures of the Third World. The label of "Third World" as an anti-imperialist rallying point implied a critique of at once European imperialism and the divided world order of the Cold War. After the 1955 Bandung Conference, a growing number of countries and ex-colonies sought to go their own way without being aligned with either the American or the Soviet hegemonic poles. The movement had initially little influence in South Korea, where it inspired but a few locals in the country's prostrate postwar situation. By the time the 1970s came around, however, South Korea was in an economic upswing along with other East Asian postcolonial countries such as Indonesia, Singapore, and Taiwan. The idea of nonalignment began then to sound appealing also from a cultural point of view. In his preface to the Korean translation of Samuel Palmer's *Understanding the Third World* (*Che-3 segye ŭi ihae*; 1979), for instance, Pyŏn Hyŏngyun wrote that the Third World movement would have concrete cultural-political implications for Koreans:

> Recently, Koreans have been taking a belated interest in the Third World. This is not just due to the growing importance of the Third World. It is also the manifestation of a historical consciousness that South Korea also belongs to the group. Indeed, understanding the Third World would signify for us much more than just the pursuit of a theoretical sort of knowledge.[17]

In this newly energized cultural climate in South Korea, the rising interest in the Third World came hand in hand with the popularity of the idea of Third World literature.

Within and without Korea, Third World theories attracted those who were critical of the United States, the Soviet Union, and, more generally, the Cold War world order and their dual hegemony. As a liberational discourse, however, the theory of the Third World as an alternative transnational political entity had its own limitations. Those who insisted on a Third World identity apart from both the capitalist and the communist bloc often ended up lending their support to tyrannical nationalist governments, while those who were wary of nationalism saw no other option than to fall back on socialism and the Soviet communist bloc. Such was the sad predicament of Third World intellectuals in the Cold War era, in which so few counterhegemonic visions seemed available. On a global scale, the consequent split among the members of many Third World movements was partly responsible for the waning of initial enthusiasm for the trend.

In spite of these controversies, the Soviet Union did play an important role in the rise of Third World discourse and Third World literature in Asia and Africa. When it hosted the first Asian and African Writers' Congress (AAWC) in Tashkent, Uzbekistan, in 1958, the USSR effectively renewed its long-standing strategy of mobilizing the forces of national liberation movements toward its own strategic goal of a global communist

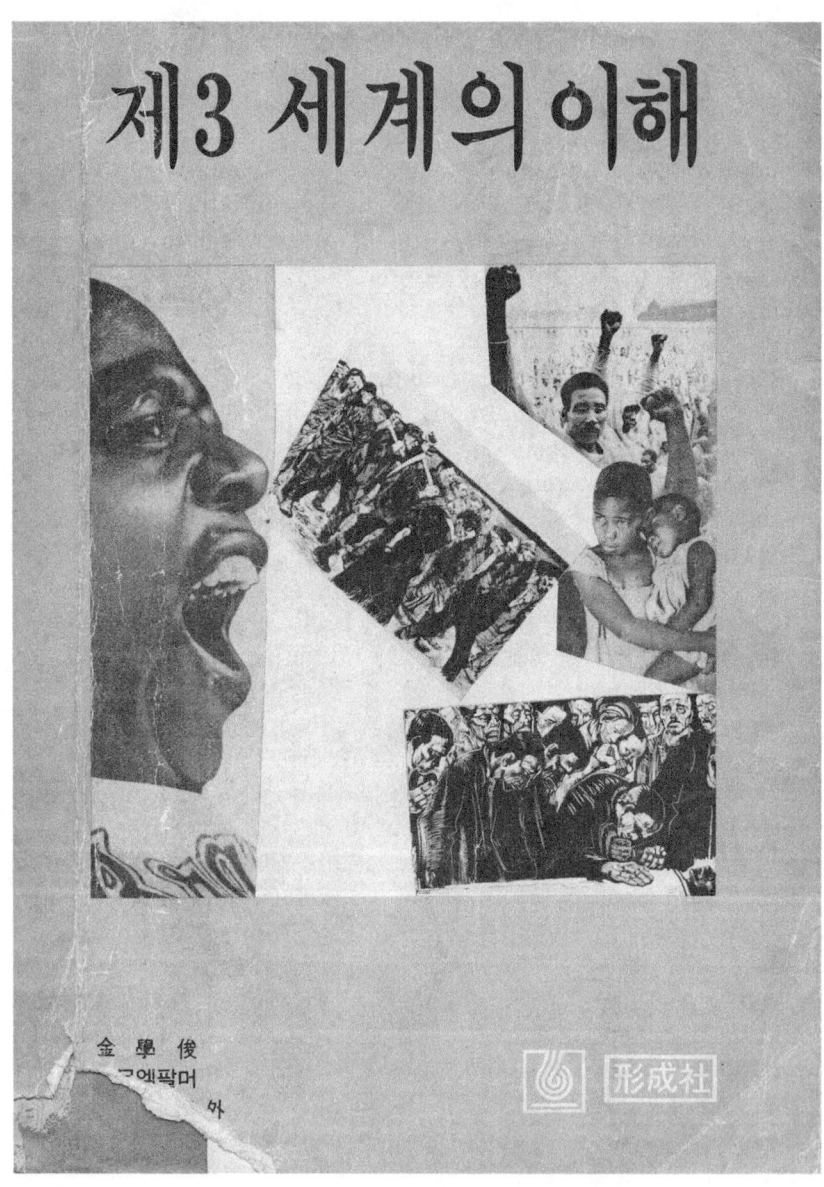

Fig. 3.1. Cover of Samuel Palmer's *Understanding the Third World* (1979), translated into Korean by Kim Hakchun. Courtesy of Hyŏngsŏng sinsŏ.

revolution. The predictable conflict between the Soviet agenda and the hopes of invited participants, however, gradually rose to the surface and soon resulted in China's objection to what it perceived to be Soviet imperialism at the second congress in Egypt in 1962. When the AAWC convened again in Beirut, Lebanon, in 1967, China was conspicuously absent and had instead started its own internationalist writers' organization. It installed its own bureau in what was then British Ceylon, later moving its seat to Peking. In retrospect, it seems clear that the USSR-China split over dominance of these conferences took away substantially from the momentum of the anti-imperialist alliance of Asian and African intellectuals that had originated in Bandung.

Korean intellectuals were likely unaware of the movement's storied past when they embraced the idea of Third World literature in the 1980s. After the journal *Ch'angjak kwa pip'yŏng* (Creation and criticism) ran a special issue on the theme in 1979, Third World literature quickly emerged as a popular topic of debate in journals and in college newspapers. Important milestones in the movement were the publication of the volume *A Theory of Third World Literature* (*Che-3 segye munhangnon*; 1982) as well as *Minjung Culture and the Third World* (*Minjung munhwa wa che-3 segye*; 1983).[18] The latter book was a translation of *How to Change the World with Minjung Culture: Records of the Intercultural Congress of Asia, Africa, Latin America* (Minshū no bunka ga sekai o kaeru tame ni: Ajia, Afurika, Raten Amerika bunka kaigi no kiroku; 1981), which offered Korean readers a record of the AAWC that had been hosted in Kawasaki, 1981, by the association's Japanese branch. At this point, however, Japan had not one but three competing local branches of the AAWC. The host of the Kawasaki conference had been the pro-Soviet branch, while the competing branches had been respectively a pro-Chinese and a Japanese unaligned one that preferred to have its own autonomous organization.[19] The publication was thus infused by the Soviet-led vision of the Third World, but that insight was lost on most of its Korean readers.

In the end, the 1980s discourse of Third World literature was expressive of South Koreans' desire to overcome the imperialist modernity that characterized the Cold War system. At stake here was the vision of an alternative modernity, in which the established hegemony of imperial powers would give way to a more plural and egalitarian world order. That vision fell short of full articulation during the 1980s because its advocates were still not free from the Cold War epistemological framework. It was only with the collapse of the Soviet Union in 1991, and with the ensuing criticism of Soviet imperialism by its ethnic minorities and satellite states, that

Korean intellectuals finally became able to clearly see Sovietcentrism as yet another variation of Eurocentrism. They then gained an insight into the historical role that was played by the USSR in undermining the political and cultural alliance of Third World countries.

Recognizing the Subimperial Self

There was an extra dimension to Korean intellectuals' quest for decolonization that became more and more important in the 1990s: South Korea's awakening to its own subimperial agency. Through the experience of colonization and national division, Koreans had become used to regarding themselves as victims of imperialism. This self-perception is key to understanding many aspects of South Korean society and culture, and it certainly has its material grounds in the country's historical experience. In more ways than one, however, this sort of self-representation has prevented South Koreans from recognizing their own oppression of other people. The country's participation in the Vietnam War as an ally of the United States was arguably the most notorious episode in the history of South Korea's own subimperialist doings.

The events of the Vietnam War challenge and complicate Korea's sense of victimhood. Critical voices were raised already as events unfolded in the 1960s. Among the most poignant literary responses to the war back then was Sin Tongyŏp's poem "My Country" (Choguk; 1969).[20] President Pak Chung Hee had justified participation in the war by citing a supposed need to "defend the free world against communists." Sin's poem countered such propaganda by suggesting that Korean soldiers were rather being dispatched in a mercenary function. And it urged readers not to participate in the fighting against the Vietcong who, it pointed out, had never done any harm to the Korean people. Considering the absence at the time of any real antiwar movement in South Korea, literary voices such as Sin's played an especially important role in shaping local intellectuals' perspectives on the war.

These early insights into South Korea's subimperial agency in Vietnam were developed further during the 1970s and 1980s, as progressive writers continued to emphasize that the war had its purpose not in the safeguarding of democracy but in the protection of America's own imperialist interests. Hwang Sok-young, an emerging writer and a veteran of the war, rose to prominence with antiwar short stories such as "Pagoda" (T'ap; 1970) and "Camel's Eye" (Nakt'a nunkkal; 1972). The 1980s also saw the appearance of full-length novels such as An Chŏnghyo's *White Badge* (*Hayan chŏnjaeng*; 1989), Yi Sangmun's *Yellow* (*Hwangsaeggin*; 1989), and Yi Wŏn'gyu's *Medal and Yoke* (*Hunjang kwa kulle*; 1987). Later in his career, Hwang wrote the novel *Shadow of Arms* (*Mugi ŭi kŭnŭl*; 1987), which probed the arms trade that was conducted by Koreans as well as Americans for the whole duration of the war.[21] Taken together, these works offered an indictment of government-sponsored militarism, and they demonstrated the maturation of antiwar literature and politics in South Korea.

In spite of all these progressions, a straightforward recognition of South Korea as a participant in imperialist aggression was largely absent in 1980s Korea. A deeply entrenched sense of victimhood in some ways allowed the Koreans to live in the comforting belief that they had been unwilling and passive participants of the Vietnam War. It was only during the 1990s, when South Korea began to actively interact with post-Doi Moi Vietnam in the trade of goods and labor, that Koreans came to confront their own subimperial self. Through the experience of the Lai Tai Han (the children of Korean fathers and Vietnamese mothers) and that of Vietnamese migrant brides to Korea, Vietnam and its people finally confronted the South Korean public with the reality and the weight of Korea's past and present subimperial status in the broader East Asian region.

Toward Alternative Modernity

South Korean intellectuals became disenchanted with the magic of Americanism through the experience of the Kwangju Uprising in 1980, and they awakened from their Soviet-philic dreams with the disintegration of the Soviet Union in the early 1990s. As these events were unfolding, along came also the dawning consciousness of South Korea's own contribution to global imperialism. It is thus that the effort to overcome colonial modernity had a new beginning. Through a process of reflection on these historical times, progressive Korean intellectuals, including myself, came to an understanding that there would be no true reform or liberation without a radical change in the world order that originated in imperial modernity, ever since the 1840s. Some lessons were hard won, and yet worth the effort. Without a critique of industrial capitalism, antiimperialism could easily slip into nationalism. And without an anticolonial consciousness, a critique of capitalism could still be in collusion with West-centrism and Orientalism.

The intellectual endeavor of reforming imperial modernity in light of the historical experiences of non-Western people is still continuing today. There are signs of it in Korea, as well as in other postcolonial societies in Asia, Africa, and Latin America. Writers from all these regions have played key roles in local anti-imperialist movements that have existed since the nineteenth century. Exemplary is the towering intellectual figure of Bengali poet Rabindranath Tagore. After witnessing the devastations of World War I, Tagore judged that Western civilization could no longer represent an ideal point of departure in reflections about the future of humanity. Believing that it was now necessary to propagate knowledge of the virtues of the non-Western world, he visited Japan on a lecture tour in 1916. As soon as Japan itself became a full-fledged empire, however, Tagore denounced it for repeating the path of European imperial modernization. He also remained critical of the Soviet Union throughout his life. Tagore found his inspiration for an alternative modernity in Goethe's theory of world literature. He proposed his own version of that theory in an essay titled "World Literature," and that essay, in turn, inspired my own pursuit of an alternative global literature within which the West is decentered.[22]

In its personal dimension, and with a few divergences and adjustments, my own journey followed the trajectory that has been laid out above for my generation of Korean intellectuals. In 1993, I was one of the authors of a volume titled *History of Modern Korean Literature* (*Han'guk kŭndae minjok munhaksa*), which retold modern Korean literary history from the viewpoint of the minjung cultural movement. The volume rightfully reinstated the proletarian and anti-imperialist literature of the colonial era to its central place after nearly half a century of censorship and neglect.[23] After that early publication, I have directed my efforts primarily toward the study of non-Western global literatures. As I traveled to many parts of the world and networked with the intellectuals of many countries, I was able to confirm that Tagore's aspiration for an alternative modernity was and is widely shared by a great number of writers in places as diverse as Okinawa, Palestine, and South Africa.

Throughout my career, I have sought ways to build and maintain collaborative relations with writers and literary intellectuals abroad. I served as the editor of the journal *Silchŏn munhak* (Letters in action) from 1996 to 2005, which has given me the opportunity to frequently invite intellectuals from Asia, Africa, and Latin America for literary forums. I have chosen to label their literature "non-Western global literature," rather than "Third World literature," in recognition of the conceptual limitations of a terminology that had its roots in the Cold War world order. In addition to founding the literary journal *ASIA* in 2008, since 2010 I have been the host

ASIA

세계인과 함께 읽는 아시아 문예 계간지

VOL. 4, NO. 4 | 2009

PHILIPPINE SPECIAL

We, who now present literature of the Philippines, a country that enjoys warm weather year round, are now entering the season of cold winter in Korea. This also contributes to the enjoyment of having *Asia* in this winter.

프란시스코 시오닐 호세
Francisco Sionil José

내 전통은 시사이고, 고통에 시달리면서도 나를 지탱하고 드높여 준 이 불행한 나라다. 아시아의 다른 나라들과 비교할 때 우리나라는 젊다. 우리에게는 이 지역 다른 곳과 같은 당당하고 유서 깊은 기념물들, 고색창연한 문화가 없다. 1521년 스페인이 향료와 금을 찾아 필리핀에 왔을 때 우리는 하나의 나라가 아니었다. 우리는 제각기 독특한 특징을 지닌 채 수천 개의 섬에 흩어져 살면서 서로 싸움을 일삼던 다양한 인종 집단들이었다.

My tradition is Sisa, and this unhappy country which has anguished but also sustained and exalted me. Compared to the other countries in Asia, my country is young; we do not have the august and ancient monuments, the hoary cultures of the region. When Spain came to the Philippines in 1521 in search of spices and gold, we were not a nation—we were several thousand islands with different ethnic groups with distinct characteristics, often at war with one another.

비르힐리오 S. 알마리오
Virgilio S. Almario

카파리스는 문학의 기준을 지우는 것은 매출이 아니라는것을 이해하지 못한다. 만일 그의 상업적 기준이 적용된다면 J. K. 롤링은 두 번째 책을 낸 뒤에 노벨상을 받았어야 마땅하며, 카파리스가 모방하는 마블사 슈퍼히어로 만화의 작가들 역시 그랬어야 마땅하다.

If his commercial standards were applied, then J.K. Rowling should have won the Nobel Prize after her second book, and so should the creators of Marvel superheroes whom Caparas imitates.

제너비브 엘 아센뇨
Genevieve L. Asenjo

필리핀으로 오지 그래, 가깝고 비용도 덜 들고, 우리나라에 가면 더 행복할 걸. 우린 외국인들을 훨씬 더 좋아하니까

Come to the Philippines, it's near, cheaper. You will be happier in my country, because we love foreigners more, you heard yourself saying.

ISSN 1975-3500
13,000원 ($15)

계간 〈아시아〉는 서로 다른 창조적 상상력이 모여 이루어내는 정신의 숲입니다. 단순히 공간으로서의 특정지역을 의미하지 않습니다. 미학적인 지역자치제를 하자는 것도 아닙니다. 자신의 눈으로 자신을 보자는 것입니다.

Asia aspires to be a forest of various creative minds. *Asia* does not mean a specific geographical region. We do not aim for an aesthetic self-governance. We do not propose a cultural separatist movement. We simply want to look at ourselves with our own eyes.

WINTER
15

Fig. 3.2. Cover of *ASIA* (2009). Private collection.

of the Asian, African, and Latin American Literary Forum that takes place annually in the city of Incheon, South Korea. The forum has recently opened a representation office that will be dedicated to managing its international organizational network. Projects of this sort are often believed to be part of the post-1990s wave of globalization in Korean culture. In fact, their ideological underpinnings go back quite directly to the era of minjung democratization in the 1980s.

More recently, however, I have grown increasingly discontented with my projects so far, which have exclusively focused on Asian or colonial literatures. I am now convinced that more desirable would be a globally inclusive project that would advance a concept of world literature that is alternative to the currently hegemonic Eurocentric version. I have to that effect launched a new journal, in 2013, whose title is *Chigujŏk segye munhak* (Global world literature). As a witness of recent neoliberalist developments in South Korean society, I am ever more conscious that my experience of the 1980s lies at the roots of all my subsequent endeavors toward the envisioning of a new, alternative, and nonimperialist modernity.

NOTES

I would like to thank Sunyoung Park for her translation and Viet Nguyen for his feedback on an earlier draft of this essay.

1. See Im Hwa, "Minjok munhak ŭi inyŏm kwa munhak undong," and An Hamgwang, "Minjok munhwaron."
2. See Mungello, *Curious Land*.
3. Sin Ch'aeho, "Manju munje e ch'wihayŏ chaeronham."
4. Sin Ch'aeho, "Chigusŏng miraemong."
5. Yi Injik, *Tears of Blood*.
6. Pyŏn Yŏngman, *Segye sam koemul*.
7. Pyŏn Yŏngman, "Isip-segi taech'amgŭk."
8. Yŏm Sangsŏp, *Hyop'ung*.
9. For the U.S. involvement, or the lack thereof, in the Kwangju Uprising, see Cumings, *Korea's Place in the Sun*, 377–78.
10. Hyŏn Kiyŏng, "Asŭp'alt'ŭ."
11. Hyŏn Kiyŏng, "Kŏrukhan saengae."
12. Cho Chŏngnae, *T'aebaek sanmaek*.
13. Such shifting sentiments among Korean intellectuals subsequently gave rise to scholarly efforts to understand the history of North Korea in alternative and less antagonistic ways. Examples within the literary scholarship include, but are not limited to, Im Hŏnyŏng's *Pundan sidae ŭi munhak* (1992) and Kim Jae-Yong's *Pukhan munhak ŭi yŏksajŏk ihae* (1994).
14. Mun Pusik, *Irŏbŏrin kiŏk ŭl ch'ajasŏ*, 93.

15. Han Sŏrya, "Moja."
16. See, for instance, Cho Chŏnghwan, "Minjujuŭi minjok munhangnon e taehan chagi pip'an."
17. Palmer, Che-3 segye ŭi ihae, 10.
18. Paik Nak-chung, Che-3 segye munhangnon, and Ilbon Asia Ap'ŭrik'a chakka hoeŭi, Minjung munhwa wa che-3 segye. The latter was translated into Korean by Sin Kyŏngnim, a poet who was most famous for his peasant-revolution-themed poetry.
19. Kurihara, Rekishi no dōhyō kara, 139–40.
20. Sin Tongyŏp, "Choguk."
21. See its English translation, Hwang Sok-young, Shadow of Arms.
22. Tagore, Selected Writings on Literature and Language, 138–50.
23. Kim Jae-Yong et al., Han'guk kŭndae minjok munhaksa.

REFERENCES

An Hamgwang. "Minjok munhwaron" [Theory of national literature]. In *Minjok kwa munhak* [Nation and literature], edited by Kim Jae-Yong, 3–24. Munhwa chŏnsŏnsa, 1947.
Cho Chŏnghwan. "Minjujuŭi minjok munhangnon e taehan chagi pip'an kwa nodong haebang munhangnon ŭi chech'ang" [Self-critique of the democratic national literature and a proposal of a labor liberation literature]. *Nodong haebang munhak* 1 (March 1989): 240–67.
Cho Chŏngnae. *T'aebaek sanmaek* [Taebaek mountains]. Han'gilsa, 1989.
Cumings, Bruce. *Korea's Place in the Sun: A Modern History.* New York: W. W. Norton, 1997.
Han Sŏrya. "Moja" [Hat]. *Munhwa chŏnsŏn,* July 1946, 198–215.
Hwang, Sok-yong. *Shadow of Arms.* Translated by Chun Kyung-Ja. New York: Seven Stories Press, 2014.
Hyŏn Kiyŏng. "Asŭp'altŭ" [Asphalt]. In *Asŭp'al'tŭ,* vol. 2 of *Hyŏn Kiyŏng chungdanp'yŏn chŏnjip* [Selected short stories of Hyŏn Kiyŏng], 33–69. Ch'angjak kwa pip'yŏngsa, 1986.
Hyŏn Kiyŏng. "Kŏrukhan saengae" [A sacred life]. In *Majimak t'euri* [The last shepherd], vol. 3 of *Hyŏn Kiyŏng chungdanp'yŏn chŏnjip* [Selected short stories of Hyŏn Kiyŏng], 24–56. Ch'angjak kwa pip'yŏngsa, 1994.
Ilbon Asia Ap'ŭrik'a chakka hoeŭi. *Minjung munhwa wa segye* [*Minjung* culture and the Third World]. Translated by Sin Kyongnim. Ch'angjak kwa pip'yŏngsa, 1983.
Im Hŏnyŏng. *Pundan sidae ŭi munhak* [Literature in the age of national division]. T'aehaksa, 1992.
Im Hwa. "Minjok munhak ŭi inyŏm kwa munhak undong ŭi sasangjŏk t'ongil ŭl wihayŏ" [In defense of the idea of national literature and the ideological unification of the literary movement]. *Munhak* 3 (April 1947): 8–16.
Kim Jae-Yong. *Pukhan munhak ŭi yŏksajŏk ihae* [A historical understanding of North Korean literature]. Munhak kwa chisŏngsa, 1994.
Kim Jae-Yong, Lee Sang-Kyung, O Sŏngho, and Ha Chŏngil. *Han'guk kŭndae minjok munhaksa.* 1993; Han'gilsa, 1998.

Kurihara, Yukio. *Rekishi no dōhyō kara: Nihon-teki "kindai" no aporia o kokufukusuru shisō no kairo* [From a signpost to history: the circuit of thoughts to overcome the aporia called Japanese "modernity"]. Tokyo: Renga Shobō Shinsha, 1989.

Mun Pusik. *Irŏbŏrin kiŏk ŭl chajasŏ* [In search for a lost memory]. Samin, 2002.

Mungello, David E. *Curious Land: Jesuit Accommodation and the Origins of Sinology*. Honolulu: University of Hawaii Press, 1985.

Paik Nak-chung. *Che-3 segye munhangnon* [A theory of Third World literature]. Hanbŏt, 1982.

Palmer, Samuel. *Che-3 segye ŭi ihae* [Understanding the Third World]. Translated by Pyŏn Hyŏngyun. Hyŏngsongsa, 1979.

Pyŏn Yŏngman. "Isip-segi taech'amgŭk" [Imperialism: The great tragedy of the twentieth century]. In *Pyŏn Yŏngman chŏnjip* 2: 42–72. Sungkyunkwan University Press, 2006.

Pyŏn Yŏngman. *Segye sam koemul* [Three monsters of the world]. Kwanghak sŏp'o, 1908.

Sin Ch'aeho. "Chigusŏng miraemong" [A dream of the future of the earth]. *Taehan maeil sinbo*, July 15–August 10, 1909.

Sin Ch'aeho. "Manju munje e ch'wihayŏ chaeronham" [Again on the issue of Manchuria]. *Taehan maeil sinbo*, January 19–22, 1910.

Sin Tongyŏp. "Choguk" [My country]. *Wŏlgan munhak*, June 1969, 162.

Tagore, Rabindranath. *Selected Writings on Literature and Language*. Edited by Sukanta Chaudhuri. New Delhi: Oxford University Press, 2001.

Yi, Injik. *Tears of Blood*. In *Korean Classical Literature: An Anthology*, edited by Chung Chong-wha, 156–221. New York: Routledge, 1989.

Yŏm Sangsŏp. *Hyop'ung* [Dawn wind]. Silch'ŏn munhaksa, 1998.

4

Political Travel at Cold War's End

International Student Exchanges between Australia and the Two Koreas

Ruth Barraclough

I flew from Hong Kong into Kimpo Airport the last summer of the Cold War, August 1989. A freshman Russian major from the University of Queensland, I had been selected by the campus group Australian Student Christian Movement (hereafter ASCM) for an "exposure tour" hosted by our sister organization in South Korea, the Korean Student Christian Federation (KSCF). Supported by progressive churches, Christian university circles across the Asia-Pacific ran exchange programs in the 1980s that allowed students to travel between societies with repressive regimes and vibrant democratization movements including the Philippines, Taiwan, Indonesia, Sri Lanka and South Korea. Political exposure tours were two-way. Students visiting Australia and New Zealand, for instance, could be introduced to current issues of feminist politics, land rights for indigenous people, and environmental campaigns to protect ancient forests, while visitors to South Korea in the 1980s touched down at the very height of the student movement. Although two years had passed since giant rolling strikes and street demonstrations brought down General Chun Doo Hwan's regime in 1987, the scattering of the opposition parties meant that an old military comrade and intimate of Chun's, Roh Tae Woo, narrowly won the nation's democratic elections for president held late that year, and the military remained deeply entrenched in state power in South Korea. The summer of 1989 would not be a quiet one.

This chapter reflects on the international student exchanges of the

1980s that provide a rare glimpse of the global dimensions of South Korea's labor and student movements. Operating with the endorsement and protection of the established churches in both countries—Catholic and Protestant—these exchanges brought foreign students into the very heart of student circles and labor organizations in Korea. In South Korea, the developmental state's rapid industrialization policies of the preceding two decades had relied upon and reproduced extreme class divisions in its pursuit of economic growth. In response to the poverty and desperation found in the slums and shanty towns that housed South Korea's young industrial workforce, the Uniting Church in Australia had by the late 1980s decided to concentrate its resources upon the Urban Industrial Mission (UIM) set up in Yŏngdŭngp'o, one of the epicenters of Seoul's factory districts. UIM's message was a compelling combination of working-class pride, Christian fellowship, and labor power. Along with the students, they would be my hosts.

For students in the 1970s and 1980s, international travel was a rare privilege. The Cold War world was globalized in ways very different from our current configuration; as recently as the late 1980s, large swathes of the world were closed off to informal travel, and visas were a complicated business. As a close ally of the United States and a capitalist country, South Korea could be included within the nomenclature "First World," but in the 1980s it was neither a travel nor a study destination and was considered a hardship posting for expatriates. Within South Korea itself the restriction on international travel was only lifted in 1989; before that, on Korean Air flights out of Seoul one seemed to encounter only businessmen, government officials, and scholarship students heading abroad.[1] These restrictions meant that South Korean youth culture in the 1980s was relatively isolated from global peers in ways that enabled them to create their own unique campus dissident culture. Furthermore, the military state's attempts to enforce the idea that the entire "First World" was complacently capitalist were systematically undermined by the domestic and transnational underground networks of solidarity and support that the student and labor movement could call upon.

The international exchanges organized by the Student Christian Movements (SCMs) only rarely intervened in large-scale political events, such as when SCMs' members facilitated the travel of Lim Su-kyung to North Korea in 1989. Nevertheless, they were an exceptional phenomenon of student-led transnational organization that operated at the heart of a vast and diverse democratization movement in South Korea. One of the striking features of the Australian-Korean exchange relationship was that even during the Cold War the program could incorporate both South and North Korea. Situated somewhere between Cold War "political tourism" and a new, bottom-up attempt at "horizontal solidarity" across the globe, these exchanges helped to disseminate the dirty secrets of both South Korea and Australia, to buttress key labor organizations in South Korea, and in 1989 to open Pyongyang up to a summer of curious youth.

The conventional narrative of globalization and international travel in South Korea is that it began when the dictatorship ended, stirred into being by a curiosity about the world that was equal parts open-minded and consumer oriented: a liberal capitalist model of globalization. But globalization in fact has a far richer history that traverses the dictatorship years with its valuable international solidarities and distinct exiles.

World Student Christian Federation and World Festival of Youth and Students

The institution behind these solidarity tours was the old and eminent late-nineteenth-century university organization the World Student Christian Federation (WSCF). The WSCF had grown out of the ecumenical spirit and "muscular Christianity" of the nineteenth-century YMCAs and YWCAs. Evangelical, self-confident, and pushing a spirit of religious ecumenism radical for the time, the YMCA and YWCA had from the beginning targeted working-class and lower-middle class youths in their championing of healthy sporting pursuits and spiritual refreshment of young laboring men and women. By contrast, the WSCF represented a rather more cerebral and intellectual stream of campus activity for coeds. Originating in Europe and North America, the movement expanded into colonial India and Ceylon (1912), colonial Hong Kong (1920s), colonial Indonesia (1932), Japan (1903), and Australia (1892).[2] The WSCF was constituted of autonomous SCMs that operated in member countries and were responsive to the social and political climate of their national contexts. With the ending of colonial rule in parts of the Asia-Pacific after 1945, local SCMs reemerged or were newly formed and, as campus organizations, represented an elite, liberal Christian leadership cadre in the 1950s and early 1960s.

Early luminaries of SCMs include Amir Sjarifuddin, prime minister of Indonesia (1947–48); Eduardo Mondlane, president of the Mozambique Liberation Front (1962–69); and M. M. Thomas, chairperson of the World Council of Churches (1968–75) and, later, governor of the Indian

State of Nagaland (1990–92). Two postwar Australian prime ministers were former members of the ASCM: the Liberal PM Robert Menzies (1949–66) and the Labour PM Bob Hawke (1983–91). The shift in campus politics from the 1950s to the more radical mood of the 1960s and '70s challenged national SCMs to look beyond their universities and engage with the many organized political movements emerging "on the streets and in the villages."[3] The turn away from the privileged arena of university politics and discussion groups to the more urgent political and economic problems found off campus was a corollary of a larger shift toward a politics of direct action in the 1970s. As progressive Christian groups shifted their focus off campus and to the more compelling problems in the streets, conservative evangelical student groups moved into the space they had vacated.

In 1972 the WSCF restructured itself around geographic regions, and the WSCF Asia-Pacific became its own entity and began to establish networks of solidarity inside the region. Each country had distinct issues that defined their political landscape in the 1970s and 1980s. Political tours facilitated by the local SCMs encountered popular prodemocracy movements against entrenched regimes in Taiwan and the Philippines. In Indonesia the local SCM students formed part of a Christian minority who were careful to abide by the government proscription on discussing the takeover of East Timor and West Papua and the 1965 massacre of communists. In Sri Lanka, while the civil war escalated from the early 1980s, SCM was the only nationwide campus organization where Tamil and Sinhalese university students could meet each other as fellow students working for peace. In Singapore the local SCM movement that had been openly critical of the Lee Kuan Yew government was accused in 1987 of staging a communist plot to overthrow the government. Members were arrested and imprisoned, a huge blow to the organization. In South Korea the local SCM was an important campus organization in the 1970s and 1980s. As part of the democratization movement under the generals, some KSCFers (their official name was Hang'uk kidok haksaenghoe ch'ong yŏnmaeng) in the 1980s abandoned the university to seek factory work in the industrial districts, or took leadership positions in the student movement that in 1987 brought down the Chun Doo Hwan government. On top of their local, national political activities, the Asia-Pacific SCMs also ran international exchanges. Both the WSCF and YMCA International were involved in the International Preparatory Committee that organized the World Festival of Youth and Students held in North Korea in 1989.

The 1989 invitation from the KSCF for the Australian SCM to send a student delegate on a solidarity exchange arrived at the same time that Pyongyang invited the students of the world to the thirteenth World Festival of Youth and Students, held that year for the first time in Asia. Both the North American YMCA and the Australian SCM would send delegates to Pyongyang in 1989.[4] Australia maintained diplomatic relations with both North and South Korea, and this year the invitation to attend one of the highlights of the student calendar proved irresistible to my fellow SCMers. That July, when everyone else was going to Pyongyang, I alone would spend the summer in the South.

A feature on the calendar of university students during the Cold War, the World Festival of Youth and Students originated in Europe and crisscrossed the Cold War divide with twelve festivals staged between 1947 and 1985, including in Prague (1947), Vienna (1959), Helsinki (1962), and Moscow (1985). The World Festival moved to Asia for the first time when Pyongyang announced it would host the students and youth of the world in 1989. Australia had been sending delegates to the World Festival for decades. In 1957, the youth wing of the Australian Communist Party had sent over one hundred delegates to the sixth World Festival in Moscow, while Trotskyites went to Helsinki in 1962 and youth of various political stripes, including indigenous Australian activists, participated in the 1968 World Festival in Bulgaria.[5]

The World Festivals were a unique expression of the Cold War's particular strain of internationalism and showed how the hearts and minds of the world's students constituted an important ideological battleground throughout the Cold War. The World Festivals also intersected in important ways with global political events. The sixth World Festival in Moscow took place only a year after Khrushchev's February 1956 secret speech denouncing Stalin. As Margaret Peacock explains, it was the staging of the Festival that allowed the Soviet Union to present "a new image of Cold War youth to the world ... to replace an older Stalinist version of insulated Soviet youngsters with new images of well-educated, independent, creative and activist youth."[6] The 1968 ninth World Festival in Bulgaria followed an extraordinary year of political events in Vietnam (the Tet Offensive), Paris (May '68), and Prague (the Prague Spring). Many delegates to the 1968 summer Festival in Sofia had stopped off in Prague on their way to Sofia, keen to savor the experience of a communist state reforming its own institutions.[7] In carefully crafted language, the Sofia Festival condemned the actions of the reformist government in Czechoslovakia.[8] Three weeks after the festival ended, Warsaw Pact forces invaded Prague. Delegates at the Sofia Festival who had been part of the democratic euphoria and street demonstrations in Prague were left devastated by this turn of events. These precedents suggest that festival organizers, despite their best efforts, were not always in control of the political experience of their guests.[9]

Political Travel in the "Free World"

The historian of Soviet Russia Sheila Fitzpatrick has used the term *political tourist* to describe those visitors to the Soviet Union from the 1920s to the 1940s who came to observe a new political system at work. She reports that just as people traveled to Italy to look at the art, people went to the Soviet Union to observe the politics of this new reorganized society. Fellow travelers as well as curious or disinterested professional scientists, journalists, feminists, musicians, and psychiatrists took Soviet agency tours to find out about developments in their field in this experimental state. As Fitzpatrick notes, while "politics was the point" of many of these tours, people also came for professional curiosity as "interesting things were going on [in] the state organization of science, economic planning, experimental theatre and the mass dissemination of high culture."[10] Although traces of the Cold War model of political tourism can be found in the WSCF exchanges whose itineraries were devoted to political meetings, cultural events, and discussions of social problems, the fact that they were often clandestine and antistate gave them an entirely different flavor. These tours might be described as possessing an added layer of "political translation" in their attempt to build horizontal solidarities in a globalizing world. Here Arjun Appadurai's notion of "cosmopolitanism from below," which regards global activism as at heart an act of translation, is useful for explaining and understanding those solidarity tours that created a mutually articulated comradeship.[11]

While political travel has conventionally referred to visitors to the communist states, in fact the "free world" had its own political travelers during the Cold War. The African American singer Paul Robeson's hugely successful tour of Australia in 1960, organized by a combination of entertainment agency and waterside and building workers unions, can be included within this category. Paul Robeson came to Australia somewhat reluctantly.[12] An international star of stage, screen, and the political platform, Robeson's travel had been curtailed between 1950 and 1958 in penalty for his outspoken support of the Soviet Union alongside criticism of racial discrimination in the United States. When his passport and traveling rights were finally returned to him, Australia—administered at that time by the anticommunist Menzies government—was not the most attractive prospect for a solidarity tour, but the money offered was spectacular. On his tour of the country, Paul Robeson's talent, celebrity, and outspoken political opinions received a rapturous response. Robeson's trip is remembered in Australia with a famous clip of him on a building site singing to the workers building the Sydney Opera House, which is in scaffolding in the background while the audience of listening workers smoke thoughtfully. Reflecting on this moment, Australian historian Jeff Sparrow writes, "It's a tiny glimpse of the Old Left's dream: the unity of black and white, proletarians and intellectuals, high culture and manual labor—a dream that momentarily became real."[13] Paul Robeson's records had sold well in Australia since the 1930s, and his tour would have a profound and lasting impact on Australian society. To Robeson's message of international working-class solidarity was added the "powerful encouragement" he gave to the many Australian indigenous people he met across the country and his outspoken support for their cause of Aboriginal rights and racial equality.[14] In the white-settler colony of Australia, politically and culturally isolated by the Cold War, Paul Robeson was a figure of extraordinary political and racial glamour whose brief tour continues to resonate to this day.[15]

Another example of unconventional political travel in the "free world" would be the London Recruits, who traveled to apartheid South Africa in the late 1960s and early 1970s under the blandest of covers: white tourists. This was a period when the apartheid regime had jailed all the top leaders of the African National Congress (ANC), including Nelson Mandela, forcing the organization to seek recruits from sympathizers outside the country. Between 1967 and 1971 the ANC in London recruited young men and women, students, workers, and tourists who traveled to South Africa on short missions to "reinvigorate resistance to apartheid within South Africa."[16] Some distributed thousands of leaflets and staged fleeting public propaganda events to keep the ANC alive in its "bleakest period"; others smuggled weapons into the apartheid state.[17] As organizer Ronnie Kasrils noted, "Apartheid, like any racist doctrine, presumed that all white people were natural allies."[18] Currently under production as a feature documentary, the story of the London Recruits reveals the varied paths of international solidarity in the ANC's history. In contrast to the World Festivals, which aspired to control political tourism in the communist world, the so-called free world had its own autonomous, sometimes spontaneous networks of connection and solidarity that provided a space of critique and even intervention across the globe. It is in this context that I turn to

Fig. 4.1. Workers listen to American singer Paul Robeson's performance at the Sydney Opera House building site on November 9, 1960. Courtesy of Sydney Opera House.

examine the South Korean and Australasian student exchanges of the 1980s.

Seoul and Pyongyang

Beginning with worker missions in the 1960s, churches in South Korea had made an effort to reach out to the thousands of young men and women coming to urban centers to find work in factories, construction sites, and sweatshop districts as Korea rapidly industrialized. These worker missions were so keenly received that a new approach of industrial mission (*sanŏp sŏn'gyo*) that tackled city poverty and labor issues was born to minister directly to young workers.[19] Worker missions have a long and distinguished history in Europe and North America. The worker-priests in France and Belgium who entered factories after the Second World War to bring a "lived theology" to the industrial proletariat were attempting to break down the divide separating the established Catholic Church from the working classes.[20] While some of these priests came from worker or peasant families, others had endured "the proletarian experience of the 4,000 French priests imprisoned in Nazi war camps,"[21] and their activities became influential throughout Western Europe. In the United States, in Chicago and Detroit, religion and civil rights activism converged in the missions that sought to reach out to the "young, Black and poor" of the industrial cities.[22] Industrial missions where clergy took on factory jobs or moved into slums and ghettos were often a complex mix of preaching and learning. This same tension characterized the urban industrial missions in South Korea, where over time the missionaries moved from ministering to the suffering of workers to advocating labor rights. By 1989 branches of the main Protestant and Catholic churches in South Korea had been engaged in industrial missionary work for nearly three decades through the Urban Industrial Missions and the Catholic organization Young Christian Workers.

The Uniting Church in Australia had been involved in the Urban Industrial Missions (UIM) of the Presbyterian Church of Korea since the 1970s. In 1978 the Australian UIM worker Stephen Lavender was deported from Korea for "spreading communism" to factory girls.[23] Tony Dawson worked at the Yŏngdŭngp'o UIM in the 1980s, followed by another Australian, Debbie Carstens, but eventually the Uniting Church would try to send young Korean Australian students and activists, many of whom were bilingual, as its representatives to the UIM. All of these young people shared formative life experiences with their peers in industrial Seoul that in some cases shaped a whole life trajectory. Debbie Carstens, whom I met in Yŏngdŭngp'o in 1992, returned to Sydney and established an organization called Asian Women at Work. This now twenty-plus-year-old organization with two thousand members advocates for the labor rights (and access to recreational activities, like swimming lessons) of women new to Australia employed in the clothing, textile, and footwear industries.[24] Yoon Yŏng-mo, who was a prominent member of the Melbourne branch of the Australian Student Christian Movement in the 1980s, went to South Korea and remained there, becoming in the mid-1990s an organizer at the Korean Confederation of Trade Unions (Minju Noch'ong), and later would hold a position with the International Labor Organization. Clearly the experience of the Urban Industrial Mission had a radicalizing impact that could be lifelong.

By the mid-1980s, ASCM and KSCF had a yearly student exchange. In 1989 the ASCM was sending delegates to the thirteenth World Festival of Youth and Students in Pyongyang. At the same time, as part of its student exchange program with the KSCF, the organization sent a student on what was dubbed an "exposure tour" to South Korea. I was approached in 1989 by the ASCM with the option of being either a delegate to Pyongyang or the guest of the KSCF in Seoul. This is both an example of the success of North Korea's "Juche diplomacy"—which sought alliances with both non-aligned and First World countries—and a reflection of the Australian government's own diplomatic approach to Northeast Asia, where both countries were accessible to us. It also reminds us of this period of time when to an outsider North Korea and South Korea appeared equally intimidating. As it turned out in the months leading up to the World Festival, an extraordinary political intervention was being quietly organized through now long-established connections of solidarity and trust built between the KSCF and its Australian partners.

When Lim Su-kyung arrived at the Pyongyang World Festival as the sole student representative from South Korea, she had been traveling for ten days. South Korea's National Union of Students (Chŏndaehyŏp) was not deterred when its application to send a delegation to the World Festival was refused by the South Korean government. Its leaders turned to the campus organization whose international links were the strongest and most viable: the KSCF. Flying first to Japan and then to Germany, Lim had journeyed on an itinerary carefully organized for her by Korean and Australian Christian activists working together outside the country. Lim herself was not a student leader. Rather, in the nature of political travel, her role was to be a messenger representing thousands just like her and carrying a common objective of solidarity and reunification.

Lim Su-kyung's remarkable journey took the South Korean state security agency by surprise. She was arrested when on August 15 she attempted to cross the border into South Korea as an act of symbolic unification of the two nations. Arrests of her associates followed swiftly. The Korean Australian dentist and missionary Kim Chin-yop was arrested on September 2, 1989. Kim Chin-yop had arrived in Pusan in April 1989, sent by the Uniting Church of Australia to head the dental clinic of the Maternal-Child Health Centre at Ilshin Hospital in Pusan.[25] His crime was helping plan the travel arrangements for Lim using contacts with student organizations in West Germany. Kim was sentenced to two years' imprisonment on charges of espionage. His arrest was protested in the Australian Parliament, and he was adopted as a prisoner of conscience by Amnesty International.[26] Kim's sentence was reduced on appeal to eighteen months; after he was released, he went on a speaking tour on university campuses around Australia. As other arrests followed, KSCF members in Seoul went into hiding, their vacated apartments ransacked by Korean Central Intelligence Agency (KCIA) agents and their family members questioned.

Fig. 4.2. Lim Su-kyung in Pyongyang, July 1989.

So when I touched down at Kimpo Airport on August 21, 1989, no one from our sister organization was there to meet me. Following Lim Su-kyung's spectacular tour, everyone had gone into hiding. After two hours of wheeling my luggage around the arrivals hall at Kimpo hoping to be claimed, I accepted that I would need to make my own way into the city. Flagging down a taxi, I tried out the only globalized brand of cheap hotels I could think of—YMCA—and the taxi driver and I were both mightily relieved that with this talisman we could understand each other. Taxis in those days commonly picked up multiple passengers along their journeys and exchanged money based on a baffling series of algorithms. After the first fright of a young mother and child opening my door to jump in, I became accustomed to the practice during the one-hour journey into the city. There was much to learn. I was astonished to be deposited not outside the welcome sign to my hotel but across an eight-lane city thoroughfare in the middle of Chongno, with kind but firm instructions to exit there with my enormous orange suitcase and take the Chonggak underpass. It was a humid, rainy, and magical summer evening.

Seoul and Puch'ŏn

Political travel such as that organized by the Student Christian Movements was not about the individual; rather, one was a messenger entrusted with stories, experiences, and messages to take back to Australian campuses. Political tourists learned that Christianity meant different things and had different levels of radicalization in each national context. In South Korea the movement had martyrs. When I finally met my Korean hosts, I was taken to the verdant green gravesite at Seoul National University of Kim Sejin, a KSCF member who had taken his own life in 1986 protesting against military violence.[27] Day after day I took notes and photographs and stayed up late hearing about the issues that South Korean students considered important and wanted us to understand: the brutality of rapid industrialization, the radical stream in the working class exemplified by Chŏn T'aeil, and the press for reunification with the North.

My three-week political tour of South Korea was spent with factory girls in Puch'ŏn, on farm stays in South Chŏlla Province, in visits to KSCF student circles on university campuses, and in meetings with former prisoners who had been arrested in Kwangju following the 1980 uprising and military crackdown. I was taken on a tour of the remnants of the slum district in Sadang-dong and stayed for a week in the industrial north of Seoul, where I enjoyed workers' literary festivals, music shows, and private conversations with new friends. I was constantly on the move because my hosts were under surveillance. Sometimes we arrived home to find a KCIA agent lolling by the door. On these occasions, as the argument spiraled into one hour, two hours, I was dispatched to buy cigarettes to keep up the comrade's stamina. One of the factory girls I met in Puch'ŏn worked for the women's labor union and was a keen reader of Russian literature. Mistrustful of translations that might dilute the power of the original, she read in Russian with the aid of a dictionary propped up beside her. Many of these encounters and experiences ended up finding their way into my book *Factory Girl Literature*.

One of the challenges of building solidarity with students and workers in South Korea was learning Korean. While students often preferred to read key Marxist texts (as well as novels) in their original English, French, or German, all the enjoyment and ferment of discussion and conversation occurred in Korean. For the foreign political tourist, learning Korean was a daunting and exhilarating invitation to solidarity. Studying political translation in this context was also an act of homage to the South Korean student movement's anti-imperialism that made English a minor language. Rather than being a symptom of a nationalist, parochial student movement, the fact that learning Korean (or trying to learn Korean) was for the political tourist the compulsory first step to building relationships and entering a committed group of fellow student activists felt like the very incarnation of transnational solidarity.

There were many acts of political and linguistic translation as I passed through conversations, circle meetings, documentary film showings, poetry nights, and testimonial drinking sessions. I envied the Korean skills of Yoon Yŏng-mo and later Debbie Carstens at the UIM, who told me she was motivated to learn so fast because none of the workers at the UIM spoke English and she desperately wanted to make friends. My Puchŏn friend labored over Dostoyevsky and Gorky at night after working in a factory all day, determined not to miss out on the richness of a foreign linguistic world. In the South Korean context of "cosmopolitanism from below," translation was no mere metaphor; it was a compelling and attractive political act on both sides. When some young musicians who were also factory workers performed a show and gave me lessons on the *jabara* (cymbal), they told me they had never spoken to a foreigner before or seen one close up. How agreeable that their first foreigner should be a Christian activist like them, they told me.[28] Appadurai writes of a "vernacular cosmopolitanism" that is not contained by boundaries of neighborhood or language and whose aim is to produce a "preferred geography of the global."[29] However ephemeral or inconclusive such concepts may seem, the lived experience of these experiments lingers on in memory, captured in the records of multiple organizations around the globe.

In asking how we might measure the impact of these circuits of transnational activism, it becomes clear how difficult it is to measure such fleeting moments of human solidarity. The political tour I experienced was undoubtedly an expression of middle-class student privilege. But it was also a unique investment by churches across South Korea and Australia that had been decades in the making. I offer this chapter as merely some preliminary reflections on what was a profound and formative experience for all of those involved. I would like to bookend this reflection with a final anecdote.

A few days before I departed Brisbane for this political adventure, I was in conversation with our neighbor, an indigenous-rights activist and evangelical Christian called Auntie Jean Phillips.[30] Jean had grown up on the Aboriginal reserve in South Queensland, Cherbourg. She lived in the caretaker cottage of a rotting old mansion owned by the Uniting Church. Chatting over our shared back fence, Jean learned that I was about to travel to South Korea on an SCM international exchange. She turned to me and said, "Why are you going over there? We have plenty of problems here that need energy and attention"—and then, most devastatingly, "Our girls never get to have a chance like that." She was right. None of the indigenous girls I went to primary school with had made it to my selective high school. Some of the boys did, but no girls. That is not the case today, but in the 1970s and 1980s in inner-city Brisbane, when racist and sexual violence against indigenous women and girls was ever present in Queensland, opportunities for political tourism or cosmopolitanism from below were monopolized by white students such as myself. Walking though the KSCF offices in the Christian Broadcasting Building in Chongno-5-ga, I recall seeing a filing cabinet plastered with political stickers, among them an Australian indigenous land-rights flag. The sticker had made it across the Pacific Ocean, but a delegate had not. The very opportunity I had received to experience a trans-Pacific world of political solidarity was built on layers of exclusions that no amount of anti-imperialist solidarity could deny.

Conclusion

The year 1989, like 1968, was an extraordinary year to be voyaging on political travels. In those days there was no direct flight from Australia to Korea, and en route to Seoul I stopped off in Hong Kong. The timing was significant: just two and a half months earlier, on June 4, 1989, the government in China had violently ended a peaceful occupation of Tiananmen Square calling for democratic reform. In Hong Kong the shock and apprehension from the Tiananmen Square killings two months earlier was palpable. In public arenas such as ferry and bus terminals, mounted televisions replayed scenes of the tanks rolling through central Beijing. People gathered to watch the same footage over and over again; the city felt anxious and subdued. By 1989 Hong Kong had long been a regional hub for exiles, fortune hunters, and booksellers whose magazines and books were banned in other parts of Asia. In its bookstores one could find accounts of antigovernment protests in Burma in 1988 and the Philippines in 1986; analyses of the transition to democracy in Taiwan following the lifting of martial law in 1987; and T. K.'s *Letters from South Korea* that reported on the democratization movement under military dictatorship.

Just as 1968 encapsulated a global mood of protest and revolution that traveled from Prague to Paris to Chicago, 1989 in East Asia was also a year of extraordinary change. Long overshadowed by events in Europe that marked 1989 as the year that communism crumbled to an ignominious end, in East Asia the dominant political mood was democratization. This chapter offers an alternative snapshot of the year 1989: a summer when Korea, North and South, was *the* place to be, where one could observe a First World nation's relentless suppression of its students and workers, while to the north a self-serving but nonetheless dazzling exercise in cosmopolitan solidarity was taking place.

NOTES

1. Jennifer Chun and Judy Han have written about these travel restrictions as satisfying the military state's desire for surveillance and economic protectionism, and the significance of the year 1989 as a "turning point in the international mobility of Korean citizens." Chun and Han, "Language Travels and Global Aspirations of Korean Youth," 571.
2. These details are drawn from the WSCF Asia-Pacific official history published on the website: http://www.wscfap.org/nationalmovements/index.html (accessed September 2015).
3. Ibid.
4. Van Mersbergen, "The Rhetorical Reduction of the 13th World Festival of Youth and Students."
5. Piccini, "'There Is No Solidarity,'" 193.
6. Peacock, "The Perils of Building Cold War Consensus."
7. Piccini, "'There Is No Solidarity,'" 192.
8. Taylor, *Let's Twist Again*, 53–57.
9. Even Australia's official Communist Party delegates sent to work for the festival's organizing committee criticized the festival for its inability to respond to the reforms emerging from Czechoslovakia. See Piccini, "'There Is No Solidarity,'" 194–95.
10. Fitzpatrick, "Australian Visitors to the Soviet Union," 24.
11. Appadurai, "Cosmopolitanism from Below."
12. Duberman, *Paul Robeson*.
13. Sparrow, "Paul Robeson."
14. Curthoys, "Paul Robeson's Visit to Australia and Aboriginal Activism, 1960."
15. Paul Robeson is bound up with the history of Australia's most iconic building, and his impromptu performance is acknowledged as the first concert at the Sydney Opera House. Plays, documentaries, memoirs, radio shows, and history books continue to document his role in Australian cultural and political life. Playwright Nancy Willis's 1987 account of Paul Robeson's life and songs and his visit to Australia, *Deep Bells Ring*, toured the country playing at theaters, universities, and construction sites. The National Museum of Australia is considering staging an exhibition of Robeson's tour of Australia (private communication with curator Sophie Jensen, August 2016).
16. Smith, "Secret London Activists."
17. On the subject of arms smuggling into Southern Africa for the ANC under cover of innocuous tourist safaris, see the 2001 documentary *The Secret Safari*.
18. Ronnie Kasrils, quoted in Jeffries, "The Leaflet Bombers."

19. Kim Won et al., *Minju nojo*, 269.
20. Arnal, *Priests in Working-Class Blue*.
21. Murphy, "Review of *Priests in Working-Class Blue*," 652.
22. Gellman, "Black Freedom Struggles."
23. Ballantyne, "Expelled Missionary Wants to Go Back," 5.
24. See Australian Labour Party parliamentarian Chris Hayes's speech congratulating Asian Women at Work on twenty years of organizing: http://www.chrishayesmp.com/index.php/media-centre/fowler-speeches/40-speeches-2013/779-14-november-2013-asian-women-at-work
25. Amnesty International, "Medical Concern."
26. *Hansard Parliamentary Debates*, November 30, 1989, 3202.
27. As Kim Won writes in *The South Korean Democratization Movement: A Sourcebook*, Kim Sejin was a Seoul National University KSCF member and one of the leaders of a campaign of "direct anti-imperialism" that protested the compulsory military training students were forced to undertake at the demilitarized border zone. As the Korean military under the Combined Forces Agreement with the United States was the subordinate partner, students argued that as conscripts they were effectively "American mercenaries." Lee and Kim, *The South Korean Democratization Movement*, 233–50. Kim Sejin's final letter to his parents before he took his own life is reproduced in this digital archive: http://m.blog.naver.com/open-archives/220695276122
28. I should note that nobody I encountered in the late 1980s in South Korea used the word "socialist" (*sahoejuŭi*) to describe their political orientation. Instead, people used a variety of phrases such as worker-centered, minjung-oriented, or prodemocracy, sometimes coupled with the mocking self-reference *ppalgaengi* (commie). The first time this political traveler encountered the term "socialist" in open parlance was during the winter 1996–97 General Strike.
29. Appadurai, "Cosmopolitanism from Below," 32.
30. In 2014 Jean Phillips was awarded a Community Service Medal for her work "advocating for Aboriginal and Torres Strait Islander people and cultivating the next generation of Aboriginal Christian leaders." See http://unitingcareqld.com.au/news-and-publications/news/2014/10/17/queensland-volunteers-recognised-for-community-service. I am very grateful to Auntie Jean Philips for allowing me to quote her unforgettable words here.

REFERENCES

Amnesty International. "Medical Concern: Continued Detention of Kim Chin-yop." September 3, 1990. Index no. ASA 25/041/1990.

Appadurai, Arjun. "Cosmopolitanism from Below: Some Ethical Lessons from the Slums of Mumbai." *Salon* 4 (2011): 32–43.

Arnal, Oscar. *Priests in Working-Class Blue: The History of the Worker Priests (1943–54)*. New York: Paulist Press, 1986.

Ballantyne, Tom. "Expelled Missionary Wants to Go Back." *Sydney Morning Herald*, June 27, 1978.

Barraclough, Ruth. *Factory Girl Literature: Sexuality, Violence, and Representation in Industrializing Korea*. Berkeley: University of California Press, 2012.

Chun, Jennifer, and Judy Han. "Language Travels and Global Aspirations of Korean Youth." *positions: east asia cultures critique* 23, no. 3 (2015): 565–93.

Curthoys, Ann. "Paul Robeson's Visit to Australia and Aboriginal Activism, 1960." In *Passionate Histories: Myth, Memory, and Indigenous Australia*, edited by Frances Peters-Little, Ann Curthoys, and John Docker, 163–84. Canberra: ANU EPress, 2010.

Duberman, Martin. *Paul Robeson: A Biography*. New York: New Press, 1988.

Fitzpatrick, Sheila. "Australian Visitors to the Soviet Union." In *Political Tourists: Travellers from Australia to the Soviet Union in the 1920s–1940s*, edited by Sheila Fitzpatrick and Carolyn Rasmussen, 1–39. Melbourne: Melbourne University Press, 2008.

Gellman, Erik. "Black Freedom Struggles and Ecumenical Activism in 1960s Chicago." In *The Pew and the Picket Line: Christianity and the American Working Class*, edited by Heath Carter, 115–42. Champaign: University of Illinois Press, 2016.

Hansard Parliamentary Debates, November 30, 1989, 3202.

Hayes, Chris. "Asian Women at Work Congratulatory Speech." *Parliament of Australia House Debates*. November 14, 2013. http://www.chrishayesmp.com/index.php/media-centre/fowler-speeches/40-speeches-2013/779-14-november-2013-asian-women-at-work

Jeffries, Stuart. "The Leaflet Bombers." *Guardian*, December 6, 2015. https://www.theguardian.com/world/2015/dec/06/ronnie-kasrils-apartheid-london-recruits-south-africa-bombs

Kim Won et al., eds. *Minju nojo, nohak yŏndae kŭrigo pyŏnhyŏk: 1980-yŏndae nodong undong ŭi yŏksa* [Democratic unions, the student-worker alliance and revolutionary change: A history of the 1980s labor movement]. Sŏngnam: Academy of Korean Studies Press, 2017.

Lee, Namhee, and Kim Won, eds. *The South Korean Democratization Movement: A Sourcebook*. Sŏngnam: Academy of Korean Studies Press, 2016.

Murphy, Francis. Review of "Priests in Working-Class Blue." *Catholic Historical Review* 74, no. 4 (Oct. 1988): 652–53.

Peacock, Margaret. "The Perils of Building Cold War Consensus at the 1957 Moscow World Festival of Youth and Students." *Cold War History* 12, no. 3 (2012): 515–35.

Piccini, Jon. "'There Is No Solidarity, Peace or Friendship with Dictatorship': Australians at the World Festival of Youth and Students, 1957–1968." *History Australia* 9, no. 3 (2012): 178–98.

The Secret Safari. Directed by Tom Zubrycki. Ronin Films, 2001.

Smith, Alex Duval. "Secret London Activists Who Became Anti-Apartheid's Un-Sung Heroes." *Observer*, July 1, 2012. http://www.theguardian.com/world/2012/jul/01/london-activists-anti-apartheid-anc

Sparrow, Jeff. "Paul Robeson: A Stellar Career Sacrificed for a Dream." *Drum*, November 25, 2014. http://www.abc.net.au/news/2014-11-25/sparrow-paul-robeson-a-stellar-career-sacrificed-for-a-dream/5913508

Taylor, Karin. *Let's Twist Again: Youth and Leisure in Socialist Bulgaria*. Vienna: LIT Verlag, 2006.

T. K. *Letters from South Korea*. Translated by David L. Swain. Tokyo: Iwanami Shoten, 1976.

Uniting Care Queensland. "Queensland Volunteers Recognised for Community Service." October 17, 2014. http://unitingcareqld.com.au/news-and-publications/news/2014/10/17/queensland-volunteers-recognised-for-community-service

Van Mersbergen, Audrey. "The Rhetorical Reduction of the 13th World Festival of Youth and Students." Paper presented at the Annual Meeting of the Speech Communication Association, Chicago, Illinois, October 29–November 1, 1992.

World Student Christian Federation. "World Student Christian Movements in the Asia-Pacific." http://www.wscfap.org/nationalmovements/index.html. Accessed September 2016.

5

Exhibiting Minjung Art Abroad

Tokyo, New York, and Pyongyang in the Twilight of the Cold War

Sohl Lee

South Korea's prodemocracy movement in the 1980s saw an unprecedented emergence of artistic language that visualized leftist ideology through art for the first time since the Korean War, a war that spatialized the ideological spectrum of the left and the right along the geographical division of the Korean Peninsula into north and south. This essay is part of a larger research project on the 1980s production of art for the democracy movement in South Korea. During the decade of the 1980s, the concept of nation (*minjok*) and ideals of democracy (*minju*) were merged in the neologistic characterization of the Korean people as the *minjung* (common people), in whose name the nation was mobilized on all fronts of culture, economy, and politics. Thus was also born the "minjung art movement" (*minjung misul undong*), which would historically become one of the most influential political and aesthetic avant-gardes in South Korea. In placing equal weight on nation and democracy, the 1980s social movement in South Korea was a movement not only for democracy and against repressive dictatorship but also for national liberation and decolonization driven by a new understanding of history (*minjung sagwan*). This historical vision, to this day a full-fledged worldview on the South Korean left, refuses to consider South Korean history as having been formed in an antagonistic relationship with North Korea and instead questions the unequal relationship between the Korean nation (the self) and the foreign powers (the other), while reconsidering the tendency to see modernization, Westernization, and capitalism as a holy trinity of social progress.[1]

The latter half of the 1980s, marked by the massive mobilization of South Korean citizens against authoritarian government, also witnessed an explosion of political art. The 1985 exhibition called *The Power of the Twenties*, which the state censored by confiscating artworks and arresting several artists in the gallery, motivated artists and artist collectives to organize themselves under the umbrella institution of Minmihyŏp (Minjok misul hyŏpŭihoe, or the Association of Korean People's Art, 1985–95). In June 1987, when more than a million citizens came out to the streets in Seoul and other big cities, forcing the military dictator Chun Doo Hwan to step down and ensure a direct presidential election, each day the protest was spatially and visually denoted by the flags and banner paintings that marched along with the citizen protesters. A banner commemorating a Yonsei University student, *Let Hanyŏl Live Again*, was featured in demonstrations against police brutality, while a gigantic banner painting, *The Great Struggle of Workers*, accompanied the largest union protests in scale in July–September, 1987.

The present essay—focusing on the exhibitions of minjung art in Tokyo, New York, and Pyongyang from 1986 through 1989—attempts to provide a balanced reassessment of the narratives of minjung art that have become established in the field. In South Korean art history, these stories of collective production and consumption of art are often told by the movement's sympathizers in ways that emphasize the artworks' contributions to the progress of the social movement. Yet, while each exhibition in Tokyo, New York, and Pyongyang was propelled by distinct circumstances, the stories behind these exhibitions reveal not only the contradictions within South Korean artists' claimed intentions and their art's visual solutions to the exigency of the domestic political climate, but also the difficulties of the international exchange—the challenges in imagining a space for political art, or political space for art, across national borders. The tales of the tensions, conflicts, and misunderstandings narrated in this chapter consider the cross section between the 1980s South Korean democracy movement and the new era of (neo-)liberal democracy around the world as a productive site where the questions of nation, ethnicity, and locality were pressed against the belief in universality purportedly embedded in the ideals of democracy, which, despite everything, gave the hope for a better future to many South Korean artists and activists.

The South Korean minjung art shown within South Korea did travel abroad; and yet the record of these physical movements is mostly left untold for reasons apparent to its practitioners. From its inception, rejecting foreign influences, Western or Japanese, and the institutional legitimacy granted by overseas exhibition opportunities worked conjointly with assuming that the intended audience for minjung art was first and foremost domestic. This study therefore constitutes the first conceptual effort to connect the fragments previously left out of the history of minjung art as unimportant or, perhaps, distracting. For the sake of clarity, I will follow a straightforward structure: first, I will explore the sociopolitical and cultural backgrounds that gave rise to the three instances of border-crossing, alongside the motivations of South Korean, Japanese, American, and North Korean actors; I will then close the essay by briefly tracing the imprints that this intercultural exchange has left behind in the three recipient locales as much as on the participating minjung artists. The present study does not focus on individual artworks but instead charts their overseas exhibition and reception history, opening up the discursive frameworks and contexts of minjung art.

Korea by JAALA (Japan, Afro-Asian, Latin American Artists' Association)

One summer day in June 1986, when artist Kim Jung-Heun rushed from Haneda Airport to the Tokyo Metropolitan Museum of Art in Ueno Park, he might have reflected back on the ordeals—the hoops to jump through—that made his first visit to Japan possible. Several months beforehand, an invitation to participate in an exhibition in Japan took him by surprise. Although he was aware of the existence of Japanese leftist intellectuals and their activities through hearsay, he had neither been informed about a type of Japanese minjung artist nor had he expected to receive an invitation for collaboration. Nor did he anticipate the difficulty in procuring a passport in Seoul, as was the case when a representative of the Information Bureau (the present-day Ministry of Culture) interrogated him because of the danger Japan always posed as a passage to the North through the operations of the Sōren, the *zainichi* Korean group connected with the Democratic People's Republic of Korea (DPRK). The attempted blockage was assuaged by Kim's claim that it would be a shame for (South Korean) national reputation if the works were to be presented in the absence of the participating artists, because the works had already been shipped. Kim had earlier rolled two dozen prints by O Yun and equally many paintings by several other artists like Min Jeongki, Song Changsup, Lim Oksang, and himself and sent them by freight to save costs. As he recounted later, when the responsibility to facilitate the first overseas exchange for minjung artists was bestowed on him, it was the lack of knowledge about transporting art (i.e., shipping under strict duty regulations or hand-handling by the artists), along with his off-the-cuff performance of national pride, that helped him retrieve his passport.

The lack of resources was not limited to Korean artists. Upon Kim's arrival at the Tokyo Metropolitan Museum of Art, he was greeted by the representatives of the Japanese organization who were installing the paintings themselves, because of the lack of proper funding. Founded in 1977, the Japan, Afro-Asian, Latin American Artists' Association (JAALA) was supported by its individual membership fees and had little success in procuring state or corporate funds.[2] In 1978 the association hosted a traveling exhibition of Palestinian art from Lebanon, which prompted its members to travel to Palestine. Subsequent travel took members to Thailand for the 1980 exhibition and to the Philippines for the 1982 and 1984 exhibitions.[3] Artists from these nations would then be invited to exhibit alongside the domestic artists in Japan every two years. It was as a continuation of this international programming that South Korean minjung artists were invited in 1986. JAALA's international exhibitions were initially titled "The Third World and Us" and kept the name well into the 1990s. Haryū Ichirō, a renowned critic and the founder of JAALA, later admitted that the title inadvertently reflected JAALA's unintended embodiment of a "Western imperialistic outlook" in naming Palestine, Thailand, the Philippines, and Korea all together as the Third World "other."[4]

As Haryū noted almost twenty years after JAALA's establishment and more than thirty years after he began his career as one of the leading leftist cultural critics, the differential treatment between Japan and the rest of Asia in the Japanese leftist circle originated not only in the difference in locational identity (i.e., host nation versus invited artists), but also in the geopolitical history in which the Japanese envisioned, time and again, a unifying entity in Asia under Japanese guidance. The opposing ideas of an Asian coalition against Western modernity went back to the late nineteenth and early twentieth centuries, with famed curator Okakura Tenshin's promotion of such ideals as "Asia as One" as well as philosopher Miki Kiyoshi's advocacy of a "Greater East Asia Co-Prosperity Sphere." In its turn, the notion of the Co-Prosperity Sphere had its origin in Prime Minister Fumimaro Konoe's proposed economic policy for Northeast Asia, which had been inflected with militarism and

Japanese nationalism.[5] The defeat of the anti–Security Treaty protests in the 1950s and 1960s postwar period gave way to a relatively modest and fragmented leftist dissent against the lasting system of Japanese imperial rule and the stealthy conservatism. By the 1970s, the desire to find coalition with other Asian countries as part of the anti–Vietnam War protest and the reinvigorated Third World discourse in Japan may have laid the groundwork for the establishment of JAALA and of its "older sister" Afro-Asian Latin American Writers' Association (AALA), also founded by Haryū Ichirō, then the editor of the leftist monthly *Shin Nihon bungaku* (New Japanese Literature). As recently characterized by curator Fumio Nanjo, the generation of Haryū Ichirō rediscovered Japan through their discovery of the Third World—that is, Japan as part of Asia, and not as an advanced nation that happens to be in Asia.[6] This prewar and postwar intellectual genealogy of the Japanese perception of its own position vis-à-vis other parts of Asia was important, insofar as it remained a dilemma, one whose language kept shifting due to the changing geopolitical alliances among nations.

The history of exchange between JAALA and South Korean minjung art represented an effort to construct an alternative network outside the normative, mainstream alliance within the Cold War axis—that of the U.S.–Japan–South Korea constituted by anticommunism and capitalist democracy. But for the South Korean invitees, the host's weak position within its own nation of Japan posed a problem. As summarized by critic Wŏn Tongsŏk, who visited JAALA in 1986 and many more times later, two main reasons for disappointment prevailed among the Korean participants. First, the Japanese artists' experimental performances and happenings held as part of the JAALA exhibition sometimes looked too "*modŏnisŭt'ŭ*" and different from works by artists invited from the Third World nations. By the term *modŏnisŭt'ŭ* or "modernist," Wŏn refers to what he believes is nothing more than derivative copies of Western art whose South Korean version propelled the birth of minjung art with an intent to develop anti-Western, national aesthetics. Second, the major complaint among Korean participants originated from their realization that JAALA was not a structured, organized movement of collective resistance like its South Korean counterpart Minmihyŏp, to which Wŏn belonged. Wŏn himself expressed his dissatisfaction when Haryū Ichirō introduced himself as a "Japanese living in Japan," a playful but rather inept pun on *zainichi* ("[Koreans] living in Japan") frequently used by Japanese antiestablishment intellectuals to express a sarcastic self-deprecation.[7] Wŏn's disappointment reflected his own perception of Minmihyŏp as a powerful opposition force that would soon replace the state or the dominant establishment, and his disregard for other models of opposition.

This point of difference in the scale and nature of opposition was acknowledged by Haryū himself, who harbored a positive evaluation of South Korea's democracy movement and a cynical view of his own nation's supposedly failed left. In Haryū's own recollection, one of his *zainichi* friends noted, sometime in the late 1980s, that with the political revolution in South Korea the time had come for Korea to export something important to Japan, ending the cycle of Japan's more advanced industrial development from which Korea benefited. Nodding in agreement, Haryū responded that it was truly unfortunate that the "Japanese receiver" was nothing but dysfunctional. For the Japanese leftist cultural practitioners living through the bubble economy, Haryū concluded, Korea, and especially the civilian uprising and sacrifice in May 1980 in Kwangju, represented a source of tremendous hope, although it was a hope located outside Japan with little chance for a successful transplantation to the Japanese soil.[8]

A more fundamental difference could be located in the divergent perceptions of "democracy" harbored by Korean artists and the Japanese organizers. According to curator and art historian Kuroda Raiji, JAALA's open platform, which operated under a membership system and invited everyone to present their works, followed to a certain extent postwar precedents such as the Yomiuri Independent (1949–63), an annual no-jury exhibition whose motto was to accept all forms of art made by any artist to arrive at the gallery in the purported spirit of American-style liberal democracy. This was supposed to provide an antidote to the suffocation experienced during wartime under Japanese military imperialism. The notion of democracy as it was translated in the artistic realm meant above all no requirements to participate except a meager membership fee, which in turn could be used to invite artists from abroad. In this spirit of democratic individualism, JAALA sought to bring to Japan many artists and artworks from Asian countries such as South Korea, Thailand, and the Philippines. Finding comrades, so scant in Japan itself, would have been possible only if JAALA had more financial resources to physically bring them to Japan. This is how we might understand Haryū Ichirō's frequent complaints about the lack of funding, as more support would have helped JAALA realize its envisioned alternative network of international solidarity.

This desire to gather as many works as possible in one place, together with JAALA's inability to rent a larger gallery in the mostly rental-based

Tokyo Metropolitan Museum of Art, might explain the practical reasons for the two-stack display method of South Korean paintings. And yet, the visual effect it created unveils another interesting point of comparison and contrast between the two groups. Back in South Korea, these paintings were hung with an ample spacing that emphasized their nature as individual, distinct "works of art." The minimal spacing in Tokyo made the paintings look connected, as if they had become a large banner that surrounded the entire wall. As recalled by Inagaki Saburo, an early member of JAALA in charge of exhibition display in those years, the South Korean artworks that arrived in 1986 were so powerful that the option of displaying two rows of paintings without much room for breathing seemed like an apt display method that also accommodated the spatial constraints.[9]

Seen in retrospect, this display method bore a similarity with a particular method of image production that would surface a couple of years later in South Korea, wherein a compilation-like composition that demonstrated the interconnection between heterogeneous episodes and icons, of the present and the past, emerged as a defining aesthetics of large protest banners. While the idea of bringing multiple images to one space and creating an environment that evoked powerful visual effects was a commonality between Japanese and Korean models of "thinking democracy and art" in the late 1980s, the difference was not insignificant. In South Korea, the production of large banners responded to the urgency to accumulate, build, and express collective power by maximizing the impact of visual images displayed in the public space. The objective was not an equal representation (i.e., the logic of horizontal distribution) but a culmination of counterhegemonic power (i.e., the logic of vertical energy). Democracy could not be untangled from resistance against dictatorship, which always required a decisive choice, and not an open door for everyone. Furthermore, a different emphasis on the spatiotemporality of resistance is notable in the two countries. Whereas the exhibition of minjung paintings in Tokyo represented South Korea as a space of powerful dissent (as if to comfort, if not enlighten, Japanese leftist intellectuals with a revolutionary message), the emphasis on history among Korean minjung artists envisioned the present conditions (*hyŏnsil*) as an entry point for resistance and the rewriting of history. Nostalgia for the past or a foreign country was a luxury that South Korean artists could not afford, and an urgency for social transformation was a point shared by the American critics who welcomed minjung art in New York just as their own city was witnessing a vibrant struggle unfolding.

Fig. 5.1. An installation at the fifth JAALA exhibition, *The Third World and Us*. Courtesy of Kim Jung-Heun.

New Eyes, New York: How the Multicultural City Saw Korea's Art for Democracy

On September 29, 1988, a large crowd gathered in Soho, New York, for the opening of *Min Joong Art: A New Cultural Movement from Korea* in Artists Space, a renowned alternative art space founded in 1972. Less than two weeks after the opening of the 1988 Seoul Olympics, a viewer in New York would have seen, among other works, Lee Jonggu's realist portraits of farmers and O Yun's woodcut prints that had been displayed in Tokyo two years before. The two years between 1986 and 1988, however, carried a tremendous weight for the development of political art on the streets. Newly included in *Min Joong Art* was the larger-than-life work *Let Hanyŏl Live Again*, a banner that artist Choe Byŏngsu had made from a press photograph of a Yonsei University student, Yi Hanyŏl, who had been fatally hit by a tear gas canister on June 9, 1987.[10] Once referred by the Artists Space curator Valerie Smith as "a Korean pietá," this majestic banner became an iconic representation of state violence while heralding the rise of a new artist who had been trained in and by the protest sites.[11] Unlike other participating artists like Lee Jonggu, O Yun, Kim Bongjun, and Lim Oksang,

Fig. 5.2. Choe Byŏngsu, *Let Hanyŏl Live Again* (1987), outdoor installation at Artists Space, New York, on September 29, 1988. Courtesy of Artists Space.

who had all graduated from art schools, Choe's education had been limited to elementary school, and he had spent his youth doing temporary manual jobs as a carpenter and a construction worker. When Choe saw the photograph of Yi in the *Joongang Ilbo* (*Central Daily*), he was reportedly inspired to draft woodblock prints of the image and distribute them among protesters—at first 180 copies. But the work's popularity compelled him to make 4,000 copies two days later, 1,000 extra copies and 4,000 four-color handkerchiefs a week thereafter, and finally a 7.5 meter by 10 meter banner, which he made with the help of Yonsei University students before Yi's eventual death.[12] In short, the story of the banner's production was interwoven with that of its immediate distribution and exhibition amid the rapidly evolving political reality, as by June 29 the man picked to succeed the dictator Chun, Roh Tae Woo, promised a direct presidential election. The question then emerges: What did it mean to hang this banner in downtown New York?

Notwithstanding the differences in art historical narratives and political situations defining New York and Seoul in 1988, American art critic Lucy Lippard noted in her catalogue essay that her goal was "to investigate the erratic convergences and divergences that relate Min Joong [*sic*] art to the art I know; to acknowledge and perhaps surrender to the porousness of such an encounter."[13] Could such an encounter really be porous, or was that only the critic's wishful thinking? At the exhibition opening, Kim Levin, a frequent contributor to the *Village Voice*, noted that the type of Korean art to which she had previously been exposed was different in content, formal language, and social context. Even her recent trip to Seoul, Levin noted, did not prepare her for the encounter with minjung art in New York, because the type of Korean art promoted by the South Korean government abroad, and particularly in the United States, had been tightly controlled by the state's logic of cultural diplomacy and export.[14] For her part, Lippard had been once before exposed to minjung art when, about a year prior, she was invited to contribute an essay for the first exhibition of minjung art in North America titled *Min Joong Art: New Movement of Political Art from Korea*. Co-curated by Um Hyuk, a Korean-born artist and recent graduate of the Ontario College of Arts and Design, and featuring only four artists (O Yun, Park Buldong, Jung Boksu, and Sung Neungkyung), the show initially opened in January 1987 at A Space in Toronto and later traveled to Minor Injury in Brooklyn. Both venues were artists-run alternative art galleries, and the modest success of this exhibition eventually served as a motivation for Um and Bahc Mo, the founder of Minor Injury and another Korean-born artist, to prepare the larger-scale show of minjung art that took place at Artists Space in downtown New York.[15]

In an exercise of art historical comparison, Lippard's 1987 essay assessed minjung art according to formal criteria mostly derived from the Euro-American art scene—referring for instance to a photo-montage technique by John Hartfield. Her second essay on minjung art, however, written for the 1988 show at Artists Space, took a different approach. The role assigned to a critic, as Lippard argued in 1988, is neither to detect the unfamiliar and the exotic among the familiar, nor to praise the similar vis-à-vis the dissimilar in minjung art. The critic's role is, rather, to consider the discursive *histories* of different locales.[16] To avoid "theoretical tourism" (Caren Kaplan's term cited by Lippard), where an excursion to the exotic is temporary, one would instead expand on the "relational models" (Carol Gilligan and Ulf Hannerz) or, in Lippard's own terms, the "liminal ground where new meanings lurk."[17] In other words, the discussion about forms gave way for Lippard to a shared concern for the history of political struggles and resistant strategies.

For Sung Wan-kyung, a South Korean critic and a founding member of the prominent art collective Reality and Utterance (Hyŏnsil kwa parŏn), it was hard to leave behind a feeling of ambivalence and discomfort. Sung had helped Um Hyuk and Bahc Mo to organize the New York exhibition, but he was torn by the dilemma of acknowledging both the inability of the New York audience to "get" South Korean political art *and* his own shortcomings in truly understanding the discursive language of the American art scene.[18] Herein we find a conspicuous difference between Lippard and Sung. Whereas Sung found an insurmountable difficulty in "seeing two cultures together and, more accurately, imagining them together," Lippard's desire to "surrender to the porousness" between cultures could perhaps be an illustration of "the admiration for the peripheral culture expressed by progressive intellectuals residing at the center," as articulated by Bahc Mo five years later.[19] At that time, Sung was striving to interrogate the relationship between the so-called center and the so-called periphery as well as the interdependence between First World intellectuals and Third World intellectuals.[20] Indeed, Levin's honest assessment of a work's visual impact left an impression on Sung, and so did Hal Foster's questions about the definition and operation of minjung art as a viable category in contemporary art. Sung saw their views as fresh; and perhaps he felt that they touched upon the ambivalence that he himself had long harbored about minjung art as a cultural movement. During a conversation with Sung at the opening, Levin for example commented that visually overwhelming paintings such as Lim Oksang's manifested a sort of self-righteousness, giving her discomfort and a sense of menace because they seemed to assume her ignorance. Her comment got to the heart of some of the later feminist critiques of the minjung social movement and its politics of representation.

An exhibition held at what Sung called a time of "a closure and a new departure," *Min Joong Art* demonstrated a diversity of subject matters, political ambitions, and cultural disciplines, and it reflected the ethos of an activist art movement at its climax in 1987–88.[21] As the first comprehensive show of minjung art to be held outside of Korea, *Min Joong Art* was also enhanced by a productive conversation with non-Korean critics like Lippard, who wrote perceptively about the integration of art and life on Korean streets: "If there is a ferocious edge to the Min Joong [*sic*] art that is absent from much U.S. antiwar and anti-imperialist art, it must be recalled that Korea is still at war."[22] Born as a visual language of dissent opposing the anticommunist, authoritarian government, minjung art thus assumed, for better or worse, an assertive presence as fierce, symbolic, nationalist, androcentric, and at times as hackneyed and didactic as the dominant power it sought to oppose. The violence during public demonstrations was perhaps a natural result of the clash between the dominant narrative and dominant counternarrative, which led artists Kim Bongjun and Kim Yongtae to note a disappointment when they encountered a march outside the White House in 1987—for it was too peaceful, too quiet, and lacking in the "volatile . . . life-threatening potential" of most Korean mass protests.[23] While the artists had been subject to temporary arrests for presenting expressions of dissent since the 1985 exhibition *Power of the Twenties*, it was always a suspicion of any connection with North Korea that gave the government an uncontested excuse for the investigation, imprisonment, and torture of artists. Even after constitutional reform was complete and a president was elected by popular vote, the nation was still at war, as shown by the imprisonment of nine artists in 1989 for crossing the border with North Korea.

Shared Authorship across the DMZ: Pyongyang, 1989

On August 12, 1989, the *Pyongyang Times*, the English-language newspaper of North Korea, reported that an art exhibition dedicated to Korean reunification had opened at the February 8 House of Culture the month prior. Art was then and is now everywhere in North Korea, and the country is

Fig. 5.3. Kim Gyeong Hui's article "Art Exhibition Dedicated to Reunification," *Pyongyang Times*, August 12, 1989. Courtesy of the *Pyongyang Times*.

known for a state-run art production system whose most well-known bureau is the Mansudae Art Studio. This exhibition in 1989, however, did not display North Korean art; instead, as the article stated, the exhibition presented "55 posters, 46 woodcuts, 26 photographs, and a flag sent by patriotic students and progressive artists in south Korea." Among the 55 posters, the article continued, "the 13-piece long work 'The History of the National Liberation Movement,' 3 meters in height and 90 meters in length, portrays the historical facts from the Kabo Peasants' War to the present struggle of the south Korean people for the reunification of the country."[24]

The rather neutral and weak English term "poster" is a curious translation, because when first presented in South Korea in April of the same year, *The History of National Liberation Movement* took the form of *kŏlgae kŭrim*, a new medium of public art invented by South Korean activist artists in 1983 and actively deployed as the democracy movement took a more dramatic and public turn in the latter half of the 1980s. As seen in the example of Choe Byŏngsu's *Let Hanyŏl Live Again*, the protest art *kŏlgae kŭrim* was also more than just an "enlarged painting," as it required a fundamental transformation in the artists' conceptualization of painting as such. The new art form promoted outdoor use to mark a gathering space and energize the participating public, as seen in *kwaebulhwa*, a Chosŏn-era Buddhist banner painting that used to be hung outside for massive-scale rituals.[25] In the days of *kŏlgae kŭrim* production, new works would usually be commissioned at the last minute for one upcoming pro-

Fig. 5.4. An image from the 1989 opening ceremony of *National Liberation Movement Paintings* in Seoul. Courtesy of the National Museum of Modern and Contemporary Art, South Korea.

test after another, and the time constraints forced artists to rely on any available labor at the site. As one South Korean artist later commented about his college days in the mid-1990s, he would sometimes be pulled by his seniors (*sŏnbae*) to paint one corner of a *kŏlgae kŭrim* before being allowed to drift away. In *kŏlgae kŭrim*, authorship was always in question; one or two main draftsmen would make the line drawings onto which an unknown number of painters joined without receiving credit. In a way, *kŏlgae kŭrim*'s performative aspects of collective production were as important as its radical public viewing practice. Art critics soon began to call this type of site-specific protest art *hyŏnjang misul* (art at the site), which included flags, posters, banners with slogans, and wearable objects like scarfs, in addition to *kŏlgae kŭrim*.

If the main characteristics of *kŏlgae kŭrim* include the rhythm of a quick public display and an easy retrieval into safety, then this rhythm of temporary viewing and consumption of *The History of the National Liberation Movement* was cut short by the state censor in Seoul. The original paintings, recorded by South Korean sources as eleven pieces, each 2.3 meters in height and seven meters in length, were planned and executed for the duration of three months by more than 200 artists belonging in seven different art collectives across the nation.[26] Unveiled in April 1989 at Seoul National University for the first time, the paintings were subsequently displayed at large-scale gatherings on college campuses and public squares like Kwangju's Kŭmnam Avenue and the Busan Train Station Plaza, until they were cut to pieces and burned by the police at Hanyang University on June 30, 1989. That day, Seoul received the news that a twenty-one-year-old female member of the National Council of Student Representatives (Chŏn'guk Taehaksaeng Taep'yoja Hyŏbŭihoe, or Chŏndaehyŏp), Lim Su-kyung, had arrived in Pyongyang via Berlin to attend the thirteenth World Festival of Youth and Students.[27]

While the existence of the communist state up north had always challenged the foundation of South Korea's identity as a legitimate nation-state, the year 1989 nonetheless posed a special challenge for the South Korean government. At the twilight of the Cold War, and only months before the fall of the Berlin Wall, prominent public figures such as writer Hwang Sokyoung and Reverend Mun Ikhwan had staged a political demonstration by crossing the border in March 1989. Lim's return on August 15, 1989 through Panmunjom, after a forty-nine-day stay in North Korea, was widely covered by the media, as she had been the first individual to officially cross the Demilitarized Zone (DMZ) on foot since the provisional end of the Korean War in 1953. Upon their return, Lim, Hwang, and Mun were arrested on charges of breaking the National Security Law's ban on any direct contact with North Korea that was not preauthorized by the South Korean government. Also put on trial and interrogation in torture chambers were Hong Sungdam and eight other artists who led the production of *The History of the National Liberation Movement*, for Hong had earlier sent to the North slide reproductions of the banner paintings via a Los Angeles-based association called Minjok Hakkyo (the National School). Out of the three international borders that South Korean minjung art crossed—to Tokyo, New York, and Pyongyang—the inter-Korean border was by far the least porous.

It is difficult to know exactly *how* the slides of *The History of the National Liberation Movement* were reproduced by the North Koreans in a scale that was slightly larger than the original *kŏlgae kŭrim*. Art historian Park Carey, thus far the most prolific writer on North Korean art in South Korea, notes only that North Korean artists "reproduced" (*chae chejak*) the work from the color slides, without explaining the exact method of reproduction.[28] Given that North Korea flaunts its own collective production method of painting called *chipch'ejak*, which involves discussions among the board members of the state art council at multiple stages of the painting's production on the subject matter and composition, one may ponder whether a collective production of a different nature might have been executed to translate the slides to paintings. To my question as to how the North Korean counterparts were able to reproduce the artwork so quickly, within six weeks, what took two hundred South Korean painters three months to finish, Park noted that "over there, reproduction as a production method comes easier than we think," speculating that "they might have projected the slides onto a large panel so as to swiftly paint."[29] One can indeed only speculate, and Park may be right about the swiftness of North Korea's unique practice of copy and reproduction. In North Korea, the copies of master paintings, be they ink or oil, are sometimes certified by the state and treated as "originals" for display in museums or for sending abroad.[30] Where a great painting makes for great propaganda, reproducing an existing masterpiece is at once a method of reinforcing the state-regulated aesthetics of socialist excellence and a daily routine for many lesser-known artists.[31]

In regard to the case in 1989, however, the most convincing account comes from An Miok, a 1986 graduate of Pyongyang Art School and a participant in the 1989 World Festival of Youth and Students who now resides in Seoul. Upon seeing the photograph of the installation that was featured in the *Pyongyang Times*, An immediately recognized the propaganda panels erected on the festival grounds as the type that is usually made for temporary use at outdoor public displays in the North. Wooden beams are laid like a grid to make a freestanding panel, over which several layers of paper are stretched with sprayed water and glue. When dried, the surface is tight and firm, giving considerable support for the printed posters that would be affixed on the panel.[32] The use of "poster" instead of "banner painting" in the newspaper article might have been accurate, if the reproduction involved printing the panels of *The History of the National Liberation Movement* on rolls of paper and then pasting them onto the prepared wooden panels. The pasting job itself would have taken only an hour or two, as artists are highly trained in such a task. Given the World Festival's purpose as overseas propaganda—for which the entire nation was mobilized for two consecutive years—it would have been a natural gesture for North Korea to reciprocate the generous gesture of a coalition from South Korea's own leftist, anti-imperialist artists, and, as An believes, it was necessary to produce a publicity photograph like the one featured in the *Pyongyang Times*. For the North Korean regime, a cynic might say, the task of reproducing the South Korean *kŏlgae kŭrim* was valuable insofar as the work would be reproduced, yet once again, on the pages of the English-language newspaper.³³ In the publicity photograph, the neatly lined-up people facing the posters in Pyongyang look stiff in their seeming disengagement with the images that had once energized the college campuses in Seoul. But in the end, this incident marks the first inter-Korean exchange in art. Reverend Mun Kyuhyŏn, who accompanied Lim Su-kyung during her border crossing, once noted that these enlarged reproductions were said to have traveled to other North Korean cities like Wŏnsan, Hamhŭng, and Kaesŏng during the World Festival.³⁴ North Koreans were the final witnesses to the paintings, even after the destruction of the South Korean originals.

Postscript: "The Funeral of Minjung Art"

To revisit the triangulated network established by overseas minjung art exhibitions is to insist on seeing the histories of both minjung art and global art in a different light. For the history of minjung art, recounting this transnational journey recuperates minjung art from two types of binaries. One is the dichotomy of center versus periphery that has for long determined South Korea's self-designated location as a marginalized, isolated victim of world politics. While artists like O Yun aspired to learn from 1930s Mexican muralism through illustrated publications as early as the late 1960s, it was only in the late 1980s that direct communication between minjung artists and foreign art scenes produced dialogues that illuminated a common ground, or what Lippard called a "liminal ground." The other binary constraining minjung art discourse is that of friend vs. foe—or sanguine brother vs. predatory colonizer—which was typically used by minjung artists and critics to place the DPRK in the first category and Japan and the United States in the second. The more subtle truth is that, within each country, there existed a leftist network regardless of its mainstream or marginalized position. As the South Korean–made works crossed the Korean-Japanese strait, the Pacific, and the DMZ, it became apparent to critics like Sung Wan-kyung that a global assessment of minjung art's leftist politics and aesthetics was not only possible but also inevitable and necessary, especially as the world that minjung artists participated in was changing and, as a result, different questions began to be asked about radical visual culture. For one thing, the democratization of South Korea (1987), the Seoul Olympics (1988), and the lifting of overseas travel restrictions for South Korean nationals (1989) marked an unprecedented era of opening.

Following this era, the decade of the 1990s was, in East Asia as well as globally, a time of realignment under the aegis of the neoliberal market economy. Rapidly forgotten, the activist art of the late 1980s represented a testament to the multiple histories of politics and aesthetics that had once existed in contemporary art. For Japan in the 1990s, the redefined relationship with the United States as a result of the emergence of China had a greater impact than the Cold War's end.[35] In New York, talk of identity politics dissipated as quickly as it once powerfully swept the city, just when the majority of participants in the 1993 Whitney Biennial—casually referred to as the American art biennial's multicultural edition—began representing the wave of the global biennial fad that lasted well into the 2000s. The stories from Tokyo, New York, and Pyongyang do not simply signal a demarcation from the decade of globalization to come; they are important albeit neglected stories of how the world and the global political commons were imagined in art—even though minjung art's formal qualities (i.e., the seeming lack of mastery of materials, folk aesthetics) and collective agenda (e.g., deemphasized individual authorship) did not prepare many minjung artists for the era of contemporary art as global commodity. Seen in light of the expanded art infrastructures for global exchanges over the past three decades, the grassroots, antiestablishment nature of the early overseas exhibitions of minjung art is nothing short of striking. It demonstrates these artists' modest beginnings and earnest yearning for a cross-cultural dialogue that put political justice before concerns over free trade agreements, even if the values of modesty and earnestness were not what Pyongyang had in mind in 1989, when its larger-than-original reproduction of *The History of the National Liberation Movement* turned the (South Korean) state-censored minjung art into (North Korean) state-approved propaganda.

In South Korea too, the relationship between minjung art and the state quickly flipped by February 1993, when Kim Young Sam took office as the first civilian president from the opposition party. In February 1994, only a short twelve months later, the state-run National Museum of Contemporary Art opened the nation's first retrospective of minjung art, staging through an official platform the formerly underground grassroots movement. Titled *15 Years of Minjung Art, 1980–1994*, the exhibition with more than 400 works by approximately 300 artists signaled an official endorsement of minjung art from the by-then democratic government whose foundation rested on the prodemocracy social movement.[36] The status of minjung art thus switched, within a few months, from antiestablishment dissent to a hub of art endorsed by the state.[37] Merely a year prior, the

Queens Museum of Art's request of South Korean government cosponsorship to fund only a fifth of the traveling budget necessary for the U.S. tour of *Across the Pacific: Contemporary Korean and Korean American Art* (1993) had been denied because of its inclusion of minjung artists.³⁸

The sense of disjointedness was not merely a temporal one. Perhaps, what was "not realistic (*pihyŏnsilchŏk*)" circa 1994, to borrow Sung Wan-kyung's impression of the exhibition, was minjung art itself.³⁹ In a very important sense, the hanging of Choe Byŏngsu's banner *Let Hanyŏl Live Again* in a museum's central hall was indicative of the museumification of minjung art that only emphasized its irrelevance to the present moment. Pervasive among artists was thus a consensus that the exhibition represented "the funeral of minjung art."⁴⁰ The blame for the death of minjung art of course should not be directed only to the exhibition, as critics like Kang Sŏngwŏn point to two significant external factors that very much affected the art movement. The first was the collapse of the Cold War system and the demise of historical socialism. The second was a change in the political landscape in South Korea itself, where the end of the minjung social movement coincided with the institution of the civilian government.⁴¹ One fault of the minjung art scene, however, including artists, critics, and curators, was the lack of a concerted effort to reinterpret the activities of the 1980s in light of the changed reality. If one were to apply the lessons of circa 1988 New York City to circa 1994 Seoul, to consider the banner rehung in the National Museum as a dead banner only highlights the narrow definition of a political site (*hyŏnjang*) that haunts the minjung practitioners. Not all decontextualizations are the same, as proven by the fruitful conversations in New York. As Sung rightly concludes his assessment of *15 Years of Minjung Art*, minjung art's hard-won "citizenship" after recurring denials of its indisputably "public existence" (*konggongjŏk silchae*) is one thing, but the "public acknowledgement (*kong'in*) is done by the people (*taejung*) and not by the state (*tangguk*)."⁴²

NOTES

1. See Namhee Lee, *The Making of Minjung*, and Sim Kwang-hyun, "The Min Joong Cultural Movement and Modernization Process in Korea."

2. It is possible to conjecture the connection between the Afro-Asian Writers' Workshop held in Tokyo in 1961 and the later establishment of JAALA. Within and outside Japan, research on JAALA is scant at best. JAALA compiled the institution's history and a list of exhibitions under the title *History of JAALA: 1977–1993* (Tokyo: JAALA, 1994).

The entire publication is available on JAALA's website: https://jaala2015.jimdo.com (accessed January 31, 2017).

3. This type of research in lesser-developed economies in Asia on the one hand inherited the colonial paths of Japanese empire and on the other hand anticipated the Japan Foundation's work in Asia starting in the 1990s. JAALA stood out, however, in its efforts to overcome a nationalist outlook. By the early 1990s Haryū Ichirō was well aware of the more mainstream international exchange programs run by the Japan Foundation and the Asian Art Museum in Fukuoka. Haryū, "The Past and the Future of JAALA," 6–7.

4. Haryū, "South Korean Minjung Art," 15. For more on Haryū Ichirō as one of the influential "Big Three" critics of postwar Japanese art—along with Tōno Yoshiaki and Nakahara Yūsuke—and Haryū's conceptualization of 1960s Japanese art as "international contemporaneity," see Reiko Tomii, "'International Contemporaneity' in the 1960s."

5. See Zachmann, "Blowing Up a Double Portrait in Black and White"; Nishida, "The Logic of the Place of Nothingness and the Religious Worldview"; and Karatani, "Japan as Museum."

6. Fumio Nanjo, interview with author in Tokyo, January 20, 2017. Even in the 1970s, South Korean art was seen as the only "other" contemporary art besides the Japanese one. *Tansaekhwa*, or South Korean monochrome paintings, might have given such an impetus for structural change in the perception of Asia among the leading Japanese art critics and gallerists, especially after these paintings' successful debuts in Tokyo in 1974–75. See Kee's study of *tansaekhwa* in *Contemporary Korean Art*, 233–59.

7. Haryū, "The Past and the Future of JAALA," 6–7. Haryū's identification with the Korean minority in Japan is reminiscent of the slogan—"We are all German Jews"—chanted on the streets of Paris in May–June 1968. As analyzed by philosopher Jacques Rancière, this ethical act of disidentification with the French self-defined the manifestation of political subjectivity for the students and workers on strike, and a parallel case can be made for the Japanese leftist' desire for disidentification and dislocation as a conceptual beginning of politicization. See Kristin Ross, *May '68 and Its Afterlives*, 57–58.

8. According to sociologist Yoshitaka Mori, the desire for Korean-Japanese leftist solidarity expressed by Haryū Ichirō is perhaps driven not only by the prodemocracy uprisings in South Korea but also by the prewar precedents in Japan like the Aso Coal Strike in 1932 and the more recent events in 1959–60 of the Miike Mine Strike, during which the participation of *zainichi* miners in the Japanese social movement left an undeletable mark on the Japanese leftist consciousness. Yoshitaka, interview with author in Tokyo, January 20, 2017. On the history of Korean miners in Japan, see W. Donald Smith, "Digging through Layers of Class, Gender, and Ethnicity."

9. Inagaki Saburo, interview with author in Tokyo, January 19, 2017.

10. Yi Hanyŏl's death, along with the death of six other student activists, was the stage for one of the largest protests during the June Uprising, where banners and enlarged funeral portraits were indispensable for the activation of the space and the participating citizens' bodies.

11. Valerie Smith, a letter sent to Reverend James P. Morton of St. John of the Divine on September 22, 1988. The Artists Space archive of NYU Bobst Library.

12. Sung Wan-kyung, "Two Cultures, Two Horizons," 14.

13. Lippard, "Countering Cultures Part II," 19.
14. Sung Wan-kyung, "Han'guk ŭi minjung misul chŏn," 39.
15. In his review for Canada's major daily, the *Globe and Mail*, John Bentley Mays describes the show as "bright, provocative, and keyed up with hip-hop high spirits, all of which set it right apart from the average run of North American activist art," in his review "Korean Works Full of High Spirits, Sharp Ironies," *Globe and Mail*, January 9, 1987. The *Varsity* of the University of Toronto featured a full-page review by its staff writer, with an installation shot of Kim Bong-jun's banner painting *Ch'ohondo* (Memorial painting). The frontal view of Kim's painting on a large central wall was featured on the front page of the Korean language semiweekly *Minjoong Shinmoon: The Korean Canadian Community Newspaper*, which published Wŏn Tongsŏk's essay "Minjung misul ŭi nolli wa chŏnmang" (The logic and prospect of minjung art), in addition to the exhibition review. See "Minjung ART chŏn e kwansim taedan kaemak chŏnnal 4-paekmyŏng mollyŏ" (Minjung art exhibition attracts public attention, 400 visitors on the opening day) in *Minjoong Shinmoon*, January 9, 1987.
16. Lippard, "Countering Cultures Part II," 22.
17. Ibid.,19, 22.
18. Sung Wan-kyung, "Two Cultures, Two Horizons," 9.
19. Bahc Mo, "T'aep'yŏngyang ŭl kŏn'nŏsŏ," 96.
20. It was Bahc Mo who articulated in 1994 these questions that Sung did not pose as questions in 1988, as Sung refuses to evaluate—"keep his mouth closed about"—the *Minjoong Art* exhibition because it still seemed to bother him to "his guts." See Bahc, ibid., and Sung, "Han'guk ŭi minjung misul chŏn," 39.
21. Sung, "Han'guk ŭi minjung misul chŏn," 36.
22. Lippard, "Countering Cultures Part II," 20.
23. Min Yong Soon, "Min Joong," 16.
24. Kim Gyeong Hui, "Art Exhibition Dedicated to Reunification," *Pyongyang Times*, August 12, 1989.
25. The neologism *kŏlgae kŭrim* is the Korean translation of the Sino-Korean term *kwaehwa*, and it is used for the first time when the art collective Turŏng produced a series of large paintings for a public gathering sponsored by the Korean Presbyterian Church that had a progressive, prodemocracy agenda. Ra Wŏnsik, "80-yŏndae kwangchang ŭi misul: Kŏlgae kŭrim," 127–28.
26. Belonging in Minmihyŏp, these collectives collaborated as a working group titled Minmiyŏn Kŏnjunwi (the Preparation Committee for Alliances of People's Artists, 1988) with a goal of forming a stronger collaboration with student activist art groups on campus.
27. For two years, Pyongyang prepared the World Festival of Youth and Students in a competition with Seoul, who hosted the Summer Olympics one year beforehand. The Festival's motto was "For Anti-Imperialist Solidarity, Peace and Friendship," and Pyongyang received representatives from 177 nations, a record for the festival. Lim Su-kyung's arrival from South Korea was unexpected given the strictness of South Korea's National Security Law. See Lim Su-kyung, *Ŏmŏni*.
28. Park Carey, "Paektusan," 56.
29. Park Carey, interview with author in Seoul, January 13, 2017.
30. The certified copies come with the state certification, and the paintings are usually adorned with the (copied) signatures of the initial painters. Overseas exhibitions of

North Korean masters are likely to include these "official reproductions," as in the case of *Contemporary North Korean Art: The Evolution of Socialist Realism* held between June 18 and August 14, 2016 at the American University Museum in Washington, DC.

31. Hoffman, "Brush, Ink, and Props," 145–80. Hoffman details the cross-medial proliferation of North Korean masterpieces, such as the case of Chŏng Yŏng-man's *Evening Glow over Kangsŏn* (1973).

32. An Miok, interview with author in Seoul, January 25, 2017.

33. The Korean-language daily *Rodong Sinmun* published a brief article unaccompanied by any image, "Nam Chosŏn chŏngnyŏn haksaengdŭl kwa inmindŭl i ponaeon t'ong'il nyŏmwŏn misul chŏllamhoe kaegwan" (Exhibition for wishing reunification sent by south Korean students and people opens) on July 23, 1989. Featured in the December 1989 issue of *Chosŏn yesul* (Korean arts) was the monotone reproduction of four select chapters from the painting series. A close examination of chapter 3, "Anti-Japanese Militant Resistance"—by comparing the South Korean–made photographic slide and the North Korean magazine's reproduction of the chapter—reveals a slightly altered detail in the cloud surrounding a fighter, leading this author to conclude that at least chapter 3 out of a total of eleven chapters was repainted by hand in North Korea.

34. Lee Sunok, "The Anger and Eager Desire Represented by *The History of the National Liberation Movement*," 109–43.

35. Harootunian, "Japan's Postwar and After, 1945–89," 21.

36. For a large-scale exhibition, the planning process and timeline was extremely brief. The plan to organize an exhibition on minjung art became official in April 1993, and the preliminary outlines were submitted in September 1993 by practitioners of minjung art upon the museum's invitation. The exhibition's large scope is testament to how the notions of "publicness" to "official status" translated into the large scale. While the absence of curatorial vision points to the desire to comply with showcasing one work by one artist in an awkward understanding of the equality principle, the Museum's curator, Choe Taeman, noted that the exhibition focused on making visible the "existence" (*silchae*) of minjung art and thus its purpose was not acknowledging minjung art's "aesthetic legitimacy" (*mihakchŏk chŏngdangsŏng*). See "Interview: Choe Taeman," 37.

37. Sung Wan-kyung, "Minjung misul 15-yŏn chŏn," 28.

38. Bahc Mo, "T'aep'yŏngyang ŭl kŏnnŏsŏ," 97.

39. Sung, "Minjung misul 15-yŏn chŏn."

40. I Juhŏn, "Minjung misul 15-yŏn."

41. Kang Sungwŏn, "90-yŏndae misul undong ŭi palchŏn," 38.

42. Sung, "Minjung misul 15-yŏn chŏn," 34–36.

REFERENCES

Bahc Mo. "T'aep'yŏngyang ŭl kŏnnŏsŏ" [Across the Pacific], *Misul segye*, April 1994, 94–97.

Harootunian, Harry D. "Japan's Postwar and After, 1945–1989: An Overview." In *From Postwar to Postmodern: Art in Japan 1945–1989*, edited by Doryun Chong et al., 17–21. New York: Museum of Modern Art, 2012.

Haryū, Ichirō. "The Past and the Future of JAALA." In *History of JAALA: 1977–1993*, 6–7. Tokyo: JAALA, 1994.

Haryū, Ichirō. "South Korean Minjung Art in My View." In *Art for Society: Realism in Korean Art 1945–2005*, edited by Ko Seongjun, 15–22. Kwachŏn: National Museum of Contemporary Art, Seoul; and Niigata: Niigata Bandaijima Art Museum, 2007.

Hoffman, Frank. "Brush, Ink, and Props: The Birth of Korean Painting." In *Exploring North Korean Arts*, edited by Rudiger Frank, 145–80. Vienna: Verlag, 2012.

I Juhŏn. "Minjung misul 15-yŏn, kŭ hoego wa chŏnmang" [15 years of minjung art: Retrospect and prospect]. *Munhwayesul* 176 (March 1994). http://www.arko.or.kr/zine/artspaper94_03/19940314.htm. Accessed January 31, 2017.

"Interview: Choe Taeman." *Gana Art*, March/April 1994, 37.

Kang Sungwŏn. "90-yŏndae misul undong ŭi palchŏn ŭl wihan pip'yŏngjŏk sogo" [A critical commentary on the 1990s development of the art movement]. *Gana Art*, March/April 1994, 38–41.

Karatani, Kōjin. "Japan as Museum: Okakura Tenshin and Earnest Fenollosa." In *Japanese Art after 1945: Screams against Sky*, edited by Alexandra Munroe, 33–39. New York: Harry N. Abrams, 1994.

Kee, Joan. *Contemporary Korean Art: Tansaekhwa and the Urgency of Method*. Minneapolis: University of Minnesota Press, 2013.

Lee, Namhee. *The Making of Minjung: Democracy and the Politics of Representation in South Korea*. Ithaca: Cornell University Press, 2007.

Lee, Sunok. "The Anger and Eager Desire Represented by *The History of National Liberation Movement*." *Journal of Democracy and Human Rights* 14, no. 1 (2014): 109–43.

Lim Su-kyung. *Ŏmŏni, hanadoen choguk e salgo ship'ŏyo* [Mother, I want to live in a unified motherland]. Tolpaege, 1990.

Lippard, Lucy. "Countering Cultures Part II." In the exhibition catalogue *Min Joong Art: A New Cultural Movement from Korea*, 19–24. New York: Artists Space, 1988.

Min, Yong Soon. "Min Joong." *Art & Artists*, June/July 1987, 3, 16.

Nishida, Kitaro. "The Logic of the Place of Nothingness and the Religious Worldview." In *Last Writings: Nothingness and the Religious Worldview*, translated by David A. Dilworth, 47–123. Honolulu: University of Hawai'i Press, 1987.

Park Carey. "Paektusan: Mandŭrŏjin chŏnt'ong kwa p'yosang" [Paektu Mountain: The invention of tradition and icon]. *Misulsa hakpo*, June 2011, 43–74.

Ra Wŏnsik. "80-yŏndae kwangchang ŭi misul: Kŏlgae kŭrim" [1980s art of public squares: Banner painting]. *Misul segye* 89 (April 1993): 126–33.

Ross, Kristin. *May '68 and Its Afterlives*. Chicago: University of Chicago Press, 2002.

Sim Kwang-hyun. "The Min Joong Cultural Movement and Modernization Process in Korea." In the exhibition catalogue *Min Joong Art: A New Cultural Movement from Korea*, 4–8. New York: Artists Space, 1988.

Smith, W. Donald. "Digging through Layers of Class, Gender, and Ethnicity: Korean Women Miners in Prewar Japan." In *Women Miners in Developing Countries: Pit Women and Others*, edited by Kuntala Lahiri-Dutt and Martha Macintyre, 111–30. Farnham: Ashgate, 2006.

Sung Wan-kyung. "Han'guk ŭi minjung misul chŏn, kŭ sŏnggwa ŭi anp'ak" [Minjung art exhibition in America: The inside and outside of its accomplishment]. *Gana Art*, January/February 1989, 39–44.

Sung Wan-kyung. "Minjung misul 15-yŏn chŏn, han sakŏn ŭi ŭimi" [15 years of minjung art: The meaning of an event]. *Gana Art*, March/April 1994, 28–36.

Sung Wan-kyung. "Two Cultures, Two Horizons." In the exhibition catalogue *Min Joong Art: A New Cultural Movement from Korea*, 9–15. New York: Artists Space, 1988.

Tomii, Reiko. "'International Contemporaneity' in the 1960s: Discoursing on Art in Japan and Beyond." *Japan Review* 21 (2009): 123–47.

Zachmann, Urs Matthias. "Blowing Up a Double Portrait in Black and White: The Concept of Asia in the Writings of Fukuzawa Yukichi and Okakura Tenshin." *positions: east asia cultures critique* 15, no. 2 (Fall 2007): 345–68.

PART III

New Labor Culture

6

Where Have All the "Shouting Stones" Gone?

South Korean Workers' Literary Clubs and Labor Literature, 1970s–1990s

Jung-Hwan Cheon

The title of this chapter draws its inspiration from Yu Tong'u's poetry collection *The Shout of a Little Stone* (*Ŏnŭ tolmaengi ŭi oech'im*; 1979), a signature product of workers' literature from 1970s South Korea. The appearance of the book, whose author had only an elementary school education, marked a high point in the nationwide movement for workers' cultural emancipation that was made possible through the cooperation of workers and intellectuals. A few years later, another milestone would be the publication of *The Life and Death of a Young Worker: The Critical Biography of Chŏn T'aeil* (*Ŏnŭ chŏngnyŏn nodongja ŭi sam kwa chugŭm: Chŏn T'aeil p'yŏngjŏn*; 1983).[1] In referring to himself as a "little stone," Yu poetically conveyed his self-image as an individual with next to no clout or power. Even so, he seemed to say, a little stone can make its voice heard, and the writing of verse represents the best way of doing that.

The present study examines the cultural movement that made these and other writings by workers unlikely bestsellers in South Korea during the decades of the country's democratization. More specifically, it documents the history of workers' literary clubs, which served, along with many reading groups at factories and at night schools, as a central locus of the 1980s progressive labor culture movement. Various forms of workers' literature, both fictional and nonfictional, had been produced in Korea since the late 1960s, but it took about a decade before this movement came to be recognized in local critical discourse. The history of workers' literature is little known outside Korea and is also being fast forgotten within Korea, to the point that today's new generations would find unfamiliar the names and events that are evoked here. This history, however, was a critical and integral part of South Korea's modern transformation.

Within the present volume, this chapter contributes to the recent surge of research interest in 1980s cultural history, which seeks to reexamine the subject anew from today's vantage point and apart from the previous focus on its *minjung* (people's) literature movement. The renewed interest in the 1980s is partly due to the fact that, at a remove of three decades, more and more scholars are beginning to look at these years as a ripe object of historical investigation. There is also another reason for revisiting the 1980s, however, and this is the necessity of reflecting on the present transformation of the post-1987, or postdemocratization, social system in South Korea. At a time of democratic crisis and increasing social inequality, the hegemony of neoliberalism in the country's rule has revealed its limitations. Suffering from this are the Korean masses, especially the working class, who find themselves once again locked out of a system of power that has little regard for citizens and for the "little stones" among them. The current status quo calls for a new critical examination of the 1980s—its workers' culture in particular.

The Birth of Workers' Literary Clubs

During the 1980s in South Korea, it was possible and not uncommon for a factory worker to spend his or her evening debating a recently published novel with colleagues in a communal space. These so-called literary clubs, which used to be important sites of intellectual development and association for Korean workers, have now become few and almost invisible. The explosive growth of the clubs between the late 1970s and the mid-1990s, and their sudden extinction afterwards, are symbolic of the radicalism of this unique historical moment. The movement for workers' literacy had a critical impact not just on workers and their lives but also on intellectuals. It is not an exaggeration to say, in this respect, that the literary club movement changed the history of literature and culture in Korea. Today, however, its memory seems to be but a bygone era—a history that we may reevaluate but cannot reenact.

With broad public support, the democratization movement of the 1970s and 1980s pursued at once a social and a political agenda. The movement grew more and more radical as time went by, drawing its inspiration from socialist doctrines and also promoting the cause of reunification with North Korea, thus outright defying the government's anticommunist policies. The propagation of Marxism and Leninism gave a theoretical grounding to the activists' aspirations for social reform. Among the prevalent ideas of the time was the goal of abolishing the division of labor and, with it, the distinction between intellectual and manual labor. Promoted through the idealistic fervor of student activists, the movement for workers' literacy was in many ways an attempt at a direct application of these ideas. The result was a remarkable shake-up in the distribution of literacy and in the intellectual and cultural hierarchies of South Korea.

The period's vibrant cultural activism produced not only a substantial body of workers' literature but also intense debates over the nature and purpose of minjung literature and culture, which inevitably attracted the attention of both critics and writers. The workers' literacy movement was in a way the result of an epochal alliance between the cultural and the social spheres. Events such as the 1970 self-immolation of a young worker named Chŏn T'aeil in protest of inhumane labor conditions and the massacre of workers and activists in the 1980 Kwangju Uprising made a deep impression on students on college campuses nationwide. They were a rallying cry for help that, once heeded, ended up changing the lives of both workers and student activists.

In the remainder of this essay, I will attempt to bring to light the activities of South Korean workers' literary clubs as a neglected but vital part of the larger history of Korea's democratization. More specifically, I will focus my analysis on the ways in which this "literature from below" movement reshaped the relationship between the sites of knowledge production, encompassing intellectual groups and college campuses, and the sites of industrial production such as workers, factories, and the societies that gravitated around them. Throughout, I seek to reexamine workers' literature and its culture from the perspective of a history of knowledge "from below" and that of the study of culture as a site of class conflict. In the theoretical background are the variegated issues that arise from two important works of cultural criticism: Richard Hoggart's *The Uses of Literacy* (1957) and Jacques Rancière's *Proletarian Nights* ([1981] 2012). Each in its own way offers important perspectives on issues at the intersection of cultural and social history, including the uses of culture, literacy as political agency, the possibility of mass intellectuality, and the relationship between activism and cultural politics.[2]

The Varieties of Workers' Literary Clubs

The study of workers' literary associations in the 1980s poses a problem of sources. Few to no publications exist on the topic, and what information can be found is typically contained in the hardly accessible archives of the associations themselves. For this reason, research on this historical reality is today in its infancy and will require much archival work. At this preliminary stage, a reasonable way of beginning is by compiling a small taxonomy of the types of workers' literary associations that existed:

A. *Small-Scale Reading Groups*: Small-scale reading groups, which were numerous but for which we now have no statistical data available, served as the most basic units of workers' intellectual organization. These groups were both the seeds and accomplishments of all labor organizational activities, and they often served as a front for other organizations such as labor unions. When students infiltrated major industrial areas in the 1980s, reading groups were organized as informal, underground organizations with multiple purposes, and they provided human, intellectual, and organizational resources to the labor movement. Reading group activities often led to the practice of writing in the form of, for instance, book reviews, and these activities helped individual workers cultivate their self-awareness as well as their writing abilities.

B. *Company-Based Literary Clubs*: Literary clubs began to be organized in the 1970s as part of employees' recreational activities to cultivate "model workers" (*mobŏm kŭlloja*). In a newspaper interview, for instance, Chŏng Inhwa, a worker-poet, remembered how he had organized a literary club with his colleagues at Hyundai Heavy Industries around 1976. He did so, Chŏng recalled, with substantial financial aid from the company.[3] Not all company-based literary clubs were, however, sponsored by the company. When the government relented on its suppression of labor unions in 1984, union activities picked up new momentum. Some of these unions established workers' literary clubs within their own companies. In these cases, union newsletters would serve as major publication outlets for workers' writings, which often advanced their critical perspectives on company policies as well as larger social issues.

C. *Regional Literary Clubs*: Regional workers' literary clubs were larger in their organizational scale and consisted of members from various workplaces in a given geographical area. During the late 1980s, more than thirty of these clubs were formed at industrial hubs such as Seoul, Inchŏn, Kwangju, Puchŏn, Pusan, Sŏngnam, and Taegu. Seoul alone had at least three clubs in the district of Kuro, Tongsŏul, and Yŏngdŭngp'o, and there was also at least one club that included workers from two industrial cities, Masan and Ch'angwŏn. The members of these clubs soon came together to found the National Association of Workers' Literary Clubs (Chŏn'guk nodongja munhakhoe yŏnhap).

D. *Night Schools*: Night schools constituted a step up in terms of complexity and institutional organization. They required a steady commitment on the part of the student activists who often ran them, and they offered workers the opportunity to pursue a systematic education in disciplines that were not necessarily restricted to literature. Night schools were often founded through the initiative of individual activists. For example, Sim Sangjŏng, now a congresswoman, first became a labor activist by opening a night school in the Kuro Industrial Complex in the winter of 1979. Tŭlbul yahak (Wild Fire Night School), which played a critical role in the 1980 Kwangju Uprising, was initiated in 1978 by student activists from Chŏnnam National University, including Yun Sangwŏn and Pak Kwanhyŏn. *Nodong yahak* (night schools for workers) proliferated between 1980 and 1983, and they grew increasingly radical in the face of oppression from the authorities.

E. *Government-Sponsored Cultural Festivals*: In the 1980s, political and economic authorities began to proactively support literary activities among workers, as they felt the need to counter grassroots movements. In this movement driven by official authorities, workers' literary activities were called *kŭlloja munhak* (workers' literature) or *munye* (literary arts). Exemplary was the Workers' Cultural Festival (Kŭlloja Munhwa Yesulche), which was founded in 1980 by the Korea Workers' Compensation and Welfare Service and the Korean Broadcasting System (KBS). In 1981 its program expanded to include a literary festival for workers.

Naturally allowing for some overlap, this classification shows the diverse forms of workers' literary clubs and is useful for our understanding of the multiplicity and breadth of their organizations. Apparent across the various types of initiatives was a strong desire for self-cultivation among the workers. The Kuro literary club, for example, appealed to its prospective membership by highlighting the idea of "self-improvement" (*chagi kyebal*) in its promotional materials. Used here as a tool of recruitment of workers to the activist cause, the ideal of self-cultivation was a zeitgeist among citizens across social classes. It tapped a social desire for intellectual emancipation, and it was a key indicator of important changes ahead for the working classes.

Originating at the intersection between minjung literature and the labor movement, the workers' literary clubs were the joint product of the cultural aspirations of the workers and the determined effort by a group of activist intellectuals to raise consciousness among the proletariat. As this type of association assumed importance on the agendas of student and labor movements, their number surged dramatically and, as a result, literary clubs frequently became a target for censure by the authorities and the media. It was only when the government relented in its suppressive approach in 1984 that workers' activities picked up new momentum, including a revitalization of literary club activities. Along the way, the causes of self-emancipation, activism, and democratization advanced in parallel in one of the most distinctive and transformative movements in South Korea's process of modernization.

A Brief Historical Overview of Workers' Literary Activities

This section will offer a brief historical overview of workers' literary activities with special attention to the interaction between workers and intellectuals. At the center of this historical account will be the literary club movement, the labor literature produced by its participants, and its impact on South Korean literature and culture.

Late 1970s–1980: Stars and Pigs

Workers' memoirs and their compilations began to be published in magazines such as *Taehwa* (Dialogue) in the mid-1970s. One of them was Yu Tong'u's *The Shout of a Little Stone*, which attracted much attention. As Yu later commented, he was encouraged to write this memoir by Kim Segyun, then a staff member of the Christian Academy who later became a professor of political science at Seoul National University. *The Shout of a*

Little Stone was Yu's first effort, and by his own admission, the author had little notion of the nature and purpose of literary writing.[4] In a way, the rise of workers' literature in late 1970s Korea was a process through which South Korean workers collectively developed a voice and a social identity. The appearance of the first volumes authored by workers, along with their intellectual mentors, transformed the indistinct industrial proletariat into a more definite political and social actor.

That transformation was keenly described by Sŏk Chŏngnam, a female worker at Tongil Textile and the well-known author of *Factory Lights* (Kongjang ŭi pulbit; 1976). Unlike Yu, Sŏk loved books and always had a desire to write. However, the more she aspired to write, the greater her frustration grew. "The unreachable star in the sky," as she called the citadel of aesthetics, seemed to actively demean people like her, that is, humble workers who had received only limited cultural exposure. Using a blunt metaphor, Sŏk sought for people like her to be able to live as humans, and not as "pigs."[5] The cultural sphere appeared to her like an exclusive property of the upper classes, and that was the reason why Sŏk's memoir had such an explosive potential for subverting the status quo. In her case, too, the writings of a worker, who came to write simply as she was encouraged to do so by an intellectual, became a powerful social document that was used to awaken and recruit many student activists. This reversal of the pedagogical relationship between intellectuals and workers reached a climax with the publication of *The Critical Biography of Chŏn T'aeil*, which appeared in 1983 but had been circulating in a photocopied version since 1976.

Around this time, labor literature was being produced in night schools, state-funded organizations, and company labor unions in the form of journals and memoirs. Further studies need to be done on the nature as well as magnitude of the phenomenon. What was the level of literacy and education among workers in the 1970s and 1980s? How much formal education did these workers receive, and how much of it was necessary for them to be able to write? The education level of female workers, for instance, is known to have ranged from elementary school dropout to middle school graduate during the 1970s. And in the 1980s, a significant number of them were elementary or middle school graduates. In some cases, they were also able to continue their education through company-affiliated special middle or high school courses. There remain plenty of records, including Shin Kyung-sook's novel *Lonely Room* (*Oettan pang*; 1995), about female factory workers' experiences at those schools.

Statistics aside, it is not an exaggeration to describe the rise of workers'

Fig. 6.1. Cover of Sŏk Chŏngnam's *Factory Lights* (1976). Courtesy of Irwŏl sŏgak.

literature as a topical moment in the history of labor relations. The zeal and passion for learning and education among workers in the 1970s and 1980s arguably represented one of the foundations for South Korea's economic and cultural development. What was really important here was neither workers' literacy rate nor their education level, but rather how much they struggled to overcome their class limitations through their interactions with intellectuals and their own efforts, because it was in this act of collective and personal overcoming that South Korea found its way to democratization and modernization.

1980–1984: Chŏn T'aeil and Kanghak (Night School Teachers)

After the Kwangju Uprising in 1980, college students became increasingly radicalized and began to infiltrate workplaces. The interactions between workers and intellectuals in this period, as well as the development of workers' consciousness thereof, are well recorded in Kim Chinsuk's memoir titled *Salt Flower Tree* (*Sogŭm kkot namu*; 2007). Kim, an iconic figure of South Korea's labor movement, described her life in the early 1980s and provided a moving account of how she came to be awakened as a "human" and a worker through literary practice. She affectingly credited two sources of inspiration, *The Critical Biography of Chŏn T'aeil* and the night school (*kanghak*) teacher who gave the book to her. She recalled how the teacher was the first male individual who addressed her with the honorific suffix *-ssi* in the early 1980s, when female factory workers were derogatorily called *kongsuni* (factory girl) and were treated with general disrespect. These two "mediators" were instrumental in Kim Chinsuk's transformation into a human rights activist.[6] Extraordinary as it seems, her experience was by no means unique in early-1980s South Korea. A great number of workers underwent a similar transformation through their reading of activist literature as well as their encounters with night school teachers and labor activists.

Things were not always easy. There were cases in which distrust and conflict developed between workers and student activists—who were often perceived as "Red Commies" in disguise who sought to brainwash and incite "innocent" workers. The mutual interaction, however, also left many good memories. Night school teachers and students-turned-workers—who took on the educational enterprise based on such books as Paulo Freire's *Pedagogy of the Oppressed* (1970) and Han Wansang and colleagues' *Popular Education in South Korea* (*Han'guk minjung kyoyungnon*; 1985)—underwent a maturation in their social consciousness and overcame their own class biases through their personal interactions with workers.[7]

The Critical Biography of Chŏn T'aeil, the book that sparked Kim Chinsuk's self-emancipation, remains today a book of special symbolic significance. Overlapping in the work are the voices of Cho Yŏngnae, an activist and a lawyer with a degree from Seoul National University, and that of Chŏn T'aeil, a worker who had barely completed elementary school but also relied on extraordinary intellectual and analytical abilities. Whose voice was it that moved readers and made them embrace the figure of Chŏn T'aeil? The voices of Chŏn and Cho were inseparably blended and, in effect, they produced the effect of an intersubjective narrative presence. The intellectual was the accomplished writer, of course, but he was also the witness and broadcaster of the worker's unheard voice. It was in collaborations such as this, where an interactive fusion transcended authorship and originality, that the ethical and cultural projects of the 1970s and 1980s minjung movement reached their culmination. Sometimes it was indeed possible for participants in the movement to cooperate intersubjectively and, through this process of sublimation, to create an unprecedentedly powerful new voice.

1985–1987: The Dawn of Labor *and the Crisis of (High) Literature*

The 1984 publication of Pak Nohae's *The Dawn of Labor* (*Nodong ŭi saebyŏk*) was a turning point of sorts for South Korea's literary and intellectual world. It marked the moment when literature by workers most clearly established its influence as a mass phenomenon. In 1985, the book was ranked among the top sellers in the very competitive category of poetry, and the poems started to be frequently republished in union newsletters and labor newspapers for workers.[8] Pak Nohae, a former bus driver who was just then starting his career as a labor poet, was acclaimed by literary critics, and that recognition in turn generated great interest in the book. In this case, too, an intellectual named Ch'ae Kwangsŏk is known to have played an instrumental role in the preparation and publication of the book. For the first time in Korean culture, however, the public endorsement and propagation of the book reversed the usual direction in the flow of cultural influence. The book not only epitomized the intellectual growth of the Korean working class independently from the influence of intellectuals, but it also compelled the local literati's renewed self-reflection and rethinking of the very idea of literature. Kim Chŏnghwan, a well-known poet and literary activist in the 1980s, wrote that literary works such as Pak Nohae's writings made intellectuals reconsider their own roles in "literary revolution" and "historical progress."[9]

The so-called Pak Nohae Phenomenon grew out of workers' increasingly intense literary activities through the mid-1980s, and such a development in turn added momentum to the labor movement. The Kuro General Strike of 1985 is widely considered today as one of the most significant events in the formation of the working class in South Korea. It came about, once again, through the close cooperation of workers and student activists. The strikers had cultivated their class consciousness and became active union members through their participation in various reading groups and literary clubs. Such communal intellectual activities fulfilled workers' zeal for cultural education. Chang Yŏngsŏn, a young female worker at Karibong Electronics, said that her work life had become so interesting and engaging with union and reading group activities that she did not regret her lack of schooling anymore.[10] Indeed, a desire to make up for insufficient formal education was one of the strongest motivators toward activism for workers in the 1970s and 1980s. The cultural politics of the prodemocracy union movement helped workers fulfill that desire to some extent. In many cases, such as that of Karibong Electronics, the union newsletter had a section titled "members' literary works" (*chohabwŏn munyeran*), which published members' book reviews and essays.

The rising tides of workers' cultural activism also urged Korean literary intellectuals' serious self-reflection. In 1987, Kim Myŏngin published his landmark essay "The Crisis of Intellectual Literature and a Plan for a New National Literature" (Chisigin munhak ŭi wigi wa saeroun minjok munhak ŭi kusang), in which he argued for the necessity of restructuring the Korean literary world in order to more earnestly embrace newly emerging people's literature.[11] As the Kwangju Uprising demonstrated, he argued, it was the working class, not the middle classes, who were the main subject of national history. A new form of Korean national literature should accordingly be developed based on the literary achievements of the minjung themselves.

Kim's proposal implied a far-reaching reconceptualization of the very idea of literature, which in Korea had often been understood as a nominally universal, supraclass form of culture. It also sought to go beyond the decades-old local debates between pure literature and engaged literature (*littérature engagée*). Instead, Kim aimed to endow the new national literature and literary criticism with a distinct class identity, differentiating it from the established literature of the middle class and the intellectuals. In Kim's analysis, even the engaged literature of the 1970s deserved to be overcome, to the extent that it lacked an explicit working class allegiance.

The subsequently developed 1980s discourse of minjung literature, however, was not completely free of the nationalist emphasis of its 1970s predecessor, perhaps because "the liberation of the Korean people," that is, anticolonial struggles against American neoimperialism and in favor of the unification of the two Koreas, still remained as a task to be resolved.

1987–1991: "Anyone Can Write"—the Dual Fronts of Revolution and Writing

A new era of labor activism was ushered in by the Great Workers' Struggle of 1987, which took place immediately following the political triumph of the democratization movement in June of that year. During the three months of these labor protests, about two million people participated in some 3,300 strikes nationwide. As a result, about 1,200 new unions were created. For its scale and intensity, this development was nothing short of revolutionary.

Between 1988 and 1989, more workers' literary clubs sprang up throughout the country, and many clubs established links that eventually evolved into a solid network of interregional solidarity. To give a few examples, Ch'amgŭl (True Words), based in Masan and Ch'angwŏn, was established on September 7, 1989. Its thirty-odd members had attended the Labor Literature Class in Masan Catholic Women's Hall, which was founded in October 1988. Kŭlmaek (Literary Power) in Kwangju was launched in May 1988 with the goal of organizing book discussions, a regular workers' literary class, and the publication of anthologies. The Pusan Workers' Literary Club, founded in July 1988, engaged in a number of activities, including the organization of literary nights, lectures, writing classes, and the posting of protest posters on the streets.[12] Finally, the Puch'ŏn Literary Club that opened in February 1990 was the subject of a detailed article in the *Hankyoreh* newspaper in 1991. The club consisted of about thirty members, most of whom were production workers at various companies in the region. Around a third of them were female workers aged between nineteen and forty. While members were divided into three groups according to different literary genres—poetry, prose fiction, and general writing—the most popular activity was poetry writing, which the workers found most accessible.[13] Such a pattern was common in other literary clubs, too.

Let us take a closer look at their activities. The Puch'ŏn Proletarian Night, which was held every Wednesday and Friday, consisted of the recitation of poems written by club members, followed by critique and discussion, and then an after-party. It had the typical format of a gathering common in college students' literary club meetings in contemporary South Korea. Other regular activities of the Puchŏn club included a weekly meeting with sessions on critical poetry review and poetry writing, a bimonthly special lecture on literature, an annual literary festival, and a biannual class on literature for workers. While the club activities were mostly of a literary nature, Kim Hyŏngsik, a club staff member, said that members came to "reflect upon their lives, develop their pride as workers, and deepen their understanding of revolutionary movements through individual and group writing and other activities."[14] In other words, the club used literature to foster a sense of class consciousness among its members. The Puchŏn club was very active, and no less than three anthologies were published within the first two years of its existence. The club also offered the opportunity for workers to publish their own collections of poems.

The Proletarian Night in Karibong-dong in Seoul was similar. Sŏng Hunhwa, a female worker, recounts vivid memories of the Kuro Workers' Literary Club, having participated in intense labor struggles including the Kuro General Strike in her early twenties. She was avowedly just searching for "a break" from her daily routine, but she also recalls how she met likeminded coworkers there. In her case, participation in a club gave Sŏng a stimulus to rekindle her activism. At the proletarian nights of the Kuro Club, Sŏng recalls, there were books and literature, camaraderie and reconciliation, and numerous discussions and debates meant to "strengthen class consciousness."[15]

In 1989, several clubs jointly published a collection of poems titled *Leaving the Thick Footprints of Work Shoes* (*Chagŏphwa kulgŭn chaguk ŭl jjigŭmyŏ*; 1989), and they also planned to create a nationwide solidarity network in time for the inauguration of the National Labor Union Council in 1990.[16] The timing had a symbolic significance. The council's formation was a culmination of the 1980s militant democratic labor union movement, and the literary clubs were then seeking to become a cultural avant-garde corresponding to the social movement.

Among the accomplishments of the workers' literature movement in the post-1987 period was the increased diversification of the kind of literature produced by workers. While memoirs and general essays on workers' everyday life (*saenghwal kŭl*) continued to be produced, such writings no longer stood as the sole representatives of workers' culture. A significant number of worker-writers emerged during this period to publish their own labor-themed novels. From a pedagogical perspective, this development meant significant progress, since writing prose fiction was believed to require a much more advanced level of writing skills, "a literary expertise," and now the proletarian masses began to take an active part in literary production beyond the genres of poetry and the personal memoir. Park Haeŭn, a worker from the Kuro district and the author of a full-length labor-themed novel, reflected on this fact as follows in an interview: "Many people want to write, but it's not easy for workers to do that. You get so tired at the end of your day, and writing can easily appear to be beyond your possibilities. It takes a lot of determination to pick up the pen."[17] His words were echoed by Kim Hansu, who was also a novelist and a worker in the Toksan district: "What's most important in writing a novel is to overcome your fear of writing. . . . Anyone can write if he/she writes step by step with confidence."[18] Kim also recommended that his fellow workers who aspired to write keep daily journals. As both quotes make clear, the struggle to write was as much physical as it was psychological and social. Ten years had passed in the workers' literature movement before workers were able to express this sanguine confidence in writing—the idea that "anyone can write."

After 1992: The Decline of the Workers' Cultural Movement

In the late 1980s, socialist realism and minjung literature seemed to hold sway over the Korean literary world. The advent of democracy, however, also marked a sort of normalization in the cultural world. The journals *Ch'angbi* (Creation and criticism) and *Munsa* (Literature and society), two literary quarterlies that represented the cultural establishment during the 1970s, had their publication ban lifted and promptly reclaimed their cultural hegemony. The previously denounced bourgeois literature was now making its full return to reclaim its cultural dominance and restore the traditional hierarchy within the literary world. Even so, the period between the late 1980s and early 1990s was when the workers' literary clubs were at their most active, and it was also the time when the theorization and practices of class-biased minjung national literature reached their peak. This period marked a watershed moment in the history of the workers' cultural movement, as proletarian culture faced a rapid decline thereafter and was eventually marginalized in the field of Korean literature.[19]

The democratization movement itself underwent a major transformation in the early 1990s partly due to the epochal collapse of the world's Communist regimes and partly due to the massive breakaway of Korean intellectuals after a series of controversies centered on the allegedly violent and undemocratic strategies of the movement. This process was exacerbated by the protests of May 1991, which were sparked by the death of Kang Kyŏngdae, a student activist, at the hands of the police. In its aftermath, a few acts of self-immolation were committed by students, prompting the media to question the culture of death that was supposedly perpetuated by the protest movement. Many former activists shifted sides. In many cases, the activist students who had been working and organizing at factories moved on to graduate schools, office jobs, teaching jobs, and to life as private citizens. The former "revolutionaries," "the friends of the people," returned to their positions as ordinary Koreans in the ranks of the bourgeoisie. Few college students were now willing to commit themselves to the labor movement. Student activism rapidly declined during the years of the Kim Young Sam government (1993–98), and solidarity with the labor movement seemed no longer an option for young people embedded in an increasingly competitive society. The alliance and collaboration between workers and intellectuals that had begun in the 1970s was then rapidly eroded.

During this period, the minjung activist culture of intellectuals and college students started being absorbed into depoliticized popular culture. The labor movement, however, inherited the militant culture of 1980s unionism and began to establish its autonomous identity. Workers' literary clubs continued to play a central role in the production of labor literature into the 1990s, but their organizational nature changed. The Kuro Workers' Literary Club and the Inch'ŏn Workers' Literary Club, for instance, remained active. A great number of workers, many of whom were well equipped with class consciousness and had a desire and need for a "better" literature, continued to join these clubs through the early 1990s.[20] Several members of the Kuro Literary Club published their poetry collections and managed to become full-time poets, although most of its founders had retired from active membership by this time. For example, Song Kyŏngdong, today a well-recognized worker-poet, had joined the Kuro Literary Club while working as a carpenter and a plumber. A high school graduate and former juvenile detainee, Song had been a rebellious but bookish teenager who had been positively influenced by a teacher's praise of his poetic talents. Around the age of twenty, he had attended an institution called the Korean Literature School (Han'guk Munhak Hakkyo), which was run by famous poets including Kim Namju, Yi Siyŏng, and Chŏng Hŭisŏng. Song then joined the Kuro club at age twenty-three in 1992.[21]

Like Song, a number of workers became poets through various literary schools and workers' literary clubs that opened between the late 1980s and the early 1990s. During this period, running a literature school (or class) was a new trend among literary magazine publishers and literary associations, and quite a few workers participated in the process. To worker-poets of the Kuro Literary Club at that time, "literature" included the works of Pak Nohae and Paek Musan, themselves workers turned poets. The workers' passion for literature and their desire to be "good" writers did not mean that they wanted to write within the established paradigm of high literature. Among the many achievements of the workers' literature movement, a towering one, we may say, was the establishment of a self-standing canon of workers' literature.

Workers' literary clubs remained active well into the late 1990s, until right before the 1997 Asian financial crisis. In the meantime, however, the literary elites (*mundan*) all but ignored the presence of workers' literature, rendering it the alienated Other of the 1990s' new intellectual literary mainstream.

Conclusion: The Significance of Workers' Literary Clubs in Korean Cultural History

The significance of the workers' literary movement during the democratization era is not limited to its most visible achievements—the works of a few exceptional individual figures such as Pak Nohae and Paek Musan. Such a view would only conform to the elite-oriented epistemology of modern literary history. Rather, the movement's true significance lies in its grassroots collective activism, the consequent transformation of the literary field itself, and its implications for a potential revolution of knowledge.

The history of workers' literature and literary clubs in the 1970s and the 1980s can be viewed as a progression from nonliteracy to literature and on to the emancipation of labor. Having started with memoirs and nonfictional writings, workers moved to produce labor poems and novels that explicitly exhibited their newly acquired class consciousness. This development, however, cannot be narrated as a linear process. Rather, it followed multiple paths and had many layers. We should also remember that this movement continued well into the 1990s.

Why did the 1980s labor movement rely so heavily on the literary clubs as a main medium and institution for its activities? And how could this period's literature and culture embrace labor so rapidly and intensely? These questions cannot be answered simply by pointing at intellectuals' renewed progressive social consciousness. To answer these questions, we need to explore other, broader issues such as modern literacy, the institutional distribution of education, and the *mentalité* of the South Korean working class. When workers needed to discover and express themselves in order to achieve an emancipated consciousness, writing, along with reading, was available to them as a powerful tool. It remains in question just how aware workers and their student mentors were of this potential inherent in literature.

We should also note that the alternative culture represented by workers' literature during the democratization decades was made possible by the existence of a vast base of readers among workers. Worker-readers participated in literary clubs and schools, read poems and novels, and wanted to write. A great number of "shouting stones" became readers of literature in the 1980s, only to be abandoned by the cultural mainstream during the 1990s.

In light of the present research, we may issue an appeal for reconsideration of a currently dominant narrative within Korean cultural history. One popular motif of 1990s new culture was the "return of the repressed"— the idea of a welcome return of individualism, aestheticism, and genre diversification. In fact, however, it was workers' culture that became repressed and marginalized with the advent of the cultural discourses of the 1990s. Today, this chapter of South Korean cultural history has become so thoroughly forgotten that it seems to have never even taken place. It is important to note that such complete erasure of the memory could happen not because of the decline of workers' social and cultural movement per se but rather because of how culture itself was redefined in 1990s public discourse. This was an era dominated by intellectuals who, typically, chose to "convert" or "clear" their past in the new decade of "liberalization" (*chayuhwa*) or neoliberalism. With the corruption and ghettoization of progressive politics, the decentering of labor in the neoliberal economy, and the demise of student activism under the pressures of the increasingly unstable job market, "literature from below" came to be forgotten, and lost along with it was our memory of its mode of being and our very intellectual capacity of thinking about the subject.

NOTES

This essay is a substantially revised and updated version of the previously published journal article of the same title, "Kŭ mantŏn 'oech'inŭn tolmaengidŭl ŭn ŏdiro kassŭlkka." I would like to thank Sunyoung Park for her translation.

1. Chŏn T'aeil kinyŏm pangmulgwan kŏllip wiwŏnhoe, ed., *Ŏnŭ chŏngnyŏn nodongja ŭi sam kwa chugŭm*. This biography has since been adapted to the screen in 1995 by director Pak Kwangsu in *Single Spark*. Terms such as "labor testimonials" (*nodong hyŏnjang sosŏl*) and "reportage fiction" (*rŭp'o sosŏl*) appeared only around 1977, while "labor novels" (*nodong sosŏl*) and "labor literature" began to be frequently used in journalism around 1983 and 1984, respectively. See Kim Sŏnghwan, "1970-yŏndae nonp'iksyŏn kwa sosŏl."

2. Richard Hoggart's pioneering work, *The Uses of Literacy*, examines the layered historical relationship between the propagation of mass culture and the formation of the working class in Britain's process of modernization, and his insight is applicable to the South Korean context as well. Rancière's *Proletarian Nights* offers a deeper and more philosophical meditation on the correlation between the Enlightenment, education, and class struggle. With his radical supposition of the equality of human intelligence, Rancière challenges the conventional assumption of the need of enlightened intellectual mentorship for the self-awakening and emancipation of workers. His egalitarian perspective enables us to reconceive the relationship between workers and intellectuals in 1980s Korea outside of elitist hegemonic discourse.

3. See "Chakka Chŏng Inhwa ssi." Chŏng turned more political later on, after learning about the 1979 Puma Protest against Pak Chung Hee's Yusin regime and the 1980 Kwangju Uprising.

4. Yu Tong'u and Kim Won, "Taedam," 87.

5. Sŏk Chŏngnam, "In'gan tapkye salgo sipta" [I want to live like a human being]. *Taehwa*, November 1976, 118. Quoted in Kim Won, *Yŏgong 1970*, 761.

6. Kim Chinsuk, *Sogŭm kkot namu*, 46–47.

7. Paulo Freire's *Pedagogy of the Oppressed* was first translated into Korean under the title of *P'edagoji* in 1979. Han Wansang et al., *Han'guk minjung kyoyungnon*. The latter was translated multiple times over since 1978.

8. P'yŏnjippu, *Pak Nohae hyŏnsang*, 182.

9. Kim Chŏnghwan, "Minjung munhak ŭi chŏnmang."

10. Quoted in Yu Kyŏngsun, "Arŭmdaun yŏndae," 76.

11. Kim Myŏngin, "Chisigin munhak ŭi wigi."

12. See "Kodan hago chich'in nodong hyŏnjang" and "Puchŏn nodongja munhakhoe."

13. "Puchŏn nodongja munhakhoe."

14. Ibid.

15. Sŏng Hunhwa, "Tŏburŏ ttattŭt hage saragal su innŭn sam," 418–19.

16. "Kodan hago chich'in nodong hyŏnjang."

17. "Nodongja chakkadŭl."

18. Ibid.

19. The year 1991 was the last year when major literary journals published articles devoted to labor literature. See Sin Sŭngyŏp, "Hyŏndan'gye nodong sosŏl ŭi kyŏnghyang," and Im Hongbae, "Hyŏnsilchuŭi nonjaeng ŭi kyohun."

20. Ha T'aesŏng, "Munhwa yesurin iyŏ!"

21. "Kŏri ŭi siin Sŏng Kyŏngdong."

REFERENCES

"Chakka Chŏng Inhwa ssi 6-wŏl hangjaeng munhak ŭro hyŏngsanghwa" [Chŏng Inhwa turns the June Uprising into literature]. *Kyŏnghyang sinmun*, November 29, 1988.
Cheon Jung-Hwan. "Kŭ mantŏn 'oech'inŭn tolmaengi'dŭl ŭn ŏdiro kassŭlkka: 1980–90-yŏndae Han'guk nodongja munhakhoe wa nodongja munak." *Yŏksa pip'yŏng* 106 (2014): 173–205.
Chŏn Sŏngho, *Han'guk yahak undongsa: Chayu rŭl hyanghan yŏjŏng 110-yŏn* [History of Korean night schools: One hundred years' journey toward freedom]. Hagisisŭp, 2009.
Chŏn T'aeil kinyŏm pangmulgwan kŏllip wiwŏnhoe, ed. *Ŏnŭ chŏngnyŏn nodongja ŭi sam kwa chugŭm: Chŏn T'aeil p'yŏngjŏn* [A young laborer's death: The critical biography of Chŏn T'aeil]. Tolbaegae, 1983.
Freire, Paulo. *P'edagoji* [*Pedagogy*]. Catholic Lay Apostle Council of Korea, 1979.
Han Wansang et al. *Han'guk minjung kyoyungnon*. 1985; Hangminsa, 1989.
Ha T'aesŏng, "Munhwa yesurin iyŏ! Chojik ŭl kŏnsŏl hara: T'ulpyŏl kihoek—Nodong munhak? Itta ŏptta 5" [Cultural workers, organize! Special feature on labor literature 5]. *Ch'amsesang kyesip'an*, October 11, 2006. http://www.newscham.net/news/view.php?board=news&id=37610
Hoggart, Richard. *The Uses of Literacy*. London: Pelican Books, 1957.
Im Hongbae. "Hyŏnsilchuŭi nonjaeng ŭi kyohun kwa nodong sosŏl ŭi chillo" [Lessons of realism debates and the future path for labor novels]. *Ch'angjak kwa pip'yŏng* 72 (Summer 1991): 79–99.
Kim Chinsuk. *Sogŭm kkot namu* [Salt flower tree]. Humanitas Books, 2007.
Kim Chŏnghwan. "Minjung munhak ŭi chŏnmang e taehan myŏt kaji saenggak" [Thoughts on the prospects for minjung literature]. *Han'guk munhak*, February 1985, 358–76.
Kim Myŏngin. "Chisigin munhak ŭi wigi wa saeroun minjok munhak ŭi kusang" [Crisis of intellectual literature and a proposal for a new national literature]. *Munhak yesul undong* 1 (1987): 62–109.
Kim Sŏnghwan. "1970-yŏndae nonp'iksyon kwa sosŏl ŭi kwan'gye yangsang yŏn'gu" [A study of the relationship between nonfiction and fiction in the 1970s]. *Sanghŏ hakpo* 32 (June 2011): 13–61.
Kim Won. *Yŏgong 1970: Kŭnyŏdŭl ŭi panyŏksa* [Factory women workers counter history, 1970]. Imaejin, 2006.
"Kodan hago chich'in nodong hyŏnjang punno tama" [Letters of indignation from the tiered and weary workers]. *Hankyoreh*, December 7, 1989.
"Kŏri ŭi siin Sŏng Kyŏngdong int'ŏbyu" [Interview with the street poet Sŏng Kyŏngdong]. *Saram sesang: Chŏn T'aeil kinyŏm saŏphoe hoebo* 118 (November/December 2008): 39–40.
"Nodongja chakkadŭl, oe ssŭgo ŏttŏk'e ssŭna" [Worker writers, why and how they write]. *Yŏnhap News*, March 27, 1990.
"Puch'ŏn nodongja munhakhoe, iltŏ esŏ saem sonnŭn ch'angjak ŭiyok chinsol" [Puch'ŏn workers' literary club members draw their creative inspirations from their workplace]. *Hankyoreh*, February 17, 1991.
P'yŏnjippu, ed. *Pak Nohae hyŏnsang* [The Pak Nohae phenomenon]. Tŭngae, 1989.

Rancière, Jacques. *Proletarian Nights: The Workers' Dream in Nineteenth-Century France.* New York: Verso, 2012.

Single Spark [Arŭmdaun chŏngnyŏn Chŏn T'aeil]. Directed by Pak Kwangsu. CINE2000, 1995.

Sin Sŭngyŏp. "Hyŏndan'gye nodong sosŏl ŭi kyŏnghyang kwa palchŏn chŏnmang" [The tendency and prospect of current labor literature]. *Sasang munye undong* 8 (Summer 1991): 34–51.

Sŏng Hunhwa. "Tŏburŏ ttattŭt hage saragal su innŭn sam ŭl wihayŏ" [To build a life of mutual care and communitarianism]. In Yu Chŏngsuk et al., *Na yŏsŏng nodongja* [I, A Female Worker], 1:386–424. Kŭrinbi, 2011.

Yu Kyŏngsun. "Arŭmdaun yŏndae—tŭlbul chŏrŏm t'aorŭn 1985-yŏn Kuro tongmaeng p'aŏp" [A beautiful solidarity: The 1985 Kuro General Strike]. Meidei, 2007.

Yu Tong'u. *Ŏnŭ tolmaengi ŭi oech'im.* Chŏngnyŏnsa, 1978.

Yu Tong'u and Kim Won. "Taedam: Tolmaengi nŭn ajik to oech'inda" [Dialogue: The little stone is still shouting]. *Silchŏn munhak* 110 (Summer 2013): 72–101.

7

Indie before Indie

Minjung Song in the History of South Korean Popular Music

Chang Nam Kim

The label of *minjung kayo* (minjung song) refers to the products of a protest song movement that flourished throughout the era of South Korea's democratization between the 1970s and the 1990s. Circulating outside the mainstream record industry, these songs enjoyed broad popularity, especially among the supporters of the minjung (people's) political movement. While the term is often used interchangeably with *undonggwŏn kayo* (activist song), *minjung kayo* connotes a certain ideological or cultural orientation of the songs, rather than their usage in a countercultural function. The heyday of the minjung song movement was without a doubt the decade of the 1980s, which was also the time minjung song existed in an independent form. Starting in the early 1990s, the genre was first integrated into the mainstream music industry and then quickly lost its popularity with the South Korean public.

Beginning in the late 1970s, several song circles started to form at colleges and, in smaller measure, at factories around Korea. Members of these circles typically composed their own songs, printed and distributed the lyrics and tabs, and made (illegal) recordings that were then circulated in a cassette-tape format. The movement gained full momentum when the affiliates of these circles began to organize off-site in alliance with activists in other cultural fields such as literature, theater, film, and art. From the mid-1980s on, a variety of musical collectives were operating at colleges, labor unions, and progressive churches, creating and disseminating a large number of what would come to be known as minjung songs.

The present chapter will provide an introduction to and an examination of the genre of minjung song within the broader context of South Korean mainstream popular music. The genre of activist song has been commonly regarded as rather antithetical to popular music (*taejung ŭmak*) and to the mainstream. It is almost definitional of minjung song that the genre is the product of a music culture created outside established marketing circuits by artists who were themselves critical of the mainstream.[1] The problem with this view, however, is that it artificially separates the history and development of activist song from that of popular music.[2] As this chapter will show, the two were closely intertwined despite widespread belief to the contrary.

This kind of endeavor is not entirely new. I have previously pointed out the problem of dichotomously opposing minjung culture to popular culture or, for that matter, opposing a subculture to hegemonic culture.[3] I have raised these objections in part because the Korean cultural milieu has undergone profound changes since the era and the process of democratization, generating a renewed understanding of the nature of popular culture today. Another important reason is that, in my view, it is incumbent on us to reexamine and refresh the very idea of minjung culture well beyond the conceptual limitations of 1980s binary thinking. Much has been written about the culture of the 1980s, but the task of reassessing the minjung movement through a new analytical lens has yet to be undertaken. This is partly because cultural activism per se has lost much momentum in post-1990s Korean society. Meanwhile, minjung culture has in a way been re-marginalized in the context of mainstream cultural history, where it is often treated as the temporary flare-up of a minority of intellectuals during the heady time of Korea's democratization. Reconsidering the genre of minjung song within the context of mainstream music, and minjung culture within popular culture, will be a way for us to reevaluate the contemporary relevance of minjung songs at the same time as we behold new interpretive possibilities for Korean popular music and culture today.

The View from the 1980s: Minjung Song as Antagonistic to the Musical Mainstream

Between the early 1980s and the 1990s, alongside the minjung song movement itself, there came into being a form of music criticism expressly devoted to reflection and commentary on activist song. Much of this criticism appeared on the pages of *Norae* (Song), a magazine that played a key role in providing a theoretical grounding to the minjung song movement as part of broader activist culture. In 1984 the magazine devoted its inaugural issue to a critique of mainstream popular music, and it followed up two years later with an issue on the critique of highbrow Western classical music and its teaching in Korea.[4] The choice of these themes, of course, reflected the activists' opposition to hegemonic music culture in both its classical and popular forms. Minjung songs were then widely regarded as "antithetical to and outside of the popular mainstream and the highbrow music." This sort of negative definition was indeed seen as sufficient at that time, as cultural debate was often shaped by a dichotomous framework that opposed quite starkly the minjung to the *taejung*, the "people" to the "masses," and, in general, "resistance" to "hegemony."

Within this framework, popular culture was typically seen as a form of hegemony that contributed to the maintenance and reproduction of the ruling regime, while the minjung movement was regarded as the counterculture to that hegemony. For all its crudeness, the binarism was widely accepted, and perhaps even inevitable at a time when activists were engaged in a sharp and all-out confrontation with an oppressive regime that often turned to censorship and repression. In such a milieu, the (resistant) people were deemed separate from the (conformist) masses, and illegal underground culture was seen as opposed to officially sanctioned popular culture. Ironically, of course, such a polarized view also attested to the failure of the regime's cultural hegemony despite its heavy-handed censorship.

In the binary analysis of activist minjung critics, then, the ideological character of minjung song was understood to be resistant as opposed to hegemonic, reformist as opposed to conformist, and nationalist rather than imperialist. This dichotomous scheme came under scrutiny in the late 1980s, just as South Korea's democratic reforms began to have an effect. With the progression of democracy, censorship barriers were lowered for the entry of minjung culture into the mainstream media, which then proceeded to gradually integrate the counterculture in their programming. Thus was born a new musical force that belonged somewhere between the two poles of hegemony and resistance. The most representative example of this new cultural formation is probably a musical collective that went by the name the Seekers of Song (Norae rŭl ch'annŭn saramdŭl).[5] Aiming at the legalization of minjung song, the Seekers performed songs of an activist spirit all the while reaching out to an audience far broader than just the members of activist organizations. Their music became a legitimate part of the popular mainstream and, in a first for activist song, was allowed to circulate legally. Things had changed quickly. Within the polarized cultural environment of the mid-1980s, a story like that of the Seekers of Song would have been inconceivable.[6]

Aside from a changing cultural milieu, another challenge to the old and rigid binary paradigm came from a renewed understanding, among intellectuals, of the idea of popular culture itself. Popular culture had up to then been mainly regarded as a passive vehicle of hegemonic ideology, as had been theorized by Theodor Adorno and Max Horkheimer in their sociocultural analysis of the culture industry.[7] In this view, the masses were deemed as the uncritical recipients of messages encoded in hegemonic culture by the ruling elites. Mainstream music itself was believed to be part of this system, and it was often regarded as little more than a tool of ideological propagation. In truth, however, even in the middle of the 1980s many individual activists and groups sang popular songs as much as minjung songs at their gatherings or on weekend trips. The resistant minjung and the conformist masses were only two among the many faces of Korean people in the 1980s, and they were never as separable as Adorno's theory would have predicted them to be. Besides, had the theory been correct, the minjung itself could not have become (as it did) a subject of progressive history. For how can counterculture exist, we may ask, where nothing escapes the crushing and uniform influence of the hegemonic system of power?

Minjung Song as a Subculture in 1990s Music Criticism

One interesting way of conceptualizing minjung song, which we may call "the subcultural theory," appeared in the 1990s when the term *subculture* itself began to be actively used in South Korean cultural discourses. Diverse cultural practices were not possible during the authoritarian era, so the very emergence of subcultural movements, along with discourse about them, signaled the transition toward a more democratic Korean society. The emergence of subcultural discourse reflected, among other things, a desire among critics to overcome the dichotomy of minjung and popular culture in order to grasp the changing cultural terrain through an alternative and more open-minded analytical lens.

Critic Yi Yŏngmi's 2005 essay "The Status and Trend of Minjung Songs in Korean Music Culture" (Han'guk norae munhwa sok esŏŭi minjung kayo ŭi wisang kwa hŭrŭm) was one of the first studies that aimed to redefine the genre of minjung song by using the concept of subculture.[8] In the essay, Yi gives three reasons why minjung song should qualify as the artistic product of a subculture. First, the songs that the minjung sang were not part of dominant culture. Unlike mainstream popular music, which was mass produced for commercial interests and was often infused with a conservative message, minjung songs existed apart from profits or ruling ideologies, circulating among a small group of people at a time of heightened social consciousness. Second, minjung song had a voluntary and active following. It was through the active support and contribution of its participants that the genre was formed and developed into an organized movement. For that same reason, the movement lost its momentum with the decline and dissipation of social activism beginning in the early 1990s. Third, according to Yi, minjung song was subcultural because it deliberately took a stance that was critical of contemporary mainstream culture. As she convincingly shows, it was this self-consciously countercultural identity that set the genre of minjung song apart from traditional folk songs. Where traditional music often responded to power in ironic and even subversive ways, Yi argues, it did not exist, as minjung song did, primarily as an act of protest and resistance against the status quo.

There is some gain in seeing minjung song as a subculture and not, as had been the case in the 1980s, as an antithetical movement that rejected the dominant culture in toto. There indeed appears to be a degree of similarity between this song movement and well-known examples of global subcultures such as, for example, 1970s punk rock in Europe and America or the 1950s Rastafarian movement in the West Indies.[9] Both these subcultures gave representation to the malaise of young people and workers who felt alienated and sought to respond through music, and both saw their styles later blooming into global cultural trends that were appropriated by the mainstream media. Similarly, minjung song was expressive of the countercultural spirit of 1980s Korean youth and laborers, and some of the artists and compositions came later to enjoy popular success upon being picked up by the media.

A subcultural interpretation of minjung song, however, leaves unaddressed the question of how we should understand the very concept of hegemonic culture. In her essay, Yi labels as hegemonic both the Western classical music taught at music schools and the popular commercial music that was controlled by major labels. It is tempting to endorse this seemingly reasonable definition of the hegemonic, but in the reality of postdemocratization Korea things were more complex and layered. A good example here was Seo Taiji. A band that was immensely popular among teenagers in the early 1990s, Seo Taiji and Boys could be seen as part of hegemonic culture in that the 1990s music market was very much dominated by teen music. At the same time, however, the band's lyrics and music gave powerful expression to the discontent of young people within South Korea's disciplinarian and crushingly competitive educational system. Seo Taiji thus had strong subcultural features, and indeed he was the first to point to the status of teenagers as a social minority and to the central role that music could play in their self-expression.[10] Moreover, the rock, punk, and hip-hop music of his generation could rely on an active and voluntary fan base, which is another of the criteria that Yi applies to the subcultural. This crossing of borders has only intensified today, in new-millennium South Korea, where so-called independent music has all the characteristics that Yi associated with the subcultural despite being to all effects integrated into the commercial distribution system.

It may be possible to limit more strictly our account of minjung song to the era of the 1980s, when its fan base among the *undonggwŏn* made it undoubtedly a movement of a subcultural nature. Even so, the need to redefine minjung song as a genre still remains. The binary, oppositional scheme of activist songs vis-à-vis mainstream music may have been useful in certain periodical circumstances, but that scheme also falsely assumes the equation of the sphere of mainstream popular culture with that of hegemonic ideology. Instead, I propose, we may now benefit from reconsidering minjung song *as an integral part* of popular music with which it has until now been contrasted. That is to say, the time may be ripe for us to gain new insights into the nature of minjung song by examining it within the same context in which we analyze mainstream music. Mainstream popular music, I contend, is far from being uniformly homogeneous, conformist, and ideologically regressive. In fact, it can be rich and diverse enough to include and account for some of the most radical of minjung songs.

A New Proposal: Minjung Song as Part of Popular Music

In proposing to reexamine minjung songs through the prism of mainstream popular music, I have two main goals in mind. First, by reintegrating the genre within the historical continuum of Korean music, rather than confining its history to an isolated time-space, one will be able to gain new insights into aspects of 1980s activist song that have until now been overlooked. Second, through such a broadening and re-contextualization, one will also be able to rethink popular music and the mainstream in order to explore their positive, if not progressive, transformative potential.

Historically, the three main measures that have been used in distinguishing minjung song from popular music have been the criteria of ideological orientation, consumer demographics, and the media and networks used in the production and circulation of the music. The first two, of course, are not entirely reliable indicators, as popular music is not necessarily all conformist and, in addition, the consumers of minjung and popular music often overlapped. Moreover, while it is true that minjung songs were circulated via an illegal network during the era of military dictatorship, that all changed after democratization in 1987, when the selling of most music became legal. Needless to say, no theory would identify popular music by the criterion of its legality alone.

In the discussion that follows, I will examine anew various textual and contextual aspects of minjung song through the analytical paradigm of popular music. My discussion is indebted to the framework outlined in *The Cambridge Companion to Pop and Rock*.[11] In my examination, as in that volume, the contextual analysis focuses on the impact of music technology, that of the industrial character of music production, and that of fandom and the market of minjung song. The more properly textual analysis, for its part, will attend primarily to the musical quality of minjung songs—instead of their much-discussed lyrical aspects—including their diverse genres and styles.

Minjung Song and Technology

Music needs electricity. The broad concept of musical technology does not just refer to the collection of instruments, recording equipment, and playback equipment. It also signals a discursive sphere, a milieu within which we encounter and consume music, share and evaluate our musical experiences, and, not least, reflect on what music is and what it could be.[12] Ranging from basic electrical devices (such as the microphone, the amplifier, and the loudspeaker), recording technologies (such as the cassette deck, the multitrack recorder, and the midi sound processor), and instrument technologies (the electric guitar, the synthesizer, the drum machine, the turntable in hip-hop) to audio technologies (including long-playing records, cassette tapes, compact discs, and MP3 files), the innovation, competition, and evolution of technologies in themselves tell a history of modern music. A new technology is often developed to rationalize and control the production and circulation of music for producers' economic interest, but it can also be appropriated to bolster the consumer's subjectivity and contest the producer's controlling power. As is exemplified by the crisis of the music industry upon the introduction of the CD, which was originally meant to increase profits but had the effect of empowering consumers, technology is neither neutral nor necessarily hegemonic in itself. Rather, its development has a dialectical relationship with social change.

Minjung songs were no less associated with technology than mainstream music was. At an early stage, practitioners of the genre used acoustic sound at a rather elementary technological level. From the mid-1980s on, however, they also began to actively incorporate electronic sound and more complex recording techniques. Needless to say, minjung musicians often could afford only cheaper, low-fidelity equipment. The single most important technology for the development of the movement was probably the cassette tape. Illegal cassettes, which first appeared in 1979 with Kim Minki's song "Light of the Factory" (Kongjang ŭi pulbit), served as the most important medium in the production and consumption of the whole genre throughout the 1980s. Enduring, cheap, easy to use, and simple to record, the cassette afforded poorer Koreans a certain degree of appropriation of the modes of musical production and consumption.[13] Its potential was brilliantly showcased by the minjung song movement that, not coincidentally, began to see its decline when the cassette tape was replaced with CD technology in South Korea.

Minjung Song and the Music Industry

The most basic attribute of mainstream popular music, especially when critics evoke the genre in a derogatory way, would be its industrial character. Popular music is industrially produced within the economic logic of capital, and for that reason it often contributes to the reproduction and perpetuation of hegemonic values. Historically, perhaps the most famous proponent of this view was Theodor Adorno, who broadly centered his concerns around the concept of "standardization." Adorno argued that elements of modern popular music are so standardized that entire musical phrases and even songs are often interchangeable. Whatever difference there may be between single compositions, he suggested, is often but a superficial variation, a "pseudo-individualization" that creates an illusion of a free choice within the limits of a brutally impoverished palette.[14] By repeatedly listening to standardized popular music, Adorno thought, the masses have their musical sensibility stunted, draw fake pleasure, and become more and more conformist with the capitalist system.

Much has been written about the elitism of Adorno's views, some of which was shared by other figures of the Frankfurt School. While I very much agree with such criticism, I also believe that Adorno's analysis is useful in dispelling the notion that minjung songs were immune to the homogenizing tendency of industrially produced popular culture. Indeed, many minjung songs closely resembled each other. The majority proceeded according to a march-style rhythm, were embellished by a sublime and elegiac melody, and had a conventional structure of intro, refrain, chorus, and finale. In all fairness, of course, it should be said that there was a material reason for this phenomenon. At a time when performers had to remain anonymous and wrote their songs in response to urgent political needs, a certain standardization gave them both a shared musical code and a degree of safety in that they could not be easily recognized. Rather surprising, perhaps, was the fact that even in these circumstances, many musicians managed to divert from the marked path to create their own individual work, thus becoming respected artists whose originality defied the constraints of the culture industry.

In addition to their structure and composition, minjung songs displayed an industrial quality also in their modes of production and distribution. The recordings of the most successful artists were sold as cassette tapes mainly through a network of activist bookstores in university areas. These sales majorly contributed to financing individual activists and their organizations. Of course, the primary purpose of making those tapes was never financial, so their production was not constrained by concerns such as copyright or market competition. Nor was their circulation volume ever comparable to that of mainstream popular music. Still, the minjung song movement was not immune to the commercial dimension that, in greater measure, also characterized the world of mainstream music.

It is natural to think of mainstream music as a phenomenon deeply embedded in the logic of market capitalism. On a global scale, however, Simon Frith reported in 1983 that only about 10 percent of all commercially produced records were ever profitable, with another 10 percent barely breaking even.[15] Indeed, in certain countries and historical conditions, the music business has often been conducted at a subsistence level rather than for profit. Major labels today tend to rely on the star system, but in some cases relying on a handful of breakout successes to subsidize the less profitable releases has also increased production costs and led to losses. By contrast, minjung song made a fairly lucrative business, as it catered to no star system, cost little in production expenses (except for the high political risk), and always tended to operate on greater demand than supply. In this sense, involvement in the minjung song movement could be a sensible business venture and not the complete break with capitalism that many of its fans believed it to be.

Minjung Song and Its Fans

Far from being homogenous, popular music spans a broad, diverse spectrum, and its various strands are enjoyed by a wide range of social subjects who, in many cases, deeply identify with the music of their choice. In consuming a particular kind of music, listeners actively project a cultural identity that goes well beyond their own individual tastes. They affiliate themselves with an affective community. A central topic in the "identity politics" of music today is that of generational difference. Young people have been the tastemakers of Western popular music ever since the appearance of rock and roll in the 1950s. Since then, the critical discourse has centered on analyzing the synergies, conflicts, and negotiations that take place between mainstream music and its diverse genres, especially in regard to the youth subcultures by which the different genres are adopted.[16]

Generational identity politics, which first played out in Korean popular music in the 1970s, was also an issue with minjung song in the 1980s. The 1970s debates over *chŏngnyŏn munhwa* (youth culture), acoustic guitar, marijuana, and long hair were reminiscent of 1950s American controversies over rock and roll.[17] Those debates continued in the 1980s, albeit in a changed form, as fans took to minjung songs in order to forge and express their identities as student activists and progressive laborers. This is not to say that these fans did not also enjoy the songs of the likes of Cho Yongp'il or Yun Sinae, two big stars who then belonged to Korea's musical mainstream. While they were often critical of mainstream culture, listeners of minjung song were never entirely alienated from it. In a way, the fans of minjung songs were also consumers of mainstream music, but many of them nevertheless performed their primary identity politics via affiliation with the minjung movement.

In spite of a common assumption, it is not clear that student and labor activists sung exclusively minjung songs at protest marches and meetings. Some of these youths may indeed have been listening to mainstream music in their private, everyday lives. As we noted already, the diffusion of tape recorders significantly contributed to the privatization of music among the public. Be that as it may, the fact that minjung songs could become the chief mode of self-expression for dissident youths and laborers suggests that those songs were also quite relevant to their everyday lives. In short, it is likely that minjung songs were routinely enjoyed by young fans who, while also liking popular music, nonetheless tended to shape their identity through their consumption of activist music.

The Musical Qualities of Minjung Song

We have examined so far the contextual factors of minjung songs through some of the main paradigms that are used for analyzing popular music. We shall now move on to some reflections about the musical qualities of minjung song, understood as the set of features that more closely pertain to the melody, rhythm, and the generic attributes of this musical form. I call attention here to musicality rather than textuality because minjung songs have often been analyzed in terms of the countercultural and political content of their lyrics. Yet the musical aspects of these songs are what affect listeners most.

The category of minjung song includes a broad swath of styles and subgenres. A retrospective anthological compilation of the genre that was recently published by the Korean Democracy Foundation demonstrates well the sheer variety of activist music.[18] The collection includes, among other things, protest songs from the 1980s; modern folk songs from the early 1970s (by Kim Minki, Han Dae-Soo, Yang Pyŏngjip, and Sŏ Yusŏk); gospels that were sung in American radical churches in the 1970s; American folk songs by the likes of Bob Dylan and Pete Seeger; children's songs such as "Our Wish Is Unification" (Uri ŭi sowŏn ŭn t'ongil); traditional Korean songs like "Harbinger" (Sŏn'guja) and "Song of Liberation"; and some classics of the *trotto* repertoire of the 1950s and the 1960s such as "Idiot Adada" (Paekch'i Adada) and "Sunhŭi Who Became an Ellen" (Erena ka toen Sunhŭi).[19] This assortment suggests that, contrary to common assumption, there was no inherent essence, not even a lyrical one, that turned certain compositions into minjung songs. Rather, different songs seem to have become invested with the spirit of resistance typical of the minjung through the practice of their performance within certain activist contexts. The most that we can do, today, is to outline the broad and general musical character of minjung song by observing the musical orientations of leading activists and the major styles of the songs themselves.

Fig. 7.1. A concert by the Seekers of Song in 2013 at Seoul's Mapo Art Center. In the background is a photograph of the June 29, 1987 prodemocracy demonstration in Pusan. Private collection.

The major composers of minjung songs were almost all members of university song circles. They belonged to a generation that had experienced the new youth culture of the 1970s, and indeed some of the most famous minjung songs of the 1980s reflected the influence of 1970s iconic singers such as Kim Minki and Han Dae-Soo. Exemplary of this influence are some of the most successful songs by the Seekers of Song, including "Pine Tree, Green Pine Tree" (Sol a sol a p'urŭrŭn sol a), "Four Seasons" (Sagye), "When the Day Comes" (Kŭ nal i omyŏn), and "In the Wide Plain" (Kwangya esŏ). For this reason, when the censors' ban on Kim's and Han's records was lifted in the late 1980s, they were welcomed with great enthusiasm by the public. In most musical aspects, we may say, minjung songs represented an evolution of the musical character of 1970s modern folk songs.

The modern folk song became the major subgenre of minjung song for a variety of reasons. First, as we just saw, the leaders of the minjung song movement had their musical tastes shaped by the modern folk of the 1970s. Second, the guitar was a relatively cheap instrument that was easy to procure and not too difficult to learn at a basic level. And third, thanks to the power of their lyrics, folk songs were a natural musical form for conveying an activist message.

The genre of minjung song became more diverse and eclectic during the latter half of the 1980s, as the number of activist bands and musicians increased amid the intensification of the democratization movement. Folk music was still the mainstream, but more and more it was played with the accompaniment of electric guitars, bass guitars, and drums. Many songs were thus now composed in a rock style or, especially among labor activists, in an updated *trotto* style. Despite these stylistic expansions, however, minjung songs never diverged too far from the spectrum of mainstream popular music. For this reason, they were sometimes criticized for being "nothing but popular songs except for lyrics" and "a lyric movement rather than a song movement."[20]

Indeed, we must realize that minjung songs were often cut from the same musical cloth as popular music. Modern music in Korea developed during the colonial period (1910–45), when traditional music declined and left room for the transplantation of Western musical influences amid the modernization process. In the West, popular music is defined today against both classical music and premodern folk music.[21] In a similar fashion, popular music in Korea is contrasted with both Western classical music and Korean traditional folk music. Minjung songs were no exception to this general paradigm of modern Korean popular music.

The Significance of Minjung Song in the History of Korean Music

Until about 1987, minjung songs circulated only via small-scale organizational networks, and they were exchanged mainly at protest meetings in the form of artisanally recorded cassettes. Regardless, they commanded a sizeable following of activist listeners, most of them affiliated with student or labor organizations, and in this way they could rely on a fan base of a considerable breadth and scope. After democratization and legalization in 1987, many of the repertoires of minjung song were adopted by the mainstream media, testifying to the remarkable desire among the general public for alternative and underground music. The 1990s explosion of minjung song was analogous, albeit in a smaller scale, to the world boom in punk and reggae, both of which had originated as lowbrow forms of cultural expression by humble people and the working class.

Fig. 7.2. The second album of the Seekers of Song (1989) included some of the group's most representative minjung songs and sold over half a million copies. Private collection.

The production and active consumption of minjung songs exerted a substantial influence, both palpable and intangible, on the Korean music industry. In its most important contribution, the activist song movement induced a reform of censorship practices in the whole field of publicly available music. Although the prepublication screening requirement was not officially abolished until 1996, the barriers of censorship had already been crumbling since 1989, when the Seekers of Song published their second album. The triumph of democratization naturally contributed to this, but more importantly, the public desire for free and alternative modes of expression was too strong to be curtailed by censorship. The biggest milestone in this process was perhaps Chŏng T'aech'un's courageous campaign for the abolition of the requirement of prepublication screening for music. In 1990, at a decisive turning point in the struggle against censorship, Chŏng deliberately skipped the screening and published an uncensored album. He eventually won a court verdict that declared mandatory prescreening to be anticonstitutional. Considering that Chŏng was a self-declared minjung musician, the legal victory can be regarded as a historical accomplishment of the minjung song movement itself.

The minjung song movement also left an indelible mark on the themes and quality of Korean popular music in general. The genre of activist song expanded the scope of musical expression by unprecedentedly encoding critical and subversive messages in musical form. Socially critical songs have since become a principal strand of Korean popular music. In what may be seen as a form of "musical realism," mainstream musicians are today able to embed a critical message in their songs, thereby challenging conventionally accepted ideas and directly engaging in social and political activism. The existence of such a trend suggests that Korean popular music has broadened and diversified its horizon, which again is in no small measure a credit to the minjung song movement.[22]

The 1990s love affair between minjung song and the mainstream media did not last long. Past the mid-1990s, South Korean listeners quickly lost interest in the activist music genre. With the appearance of Seo Taiji, teen pop emerged as a new mainstream sensation, and inevitably the phenomenon cut into the popularity of most genres except pop and dance. This was the time when alienated musicians began to form an independent music scene around Hongik University in Seoul. Many minjung artists became part of the "indie" (*indi*) scene, a loan word from English new in 1990s Korea. To a large extent, it is this dwindling but lively movement that today carries forward the tradition of minjung song in South Korea.

The creation of an independent music scene is indeed another important legacy of the minjung song movement. Even today, many musicians—such as Mun Chino, Paekcha, Son Pyŏnghwi, Yŏn Yŏngsŏk, Yi Chisang, and the band Kkottaji—would explicitly describe themselves as belonging to the minjung movement, even though their scene is small in comparison with the minjung movement at its high tide in the 1980s. These musicians still compose socially critical songs, publish albums, stage concerts, and sing at protest meetings. Alongside them are also other musicians, including new-generation independent singers, who are socially conscious and encode a critical message in their music. Needless to say, the contemporary independent scene is mostly marginalized in mainstream media. But it commands a small but devoted group of active fans. In this sense, minjung song and independent music in today's South Korea are not easily distinguishable from each other. The spirit of 1980s minjung song, we may say, continues to live on in today's independent music.

The questions for organizers of musical activism today are how to mobilize supporters and how to cultivate more of them. In this sense, as Tony Bennett once said, "the point is not to define 'the people' but to *make* them."[23]

NOTES

This essay is an updated and revised version of "Minjung kayŏ ŭi taejung ŭmaksajŏk ŭiŭi." I would like to thank Sunyoung Park for the essay's translation.

1. Yi Yŏngmi, "Minjung kayo chakp'um kyŏnghyang."
2. For instance, minjung songs are absent from Kim Yŏngju's study "1990-yŏndae ihu Han'guk chŏngnyŏn taejung ŭmak," and Chang Yujŏng and Sŏ Pyŏnggi, *Han'guk taejung ŭmaksa kaeron*. In other studies, minjung songs have been treated as *undonggwŏn* songs only or as a minor phenomenon of college song circles. See, for instance, Yi Yŏngmi, *Han'guk taejung kayosa*, and Yi Hyesuk and Son Usŏk, *Han'guk taejung ŭmaksa*.
3. See Kim Chang Nam, *Taejung munhwa wa munhwa silch'ŏn*.
4. See Kim Chang Nam et al., *Norae 1* and *Norae 2*.
5. *The Seekers of Song* was at first the name of the 1984 music album produced by a group of activist musicians who then went on to formally organize a collective in 1987 under the same name.
6. For the historical account and assessment of the Seekers of Song, see Han Tonghŏn et al., *Norae rŭl ch'annŭn saramdŭl*.
7. Horkheimer and Adorno, *Dialectic of Enlightenment*.
8. Yi Yŏngmi, "Minjung kayo 30-yŏnsa," in vol. 3 of *2005 Kwangmyŏng ŭmak ch'ukche belli rek'odŭ*. This three-volume title was published by the city of Kwangmyŏng and was distributed at the festival without any public sale.
9. See Hebdige, *Subculture*.
10. For the subcultural approach to Seo Taiji's music, see Kim Hyŏnsŏp, *Sŏ T'aeji tamnon*, and Maliangkay, "The Popularity of Individualism."
11. Frith, Straw, and Street, *The Cambridge Companion to Pop and Rock*. This book has been translated into Korean by Chang Hoyŏn in 2005 under the title of *K'eimbŭriji taejung ŭmak ŭi ihae*.
12. Ibid., 133.
13. For its low cost and mobility, cassette technology was widely used in the developing world throughout the 1970s to exert a profound influence on the development of local music cultures, as it did in 1980s South Korea. See Wallis, *Big Sounds from Small Peoples*.
14. Adorno, "On Popular Music."
15. Frith, *Saundŭ ŭi him*, 139.
16. For the subcultural character of rock and roll, see Frith, *Sound Effects*, 139.
17. For the 1970s rock music culture, see Pil Ho Kim and Hyunjoon Shin, "The Birth of 'Rok': Cultural Imperialism, Nationalism, and the Glocalization of Rock Music in South Korea, 1964–1975."

18. Minjuhwa undong kinyŏm saŏphoe, *Norae nŭn mŏlli mŏlli*, 5 vols. This multivolume anthology includes minjung songs from 1977 through 1992.

19. *Trotto* (t'ŭrot'ŭ) is a genre of Korean popular music that originated during the colonial era from the indigenization of the Japanese *enka*, a form of sentimental ballad music.

20. Minjung activists called for the creation of songs composed in the style of a traditional Korean folk song, rather than that of Western popular music, while classical musicians disregarded minjung songs as nothing musically new but for their political lyrics. See Kim Chang Nam, "Norae undong, noraemal undong, ŭmak undong."

21. Both Western classical and traditional folk music can be regarded as part of popular music in a broad sense, yet commonly speaking, the three categories are largely still distinct.

22. The 1990s critical debates over "the spirit of rock," for instance, was related to the quest for a new activist musical culture. In retrospect, despite their stylistic difference, 1990s rock music provided a new musical language for minjung songs. See Kang Hŏn, "Munje nŭn rok chŏngsin ida," 29.

23. Bennett, "The Politics of the Popular and Popular Culture," 21.

REFERENCES

Adorno, Theodor. "On Popular Music." In *On Record: Rock, Pop, and the Written Word*, edited by Simon Frith and Andrew Goodwin, 256–67. New York: Routledge, 1990.

Bennett, Tony. "The Politics of the Popular and Popular Culture." In *Popular Culture and Social Relations*, edited by Tony Bennett, Colin Mercer, and Janet Woollacott, 6–21. New York: Open University Press, 1986.

Chang Yujŏng and Sŏ Pyŏnggi. *Han'guk taejung ŭmaksa kaeron* [Introduction to Korean popular music]. Sŏngandang, 2015.

Frith, Simon. *The Cambridge Companion to Pop and Rock*. Cambridge: Cambridge University Press, 2001.

Frith, Simon. *Saundŭ ŭi him* [Sound effects]. Translated by Kwŏn Yŏngsŏng and Kim Kongsu. Hannarae, 1995.

Frith, Simon. *Sound Effects: Youth, Leisure, and Politics of Rock*. London: Constable, 1983.

Frith, Simon, Will Straw, and John Street, eds. *K'eimbŭriji taejung ŭmak ŭi ihae* [Understanding popular music by Cambridge]. Translated by Chang Hoyŏn. Hannarae, 2005.

Han Tonghŏn, et al. *Norae rŭl ch'annŭn saramdŭl chigŭm yŏgi esŏ* [Seekers of songs here and now]. Homi, 2005.

Hebdige, Dick. *Subculture: The Meaning of Style*. New York: Methuen, 1984.

Horkheimer, Max, and Theodor W. Adorno. *Dialectic of Enlightenment*. 1969; New York: Continuum, 1994.

Kang Hŏn. "Munje nŭn rok chŏngsin ida" [On the question of the spirit of rock music]. *Ribyŭ* 1 (Winter 1994): 26–35.

Kim Chang Nam. "Minjung kayo ŭi taejung ŭmaksajŏk ŭiŭi" [Minjung songs in the context of Korean popular music history]. *Minjok munhwa nonch'ong* 35 (2007): 55–81.

Kim Chang Nam. "Norae undong, noraemal undong, ŭmak undong" [Song, lyric, and music movements]. In *Norae* 2 (1986): 26–35.

Kim Chang Nam. *Taejung munhwa wa munhwa silch'ŏn* [Popular culture and cultural practices]. Hanul, 1995.

Kim Chang Nam et al. *Norae 1: Chinsil ŭi norae wa kŏjit ŭi norae* [Song 1: Songs of truth and songs of lies]. Silch'ŏn munhaksa, 1984.

Kim Chang Nam et al. *Norae 2: In'gan ŭl wihan ŭmak* [Song 2: Music for humanity]. Silch'ŏn munhaksa, 1986.

Kim Hyŏnsŏp. *Sŏ T'aeji tamnon* [Seo Taiji discourse]. Ch'aek i innŭn maul, 2001.

Kim, Pil Ho, and Hyunjoon Shin. "The Birth of 'Rok': Cultural Imperialism, Nationalism, and the Glocalization of Rock Music in South Korea, 1964–1975." *Positions: East Asia Cultures Critique* 18, no. 1 (2010): 199–230.

Kim Yŏngju. "1990-yŏndae ihu Han'guk chŏngnyŏn taejung ŭmak munhwa ŭi t'ŭksŏng: Changnŭ sang ŭi t'ŭksŏng ŭl chungsim ŭro" [The popular music of 1990s Korean youths and its generic characteristics]. *Norae 5: Taejung ŭmak kwa norae undong kŭrigo chŏngnyŏn munhwa* [Song 5: Popular music, the song movement, and youth culture] (2004): 125–58.

Maliangkay, Roald. "The Popularity of Individualism: The Seo Taiji Phenomenon in the 1990s." In *The Korean Popular Culture Reader*, edited by Kyung Hyun Kim and Youngmin Choe, 296–313. Durham: Duke University Press, 2014.

Minjuhwa undong kinyŏm saŏphoe [The Korean Democracy Foundation]. *Norae nŭn mŏlli mŏlli* [Song goes far far away]. 5 vols. 2006–8.

Wallis, Roger. *Big Sounds from Small Peoples: The Music Industry in Small Countries.* Hillsdale, NY: Pendragon, 1984.

Yi Hyesuk and Son Usŏk. *Han'guk taejung ŭmaksa* [History of Korean popular music]. Lijŭaenbuk, 2003.

Yi Yŏngmi. *Han'guk taejung kayosa* [History of Korean popular songs]. Sigongsa, 1999.

Yi Yŏngmi. "Minjung kayo 30-yŏnsa: Han'guk norae munhwa sok esŏŭi minjung kayo ŭi wisang kwa hŭrŭm" [The 30 years history of minjung song: The status and trend of minjung song in Korean song culture]. In *2005 Kwangmyŏng ŭmak ch'ukche belli rekŏdŭ* [2005 Kwangmyeong music festival valley records], vol. 3, edited by Pak Chunhŭm, 8–19. Kwangmyŏng: Kwangmyŏng ŭmak beli ch'ukche ch'ujin wiwŏnhoe, 2003.

Yi Yŏngmi. "Minjung kayo chakp'um kyŏnghyang ŭi hŭrŭm kwa hyŏn sanghwang" [Trends in minjung songs and their status quo]. In *21 segi minjung ŭmak ŭi saegil ch'akki* [New prospects for minjung songs], edited by Han'guk minjok ŭmagin hyŏphoe, 25–32. Han'guk minjok ŭmagin hyŏphoe, 2003.

PART IV

Intersectional Feminism

8

Bright Constellation

The Rise and Significance of Women's Liberation Literature in 1980s South Korea

Hye-Ryoung Lee

A classic narrative of modernity features as its protagonist an enterprising young man who leaves his family and community to go out into the world, where he becomes a pioneer, a revolutionary, a missionary, an intellectual, an artist, or something similarly august and uplifting.[1] In South Korea, too, in a variant on this narrative, the 1980s saw the literary rise of an unlikely and yet powerful kind of protagonist: a college woman student who leaves her middle-class family to devote herself to social activism.[2] When historian Kim Won wrote a novel that dramatized the civil uprisings of June 10, 1987, for instance, he chose as his main character a female *hakch'ul*: a college student who, in rejection of her privilege, temporarily abandons her studies to turn into a factory worker and a labor activist.[3]

A rebellious daughter of a middle-class family was also a regular heroine in some of the bestselling novels written by women during the 1980s— such as *Room in the Woods* by Kang Sŏk-kyŏng and *A Most Beautiful Wandering* by Gong Ji-young.[4] This unique figure presents a feminist subject whose identity is not defined by gender alone but also by other factors such as class, age, and education. This sort of multifaceted, composite, and, one might say, intersectional feminist identity was rather representative of the nature and character of the women's movement as a whole during the 1980s.[5] In her early study of minjung feminism in 1980s Korea, for instance, Miriam Louie observed how women's and minjung activism were closely intertwined from the days of the 1970s labor movement on.[6]

The complex figure of a *hakch'ul* was ridden with internal tensions and conflicts, pulled as she was between the often irreconcilable stances of gender, class, and the nation. The tensions indeed came to national prominence in Korea in the real-life case of Kwŏn Insuk, a student-turned-labor-activist who suffered sexual torture at the hands of the police during an interrogation. In a later speech on the much-publicized case, Kwŏn emphasized that the violence committed against her should be regarded as the oppression of a worker rather than the violation of a woman.[7] Apparently, she gave such a caution in order to avoid her gender identity overshadowing the cause of labor activism. This may sound disingenuous by today's standards, but it demonstrates the extraordinary complexity attached to the figure of a woman activist in South Korea at the height of the democratization era in the 1980s.[8]

The layered reflection on women's multiple identities is what characterizes the 1980s women's movement and literature as its main cultural medium. As I will suggest in this chapter, I believe that the decade's activist social milieu both complicated and enabled the rise of a strong women's movement in 1980s Korea: while the politically charged atmosphere in many ways obfuscated women's identity politics, I submit that it also and at the same time generated an unprecedented constellation of social and cultural forces that, taken together, had the effect of significantly advancing women's voices in South Korea. This achievement was symbolically reflected in the mid-1980s terminological replacement of *yŏryu munhak* (feminine literature) with *yŏsŏng munhak* (women's literature) as the label for literature written by women. In historical perspective, the label *yŏryu munhak* dated back to the 1930s, when the term was institutionalized in women's magazines, whose male editors and publishers used the term *yŏryu* to connote elite women who were writers, artists, or professionals. *Yŏsŏng munhak*, by contrast, was introduced in the 1950s as a more inclusive, and less sexually stereotyped, alternative to the upper-class label. Both terms were still in use in the early 1980s. It was only through the decade's radical movement of "women's liberation literature" (*yŏsŏng haebang munhak*)—named after "women's liberation ideology" (*yŏsŏng haebang sasang*), the periodical translation of feminism with a leftist inflection—that *yŏsŏng munhak* came to fully replace the older terminology, thus redefining women's literature as a more open space for a public forum on gender-related issues.[9]

As an integral part of the minjung democratization movement, the South Korean women's movement of the 1980s included women from all walks of life, including intellectuals, students, factory workers, urban laborers, peasants, and housewives. It also ranged across generations, all the way from Pak Wansŏ (b. 1931) to Gong Ji-young (b. 1962). Reflective of this diversity, 1980s Korean women's literature presented an unprecedentedly wide array of voices. With its analytical focus on 1980s women's literary magazines, this chapter examines their critical arguments and creative orientations. In the process, it also probes how and why women activists came to turn to literature as their favored medium and what they aspired to by adopting the new paradigm of women's liberation literature.

The Formation of a Bright Constellation: 1980s Women's Social Movements and Cultural Activism

President Chun Doo Hwan's military regime, which was built upon the bloody suppression of the 1980 Kwangju Uprising, relented its iron grip over democratic forces around 1983, allowing the release and reinstatement of dissident politicians, professors, and students. Democratic forces took this opportunity to consolidate and launched a series of activist organizations. The Yŏsŏng p'yŏnguhoe (Women's Equality Council; henceforth WEC) took off in June 1983, a full three months before the founding of its male counterpart, the Minjuhwa undong ch'ŏngyŏn yŏnhap (Youth Association for the Democratic Movement; henceforth YADM). The Council was led by women intellectuals who pursued women's studies at Ewha Womans University or participated in the Christian Academy, a center of the 1970s social movement, or did both.[10] More women soon followed with self-organized efforts to pursue their gendered interests. Yŏsŏng ŭi chŏnhwa, a national women's phone hotline addressing the needs of the victims of domestic violence, began its service in June 1983. And the feminist group Tto hana ŭi munhwa (Another Culture), which was to play an important role in later years, was formed in December 1984.

Unlike the YADM, which attracted close police surveillance from the beginning, the WEC received little political pressure, mainly because women were so marginalized politically and socially. Taking advantage of its marginal status, the council hosted the first Women's Grand Cultural Festival, which combined exhibitions with performances, on October 27 and 28, 1984, in Seoul. The event attracted as many as two thousand attendees as well as media attention, and it thereby sent a powerful signal about the rumblings of a women's movement. The council indeed went on to serve as a façade for political gatherings of workers and students across South Korea. In June 1985, for instance, the WEC held a convention in

Fig. 8.1. Some issues of *Yŏsŏng p'yŏngu* (1984–86), the journal of the Women's Equality Council. Courtesy of the Korea Democracy Foundation.

Pusan in collaboration with the local Catholic center and with the sponsorship of the city's newspapers. The gathering provided, among others, an outlet and a stage for women workers who had been recently laid off from the local rubber factories.[11] In this way, the WEC managed to deploy gender politics in the service of a shared constituency of women's and labor movements, subverting their traditional divisions in favor of a stronger political effect.

An illustration of the WEC's hybrid, intersectional approach to feminist politics is provided by the association's inaugural manifesto from 1983. The document characterized Korean women as, in this order, "victims of patriarchy," "the alienated class in industrial society," and "tragic victims of national division." The manifesto also gave a nod to class consciousness by classifying Korean women into categories such as "working women," "rural women," "the urban poor," and "urban housewives," all the while endowing each category with its historical role. Hence, the manifesto not only reclaimed women's political and historical subjectivities but also acknowledged their diversity.[12]

The WEC dissolved in 1986 after a series of internal debates over its mission in the current state of Korean society and its historical orientation. In a larger context, the debates were part of the then-ongoing *sahoe kusŏngch'e nonjaeng* (social composition debate), which engaged the interest of many leading activist groups. Provoked by the spreading influence of Marxism and the overall intensification of rapid sociopolitical changes in 1980s South Korea, the participants in the debate were divided over how to assess Korea's place in the capitalist world-system. Depending on their perspectives, some would, for instance, choose to focus on achieving a "proletarian democracy" against state monopoly capitalism, while others wanted to give priority to the cause of "national liberation" from American neoimperialism through the unification of the two Koreas. Although one might blame the ideological rifts for the early demise of the important women's organization, we may also say that the debates were an inevitable part of the competitive process of knowledge production for the cause of women's liberation, as women were no more immune than other groups to the geopolitical-economic conditions of South Korea.[13]

In addition to the WEC experience, another milestone in the women's movement of the 1980s was the appearance of the journal *Yŏsŏng* (Women), which was first published by the influential activist collective Ch'angjak kwa pip 'yŏng (Creation and Criticism) in December 1985. The journal's editorial team consisted of Marxist feminists from different universities, including those who launched women student organizations at Seoul National University in the early 1980s in protest of patriarchal biases among their male comrades.[14] Echoing the hybrid approach of the WEC, the inaugural editorial preface of *Yŏsŏng* declared that the journal would "overcome the separation of women's issues from other issues" and maintain the view that "women's oppression is intimately related to the general structure of social inequality."[15] "General structure" here could be read as referring to the military dictatorship, the capitalist system, or both.[16] Lee Sangkyung, a historian of women's literature and coauthor of its special feature, "The Current State of Korean Literature from Women's Perspectives" (Yŏsŏng ŭi nun ŭro pon Han'guk munhak ŭi hyŏnsil), would later recall that the magazine "was made by women activists who were reconceptualizing the women's movement within the larger social movement, as they were transitioning from student activism to social movements."[17]

Yŏsŏng's second issue, published in 1987, was edited by the Yŏsŏngsa yŏn'guhoe (Society for Women's Historical Studies), which was formally launched in May of that year as an interdisciplinary organization of women scholars across the fields of history, literature, sociology, law, and women's studies. The society purported "to study the particularities of Korean women's problems across disciplines, instead of just relying on

Western feminist theories."[18] The *Yŏsŏng* issue carried articles about the living conditions and the activist initiatives of women factory workers in South Korea as well as theoretical essays and reports about the international women's movement. In lieu of fictional works, the issue contained roundtable debates over feminism, biographies of renowned women figures, and reportage on grassroots women who were absent from the contemporary social movements.[19] The perhaps most notable article, titled "A Critique of the Current Theoretical Development of Korean Women's Liberation" (Han'guk yŏsŏng haebang iron ŭi chŏn'gae e taehan pip'anjŏk kŏmt'o), advanced a cogent analysis of so-called dual systems theory, according to which the origin of women's oppression was patriarchy and that of general social ills was capitalism. In response, the authors of the article suggested, looking back at Friedrich Engels's *The Origins of Family, Private Property, and the State*, that capitalism and patriarchy were inseparable from each other. The article also took critical aim at the "West-centric" women's studies establishment for allegedly lacking a historical consciousness and for thus undermining the alliance between democratization and the women's movement.[20] These arguments, which were directed against the perceived conservative mainstream of the women's movement, had the effect of dividing and polarizing a field of women's organizations that had been quite collaborative up to that point.[21] In a way, the second issue of *Yŏsŏng* marked the maturation of the Marxist influence over the Korean women's movement. The major Marxist feminist voices, who at first remained anonymous for fear of censorship, had a divisive effect but also undoubtedly galvanized Korean debates over feminism and women's liberation.[22]

Class consciousness was thus central and increasingly influential in the 1980s women's movement of South Korea. The emphasis on class was not just a case of the "return of the repressed"—namely, the revival of Marxism that became possible only after its decades-long suppression under Cold War anticommunism. In fact, all women's magazines, including the liberally oriented *Tto hana ŭi munhwa*, strove to draw their contributors, authors, and interviewees from all walks of life. In 1986 the second issue of *Tto hana ŭi munhwa*, titled "Open Society and Autonomous Women," included among its women contributors a journalist, a union leader and factory laborer, and a rural worker. Which class of women was speaking, and which women were being represented? Never before were class boundaries treaded with such ease among women intellectuals. A possible explanation for this is that the emergence of women masses amid social activism—from students, to laborers, to educated housewives—compelled

Fig. 8.2. *Tto hana ŭi munhwa* (Another Culture) 2: "Open Society and Autonomous Women" (1986). Courtesy of *Tto hana ŭi munhwa*.

women intellectuals to extend their attention beyond the conventional middle-class boundaries of liberal feminism. This was so even when these intellectuals were not in full agreement with the minjung democratization movement. Regardless of political orientation, the women's magazines from this period were unparalleled in providing insights into women's lives across social classes.

It is against the background of the rise of this socially heterogeneous alliance of women that women intellectuals could form their own groups and attain social visibility. Most of the contributors to *Yŏsŏng* were elite young women who had received an education at either Ewha Womans University or Seoul National University, whereas the writers of *Tto hana ŭi munhwa* were typically older women academics with graduate degrees from America. Across disciplines, age, and ideology, the women's movement could coalesce because of a shared interest in the formation of a new knowledge and culture for women of all walks of life. Women's studies was one of the academic disciplines that thrived the most after 1987. It emerged as an independent field of study early in the 1980s, and by the end of the decade it had become part of the general core curriculum in at least thirty universities across South Korea.[23]

In spite of these achievements, the women's movement did not have an easy existence in the context of the democratization process in 1980s South Korea. There was at the time an implicit consensus that the interests of the minjung ("the people," and, more specifically, the working class) should be given priority over the gendered interests of women, even though it was women who were suffering the most from discrimination and abuse at home, at work, and at college campuses within South Korea's militarized modernity. Beginning in 1985, college women activists formed their own student associations (Ch'ong yŏhaksaenghoe), often in alliance with but still independent from the general student associations (Ch'ong haksaenghoe), but the mainstream student movement remained for the most part indifferent to their perspectives. The general culture of student activism—its organizational hierarchy and daily operations—continued to force women members to deny their own gender identities and conform to male-oriented norms. Such neglect also prevailed in other fields of social activism, including within the labor movement.

In such an adversarial milieu, the advocacy of the cause of women in and for itself, independently from class or national issues, was apt to be regarded as the liberal voice of "privileged" middle-class women. In response, the link between feminism and the middle class only became stronger, as more and more women recognized the dangers of diluting the feminist cause into that of class or the nation. This had the effect of stirring more debates within the democratization movement, and it was often literature that mediated the renewed attention to middle-class women as the potential subjects of progressive history.

The Woman Question in the Minjung Movement

The 1980s subordinate status of women's literature in relation to the women's movement is best illustrated by *Yŏsŏng undong kwa munhak* (Women's movement and literature), a periodical launched in 1989.[24] This magazine was inaugurated by a group of women writers, yet starting from the title, it gave priority to social activism. The second issue, in January 1990, featured prominently a photo reportage titled "Episodes from the 1989 Women's Movement." It displayed images of women activists across Korea, including the wives of strikers at Hyundai Heavy Industries, women crying at the funeral of a worker who had immolated himself, and women college students demanding the right to participate in the Pyongyang World Festival of Youth and Students. Such representation of the women's movement inevitably gave the impression that women's literature was but a small and integrated part of its broad spectrum.

The editorial preface of the issue, "For Women's Progress alongside National Progress" (Minjoksa ŭi chinbo wa hamkke yŏsŏng ŭi chinbo rŭl), also reflected such a critical perspective. In it, the magazine's editorial board upheld the 1970s women's labor movement as the prime example of "how women should struggle as an oppressed minority in a society with multiple contradictions." Reviewing the accomplishments of women's social and academic activism in the 1980s, the editors announced that the time was ripe for "a cautious call for a new women's literature (*yŏsŏng munhak*)." And they took the opportunity to criticize "the deviant trend of current women's literature," which in their view "has been slow in responding to historical developments and has consequently lost its critical edge and drive through its compliance with the commercial logic of the ruling system."[25] From their perspective, women's literature was only belatedly catching up with the women's movement and was not able to produce a model to emulate due to its co-optation by the capitalist hegemony.

Such diagnosis partly resulted from the self-criticism of women writers, most of whom were of a middle-class origin. This is corroborated by the fact that stories published in the inaugural issue of *Women's Movement and Literature* sought mostly to represent the life experiences of working-class women within the democratization movement. Ch'oe Minhŭi's "Circle" (Tongŭrami) gave a stirring description of a peasant woman who turned into a fighter after her son became a martyr of the labor movement; Kim Taesuk's "An August Diary" (8-wŏl ŭi ilgi) portrayed a laborer's wife joining her husband at a labor strike; Yu Sich'un's "Mrs.Yuli" (Yulidaek) told the story of a poor elderly widow campaigning to have her youngest son released from prison, after having lost two sons under the fake charge of espionage.[26] All of these stories treated women who were either active or potential participants in the democratization movement.

It is important to note that women's organizations were then turning their attention to women laborers precisely because, out in society, women factory workers were being replaced as the main protagonists of the Korean labor union movement by male laborers from heavy industry. According to historian Kang Insun, the launching of the Yŏsŏng nodongja hoeŭi (Women Workers' Congress) after the Great Labor Struggle in the summer of 1987 was partly a response to the sidelining of women in the national labor movement. Ironically, women's marginalization facilitated the long-delayed advancement of their gendered interest within the labor movement.[27]

Within literature, too, male laborers increasingly came to represent the working class as a whole. As Jung-Hwan Cheon has documented, the 1980s was the heyday of labor literature.[28] Workers produced their own writings, organized reading groups, and widely published testimonial writings both in and out of their coterie anthologies. At the origin of this "writing from below" movement were actually women who had been active in the 1970s labor union movement. And yet, as Ruth Barraclough and Namhee Lee have pointed out, leading male critics and guardians of the 1980s labor literature movement would rather lionize the works of male writers, such as Pak Nohae, Chŏng Hwajin, and Pang Hyŏnsŏk, all the while dismissing women's writings merely as a precursor or an immature attempt at "true" labor literature.[29] For this reason, Marxist feminist critics such as Yi Myŏngho, Kim Hŭisuk, and Kim Yangsŏn criticized 1980s labor literature for failing to "relate the question of class liberation to that of women's liberation." They noted, at the same time, "the labor literature from the late 1970s and the early 1980s, mostly produced in the form of memoir and reportage, was written by women workers, but it failed to give fair representation to their struggle partly due to the movement's own limitation and partly due to the shortcomings of literary forms themselves," which relied on the aesthetic of immediacy.[30] Whether critics pursued the ideal of workers' liberation or women's liberation, it seems, the critics found existing literary representations of women laborers unsatisfactory.

In the meantime, the literary trope of the female sex worker emerged as a newly favored subject of minjung national literature as a personification of the social contradictions of South Korea under neocolonial rule.[31] The best-known works in the genre were Yun Chŏngmo's *Your Mother the Korean Whore* (*Emi irŭm ŭn Chosenppi yŏtta*), which treated colonial Korean women's experience of forced prostitution in Japan's military, and, by the same author, *Bridle* (*Koppi*), which instead focused on military prostitution to American soldiers in the period after the Korean War. Both stories gave ample representation to the suffering of Korean women at the hands of foreign military forces.[32] Yun, however, also attracted the criticism of other women intellectuals for endorsing an ultimately masculinist nationalist position in the context of her anti-imperialist novels. She was thereby accused of obscuring the gendered nature of the issue of military prostitution via its dissolution into the larger question of international relations.[33]

Yun's fame and controversy speak volumes about the difficulty of identifying ideal literary works that could advance the cause of the women's movement in the late 1980s. In this period, some women's socially critical novels, in particular Yi Kyŏngja's *Half a Failure* (*Chŏlban ŭi silp'ae*) and Pak Wansŏ's *Are You Still Dreaming?* (*Kŭdae ajikto kkum kkugo innŭnga*), drew much attention from critics and general readers alike and were even adapted into television series. Both stories gave fresh treatment to the emotional agony of broken relationships that led to extramarital affairs and divorce. Advocates of women's liberation literature, however, found these works unsatisfactory in their nearly exclusive focus on gender relations. As Yi Myŏngho wrote, in a pun on *Half a Failure*, "unless [the writers of] women's literature adopt the perspective of working-class women, who are carrying the heaviest burden of gender, class, and national contradictions of our society, they will end up being not a half but a total failure."[34] The ideal model of women's liberation literature, which should pursue the cause of women's liberation as a human rights issue yet without losing a working-class perspective, was still to be found.

Tto Hana ŭi Munhwa and Women's Liberation Literature

The 1980s women's liberation literature movement gained renewed momentum with the appearance of the journal *Tto hana ŭi munhwa* (*Another culture*), which advocated from the start the necessity of developing a different mode of activism from existing social movements. The *mook* (a word combining magazine and book) magazine was launched in December 1984, after an eight-month-long preparation process that involved over a hundred volunteer contributors.[35] This group is often acknowledged only marginally in the history of the women's democratization movement.[36] Yet it played a crucial role in the 1980s women's movement, with its members leading the effort to cultivate a feminist reading culture, publishing relevant titles, and thereby significantly influencing the next generation of feminists who would populate college campuses in the late 1990s. Its founding leader, Cho Haejoang, later recalled: "The group's founding members consisted of women's studies professors, poets and novelists who began to take renewed interest in women's oppression as a particular form of human oppression, as well as graduate students who were dissatisfied with previous student movements. The fundamental purpose of this group was to change patriarchal culture through the promotion of a humane and communitarian cultural discourse."[37] Among the most prominent women writing for *Tto hana ŭi munhwa* were Ko Chŏnghŭi and Pak Wansŏ, who had both also been founding members of the group. These writers had their literary fame already established, but they would reach the peak of their career and productivity through their active participation in this new branch of the women's liberation movement.

Whereas *Yŏsŏng undong* had in some ways emphasized activism over the practice of literature, *Tto hana ŭi munhwa* gave instead much attention to writing by women as an important medium for social change. Cho Haejoang affirmed in the inaugural preface that the magazine had the goal of supporting an inclusive culture of diversity, with an emphasis on gender equality, and that it would reach that goal by "generating new symbols and meanings in our society through the print media."[38] If previous social movements had mainly taken the form of interpersonal collaborations and collective efforts, Cho reflected, *Tto hana ŭi munhwa* differed in its recognition of the need to "cultivate women's self-expression in print or visual media."[39] In a similar vein, magazine editor Chu Ŭn described *Tto hana ŭi munhwa* as a space dedicated to "encounters in print" which, she suggested, would enable creative exchanges that would eventually create "another culture" out of all the individual ideas.[40]

The idea that a woman could contribute to the creation of "another culture" by expressing herself through writing and publishing was radically alternative to the previous practices of social activism. Within the democratization movement, the emphasis had rather been on self-sacrifice for a common cause. Cho's comments, by contrast, drew attention to the effectiveness of self-expression in provoking change and developing an awareness of self and society. In her later, more direct critique of contemporary social movements, Cho Haejoang pointed out how activists had given much focus to critiquing the structural ills of society all the while remaining silent on the necessity of reforming everyday life. The popularity of economic determinism and revolutionary theory among activists, Cho wrote, had led to the rejection of cultural reformism and to the prevalence of a goal-oriented attitude that neglected the necessity of fostering democratic habits in both individual and communal life.[41]

The third issue of *Tto hana ŭi munhwa*, which appeared in April 1987, was titled "Women's Liberation Literature." Its main featured article was the transcript of a roundtable involving the issue's special editors, among whom were well-known women writers such as Kang Sŏk-kyŏng, Pak Wansŏ, and Ko Chŏnghŭi. The discussion gave some emphasis to the idea that "to live is to protest" (sam i kot undong ida), a motto that in some ways was reminiscent of the Western feminist dictum that "the personal is political." Accordingly, the roundtable offered a sharp critique of the absent representation of women's everyday experience in contemporary Korean literature. Panelists drew here a negative comparison to Western cases, the German one in particular, in which the 1960s women's movement had grown organically along with women's literature. And Pak Wansŏ remarked on the exclusion of women's literature from the minjung literary canon, which was symptomatic of the broader exclusion of women from the minjung:

> We can draw an analogy between the oppression of the minjung [by the Korean government] and the oppression of women by the Korean patriarchy. In both cases, an elite group of people is fighting to keep the status quo and to maintain its own privileges. But we often discuss the minjung without mentioning women, and with every passing day, that discussion sounds more hopelessly incomplete.[42]

In addition, Ko Chŏnghŭi emphasized the necessity of maintaining a continuity between activism and everyday life: "We need to keep searching for an alternative way of living, instead of existing as victimized, suicidal women at the side of men who understand women's problems only as an intellectual issue."[43]

Women's liberation literature, as it was theorized at the *Tto hana ŭi munhwa* roundtable, was a broad, inclusive, and ambitious genre. Described as "a literature that demystifies the gendered social structure and

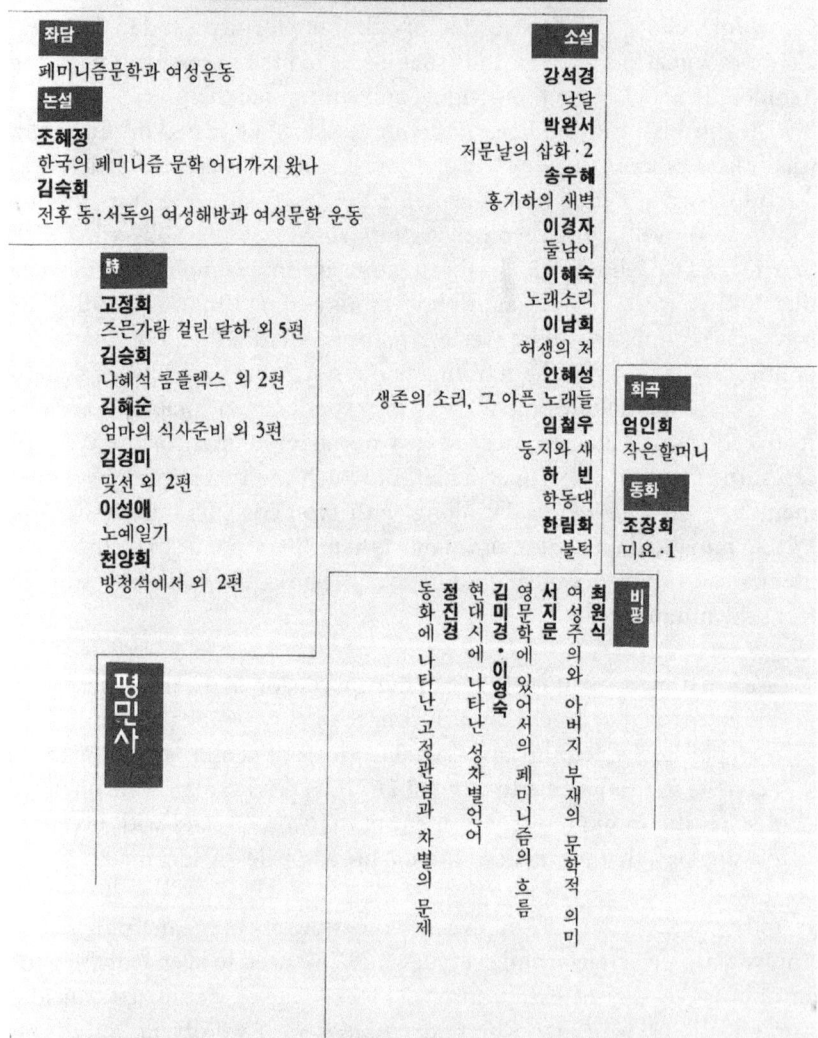

Fig. 8.3. *Tto hana ŭi munhwa* (Another Culture) 3: "Women's Liberation Literature" (1987). Courtesy of *Tto hana ŭi munhwa*.

its oppressive patriarchal ideology," this artistic practice was expected to "critique, for the sake of liberating all humans, the customs and conventions that have justified subordination and alienation."[44] What kind of works, however, were then considered as belonging to women's liberation literature? And how did writers actually translate these lofty theoretical ideals into their creative practice? While the editors of *Tto hana ŭi munhwa* found the short stories included in the issue not fully satisfactory, they also appreciated their representation of women's issues as part of human rights issues, regarding the new approach as a sign of the advancement of Korean literature and society.[45] In the next section, we will take a closer look at one of these stories, namely, Pak Wansŏ's "An Episode from Bygone Days" (Chŏmun nal ŭi saphwa), as one of the most successful examples of the new women's literature.

Against State and Domestic Violence: Pak Wansŏ's "An Episode from Bygone Days"

The theme of domestic violence was a frequent feature in the fiction by women writers in 1980s Korea. Among the poems published in *Tto hana ŭi munhwa*, for instance, one renders the anguish of a woman who prepares dinner by "pounding" and "frying" after having been heavily beaten by her husband, while another is written in the enraged voice of a woman who, having left her husband, has finally escaped from a daily cycle of abuse.[46] Ko Chŏnghŭi's "God Being Beaten" (Mae mannŭn hananim) began with the line "[a] wasted woman under the eaves, being beaten by a drunkard." Battered housewives and other women trapped in everyday violence were also frequently featured in prose fiction. Kang Sŏk-kyŏng's "Daytime Moon" (Nattal), for instance, told the story of a divorcee woman who plans to move to another apartment because of the terrifying nightly sounds of her neighbor beating his wife.[47] Yi Kyŏngja's "Tullami" (Tullami) had at its center the death of a working class woman in a fishing village at the hands of her abusive husband, a husband who is nevertheless released by the village after a mere two months' detention.[48] And Yi Hyesuk's "The Sound of a Song" (Norae sori) featured a factory manager's wife, Yŏnhŭi, who is beaten by her husband after standing up to him for his mistreatment of women workers at the factory.[49]

In "An Episode from Bygone Days" (hereafter, "Episode"), Pak offers a subtle and layered treatment of the theme of a battered housewife by interrelating the issue of domestic violence with that of state violence. "Escape" tells the story of Kayŏn, a college-educated housewife whose life is recounted by her neighbor and former middle school teacher in a first-person narrating voice. In the prologue, the reader learns that the narrator has a son who was tortured and traumatized by the police for his involvement in student activism. Although the son looks normal, he has developed paranoias and has been forced to live in an asylum for the last few years. As the reader soon discovers, this theme of violence and trauma resonates with the story of Kayŏn's abusive marriage.

After the acquaintance of their school days, Kayŏn and the narrator meet again when the young woman moves into the apartment just above her former teacher. One day, having found some objects that fell on her balcony, the teacher pays a visit to Kayŏn with the intention of returning them. She learns that Kayŏn's husband is a social activist, which immediately puts her in a sympathetic mood. Kayŏn explains that, due to her husband's economic difficulties, the couple is currently dependent on her own family for their living expenses. This does not prevent the narrator from advocating for the husband, encouraging Kayŏn to herself find a job as a teacher. In so doing, the narrator conveys her deep sense of respect for activists who, like her son, have sacrificed their personal well-being to fight against a dictatorial state.

The teacher's attitude toward the couple changes, however, when she learns that Kayŏn has been regularly beaten by her husband (the objects on the balcony had been thrown by the husband in his violent fits). The couple has been fighting because he wants Kayŏn to stay home and not get a job, even when they are faced with eviction due to the declining fortune of Kayŏn's father. The husband, the teacher discovers, has even burnt Kayŏn's thigh with a cigarette. Upon learning this, the narrator starts putting Kayŏn on a par with her son as a victim of violence. In this way, the story draws a rare analogy between the hushed topic of wife battering and the state violence that had been openly criticized by the democratization movement: "How can you trust a man who cares for the minjung, yet he cannot recognize women as belonging to it? Women, who have been oppressed and deprived for so long?"[50] The narrator then encourages Kayŏn to become independent not for his but for her own sake, in order to stand up to him as an equal: "'You will have time later on to determine whether he is [a] real [activist] or not. But you should no longer postpone your independence,' I pleaded with Kayŏn, hoping to convey my camaraderie to her."[51] The narrative thus draws a direct link between state violence and domestic violence, suggesting that however noble a man's cause may be, an activist is not immune from ethical responsibility for his own violent actions.

Pak's story ends with the narrator urging Kayŏn to gain economic independence from her husband as a way of breaking out of the cycle of violence and also to exercise her own judgment and autonomy. This rather straightforward feminist ending, however, has an extra, critical twist in the periodical milieu, because the husband is a social activist and a supposed hero in the struggle for the Korean people's emancipation from dictatorship. The twist allows Pak to foreground an issue that had been tentatively raised by minjung activists but remained to be fully addressed. Without a concurrent reflection on women and their role in the family, Pak is telling us, no democratic movement can hope to fully realize its goal of social change.

An exemplary work of 1980s women's liberation literature, "Episode" is a layered text that projects the multiple, intersecting subjectivities of a socially conscious middle-class woman. Kayŏn's ex-teacher is sympathetic to the cause of democratization, but she is also critical of the capitalist system of private property: she does not think ill of Kayŏn's husband living on her father's money, and she also at one point regrets her own past lack of generosity toward her adopted son. Her endorsement of a more egalitarian society indeed suggests great potential in the political subjectivity of a middle-class housewife such as the narrator. At the same time, however, this character also understands that a male-centered and class-based movement such as the minjung will not by itself guarantee women's liberation, which can be attained only by pursuing both greater gender equality and social reforms within the framework of a more egalitarian political and economic system.

The fight against domestic violence had famously been one of the rallying points in the second-wave feminist movements of the 1970s in the West. At stake was the idea of politicizing what had been previously regarded only as personal matters. In 1980s South Korea, too, the issue of domestic violence came to prominence in conjunction with other forms of gendered violence such as the sexual abuse of women laborers by factory managers, the harassment of college women students by the police, the sexual torture committed in the name of the state, and, more generally, the issue of "violence against women" as the sum total of the bodily subjugations of women.[52] In spite of this topical focus, however, the intersectional character of 1980s feminist discourse in Korea often also ran the risk of diluting the women's question in some supposedly "bigger" issues. Illustrative of this was the activists' rendering of the sexual torture of Kwŏn Insuk by the police as a generic case of "police brutality," albeit of the most egregious kind. Once a woman was turned into just "a victim of violence," one could easily ascribe the blame for it to the military dictatorship or other ruling authorities, thereby neglecting the gendered form of violence and letting its patriarchal agents elude their responsibilities.[53]

Read against this background, a tale of domestic violence such as "Episode" had the feminist critical significance of making visible the elusive agents of patriarchal violence, along with the power relations out of which such violence is constructed. The image of a wounded, traumatized, and frightened woman epitomized a subversive political imagination that aimed to reconstitute the collective subjectivity of the minjung into the individual subjectivity of citizen activists, including feminists, without forgoing their political vigor.

Conclusion

In the 1980s, women writers, intellectuals, and workers in Korea reshaped the traditional field of women's literature by reappropriating it into a communal space and a public forum, a forum in which they advanced a new historical and political consciousness by mobilizing their gender identities along with their class subjectivities. The resulting composite, intersectional feminist subjectivities found expression first and foremost in the quest for *yŏsŏng munhak* (women's literature), a period-specific term that connoted the radicalization of the women's movement in resonance with the decade's unprecedented political urgency. As we saw in the last section, most representative of women's liberation literature were the stories of battered housewives that denounced the plague of domestic violence by recasting the phenomenon from a private matter into a full-fledged human rights abuse on par with state violence against civilian protestors. The women's movement had as its outlets mook magazines such as *Yŏsŏng undong kwa munhak* and *Tto hana ŭi munhwa*, which served as the forums for leftist and liberal feminist agendas while providing support and a community to the budding field of women's literature and giving representation to diverse social minorities. Literature written by women was in this way reborn in an expressly political key amid the struggles and social upheavals of the minjung movement for democratization in South Korea.

For this rebirth of women's literature and the constellational formation of women's social groups and cultural communities that enabled it, the 1980s was a unique and singularly important decade in Korean cultural history. Crucially, the advancement of women's issues in the period went far beyond women serving as traditional symbols of the nation or even the doubly burdened—politically and sexually—minjung of the minjung, as it compelled the public to contest the ontological realities of "universal" subjects, such as citizens and individuals, in the rapidly democratizing society.

Now, three decades later, Korean women's literature as a feminist practice is having a crisis. While writing this essay, I had the opportunity of asking Sim Ching'yŏng, a leading feminist critic, whether there still existed women's literature as a feminist practice. In giving a negative response, Sim pointed to the problematic influence of the ways in which women's literature came to be conceptualized in the 1990s.[54] Often referred to as the "golden age" of women's literature (*yŏsŏng munhak*), the decade of the 1990s saw a transition of literary discourse from history to everyday life, as it were. In the work of new writers such as Shin Kyungsook, the treatment of women's problems through a sociopolitical lens gave way to a more intimate and personal reflection on the experiential aspects of women's life.[55] The shift brought new life and readership to the field, but it also came very close to confining women's literature to a set of gendered paradigms such as everyday life, interiority, sensibility, and the personal—all of which had been traditionally regarded as "feminine" concerns. In addition, as women writers enjoyed increasing popularity, women's literature came to be widely regarded as yet another commercialized literary genre. In this atmosphere, it did not take long for women writers to publicly disavow their affiliation with the women's literature of the previous decade (*yŏsŏng munhak*)."[56] As critic Kim Yŏngok has observed, the emphasis on the everyday and the feminine in the end exposed women's literature to the mortal risk of disregarding the political substance and the historicity of women's life experiences.[57]

I agree with these analyses and have sought in this chapter to further the critical reflection on today's crisis of women's literature in Korea by turning our attention to the 1980s. As the chapter has shown, 1980s women's literature was often torn between national, class, and gender interests. In retrospect, the tension, whether it was real or perceived, in many ways hindered the advancement of the cause of feminism within the democratization movement.[58] At the same time, it was precisely out of the fraught sociopolitical circumstances of the 1980s that an unprecedented constellation of women intellectuals emerged to form the dynamic field of women's literature, in which diverse women's voices were actively sought out in the effort to cultivate a critical consciousness and a movement for a better society.

The flourishing of women's literature in the 1990s has been in many ways made possible by the complex and conflictual subjectivities of women represented in the 1980s women's literature and movement. A frequent plot within 1990s women's literature has been that of a female protagonist who, having spent her youth on social activism, decides to keep fighting and takes leave of her husband's home. In hindsight, this common narrative of the 1990s is not so much an antithesis as a variation and successor of 1980s women's liberation literature.

NOTES

This essay is a revised version of "Pinnanŭn sŏngjwadŭl: 1980-yŏndae, yŏsŏng haebang munhak ŭi t'ansaeng." The research on this essay has been supported by the generous grant of the National Research Foundation of Korea. I would also like to thank Sunyoung Park for translation and Ruth Barraclough, Son Yugyŏng, and three anonymous reviewers of the original manuscript for their feedback on earlier drafts.

1. Felski, *The Gender of Modernity*. I have referenced its Korean translation, *Kŭndaesŏng kwa chendŏ*.
2. For this insight, I am indebted to O Chaŭn, "Chungsanch'ŭng ŭi temo hanŭn ttaltŭl."
3. Kim Won, *87-yŏn 6-wŏl hangjaeng*, 46–61.
4. Kang Sŏk-kyŏng, *Sup sok ŭi pang* (1985), and Gong Ji-young, *Tŏ isang arŭmdaun panghwang ŭn ŏpta* (1989). Kang's novel was later adapted to the screen in 1992 under the same title. The protagonist Soyang is a student activist torn between her middle-class family background and her social conscience who eventually commits suicide. In this novel, too, Soyang is contrasted with her pianist sister whose youthful musical aspiration gives way to a regular office job at a bank after her graduation and soon to housewifery. Kong, a younger writer of the 386 generation, leaves her novel on a more optimistic tone, as Minsu, a woman college student, overcomes her psychological conflict and leaves her family to commit herself to the labor movement. See Kang Sŏk-kyŏng's novel in English translation, "Room in the Woods."
5. Kimberlé Crenshaw coined "intersectional feminism" in reference to black feminist theories that took into consideration both race and gender. See Crenshaw, "Demarginalizing the Intersection of Race and Sex." I am reappropriating Crenshaw's term here to refer to the layered perspectives of the 1980s women's movement, which attended, to varying degrees, to race, class, and gender issues, although this complexity was admittedly often lost in practice, with its internal tensions repressed and subsumed under the paradigm of the minjung.
6. Louie, "Minjung Feminism."
7. Kwon Insuk, *Hana ŭi pyŏk ŭl nŏmŏsŏ*, 231 and 271–73. The original speech was given in 1987 at the ceremony of the Today's Woman Award hosted by the Association of Korean Women's Organizations (Han'guk yŏsŏng tanch'e yŏnhap).
8. See Cho Chuhyŏn, "Yŏsŏng chŏngch'ehak," 11.
9. Regarding critical alternatives to *yŏryu munhak*, Im Sundŭk, a leftist woman writer and critic, also proposed in the late 1930s to use *puin munhak* instead of the "bourgeois" term. See Lee Sangkyung, *Han'guk kŭndae yŏsŏng munhaksaron*, 237. *Yŏsŏng munhak* dates back at least to the late 1940s, but the term received renewed attention in the 1980s with the publication of women's literary magazines such as *Yŏsŏng*

munhak (1984) and *Tto hana ŭi munhwa*, which I discuss in detail in this essay. The latter published, among others, Ko Chŏnghŭi's essay that aimed to reconstruct the women's literary canon according to the new paradigm, emphasizing the historicity of womanhood, which had often been neglected in male-oriented critical discourse. See Ko Chŏnghŭi, "Han'guk yŏsŏng munhak ŭi hŭrŭm."

10. For Minister Kang Wŏnyŏng's contributions to the Christian Academy and the ideological influence of the Academy's humanist critique of modernity on feminists, see Pak Inhye, "Yŏsŏng in'gwŏn undong."

11. No Hyegyŏng, "Tu kyŏp ŭi sŭch'im."

12. Yŏsŏng p'yŏnguhoe, "Palgi ch'wijimun" [Inaugural statement], in *Yŏsŏng p'yŏnguhoe palchach'wi*, 3.

13. See Kang Namsik, "Yŏsŏng p'yŏnguhoe," 53–58, and Minjok minju undong yŏsŏng pun'gwa, "80-yŏndae yŏsŏng undong kwa 90-yŏndae yŏsŏng undong."

14. I thank the two former editors of *Yŏsŏng*, Kim Yŏng, professor of sociology at Pusan National University, and Nam Hee Lee, policy advisor at the South Korean Ministry of Gender Equality and Family, for their phone interviews regarding the history of the journal.

15. Yŏsŏng p'yŏnjip wiwŏnhoe, "Yŏsŏng 1-chip ŭl naemyŏnsŏ" [Inaugural preface], *Yŏsŏng* 1 (1985): 5.

16. See Sim Chŏngin's support of Engels's theorization of private property as the cause of gender inequality and women's oppression in her essay, "Yŏsŏng undong ŭi panghyang," 201–2. For the Korean translation of Marxist feminist theories, see Hŏ Yun, "1980-yŏndae yŏsŏng haebang undong."

17. Lee Sangkyung, "Han'guk yŏsŏng munhangnon ŭi yŏksa wa iron" [The history and theory of Korean women's literature] in Lee's *Han'guk yŏsŏng munhaksaron*, 9–34, esp. 21.

18. "Yŏsŏng yŏn'guhoe ch'angnip."

19. After the publication of its third issue, *Yŏsŏng* was reborn, in post-1989 democracy, into the annual journal *Yŏsŏng kwa sahoe* (Women and society), which was published by the Han'guk yŏsŏng yŏn'guso (Korean Women's Research Center), a successor of Yŏsŏngsa yŏn'guhoe.

20. Yŏsŏngsa yŏn'guhoe p'yŏnjippu, "Han'guk yŏsŏng haebang iron," 174–200, esp. 182.

21. For the consequent divide between liberal and leftist feminists, see the following accounts of respective positions: Chi Ŭnhŭi and Kang Isu, "Han'guk yŏsŏng yŏn'gu ŭi chasŏng," and Cho Haejoang, "The 'Woman Question.'"

22. When the government relented its censorship policy and allowed the circulation of 431 of 650 banned titles on October 19, 1987, they included such books as *Yŏsŏng*, *Chungguk yŏsŏng haebang undong* (Chinese women's liberation movement), *Yŏsŏng haebang ŭi nolli* (The rationale for women's liberation), *Yŏsŏng haebang ŭi sŏn'gujadŭl* (Pioneers of women's liberation), *Ŏmŏnidŭl* (Mothers). Under review were also *K'ŭllara Jet'ŭk'in sŏnjip* (Selected writings of Clara Zetkin), *Yŏsŏng kwa hyŏngmyŏng undong* (Women and the revolution), and *Roja Ruksemburŭk'ŭ* (Rosa Luxemburg). See "Kŭmsŏ 431-chong haeje" and "Haegŭm ch'aek."

23. The first women's studies class was offered in 1977 at Ewha Womans University, which also began to admit graduate students in 1982. By June 1988, over thirty universities were offering women's studies classes, and in early 1999, the number increased to sixty-one schools. See Cho, "The 'Woman's Question,'" 332.

24. The publication soon became one of the most successful examples of a *mook* magazine, where the term "mook" is a neologism in English that combines the word *magazine* with *book*. Mooks became popular in late-1980s Korea because their irregularity allowed publishers to circumvent the strict policies for the publication of periodicals. The Creation and Criticism collective, whose homonymous flagship journal had been banned from publication, introduced the first mook in 1985 under the title *Hamsŏng* (Outcry). See "Ch'angbisa tŭngnok ch'wiso."

25. Minjok munhak chakka hoeŭi yŏsŏng munhagin wiwŏnhoe (Women Writers' Committee of the National Literature Writers' Congress), "Minjoksa ŭi chinbo wa hamkke yŏsŏng ŭi chinbo rŭl."

26. See Ch'oe Minhŭi, "Tongŭrami"; Kim Taesuk, "8-wŏl ŭi ilgi"; and Yu Sich'un, "Mrs.Yuli."

27. Kang Insun and Yi Okchi, *Han'guk yŏsŏng nodongja undongsa*, 322.

28. See Jung-Hwan Cheon's essay included in the present volume.

29. Ruth Barraclough, quoted in Namhee Lee, *The Making of Minjung*, 272.

30. Yi Myŏngho et al., "Yŏsŏng haebang munhangnon esŏ pon 80-yŏndae munhak," 55–56.

31. See Jin-kyung Lee's extended discussion of the body of camptown literature in *Service Economies*. This title has been translated into Korean as *Sŏbisŭ ik'onomi*.

32. Yun Chŏngmo, *Emi irŭm ŭn Chosenppi yŏtta* and *Koppi*.

33. See Kim Yŏnghae, "Yŏsŏng munje ŭi sosŏlchŏk hyŏngsanghwa," 67.

34. Yi Myŏngho et al., "Yŏsŏng haebang munhangnon," 67.

35. "Tto hana ŭi munhwa t'ansaeng."

36. See, for instance, Kim Yŏnghŭi, "Chinbojŏk yŏsŏng undong ŭi chaegŏmt'o."

37. Cho Haejong, "The 'Woman Question,'" 333.

38. Reflective of the organization's communal spirit, the magazine's inaugural preface was replaced by a roundtable report, "Chwadam: 'Tto hana ŭi munhwa' rŭl p'yŏnaemyŏ," 17.

39. The editorial board of *Tto hana ŭi munhwa* spent its first two meetings on the special lectures on composition. Ibid., 27.

40. Ibid., 28.

41. Cho Haejoang, "Munhwa wa sahoe undong ŭi yangsik."

42. Pak Wansŏ et al., "Chwadam: P'eminijŭm munhak kwa yŏsŏng undong," 26. In agreement with Pak, critic Chŏng Chin'gyŏng cited Pak Nohae's "Sawing the Blanket" (Ibul ŭl kkoemaemyŏnsŏ), a poem about a male laborer's realization that his employer's tyranny towards him closely resembles his own patriarchal behavior toward his wife.

43. Pak Wansŏ et al., "Chwadam," 26.

44. Ibid.

45. See "P'yŏnjip ŭi mal," 13.

46. See, respectively, Kim Hyesoon, "Ŏmma ŭi siksa chunbi"; Chŏn Yanghŭi, "T'alch'ulgi"; and Ko Chŏnghŭi, "Mae mannŭn hannanim."

47. Kang Sŏk-kyŏng, "Nattal."

48. Yi Kyŏngja, "Tullami."

49. Yi Hyesuk, "Norae sori."

50. Pak Wansŏ, "Chŏmŭn nal ŭi saphwa 2," 127.

51. Ibid.

52. Sin Sangsuk, "Chendŏ, seksyuŏlit'i, p'ongnyŏk," 11.

53. Ibid., 14-16, 19.
54. See also Sim Chin'gyŏng, *Yŏsŏng kwa munhak ŭi t'ansaeng*, 221-25.
55. For the discussion on the transitional orientation of women's literature and Shin Kyung-sook's place in it, see Hwang Chongyŏn et al., *90-yŏndae munhak ŭl ŏttŏk'e pol kŏsin'ga*.
56. For instance, see Ŭn Hŭigyŏng, "Yŏksŏl ŭi yŏsŏngsŏng" [Ironic femininity], in Kim Kit'aek et al., *21-segi munhak iran muŏsin'ga* [What is twenty-first-century literature?] (Minŭmsa, 1999), 350. Quoted in Sim Chin'gyŏng, *Yŏsŏng kwa munhak ŭi t'ansaeng*, 222.
57. Kim Yŏngok, "90-yŏndae Han'guk munhak tamnon," 97.
58. For the post-1990s development of the Korean women's movement and the 1980s legacy in it, see Nicola Anne Jones, *Gender and the Political Opportunities of Democratization in South Korea*.

REFERENCES

"Ch'angbisa tŭngnok ch'iwso ŭi ŭimi" [The meaning of Ch'angbi's revoked license]. *Dong-a Ilbo*, December 10, 1985.
Chi Ŭnhŭi and Kang Isu. "Han'guk yŏsŏng yŏn'gu ŭi chasŏngjŏk p'yŏnga" [A self-reflective evaluation of Korean women's studies]. In *80-yŏndae Han'guk inmun sahoe kwahwak ŭi hyŏndan'gye wa chŏnmang* [The status quo and prospect of Korean humanities and social sciences in the 1980s], edited by Haksul tanch'e yŏnhap simp'ojium chunbi wiwŏnhoe, 136-64. Yŏksa pip'yŏngsa, 1988.
Cho Chuhyŏn. "Yŏsŏng chŏngch'ehak ŭi chŏngch'ihak: 80-90-yŏndae Han'guk ŭi yŏsŏng undong ŭl chungsim ŭro" [Women's identity politics in the 1980s and 1990s women's movements]. *Chinbo p'yŏngnon* 7 (2000): 126-48.
Ch'oe Minhŭi. "Tongŭrami" [Circle]. *Yŏsŏng undong kwa munhak* 1 (1989):148-68.
Cho Haejoang. "Munhwa wa sahoe undong ŭi yangsik" [Culture and the mode of social movement]. In "Yŏllin sahoe chayulchŏk yŏsŏng," 91-95.
Cho Haejoang. "The 'Woman Question' in the Minjok-Minju Movement: A Discourse Analysis of a New Women's Movement in 1980s Korea." In *Gender Division of Labor in Korea*, edited by Cho Hyoung and Chang Pil-wha, 324-58. Ewha Womans University Press, 1994.
Chŏn Yanghŭi. "T'alch'ulgi" [A record of escape]. In "Yŏsŏng haebang ŭi munhak," 89.
"Chwadam: 'Tto hana ŭi munhwa' rŭl p'yŏnaemyŏ" [Roundtable, launching *Another Culture*]. In "P'yŏngdŭnghan pumo chayuroun ai," 13-28.
Crenshaw, Kimberlé. "Demarginalizing the Intersection of Race and Sex: A Black Feminist Critique of Antidiscrimination Doctrine, Feminist Theory, and Antiracist Politics." *University of Chicago Legal Forum* (1989): 139-67.
Felski, Rita. *The Gender of Modernity*. Cambridge: Harvard University Press, 1995.
Felski, Rita. *Kŭndaesŏng kwa chendŏ*. Translated by Sim Chin'gyŏng and Kim Yŏngch'an. Chaŭm kwa moŭm, 2012.
Gong Ji-young, *Tŏ isang arŭmdaun panghwang ŭn ŏpta* [A most beautiful wandering]. P'ulbit, 1989.
"Haegŭm ch'aek" [List of unbanned books]. *Dong-a Ilbo*, October 19, 1987.
Hŏ Yun. "1980-yŏndae yŏsŏng haebang undong kwa pŏnyŏk ŭi yŏksŏl" [The 1980s

women's liberation movement and the irony of translation]. In *Chendŏ wa pŏnyŏk* [Gender and translation], edited by Pak Chiyŏng et al., 377–84. Somyŏng ch'ulp'an, 2013.

Hwang Chongyŏn et al. *90-yŏndae munhak ŭl ŏttŏk'e pol kŏssin'ga* [How to assess 1990s literature]. Minŭmsa, 1999.

Jones, Nicola Anne. *Gender and the Political Opportunities of Democratization in South Korea*. New York: Palgrave Macmillan, 2006.

Kang Insun and Yi Okchi, *Han'guk yŏsŏng nodongja undongsa* [A history of the Korean women's labor movement]. Hanul ak'ademi, 2001.

Kang Namsik. "Yŏsŏng p'yŏnguhoe ŭi hwaldong kwa yŏsŏng undongsajŏk ŭiŭi" [The activities of the Women's Equality Council and its historical significance]. In *Yŏsŏng p'yŏnguhoe palchach'wi*, edited by Yŏsŏng p'yŏnguhoe ch'angnip 20-chunyŏn kinyŏm haengsa chunbi wiwŏnhoe, 53–58.

Kang, Sŏk-kyŏng. "Nattal" [Daytime Moon]. In "Yŏsŏng haebang ŭi munhak," 90–109.

Kang, Sŏk-kyŏng. "Room in the Woods." In *Words of Farewell and Other Stories*, translated by Bruce and Ju-Chan Fulton, 28–147. Berkeley, CA: Seal Press, 1993.

Kang, Sŏk-kyŏng. *Sup sok ŭi pang* [Room in the woods]. Minŭmsa, 1985.

Kim Hyesoon. "Ŏmma ŭi siksa chunbi" [Mother's cooking]. In "Yŏsŏng haebang ŭi munhak," 74.

Kim Taesuk. "8-wŏl ŭi ilgi" [An August diary]. *Yŏsŏng undong kwa munhak* 1 (1989): 169–87.

Kim Won. *87-yŏn 6-wŏl hangjaeng* [The June 1987 uprising]. Ch'aeksesang, 2009.

Kim Yŏnghae. "Yŏsŏng munje ŭi sosŏlchŏk hyŏngsanghwa" [Novelistic representations of the women's question]. *Ch'angjak kwa pip'yŏng* 64 (1989): 55–74.

Kim Yŏnghŭi. "Chinbojŏk yŏsŏng undong ŭi chaegŏmt'o" [Review of the progressive women's movement]. *P'eminijŭm yŏn'gu* 2 (2002): 11–42.

Kim Yŏngok. "90-yŏndae Han'guk munhak tamnon e taehan pip'anjŏk koch'al" [A critical reflection on 1990s Korean literary discourse]. *Sanghŏ hakpo* 9 (2002): 93–130.

Ko Chŏnghŭi. "Han'guk yŏsŏng munhak ŭi hŭrŭm—si wa sosŏl ŭl chungsim ŭro" [A historical outline of Korean women's literature with a focus on poetry and prose fiction]. In "Yŏllin sahoe chayulchŏk yŏsŏng," 96–125.

Ko Chŏnghŭi. "Mae mannŭn hananim" [God being beaten]. In "Yŏsŏng haebang ŭi munhak," 61–62.

"Kŭmsŏ 431-chong haeje" [Publication ban lifted for 431 titles]. *Dong-a Ilbo*, October 19, 1987.

Kwon Insuk. *Hana ŭi pyŏk ŭl nŏmŏsŏ—Puch'ŏnsŏ sŏng komun sagŏn chuingong ŭi chap'il sugi* [Beyond a wall: My memoir of the Puchŏn sexual abuse controversy]. Kŏrŭm, 1989.

Lee Hye-Ryoung. "Pinnanŭn sŏngjwadŭl: 1980-yŏndae, yŏsŏng haebang munhak ŭi t'ansaeng" [Bright constellation: The birth of women's liberation literature in the 1980s]. *Sanghŏ hakpo* 47 (2016): 411–57.

Lee, Jin-kyung. *Service Economies: Militarism, Sex Work, and Migrant Labor in South Korea*. Minneapolis: University of Minnesota Press, 2010.

Lee, Jin-kyung. *Sŏbisŭ ik'onomi*. Translated by Na Pyŏngch'ŏl. Somyŏng ch'ulp'an, 2010.

Lee, Namhee. *The Making of Minjung: Democracy and the Politics of Representation in South Korea*. Ithaca: Cornell University Press, 2009.

Lee Sangkyung. *Han'guk kŭndae yŏsŏng munhaksaron* [A study of the history of modern Korean women's literature]. Somyŏng ch'ulp'an, 2002.

Louie, Miriam Ching Yoon. "Minjung Feminism: Korean Women's Movement for Gender and Class Liberation." *Women's Studies International Forum* 18, no. 4 (1995): 417–30.

Minjok munhak chakka hoeŭi yŏsŏng munhagin wiwŏnhoe. "Minjoksa ŭi chinbo wa hamkke yŏsŏng ŭi chinbo rŭl" [For women's progress alongside national progress]. *Yŏsŏng undong kwa munhak* 2 (1990): 2.

Minjok minju undong yŏsŏng pun'gwa. "80-yŏndae yŏsŏng undong kwa 90-yŏndae yŏsŏng undong ŭi chŏnmang 2" [The 1980s women's movement and the prospect of the 1990s women's movement 2]. *Chŏngse yŏn'gu* 10 (1990): 53–54.

No Hyegŏng. "Tu kyŏp ŭi sŭch'im, Yŏsŏng p'yŏnguhoe wa Pusan" [Double Encounter: The Women's Equality Council and Pusan]. In *Yŏsŏng p'yŏnguhoe palchach'wi*, edited by Yŏsŏng p'yŏnguhoe ch'angnip 20-chunyŏn kinyŏm haengsa chunbi wiwŏnhoe, 138–41.

O Chaŭn. "Chungsanch'ŭng ŭi temo hanŭn ttaltŭl—1980-yŏndae Kim Hyangsuk sosŏl e nat'anan monyŏ kwan'gye rŭl chungsim ŭro" [Rebellious daughters of the middle class: Mother-daughter relations in Kim Hyangsuk's novels]. *Han'guk hyŏndae munhak yŏn'gu* 45 (2015): 413–49.

Pak Inhye. "Yŏsŏng in'gwŏn undong ŭi p'ŭreim kwa chuch'e pyŏnhwa e taehan yŏn'gu" [Study of the theoretical framework of the women's human rights movement and the transformation of its subjectivities]. PhD diss., Sungkonghoe University, 2011.

Pak Wansŏ. "Chŏmŭn nal ŭi saphwa 2" [An episode from bygone days 2]. In "Yŏsŏng haebang ŭi munhak," 110–27.

Pak Wansŏ et al. "Chwadam: P'eminijŭm munhak kwa yŏsŏng undong" [Roundtable: feminist literature and the women's movement]. In "Yŏsŏng haebang ŭi munhak," 14–29.

"P'yŏngdŭnghan pumo chayuroun ai" [Equal parents, free children]. Special issue, *Tto hana ŭi munwha 1*. P'yŏngminsa, 1985.

"P'yŏnjip ŭi mal" [Editorial comments]. In "Yŏsŏng haebang ŭi munhak" [Women's liberation literature]. Special issue, *Tto hana ŭi munhwa* (1988): 13.

Sim Chin'gyŏng. *Yŏsŏng kwa munhak ŭi t'ansaeng* [Women and the birth of literature], 219–48. Chaŭm kwa moŭm, 2015.

Sim Chŏngin. "Yŏsŏng undong ŭi panghyang chŏngnip ŭl wihan koch'al" [A reflection on the reorientation of the women's movement]. *Yŏsŏng* 1 (1985): 200–55.

Sin Sangsuk. "Chendŏ, seksyuŏlit'i, p'ongnyŏk—sŏng p'ongnyŏk kaenyŏmsa rŭl t'onghae pon yŏsŏng in'gwŏn ŭi sŏng chŏngch'ihak" [Gender, sexuality, and violence: Gender politics of women's human rights through the conceptual history of sexual violence]. *P'eminijŭm yŏn'gu* 10 (2008): 1–45.

"Tto hana ŭi munhwa t'ansaeng" [The birth of *Another Culture*]. *Dong-a Ilbo*, December 11, 1984.

Yi Hyesuk. "Norae sori" [The sound of a song]. In "Yŏsŏng haebang ŭi munhak," 172–89.

Yi Kyŏngja. "Tullami" [Tullami]. In "Yŏsŏng haebang ŭi munhak," 150–71.

Yi Myŏngho, Kim Hŭisuk, and Kim Yangsŏng. "Yŏsŏng haebang munhangnon esŏ pon 80-yŏndae munhak" [1980s literature from the perspective of women's liberation literature]. *Ch'angjak kwa pip'yŏng* 67 (1990): 48–74.

"Yŏllin sahoe chayulchŏk yŏsŏng" [Open society, autonomous women]. Special issue, *Tto hana ŭi munwha* 2. P'yŏngminsa, 1986.

"Yŏsŏng haebang ŭi munhak" [Women's liberation literature]. Special issue, *Tto hana ŭi munwha* 3. P'yŏngminsa, 1988.

Yŏsŏng p'yŏnguhoe ch'angnip 20-chunyŏn kinyŏm haengsa chunbi wiwŏnhoe, ed. *Yŏsŏng p'yŏnguhoe palchach'wi* [The trajectory of the Women's Equality Council]. Yŏsŏng p'yŏnguhoe, 2003.

Yŏsŏng p'yŏnjip wiwŏnhoe. *Yŏsŏng*. Vol. 1. Ch'angjak kwa pip'yŏngsa, 1985.

Yŏsŏng p'yŏnjip wiwŏnhoe. "Yŏsŏng 1 chip ŭl naemyŏnsŏ" [Inaugural preface]. *Yŏsŏng* 1 (1985): 2–4.

"Yŏsŏng yŏn'guhoe ch'angnip" [The founding of Women's Studies Society]. *Dong-a Ilbo*, May 19, 1987.

Yŏsŏngsa yŏn'guhoe p'yŏnjippu. "Han'guk yŏsŏng haebang iron ŭi chŏn'gae e taehan pip'anjŏk kŏmt'o" [A critique of the current theoretical development of Korean women's liberation]. *Yŏsŏng* 2 (1988): 174–200.

Yŏsŏngsa yŏn'guhoe p'yŏnjippu. *Yŏsŏng*. Vols. 2 and 3. Ch'angjak kwa pip'yŏngsa, 1988–89.

Yun Chŏngmo. *Emi irŭm ŭn Chosenppi yŏtta* [Your mother the Korean whore]. Inmundang, 1982.

Yun Chŏngmo. *Koppi* [Bridle]. P'ulbit, 1988.

Yu Sich'un. "Yulidaek" [Mrs.Yuli]. *Yŏsŏng undong kwa munhak* 1 (1989): 72–92.

9

Queering the Dreams of a Third-World Brotherhood

Black Women in Early 1980s South Korean Literature and Film

Kyunghee Eo

In 1947, Pae Inchŏl published an impassioned ode to Joe Louis, the American heavyweight boxing champion who had inspired the young and feisty poet to take up boxing lessons himself: "Be strong, your body / Is not just yours / Fighting with you / For a new world / Are not only Black America / But all the smaller and weaker nations around the world."[1] Pae had shown a strong interest in African American literature and history since his years as an English literature student in Tokyo, and is known to have befriended many black soldiers on the U.S. military bases at Inchŏn harbor after his return to postwar Korea. Through these direct and indirect encounters Pae developed a kind of proto-Third World consciousness, an imagined Afro-Korean brotherhood that stood against all forms of colonial and racial oppression. Such feelings of solidarity, presented in the five "black poems" Pae published before his death in 1949, were often highly romanticized, and sometimes rather misguided due to his limited understanding of the complex history and politics of the African diaspora.

It is also important to remember how despite all the knowledge and friendships he accumulated during his short lifetime, it is highly likely that Pae never met a single black woman in person or read any of their published writings: "After sending you off / I am lonely, yet take joy in remembering / The nights we used to sing together / In this room / Where all the black troops sang and slept / *And I picture your womenfolk whom I've never met.*"[2] Indeed, he does try to imagine them, but the way he does so in his poem "Black Woman" (Hŭginnyŏ) is quite interesting, as it foreshadows how the figure of the "Third World woman" is to be represented in Korean literature for the coming decades: "Your beautiful homeland, its mountains and fields / But once the white man's slave ships set shore— / Now / When night visits the friendly waters of the Nile / The wind carries a song / The voice of an unsullied maiden, like the forests of nature."[3] His poetic imagination takes him centuries back to an obscure African landscape, haunted by a woman's voice mourning the violation of her body and homeland by white slave merchants. That being the case, Pae's imagination is already mediated through colonial literary and visual representations of black women, in which black femininity is figured as exotic, primitive, victimized, bound to nature, and thus more or less removed from modernity.

Approximately three decades after Pae's death, a new generation of writers and literary scholars in South Korea began to develop their own ideas of what a transnational Third World alliance might look like, and what this vision could do for the nation in political turmoil. The 1970s literary world had more or less dedicated itself to debates on national literature, the final goal being the creation of a new historical consciousness and the cultural emancipation of the nation from the neoimperial Cold War order. Quite naturally, such a project led to a pressing need to look outward, to locate national literature in relation to those of other nations and peoples who seemed to be engaged in a similar struggle for their own cultural identity. As Namhee Lee argues, the 1970s was a decade in which Korean minjung intellectuals sought to plug the nation into Third World discourses as a means of redefining its position within the global Cold War order.[4] With the rising popularity of the North Korean *Chuch'e* (self-reliance) ideology in the mid-1980s, however, the intellectual community took a much more decisively nationalistic and anti-American turn, especially because of the belief in the American complicity in the Kwangju massacre.[5] It could be said, then, that the early 1980s was a crucial historical moment in which internationalist Third World discourse reached its moment of effervescence within the Korean literary and political imaginary.

Meanwhile, Korean feminist scholars and writers of the late 1970s to the early 1980s, who had often found themselves in a tangential relationship with the largely masculinist minjung movement, also began to realign their politics by looking outward to other women of color around the world. While the institutionalization of women's studies took place in Korea during the early 1970s with the influx of Western feminist scholarship, many Korean feminist historians point to the 1975 World Conference of the International Women's Year in Mexico City as a watershed moment for Korean feminism.[6] It was through the experience of attending this conference and interacting with feminist leaders from other non-Western countries that Korean feminists began to actively respond to Third World feminist thought. The idea of a transnational "sisterhood" was exciting for many of them, as it offered the possibility of forming a united front not only against imperialism but also against patriarchy within domestic borders. Kang Sŏk-kyŏng's 1983 "Days and Dreams" (Nat kwa kkum) deserves critical attention in that this short story is one of the first literary texts that attempts to address the intersectional structures of oppression that Korean women shared with other women of color. A pressing question that arises here is why Kang decided to take yet another radical leap: to establish two female characters of different races not as sisters or friends but as *lovers*, which was a form of intimacy that was in a way even more foreign and incomprehensible than bodies of different colors.

A meaningful way to approach the black lesbian character in Kang's story might be to remember how the 1970s and 1980s was a time in which the Korean public was being exposed to newer representations of black people through the influx of U.S. popular culture and media. Despite the strict import quota placed on foreign cultural products by the dictatorial regime, the newly emerging middle class was eager to consume Hollywood action flicks, American television dramas, and popular music. One thing worth noting here is the significant increase in black female representation that was happening in U.S. popular culture during the decade. Film and media icons such as Pam Grier and Grace Jones performed a new urban "bad-ass" black female subjectivity that radically departed from previous cinematic stereotypes of the victimized slave or submissive house servant. The fact that in 1982 the Korean director Kang Tae-sŏn released a feature-length film titled *Black Woman* (*Hŭngnyŏ*), then, immediately draws our critical attention, and leads to the question of how representations of black femininity within popular texts converged with—or departed from—those within Third World intellectual discourse.

In this chapter I argue that cultural representations of black women during the earlier half of the 1980s not only expose the many contradictions within idealistic and masculinist conceptualizations of an anticolonial Third World alliance but also embody various forms of transnational feminist and queer desires that lay hidden beneath minjung intellectual discourse. Because black characters in modern Korean literature and film were predominantly male African American troops, the political and cultural interpretation of blackness in Korean society has been very much distorted by gendered racial stereotypes of black hypermasculinity, thus often leading them to function as symbols of U.S. military aggression. Even as minjung intellectuals experimented with the idea of an anticolonial Third World coalition, their romanticized notions of an Afro-Asian brotherhood lacked a fuller reflection on how Korean society actually made sense of racial others as embodied, sexual beings. Despite—or perhaps *precisely because of*—the cultural invisibility of black women within Korea, black femininity was treated in a much more incoherent, amorphous, and fluid manner within cultural texts. By placing black women at the center of critical examination, this chapter shows how the elusiveness of black femininity allowed it to function as a type of symbolic receptacle for various obscure desires as well as political ideals—patriarchal, feminist, queer—within early 1980s Korean society.

The four main sections of this chapter each discuss Third World women as imagined within minjung intellectual discourse—Vietnamese women as objects of rural nostalgia in eighties Vietnam War novels, the figure of the African American woman as a feminist fantasy in women's literature, and (queer) cinematic imaginations of black female sexuality. By examining Ch'a Pŏmsŏk's 1965 play *Tropical Fish* (*Yŏldaeŏ*) in relation to the work of minjung scholars and writers such as Paik Nak-chung and Ahn Junghyo, I account, in the first and second sections of this chapter, for a long heritage of repeated but failed attempts made by male thinkers to confine the female racial other within the boundaries of Korean heteropatriarchal political discourse. In the third section I discuss Kang Sŏk-kyŏng's "Days and Dreams," a short story that portrays the relationship between a black lesbian soldier and a Korean sex worker, and presents the former as a savior figure who can potentially rescue Korean women from the violence of both U.S. imperialism and domestic patriarchy. I then focus on the cinematic appearance of a queer black femininity in Kang Taesŏn's 1982 *Black Woman*, an erotic film in which the mixed-race (*honhyŏl*) heroine's hypersexualized body dangerously veers toward a "butch" lesbian image that disrupts the film's patriarchal narrative. I conclude this chapter by examining what we have to garner from such fantasies in all their limited understanding of racial difference and queer desires, especially considering the present context of a neoliberal state in which First World expats, marriage migrants, and a transnational workforce are becoming increasingly visible within the cultural landscape.

Tracing the Third World Woman in Minjung Nationalist Discourse

The postwar playwright Ch'a Pŏmsŏk's 1965 *Tropical Fish* provides a good entry point for our discussion, as the play's lead female character, Gloria, illustrates the way in which Korean male intellectuals struggled to incorporate black women into the nation's heteropatriarchal cultural imaginary. The story focuses on the homecoming of Jinwoo, who returns to Korea to inherit his father's hospital after studying medicine in the United States. To the horror of his upper-middle-class family, he brings with him an American wife, Gloria, who falls prey to the racist abuse of her mother-in-law. Though Gloria struggles to fit in with her new Korean family, the conflict reaches a climax when she becomes pregnant, and the in-laws devise a plan to forcibly abort her baby by feeding her poison. Gloria miraculously escapes this plot, but she is traumatized by the cruelty and violence of her husband's family, and suffers a nervous breakdown and subsequently goes mad. The play does manage to raise some interesting questions about race and racism in postwar Korean society, especially in a scene where Jinwoo challenges his father to compare their treatment of Gloria with his own experience of discrimination under Japanese colonial rule: "Father . . . You are inflicting on her the same pain that you felt when you were a student in Tokyo and no one wanted to rent you a room because you were Korean."[7] Nevertheless, it fails to draw more explicit connections between Gloria and a whole generation of neglected mixed-race "G.I. babies" in Korea, even as the racist rants of the mother-in-law character dangerously veer toward the same kind of abusive rhetoric that was often used against the latter within postwar Korean society.

What is most interesting about the play is its incoherent, unrealistic construction of the character of Gloria, and the male protagonist's ambivalent attitude toward her. She is introduced as a law student who comes from an affluent South Carolinian landowning family who grow "rice, cotton, tobacco and fruit" on their plantation. She claims to have been born to a Chinese father and a Portuguese mother of African descent, and this rather uncommon ethnic heritage seems to have been devised for very specific purposes: to add credibility to her higher-class background by dissociating her blackness from the history of American slavery, and to suggest that her Asianness is a source of romantic attraction between the two lead characters. When confronted with his family's racist rejection of Gloria, Jinwoo criticizes them for being irrational, authoritarian, and culturally backward, and considers his embrace of Gloria's racial otherness as proof of his own successful internalization of liberal Western values. Nevertheless, the couple's relationship is still heavily dependent upon patriarchal gender roles of dominant husband and deferential wife; it seems, then, that Gloria's sexual appeal to Jinwoo derives from a careful balance between the symbolic currency of her U.S. nationality as well as an expectation of feminine submissiveness stemming from her nonwhite "ethnic" background. Overall, Gloria as a character is obscure and fragmented, a mechanical sum of all the conflicting desires of a U.S.-friendly, politically progressive, middle-class Korean male intellectual of the mid-1960s: she is from an affluent yet nostalgically rural background, black but also Asian, and a First as well as Third World citizen.

Perhaps it is because of these complicated and somewhat unsettling power dynamics surrounding race, class, and family that Korean male intellectuals of the 1980s opted for a "brotherhood" rather than a "marriage" with the Third World. While the publication of Paik Nak-chung's "The Third World and *Minjung* Literature" in 1979 could more or less be considered as the definitive starting point of this project, much of the groundwork had already been laid down during the 1970s. The South Korean public had watched with great interest as Eldridge Cleaver and the Black Panthers visited China, Vietnam, and North Korea in 1969 and 1970. Between the years of 1976 and 1982, foundational texts by black writers such as Léopold Sédar Senghor, Aimé Césaire, Frantz Fanon, Malcolm X, Chinua Achebe, Rabindranath Tagore, and Richard Wright were translated and published in Korean for the first time. While acknowledging the political significance of reading texts from such geographically and culturally remote locations, Paik warned his readers: "solidarity that is not based on a mutually fuller understanding of one another's political reality is, in essence, just a solipsistic ideal."[8] Ch'oe Wŏnsik also argued that the more urgent matter at hand is to create our own version of a Third World theory with neighboring nations such as Japan and China, rather than to celebrate the idea of a far-reaching international solidarity for its own sake.[9] Nevertheless, there definitely existed in this period a certain degree of excitement and romanticization around this notion of a transcontinental anticolonial alliance. After all, establishing cultural ties with another nation or racial group in a noncoercive, nonhierarchical manner was a relatively new experience for the postcolonial nation state, and the reading public's enthusiastic response to translated Third World literature suggests that identifying with foreign voices that validated their own historical experiences of colonialism and formation of nationalist identity was a great source of political inspiration and empowerment.

While the rising tide of internationalism also led to a heightened sense of compassion for antiracist struggles in other parts of the world, intellectuals involved in Third World discourses seemed unable to channel these thoughts into a critical reflection of Koreans' own racial identity or the existence of racism within its national borders. In his 1979 essay, Paik offers a fairly accurate and exhaustive overview of the *négritude* movement and African American literary history, as well the black empowerment struggles during the civil rights movement in the United States. While he discovers grounds for solidarity in that "we [colonial Koreans and African Americans] both suffered political discrimination and were forced to internalize feelings of cultural inferiority," he acknowledges the fact that "white racism operates under a universalist logic that is on an entirely different scale and dimension from that of Japanese imperialism."[10] He also compares the U.S. Black Arts movement and Senghor's emphasis on black culture with the 1920s culturalism of colonial Korea, and argues that the political impact of the former pales in comparison to the more militant black nationalisms of Fanon and Césaire, which he groups together with the radicalism of Sin Ch'aeho.[11]

What is important here, however, is that Paik defines racism and imperialism as two distinct, separable modes of oppression, suggesting that the black experience belongs to the former category, while the Korean and Irish experiences of intraracial oppression fall into the latter. His position remains more or less constant throughout the decade; in a 1988 roundtable talk, Paik again brings up the subject of racism in his discussion of U.S. imperialism in the wake of the Kwangju massacre. He harshly criticizes Anglo-Americans' exploitation of the indigenous and African American populations as "a form of chauvinism that is in a way much more insidious and unbearable than Nazism or Japanese militarism."[12] Another discussant echoes this critique, pointing out how the discrimination against "blacks, the Chinese, Mexicans and Latin Americans" in the States exposes the fictiveness of its liberal democratic ideals.[13] Neither of them, however, contemplates the effect of U.S. racism on Korean society or on diasporic Koreans within the United States. There seems to exist a willful blindness toward Koreans' own racial identity in relation to whiteness, which then leads to a complete lack of interest in problems of racial discrimination toward mixed-race children within Korea. Racism, as far as these intellectuals were concerned, was a foreign, black-versus-white issue that had little to do with their own immediate agendas.

It is also important to note how Third World women of other races were mentioned very rarely in literary criticism, and, when they were discussed, it was only through the translated work of writers who were predominantly male. Though black American women writers such as Toni Morrison and Alice Walker were introduced to Korean readers in the early eighties, they went relatively unnoticed by influential minjung critics such as Paik or Kim Myŏngin, and it was another decade before the work of contemporaneous black feminist theorists such as Barbara Smith or Angela Davis was translated and commented upon in Korea. However, an interesting pattern arises when we do gather the bits and pieces of writings on Third World women by Korean male intellectuals of the period. In his reading of Mahmoud Darwish's *A Lover from Palestine*, for example, Paik praises the poet's use of the Palestinian virgin as a metaphor for the colonized nation. Compared to Manhae's love poems, Paik argues, Darwish's metaphorical use of the female lover is more sophisticated in that it elucidates more clearly the speaker's nostalgia toward the countryside, the folk, and the lost motherland.[14] In the essay "The Social Function of African Literature," Lee Jong-uk also introduces the Ugandan poet Okot p'Bitek's *Song of Lawino*, a satirical long poem in which a "wise and humorous voice of an African woman describes to the reader the absurdities of her husband, who prides himself a civilized modern man and criticizes her for not knowing how to dance, cook, or dress her hair like white women."[15] The women in both poems are placed in opposition to Western civilization and function as receptacles of what is considered "authentic" traditional culture. By embracing such patriarchal, nationalist narratives from abroad, Korean male scholars and activists seem to be displacing onto these foreign women of color their nostalgia for a female figure who loyally supports the remasculinization of Third World anticolonial fighters.

Rural Nostalgia and Heteropatriarchy in 1980s Vietnam War Novels

This projection of nostalgic patriarchal desire onto Third World women becomes more evident in the Vietnam War novels of the 1980s. In Ahn Junghyo's 1983 novel *White Badge* (*Hayan chŏnjaeng*), for instance, this rural nostalgia is written into a Vietnamese female character, Hai. As Jinkyung Lee rightly observes, the novel condones the way in which South Korean soldiers made sense of their military activity in Vietnam through the gendered logic of (sub)imperial orientalism, how they considered

Vietnam to be "racially inferior [and] effeminate . . . in comparison to a robust South Korean masculinity."[16] It is within this gendered construct of war that the narrative goes on to endorse the male protagonist Han's sexual relationship with Hai under the pretense of romance. From the very first moment she appears in the story, Hai's body is subject to a racializing gaze that sees her as pure, untainted, and virginal: "Her long black hair cascaded over her shoulders, and though she had no makeup on, her face was well kempt enough to make her seem like an unmarried virgin. Her large black eyes looked like those of wild geese."[17] More importantly, their romance takes place in a drowsy seaside village populated by barefoot children and shabby farmers, an idyllic, fairy-tale-like space that Han imagines would be the perfect home for a newlywed couple.

Han, however, refuses to take Hai back to Korea with him, and the way in which the erosion of his love is narrated suggests that by the time this novel was written, there already existed an incommensurable distance between the Third World as a romanticized political ideal and South Korea as a burgeoning capitalist economy. Though Hai embodies a type of femininity that is palatable for his heteropatriarchal desires, she cannot amount to anything more than a fantasy that must be left behind as Han reinserts himself into the fast-paced, rapidly industrializing cityscapes of South Korea, which was being built up with the blood money that the Vietnam War was bringing into the nation. This is most likely where the rural nostalgia toward Third World femininity in *White Badge* departs from that of pre–Vietnam War texts such as *Tropical Fish*. Unlike Gloria in Cha's play, there inheres in Hai's racial otherness an imbalance of power, as it signifies a poverty-ridden past that Korea had already moved away from by the early eighties, much of it thanks to the economic boost from war profits. The Third World represented in Han's memory of Hai, therefore, is a place of momentary nostalgic retreat, a guilty pleasure for heterosexual middle-class men who were becoming increasingly fatigued by the accelerating demands of a capitalist society.

Moreover, the way in which many of these novels present negative portrayals of Korean female characters as overindustrialized, artificial, and sterile makes us question whether male writers' casting of the Third World woman in nostalgically feminine roles have anything to do with the changing power dynamics between Korean men and women within an industrializing nation state. In *White Badge*, for example, Han's wife makes her first appearance in the text by badgering him to bring home more money for their savings account. She is urban, economic, educated, a devout reader of the German news magazine *Stern*, and, much to Han's anguish, four centimeters taller than her husband. The couple's dysfunctional relationship is symbolized by their inability to conceive, and even though Han realizes toward the end of the novel that he was the one to blame for the infertility, he persistently describes his wife as a cold, inhumane, and inorganic woman who cannot inspire the sort of affective response in him that Hai had done in the past. Even so, Han does choose to live his life with his "sterile" Korean wife instead of Hai, which implies that ethnocentric nationalism trumps all, even if it requires a certain degree of emasculation on the part of the male subject.

A similar pattern arises in Yi Sang-mun's 1987 novel, *Yellow* (*Hwangsaegin*), though with a more pronounced focus on the subject of female reproductivity. After "rescuing" a Vietnamese prostitute, Ninh, from the cruelty of her pimp, Sergeant Kim Yu-bok develops an emotional and sexual attachment to the woman, whom he later discovers is a soon-to-be single mother, pregnant with child. Even though he has a fiancée in Korea, Sŏng Suran, awaiting his return, he delays his discharge from Vietnam in the hopes of seeing Ninh through her moment of childbirth. In fact, Kim shows very little motivation to return to Sŏng; he is put off by her greed and worldliness, and blames her for making him serve in Vietnam for monetary gain. What really disgusts him, however, is the way in which she had thrice aborted their children without telling him, for fear of the pregnancies leading to an impoverished marriage. Ninh's feminine deference and fertility are placed in contrast to the moral deprivation and shallow-mindedness of Sŏng, but Kim ends up dying a tragic death at the hands of Ninh's husband, almost as a punishment for forgetting the fact that human reproduction is first and foremost a duty to the ethnonation, and that indulging in sexual desires that do not fit into the heteropatriarchal, racially "pure" family unit is an unforgivable transgression.

The tentative conclusions that I draw from my readings of such academic and literary texts from the early eighties are as follows: first, even as minjung intellectuals dreamed of forming an anticolonial Third World brotherhood, such political agendas failed to make meaningful inquiries into the relationship between imperialism and racism, and how postcolonial South Korean society really made sense of racial others. Second, although scholars such as Paik Nak-chung sought to reidentify postcolonial Korea as a member of a transnational Third World alliance, literary texts like *White Badge* and *Yellow* illustrate how, by the early eighties, South Koreans were aware that participation in the Vietnam War—and the economic profit derived from it over the previous decade—had already placed the nation-state in a relative position of power over its imagined Third

World allies. Third, and most important, despite highly idealized notions of a Third World alliance, the way in which minjung intellectuals repeatedly attempted and failed to insert women of color into the Korean family structure shows that their internationalist visions did not necessarily lead them to revise their own heteropatriarchal gender ideologies. Their romanticized representations of women in Palestine, Uganda, and Vietnam revealed how their relationship to the so-called Third World was one not of identification but rather of nostalgia.

The Black Lesbian as Feminist Fantasy in "Days and Dreams"

The so-called "camptowns" surrounding the U.S. military bases in South Korea were often thought to be the physical embodiment of U.S. neocolonial violence in the peninsula. However, it was not until anti-American sentiments took a stronger hold of minjung discourse during the late 1980s that activists and intellectuals began to pay greater attention to the location. And as exciting as the idea of a Third World alliance might have seemed from a distance, the actual Afro-Korean racial dynamics within the U.S. military camptowns were telling a significantly different story. Katharine Moon details the long history of racial conflict between black American soldiers and local Korean residents, and points out how Korean camptown business owners often adopted the racist ideologies of the U.S. military and discriminated against their black clientele, eventually leading to a series of violent conflicts such as the Camp Humphrey riots in the early 1970s.[18] Camptown narratives (*kijich'on munhak*) had existed as a subgenre of literature since the mid-1960s, but most of them used the camptown as a metaphor for Korea's submission to U.S. neocolonial power. Because of their deep preoccupation with masculinist nationalist themes, problems of racial discrimination against black soldiers and mixed-race children within the camptown went largely unnoticed within such texts. In fact, many of these novels equated their black G.I. characters with moral degeneracy, predatory sexuality, and physical violence. In other words, these writers displaced their nationalist animosity against U.S. imperial violence onto globally circulating stereotypes of violent black men.

Kang Sŏk-kyŏng is a writer whose work covers a wide range of political issues that were prominent on the minjung activist agenda during the period, such as class disparity, college campus movements, and anticolonial discourse. Her best-known novella, "A Room in the Woods" (Sup sok ŭi pang), is a semiautobiographical text that details her relatively affluent middle-class upbringing as well as her experiences in the student democratization movements during her college years. After quitting her job to become a full-time writer in the late seventies, she began doing field research in the U.S. camptowns, based on which she wrote a collection of short stories that was later published under the title *Night and the Cradle* (*Pam ŭi yoram*). This book deserves critical attention in that it is one among very few camptown narratives written by a woman writer during the period, thus offering what Jin-kyung Lee defines as a "feminist revisionist" perspective to the otherwise male-dominated genre.[19] It includes a short story titled "Days and Dreams," which is one of very few modern Korean literary texts where a black female character is given a prominent role in the story. Because of her female-gendered body, the character of Barbara—an African American servicewoman stationed in Korea—has a radically different function from the more typical hypermasculine black male G.I. figures in conventional camptown narratives. A closer analysis of her role within the text allows us to see the nuanced approach Kang is taking to the intersections of nationality, race, and sexuality as lived and experienced by the Korean sex workers in the camptown. But more importantly, it gives us a glimpse into a type of sexual fascination in Korean society toward black female bodies, and how this curiosity about racial otherness sometimes led to the expression of desires that went against heteronormative bounds of female sexuality.

"Days and Dreams" is essentially a story of a lesbian relationship between an African American soldier, Barbara, and an impoverished Korean military prostitute, Sun-ja, told from the first-person perspective of another, onlooking prostitute, Baek. The reader first encounters Barbara as Baek gossips with her coworkers about how she had once had a black female soldier as a client. According to Baek, Barbara was a "beautiful young black woman" who offered Baek a generous monthly stipend, as long as Baek would accept her marriage proposal and someday relocate with her to the United States. When Baek refuses this proposal, Barbara's love interest promptly shifts over to Sun-ja, a plain and aging sex worker who accepts Barbara's courtship out of financial desperation. Differences between the two women in terms of nationality and social status are evident in the following love letter written by Barbara to Sun-ja: "I love you and your agony. I hope I can be your savior."[20] In her reading of this story, Jeehyun Lim focuses on the use of the word "savior" in this letter, and points out how within the camptown genre, black American soldiers sometimes appear as benevolent savior figures who "rescue" Korean prostitutes from Third World poverty and patriarchy.[21] Their status as racial minorities within the United States absolves them from allegations of First World interventionism; their romantic attachments to Korean women are seen to be driven more by a type of racial sympathy or fellow-feeling. Barbara's self-identification as "savior" could be seen as a variation of this trope, but her female gender adds another layer of cushion, the implication being that a lesbian relationship that is not routed through masculine authority can potentially enable a more genuine and nonhierarchical form of intimacy between an American and a Korean.[22] In short, the narrative presents a First World savior that is much more benign, nonimperialistic, and nonpaternalistic through the figure of Barbara as a black lesbian woman.

It is for this reason that the lesbian relationship in this story is more often interpreted as a convenient feminist allegory for interracial solidarity among women of color rather than a conscious portrayal of homosexual desire. The fact that Barbara never appears in the present time and space of the narrative and is instead visible only through "nested narratives" such as rumors, undelivered letters, or Baek's own retrospect, signals that Barbara as a character is never really meant to have full agency within the story. What remains most difficult to fathom, moreover, is why this attractive, financially stable black lesbian woman from the United States would want to propose marriage to one Korean prostitute after another, both of whom she had only known for several days. Jin-kyung Lee acknowledges how likely it is for lesbian desires and fluid gender performance to arise within the liminal space of camptowns, not only due to prostitutes' "loss of erotic and romantic desire in the context of the commercialized nature of their relations with men" but also because "in the more or less exclusively female society of camptowns, women seem to take on dual gender and sexual roles . . . play[ing] either more masculine or feminine roles, depending upon the circumstances."[23] In "Days and Dreams," however, Barbara is the one who consistently occupies what is conventionally understood as the "masculine" position within a relationship. In her interactions with Baek, she initiates physical contact in bed, takes the lead when they dance, and, most importantly, offers to her partner financial security through marriage. It could be said, then, that the female masculinity of Barbara is less of a conscious representation of lesbian identity than it is a convenient device for her to function as a type of surrogate male figure in her relationships with Korean women. Seen in this light, Barbara as a black lesbian character does very little to legitimize female homosexuality and its distinct forms of desire and relating.

Nevertheless, I suggest that the text's presentation of Barbara as lesbian is also a result of the Korean female subject's fascination with the black female body manifesting itself in a form of queer gaze. Various scholars have examined the cultural phenomenon of female bodies of color being eroticized into objects of homoerotic desire. Sander L. Gilman, for instance, points out how the presumed "excessive" sexuality of black women has historically been associated with lesbian sexuality in the white imagination.[24] Robin Hackett further coins the term "Sapphic primitivism" to describe the way in which white middle-class women writers of the modernist period often cast a fetishizing gaze toward black female bodies, so as to articulate the nonnormative dimensions of their own sexualities.[25] There is a way in which the character of Barbara in "Days and Dreams" is also a result of the conflation between racial and sexual objectification. For example, when the subject of lesbianism arises among a group of gossiping prostitutes, one of them remarks, "I'd say lesbians are better [than gay men]. They look better too." To this Baek responds, "Well, I know a lesbian. She's a real beauty. I can see where even a woman would fall for her." To these women, however, Barbara's sexual appeal derives equally from her blackness and her queerness: "Black women are sexy, aren't they?" they inquire,[26] and the answer to this question is provided in Baek's precise descriptions of Barbara's appearance: "Her body looked smooth and slippery, like a seal's . . . She looked as beautiful as a black pearl."[27] Hence the ambivalence of the text's political implications: there is no doubt that the Korean female characters' exploration of lesbianism in "Days and Dreams" comes at the expense of Barbara's narrative agency. It could also be said, however, that the inclusion of this female character of color is politically generative, insofar as Barbara becomes the catalyst that encourages the text to challenge not only the ethnic homogeneity of national literature but also the heteropatriarchal social order.

The Cinematic Appearance of Queer Black Femininity in Kang Taesŏn's *Black Woman*

Let us now return to Ch'a Pŏmsŏk's *Tropical Fish*, or, more precisely, its 1971 film adaptation titled *I Want to Be in Your Arms Again* (*Kŭdae kasŭm e tasi han pŏn*), as a precedent and contrasting example to Kang Taesŏn's 1982 debut film, *Black Woman*. For the role of Gloria, the production team scouted an African American woman named Susan Jackson, who, at the time, was an employee at a U.S. military base in Pusan. The film was a box-

Fig. 9.1. Gloria is introduced to her new Korean family in *I Want to Be in Your Arms* (Kim Sagyŏm, 1971). Courtesy of the Korean Film Archive.

office flop with the final audience count reaching a meager 2,135, which hardly comes as a surprise for various reasons. First of all, there is a visible absence of rapport between Jackson and the male lead actor, Lee Sunjae, most likely due to linguistic barriers and the lead actress's lack of professional acting experience prior to the making of this film. But more importantly, the camera completely fails to present Jackson to its Korean spectators as what Laura Mulvey calls the object of scopophilic desire.[28] It is evident that the production team was deeply inexperienced with filming women with non-Asian skin tones and facial structures: not only does Jackson's body language remain stiff and impassive but the camera angles, lighting, and even color choices in her wardrobe fail to bring out the actress's natural physical beauty. This exacerbation of her body's foreignness thus works against the melodramatic narrative, whose success heavily depends upon audience sympathy for the tragic heroine. One aspect of the film that does pique our interest, however, is the fact that Kang Taesŏn participated in the production of *I Want to Be in Your Arms Again* as assistant director. It could be presumed, then, that Kang's firsthand experience of the failure of *I Want to Be in Your Arms Again* might have been what motivated him to try his own hand at a film that features a woman of African descent.

Black Woman, which can loosely be categorized as a hostess film, chose the popular singer-entertainer Insooni as its heroine, thus becoming the first Korean feature film with a mixed-race black actress in the female lead role. The seventies was the decade during which the first generation of Amerasian children had reached their adulthood within a racially hostile society that failed to acknowledge their presence. Many mixed-race Koreans experienced severe discrimination in terms of education, employment, and full citizenship, and only a handful of exceptional individuals managed to craft successful careers as entertainers or athletes.[29] Similar to other mixed-race entertainers of her time, such as Park Il-Joon and Yoon Soo-Il, Insooni gradually transitioned from an obscure singer in the small musical venues near the U.S. Eighth Army Base to a mainstream performer after her debut in 1978. The cultural visibility of these figures did to some extent contribute to a better representation of mixed-race people within Korean popular culture, but their mainstream success often depended very heavily upon the exotification and sexual fetishization of their bodies, especially in the case of Insooni as a female performer.[30] Ahn Ji-Hyun points out this ambivalence in her discussion of *Black Woman*: "It was the first time ever that the black mixed-race female was represented as a protagonist in the genre of melodrama/erotic movie. At the same time, however, the film is also problematic in the sense that the film consumes Insooni's black body as a way to arouse exotic/erotic desire."[31] This is probably why, in an interview, the actress herself conceded that although she initially refused the role for fear of the erotic film taking advantage of her mixed-race female identity, she ultimately decided to do the film in the hopes of helping to portray the "difficult reality of living as a mixed-raced person in Korea."[32]

The overall storyline of the film itself pretty much adheres to the conventions of 1970s and '80s hostess films. Nan, who works as the only mixed-race hostess in a nightclub offering sexual service to Korean male customers, utilizes her exotic femme fatale charm to solicit money from her rich clients. After accumulating a large amount of wealth, Nan one day decides to call a masseur to her mansion, only to realize that the blind and penniless man is actually her ex-fiancé, Hyŏn Sŏk, whose abandonment of her had been the primary cause of her fall into prostitution. After a melodramatic process of conflict and reconciliation the two characters rediscover their love, only to realize their interracial relationship has no future and then commit joint suicide in a fit of despair. For the majority of the film's running time, the audience's viewing pleasure very much depends on Nan's performance of a sexually unruly and disobedient female subjectivity, which is why her sudden transformation into a melodramatically loyal lover toward the end of the film feels rather abrupt and anticlimactic.

In the end, her unrelenting desire to transgress the racial and class boundaries of Korean society is contained; social order is restored in the final scene as the couple holds hands and slowly disappears into the ether.

One of the most notable aspects of this film is the insertion of a markedly *urban* black female character to the Korean cinematic imagination, whose sass and spunk effectively draw the spectators into an empathetic engagement with her fight for dignity, wealth, and love. The film makes it very clear from the outset that Nan is not some tragically victimized mixed-race heroine in need of the audience's sympathy. In the opening sequence, the viewers first encounter Nan in a moment of confrontation with three of her Korean male clients in the nightclub. The camera angle is from the point of view of the men, who, huddled around their table, are cowed by the charismatic Nan, standing tall and regal in a glamorous dress. The suspense builds as the camera slowly pans her from toe to head, and is released with a sudden zoom-in shot to the icy expression on her face as she asks defiantly, in fluent, slang-ridden Korean: "Did you think because of my skin color you could treat me like dirt?" Here she is speaking not only to the men but also to the audience outside the screen, thus puncturing the initial tension surrounding her "foreign" body by explicitly acknowledging and then ridiculing unspoken racial assumptions that abound within Korean society. In the ensuing nightclub scenes, moreover, Nan's "take-no-shit" attitude is her primary means of self-protection as she navigates her way through a space built upon the exchange of money, alcohol, and sex. She blackmails her boss into paying her off when she sees him cheat on his wife, unapologetically exercises the art of seduction over her clients, and preaches to her hostess colleagues the ABCs of making "big bucks." In short, Nan is portrayed as a strong black woman who knows her way around the urban jungle and can outsmart its cunning inhabitants by tightrope-walking on the borders of criminality herself. Many aspects of her body language and manner of speech suggest that Insooni's performance was inspired by the feisty heroines of 1970s blaxploitation cinema such as Pam Grier and Tamara Dobson. In this regard, Kang does manage to exceed his protégé by constructing a lively and personable black female protagonist who strays far from Gloria in *Tropical Fish* and whose silent suffering, victimhood, and rural background are vaguely reminiscent of the stereotypical black femininity portrayed in the Hollywood plantation genre.

Another unique aspect of this film is that it reverts back to primitivist aesthetics of the early twentieth century to secure Nan's sexual desirability in the eyes of Korean viewers, primarily through the means of fashion. As Kang must have learned from his experience in *I Want to Be in Your Arms*

Fig. 9.2. Insooni on the VHS cover of *Black Woman* (1989). Private collection.

Again, the success of a mainstream melodramatic film heavily hinges upon the lead actress's legibility within the circuit of heterosexual desire, since it is only then that she gains personhood and becomes worthy of sympathy in the eyes of the spectator. How is this to be done in an erotic film, when darker skin is perceived as a sign of social and aesthetic inferiority and insurmountable otherness? The fact that Insooni personally invested an extensive amount of money in her wardrobe for this film suggests that the answer may be found in the excessive stylization of Nan. Unlike the other Korean hostess characters, who are seen in standard 1980s fashion, Nan embodies the glitz and glamour of a Josephine Baker-esque flapper girl with her outlandishly elaborate nightgowns, headdresses, and pearls. Nan's sexual currency is secured only insofar as she remains foreign, exotic, and thus symbolically removed from reality—a fantasy that stands outside of the here and now of Korean society.

This fetishization of Nan's racial otherness builds up into an excessive erotic vitality, an energy that ends up threatening the heteropatriarchal authority of the Korean male characters. In her study of the eighties *ero yŏnghwa* genre, Yun-Jong Lee points out how the "foreground[ing of] the facial expressions of orgasmic women" is what mainly constitutes the eroticism of these films.[33] In the case of *Black Woman*, however, we see a peculiar divergence from this rule; in scenes of erotic tension, the camera tends to take extreme close-up shots not of Nan but rather of the male characters and the looks of awe, curiosity, and enchantment on their faces. In these moments a strange reversal of power occurs, as the men's expressions suggest that they are neutralized and overpowered by her sexual charisma. I argue that these scenes expose a very important aspect of the relationship between Korean masculine sexuality and racial difference that is often obscured by discourses of nationalism and imperialism: there is a way in which the stability of the masculinist social order meets a crisis in its encounter with a racial other. In other words, sexual contact with the exotic, darker-skinned woman can entail the risk of demasculinization on the part of the male subject, whose gender authority extends only as far as the boundaries of Korean ethnicity and culture.

Perhaps this explains why the film is so laden with scenes of homosocial or homoerotic intimacy between Nan and other Korean female characters. To begin with, the film repeatedly suggests that, with her queen-bee attitude and physical beauty, Nan stands in a position of power over her Korean hostess colleagues. In the numerous scenes where Nan gets physically intimate with her coworkers, there exists a certain butch-femme dynamic between the two female characters. For example, when Nan makes a lewd joke while leaning in and sniffing the body of another hostess, erotic tension arises as the other hostess responds with demure and coquettish body language. In another scene, we see Nan initiating sexual acts with a man while two other, giggling hostesses are lying in the same bed with them, implying that an orgy ensued after the fade-out of the sequence. This is not to say that such scenes of girl-on-girl eroticism consciously represent lesbian relationships; they are above all designed for male titillation. However, it must be noted that although the typical *ero yŏnghwa* "is riddled with dozens of pornographic sexual spectacles that heavily rely on female nudity, it never exhibits such essential American softcore numbers as girl-girl segments, threesomes, and orgies, which are not sexual spectacles that South Koreans particularly fancy."[34] What, then, causes this type of anomaly in *Black Woman*? The simplest explanation would be that Kang was consciously or unconsciously influenced by representations of queer black femininity in American blaxploitation cinema. The way in which 1970s Pam Grier flicks struggled to contain the lesbian subtext deriving from her "strong black dyke" persona has already been examined by various scholars.[35] We could also assume, however, that in the case of *Black Woman*—a film that embodies the racially fetishizing gaze of Korean society—Nan as a mixed-race subject disrupts the phallocentric order of the ethnonation and becomes the queer signifier through which various nonnormative forms of desire are articulated.

What *Black Woman* ultimately suggests to us is that, compared to contemporaneous intellectual and literary discourse, popular texts were in some ways much less resistant to new cultural representations of black femininity. Unlike the minjung theorists and writers whose representations of women of color remained more or less stuck in nostalgic, outdated stereotypes of the rural and submissive Third World woman, Kang's film displays a much keener awareness of the appearance of new urban and queer black female subjectivities in foreign cinema; it even found a way to translate these images into a Korean vernacular. In all its cringeworthy objectification and dehumanization of the black female body, *Black Woman* is a prime example of the transformative powers of erotic imagination, of how the fetishistic gaze toward the racial other can inadvertently end up articulating queer desires that would otherwise have been left unexplored.

Conclusion

The early 1980s was a unique moment in the history of South Korea, when the country's critical intellectuals were trying to redefine its postcolonial identity in relation not just to the First World but also to other non-Western nations and communities that shared the historical experiences of imperial violence. Although leftist thinkers' dreams of a Third World brotherhood in itself had vast political potential, these dreams had their own discursive limitations, in particular their decisively masculinist nationalism. The fact that major minjung scholars such as Paik Nak-chung overlooked questions of racial difference and discrimination within Korean society is especially problematic. The Third World that appeared in their conversations was, therefore, more of an abstract political ideal than a community of real, embodied beings. This racial blindness is especially evident in representations of black American men in nationalist camptown literature and Vietnam War novels. It is curious to see how among the progressive intellectuals who argued for the formation of transnational anticolonial alliance, none of them spoke out against the proliferation of negative racial stereotypes in portrayals of black soldiers in Korean literature.

Tracing the figure of the Third World woman is an effective way to reveal how differences in race, gender, and sexuality were really articulated within the early 1980s Korean cultural imaginary. This is because, when thinking about women, matters of the body are less prone to be obscured by the political ideals of nationalism or anticolonialism. For example, in the recurrent "romance with a Vietnamese woman" narratives of male writers such as Ahn Junghyo and Yi Sang-mun, it seems as though the female characters function mainly as symbols of an alliance between Korea and the Third World. However, what the nation-state's ultimate rejection of these women really exposes to us is the rigidity of the Korean heteropatriarchal social order, as well as its subimperial belief in its own superiority over racial others. Kang Sŏk-kyŏng's "Days and Dreams," however, shows us how despite the persisting problem of racial exotification of the foreign body of color, the feminist orientation of the text allows it to present a more successful vision of a transnational Third World alliance between an African American and a Korean female subject. Moreover, the fact that the two female characters were portrayed in an interracial lesbian relationship suggests that the inclusion of a female racial other into a feminist narrative can be an occasion to challenge not only patriarchal but also the heteronormative social structures that sustain the nation-state. Perhaps what is most ironic in my analysis of early eighties culture is the fact that as a lowbrow erotic film targeting a more mainstream audience, Kang Taesŏn's *Black Woman* offers a female character of color who is in many ways more up-to-date and self-empowered than the idealistic yet anachronistic characters created by contemporaneous scholarly and literary writers. It seems that as the erotic imagination ran wild, along with it dwindled the stronghold of nationalist ethnocentrism and masculine authority. We might say, then, that this departure from conventional heteropatriarchy is the saving grace of a film that is otherwise rather troubling for its excessive sexual fetishization of the mixed-race female body. Nevertheless, *Black Woman* urges us to question the prioritization of minjung political theory and literature over popular culture in our understanding of what the 1980s truly was, especially when it came to matters of race, gender, and sexuality.

The narrative structures of the aforementioned works reappear in variations in new millennium Korea, where "multiculturalism" is celebrated as a futuristic symbol of globalization. For example, Mun Sunt'ae, who was a prominent minjung writer during the eighties, published "Mother and the Zelkova Tree" (Nŭt'inamu wa ŏmŏni) in 2006, a short story describing a middle-class Korean man revisiting his mother after marrying an African American woman. With its tentative happy ending, the story celebrates the male protagonist's successful transformation from a poverty-ridden child of postwar Korea to an educated cosmopolitan man of the twenty-first century. This text repeats the same "homecoming with foreign woman of color" structure seen in *Tropical Fish* or *White Badge*, and thus focuses primarily on the integration of his multiracial family into Korean society. In Chŏng Han-a's 2012 novel, *Little Chicago* (*Lit'ŭl Sik'ago*), we see how, three decades after the publication of "Days and Dreams," another woman writer chose an Afro-Korean lesbian romance as the main subject matter for her camptown narrative. While the Afro-Korean butch-femme dynamics in *Little Chicago* also seem somewhat conditioned by the stereotypical association between black female bodies and masculinity, the text takes a much more nuanced approach to black lesbian identity and the process of its becoming an object of desire to a queer Korean female subject. Last, the young Afro-Korean mixed-race singer Lee Michelle, who came into the national spotlight through the celebrated reality TV show *K-Pop Star*, has recently starred in *The Goose's Dream* (*Kŏwi ŭi kkum*), a jukebox musical that has been inspired by stories of Insooni's childhood as a mixed-race girl overcoming racial prejudice and discrimination. These literary and cultural influences suggest that a reconsideration of the early 1980s is desirable and even necessary for a better understanding of the racial and gender politics of today's neoliberal South Korea.

NOTES

1. Pae Inch'ŏl, "Tcho Ruisŭ ege," 19.
2. Pae Inch'ŏl, "Hŭgin pudae," 298 (emphasis added).
3. Pae Inch'ŏl, "Hŭginnyŏ," 86.
4. Namhee Lee, *The Making of Minjung*, 232.
5. Ibid., 135.
6. Lee Gi-suk, "Taehak pusŏl yŏsŏng yŏn'guso ŭi hwaldong hyŏnhwang," 16; Kim Young-Sun, "1970-yŏndae Han'guk yŏsŏnghak haksul undong," 126.
7. Ch'a Pŏmsŏk, "Yŏltaeŏ," 187.
8. Paik Nak-chung, "Che-3 segye wa minjung munhak," 44.
9. Ch'oe Wŏnsik, "Minjung munhangnon ŭi pansŏng kwa chŏnmang," 359.

10. Paik, "Che-3 segye wa minjung munhak," 60–61.
11. Ibid., 62.
12. Pak Hyŏnch'ae et al., "Chwadam: Minjok t'ongil undong kwa minjuhwa undong," 54.
13. Ibid., 54.
14. Paik, "Che-3 segye wa minjung munhak," 72–73.
15. Lee Jong-uk, "Ap'ŭrik'a munhak ŭi sahoejŏk kinŭng," 110.
16. Jin-kyung Lee, *Service Economies*, 51.
17. Ahn Junghyo, *Hayan chŏnjaeng*, 117.
18. Moon, *Sex among Allies*, 73.
19. Jin-kyung Lee, *Service Economies*, 181.
20. Kang Sŏk-kyŏng, "Days and Dreams," 24.
21. Jeehyun Lim, "Black and Korean," 7.
22. Ibid., 8.
23. Jin-kyung Lee, *Service Economies*, 158–59.
24. Gilman, *Difference and Pathology*, 89.
25. Hackett, *Sapphic Primitivism*, 3.
26. Kang, "Days and Dreams," 9.
27. Ibid., 11, 24.
28. Mulvey, "Visual Pleasure and Narrative Cinema," 346.
29. Gage, "Pure Mixed Blood," 134.
30. Ibid., 134.
31. Ahn, "Visualizing Race," 60.
32. Pae Chaesŏng, "Insuni 'Hŭngnyŏ.'"
33. Yun-Jong Lee, "Cinema of Retreat," 51.
34. Ibid., 14.
35. Keeling, *The Witch's Flight*, 109; Mask, *Divas on Screen*, 84–85.

REFERENCES

Ahn, Ji-Hyun. "Visualizing Race: Neoliberal Multiculturalism and the Struggle for Koreanness in Contemporary South Korean Television." PhD diss., University of Texas at Austin, 2013.
Ahn Junghyo. *Hayan chŏnjaeng* [White badge]. Segyŏng, 2009.
Ch'a Pŏmsŏk. "Yŏltaeŏ" [Tropical fish]. In *Taeriin: Ch'a Pŏmsŏk hŭigokchip*, 139–206. Sŏnmyŏng munhwasa, 1969.
Ch'oe Wŏnsik. "Minjung munhangnon ŭi pansŏng kwa chŏnmang" [Reflections on and future prospects of national literature]. In *Minjok munhak ŭi nolli*, 346–70. Ch'angjak kwa pip'yŏngsa, 1982.
Chŏng Han-a. *Lit'ŭl Sik'ago* [Little Chicago]. Munhak tongne, 2012.
Gage, Sue-Je Lee. "Pure Mixed Blood: The Multiple Identities of Amerasians in South Korea." PhD diss., Indiana University, 2007.
Gilman, Sander L. *Difference and Pathology: Stereotypes of Sexuality, Race, and Madness*. Ithaca: Cornell University Press, 1985.
Hackett, Robin. *Sapphic Primitivism: Productions of Race, Class, and Sexuality in Key Works of Modern Fiction*. New Brunswick, NJ: Rutgers University Press, 2004.

Halberstam, Jack. *Female Masculinity*. Durham: Duke University Press, 1998.
Hŭngnyŏ [Black woman]. Directed by Kang Taesŏn. Samyŏng Film, 1982. DVD.
Kang, Sŏk-kyŏng. "Days and Dreams." In *Words of Farewell: Stories by Korean Women Writers*, 1–27. Translated by Bruce and Ju Chan Fulton. Seattle: Seal Press, 1989.
Keeling, Kara. *The Witch's Flight: The Cinematic, the Black Femme, and the Image of Common Sense*. Durham: Duke University Press, 2007.
Kim Young-Sun. "1970-yŏndae Han'guk yŏsŏnghak haksul undong ŭi kyebo wa changsosŏng" [The genealogy and development of the Korean women's studies movement during the 1970s]. *Hyŏnsang kwa insik* (Spring 2015): 113–37.
Kŭdae kasŭm e tasi han pŏn [I want to be in your arms again]. Directed by Kim Sagyŏm. Haptong yŏnghwa, 1971. DVD.
Lee Gi-suk. "Taehak pusŏl yŏsŏng yŏn'guso ŭi hwaldong hyŏnhwang kwa kŭ kwaje" [The activities and goals of university-affiliated women's studies research institutes]. *Pusan taehak yŏsŏng yŏn'gu* 1 (1989): 7–44.
Lee, Jin-kyung. *Service Economies: Militarism, Sex Work, and Migrant Labor in South Korea*. Minneapolis: University of Minnesota Press, 2010.
Lee Jong-uk. "Ap'ŭrik'a munhak ŭi sahoejŏk kinŭng" [The social function of African literature]. *Ch'angjak kwa pip'yŏng* 14, no. 3 (1979): 96–117.
Lee, Namhee. *The Making of Minjung: Democracy and the Politics of Representation in South Korea*. Ithaca: Cornell University Press, 2007.
Lee, Na Young. "The Construction of United States Camptown Prostitution in South Korea: Transformation and Resistance." PhD diss., University of Maryland, College Park, 2006.
Lee, Yun-Jong. "Cinema of Retreat: Examining South Korean Erotic Films of the 1980s." PhD diss., University of California, Irvine, 2012.
Lim, Jeehyun. "Black and Korean: Racialized Development and the Korean American Subject in Korean/American Fiction." *Journal of Transnational Studies* 5, no. 1 (2013): 1–27.
Maeng Mun-Jae. "Pae Inch'ŏl ŭi hŭginsi e nat'anan chuje ŭisik koch'al" [A study on the theme of African American traits in Pae Inch'ŏl's poems]. *Han'guk sihak yŏn'gu* 42 (2015): 99–126.
Mask, Mia. *Divas on Screen: Black Women in American Film*. Urbana: University of Illinois Press, 2009.
Moon, Katherine H. S. *Sex among Allies: Military Prostitution in U.S.-Korea Relations*. New York: Columbia University Press, 1997.
Mulvey, Laura. "Visual Pleasure and Narrative Cinema." In *Media and Cultural Studies: Keyworks*, edited by Meenakshi Gigi Durham and Douglas M. Kellner, 342–52. Oxford: Blackwell, 2006.
Mun Sunt'ae. "Nŭt'inamu wa omŏni" [Mother and the zelkova tree]. In *Ult'ari*, 73–104. Irum, 2006.
Pae Chaesŏng. "Insuni 'Hŭngnyŏ'" [Insooni's *Black Woman*]. *Joongang Ilbo*, June 25, 2014, http://news.jtbc.joins.com/article/article.aspx?news_id=NB10509314
Pae Inch'ŏl. "Hŭginnyŏ" [Black woman]. *Paekche* 2 (1947): 86–89.
Pae Inch'ŏl. "Hŭgin pudae" [Black troops]. *Hyŏndae munhak* 9, no. 2 (1963): 295–99.
Pae Inch'ŏl. "Tcho Ruisŭ ege" [To Joe Louis]. *Munhwa ch'angjo* 2 (1947): 17–19.
Paik Nak-chung. "Che-3 segye wa minjung munhak" [The Third World and minjung literature]. *Ch'angjak kwa pip'yŏng* 14, no. 3 (1979): 43–79.

Pak Hyŏnch'ae et al. "Chwadam: Minjok t'ongil undong kwa minjuhwa undong" [Roundtable talk: The national reunification movement and democratization movement]. *Ch'angjak kwa pip'yŏng* 16, no. 3 (1988): 6–63.

Paquet, Darcy. "The Korean Film Industry: 1992 to the Present." In *New Korean Cinema*, edited by Chi-Yun Shin and Julian Stringer, 32–50. Edinburgh: Edinburgh University Press, 2005.

Yi Sang-mun. *Hwangsaegin* [Yellow]. Han'guk munhwasa, 1987.

PART V

Popular Culture

10

Between Progression and Regression

Ero Film as Cinema of Retreat

Yun-Jong Lee

Ero, an abbreviation of "erotic" or "eroticism," was *the* keyword of the South Korean film industry in the 1980s. Almost all the mainstream films of the decade, namely the domestic 35mm films distributed through first-run movie theaters, bore in one way or another the label of ero films (*ero yŏnghwa*). Because of this prevalence of the erotic, the Chungmuro film district, the hub of South Korea's movie industry, was then widely criticized for its commercial, unethical, apolitical, and inartistic filmmaking. The ero film genre thus came to be seen as emblematic of "the film industry's . . . conspiracy against wholesome social consciousness," it was called "the malady of South Korean cinema," and it was even blamed for the "regression" of national cinema.[1] As a result, the ero film—and by extension the 1980s as a whole—historically became one of the most understudied and misunderstood genres within Korean film studies.

In this chapter, I propose to rethink and reappraise the ero film of South Korea as a genre, a trend, and a style that resonated with the cultural politics and the aesthetics of the country during the 1980s. In doing so, I will characterize the ero film as a "cinema of retreat" that oscillated between progression and regression not only in its position in the Korean and global film history but also in the politico-economic and cultural development of South Korean society in the era, especially regarding women's status in it. The oscillation is particularly observable in the ero film's confrontation with two major cultural forces, namely, the minjung nationalist ideology of the 1980s and the then emerging discourse of radical feminism.[2] As two of the most influential discourses of 1980s Korea, minjung nationalism and feminism were particularly vocal in criticizing the ero film for its alleged lack of political and ethical engagement and for its sexploitative style.

Given the apparent antagonism between minjung critics and the ero film, it seems ironic that Chungmuro in the 1980s, including its ero filmmakers, in many ways supported the minjung movement's rejection of developmentalism and economic growth at all costs. Relatedly, despite their commercial exploitation of half-naked women, many ero films were actually sympathetic to the feminist cause, and many were melodramas with female protagonists that were also categorized as "women's films" (yŏsŏng yŏnghwa).[3] This female-friendly tendency of the ero film is even more resonant if we contrast it with today's filmmaking trends in Korea, which lean toward all-male casts and a rather antagonistic approach to women in general. In this respect, even when the ero film was socially regressive, that was not so much due to its sexploitation or its political and moral indifference, but rather due to its subscription to a chauvinistic nationalism that, in different measures, was shared by both minjung intellectuals and feminist critics in 1980s Korea. As a "cinema of retreat," I will suggest in this chapter, the ero film was never fully progressive nor completely regressive. Rather, it was a genre that distinguished itself for its refusal to endorse the violence intrinsic in the state-driven process of modernization and industrialization between the 1960s and the 1980s. We may see the retreative sensibility, in this sense, as a "counter-developmentalist" structure of feeling, in Raymond Williams' terms, that was ultimately antagonistic to South Korean society's rushed endorsement of capitalism, dictatorship, militarism, and, in short, developmentalist modernization.[4]

The Erotic Movie in International Film History

The erotic movies of the 1980s have long been denounced by film critics as low-quality commercial ventures that were produced in the "dark age" between the golden era of the 1960s and the postdemocratization renaissance of the 1990s. The eroticization of Chungmuro, however, had been underway since the mid-sixties in line with the post-1968 international filmmaking trend that had popularized soft-core pornography, often equating political revolution with sexual revolution. Moreover, the erotic films of the 1990s and on, which were technically much more sexually explicit than ero films, were neither dismissed nor labeled with the notorious generic prefix *ero-*. Why, then, does the "ero" label carry so much prejudice, and why has ero film itself been so ostracized in South Korea? One explanation may be that the term "ero" has a Japanese etymological origin that is widely regarded as kitsch in South Korea, even more so than Konglish (Koreanized English) words.[5] While in Japan the label did not become exclusively associated with the adult film genre, its South Korean counterpart became the choice designator of 1980s erotic films as well as the ero videos of the 1990s.[6]

Compared with its South Korean kin, Japanese cinematic eroticism has a longer history and, over time, it has diversified into more genres. Its history stretches back to the late 1950s, when the first *eroduction* (erotic production) films were commercialized as low-budget independent ventures for adult viewing. Beginning in 1963, however, the prefix *ero-* became gradually displaced by the less explicit "pink" label.[7] Very rapidly, *pinku eiga* (pink film) began to dominate the Japanese film industry in the sixties, to the extent that they comprised 40 percent of all domestic production by 1965. Japanese erotic cinema then further developed into *roman poruno* (fictional pornography) during the 1970s, when the Nikkatsu studio introduced relatively high-budget, artistically ambitious mainstream films under that label. Yet another evolution came in the late 1980s with the rise of the direct-to-video films that were called *AV* (adult video).[8]

Beyond Korea and Japan, the eroticization of mainstream cinema was an international phenomenon. One reason for this was that many auteur filmmakers began to devote serious attention to cinematic eroticism as a tool for political and cultural activism. Hence, the European and American politico-sexual revolutions of the late 1960s encouraged directors to make intensely sexual art films such as *Last Tango in Paris* (1972, dir. Bernardo Bertolucci) and *Salò* (*Salò, or 120 Days of Sodom*, 1975, dir. Pier Paolo Pasolini).[9] The latter movie was memorably described by Linda Williams as one of the "high-culture Marquis de Sade films." Japan, too, had its own erotic art film in director Oshima Nagisa's *In the Realm of the Senses* (*L'empire des Sens*, or *Ai No Corrida*, 1976).[10] The leftist and progressive rubric of the May 1968 protests in France encouraged film critics to approach and promote these films in high-concept modernist terms. Consequently, sexual freedom and sexual revolution were equated with political resistance, and both became embedded in America in the anti–Vietnam War movement and in hippie culture. "Make love, not war" thus became a political slogan that urged intellectuals, students, urban laborers, and middle-class workers to revolt against state authorities and the politico-economic ruling class.[11]

Another reason for the international rise of erotic film was the motion pictures' commercial competition with television. Up until the home video revolution of the 1990s, when erotic content began to be packaged in direct-to-video format, the injection of sexually explicit scenes in theatrically distributed 35mm films made for good business. This accounts for the rise of many successful genres and films. Examples are Hollywood erotic thrillers such as Lawrence Kasdan's *Body Heat* (1981) and Adrian Lyne's *9 1/2 Weeks* (1986) and *Fatal Attraction* (1987); China's Fifth-Generation sexually metaphoric films such as Zhang Yimou's *Red Sorghum* (1987) and *Ju Dou* (1990); Japan's own *pink eiga* film wave; and Just Jaeckin's 35mm French soft-core films such as *Emmanuelle* (1974), *Story of O* (*Histoire d'O*, 1975), and *Lady Chatterley's Lover* (1981). Jaeckin's *Emmanuelle* was one of the most famous and internationally successful French films of all time, generating dozens of its own sequels as well as international imitations. Indeed, in South Korea, the title of the first ero film, *Aema Puin* (*Madame Aema*, dir. Jeong In-yeob), is said to have been chosen by its producer to remind Korean cinemagoers of *Emmanuelle*.[12]

South Korean Ero Film: A Brief Historical Overview

Against this international background, the eroticization of South Korean cinema from the 1960s on, which technically began with the first kiss scene in 1956, was neither a culturally degenerate nor a historically regressive phenomenon. It did, however, cause controversies that had sometimes to be settled legally. The 1956 kiss scene, which was presented in the spy melodrama film *The Hand of Destiny* (*Unmyŏng ŭi son*, dir. Han Hyŏng-mo), involved just a brief brush of the two performers' lips, but it was enough to stir trouble.[13] The first display of cinematic nudity, in the 1965 experimental film *The Empty Dream* (*Ch'unmong*), led to a lawsuit by censors against director Yu Hyun-mok. Yu indeed lost the suit and was subsequently imprisoned for "obscene film production," an unprecedented charge in Korean film history.[14] At the end of the sixties, the obscenity charge was again leveled against three other directors, Shin Sang-ok, Park Jong-ho, and Lee Hyung-pyo for *Eunuch* (*Naesi*, 1968), *A Woman in the Wall* (*Pyŏk sok ŭi yŏja*, 1969), and *Your Name Is Woman* (*Nŏ ŭi irŭm ŭn yŏja*, 1969), respectively. In the sixties, "obscenity" and "ideology" were politically and judicially the most sensitive issues in South Korean film censorship. Film director Kim Soo-yong thus recollects that the aggressive state censorship was "viciously and severely discouraging" the national film industry that was in full bloom in the 1960s.[15]

How bad was all this for South Korean cinema? There is no question that, by many measures, the South Korean film industry experienced a prolonged slump from the end of the 1960s through the early 1990s. The eroticization of Chungmuro, however, was to a great extent a response to, and not a cause of, this crisis. The decline was owed partly to the rigidly puritan cultural policy of the Park Chung Hee regime, partly to the New Hollywood invasion of the seventies and eighties, and partly to the propagation of television sets in South Korean households beginning in the late 1960s. Under these circumstances, Chungmuro sought for respite in the depiction of partial nudity and the inclusion of sexual themes that would hopefully bring the audiences for television and foreign films back to domestic cinema.[16]

During the 1970s, perhaps the most prominent subject of South Korean ero film was the "dissolute" but titillating life of sex workers. Indeed, the modern concept of pornography was formulated in eighteenth-century Europe as that of an obscene writing or painting concerning prostitution.[17] Known generically as the "hostess film" (*hosŭtisŭ yŏnghwa*), this quasi-pornographic type of movie keenly exploited the curiosity, hypocrisy, and taboos that then surrounded female sex work. A common plot followed the supposed corruption of an innocent rural girl as she became an urban prostitute, featuring various sex workers including barmaids, club hostesses, call girls, and red-light-district workers. The filmmaking trend of the hostess genre was originated from two record-breaking hits and critical successes: *Heavenly Homecoming to Stars* (*Pyŏltŭl ŭi kohyang*, 1974, dir. Lee Jang-ho) and *Yeong-ja's Heydays* (*Yŏng-ja ŭi chŏnsŏng sidae*, 1975, dir. Kim Ho-sun). The two movies were also frequently categorized as youth film (*chŏngch'un yŏnghwa*), another trendy genre at the time, for their attention to the shattered lives of young rural migrants under the nation's rapid industrialization and urbanization. Their style and themes influenced many younger filmmakers who emulated Lee and Kim by shifting the cinematic protagonists of their movies from conventionally cheerful youths to the more somber and gloomy hostesses and their clients. The hostess film culminated in the late seventies and merged into the ero film, as one of its subgenres, in the early 1980s. Contributing to the genre were also auteur directors such as Kim Ki-young and Ha Gil-jong, who attempted to blend eroticism and high-concept artistry through original styles and themes.[18] In this respect, artistic eroticism in 1970s South

Korean cinema was in many ways inspired by and aligned with contemporary European erotic modernist films.

Following the cinematic eroticism of the 1970s, the ero film turned into a supergenre of Chungmuro in the 1980s. It did so by absorbing the contiguous genres of hostess film and traditional Korean melodrama, and in addition it merged with distinct genres such as comedy, thriller, horror, crime drama, and costume drama. The ero film thus expanded its erotic characters from hostesses to widows, divorcees, housewives, college students, office workers, and women professionals. While Chungmuro in the seventies had been rather discreet when representing eroticism outside the boundaries of sex work, the expansion in the eighties was unprohibited by the military regime of Chun Doo Hwan (1980–87) and, by all appearances, it was unresistingly accepted by South Korean audiences.[19]

What was the role of the Chun regime in the emergence of the ero film? According to many critics, the rise of the genre was inseparable from the so-called 3S policy (*sam esŭ chŏngch'aek*): the promotion of sex, screen, and sports by the government in the attempt to distract citizens from politics and civic engagement. Indeed, lacking in political legitimacy and faced with popular protests, the regime sought to quell its critics by diverting South Koreans' political passions through mass entertainment. The regime thus relented on censorship, especially that of eroticism, and it allowed cinema owners to open late-night theaters for special screenings to adult audiences.

One of the greatest prejudices against the ero film, however, is that the genre was quite entirely the product of the 3S policy. In fact, even granting the importance of the policy, the ero genre would not have thrived but for its cinematic achievement joined with the extraordinary enthusiasm of Korean audiences. On February 6, 1982, *Madame Aema*, arguably the very first true ero film, was screened in a night showing at the Seoul Theater. After thirty-seven years of nationwide curfew, which had been effective every day from midnight to 4 a.m. since 1945, thrilled cinemagoers swarmed the theater. *Madame Aema* was screened for three months at this first-run theater, attracting a record 300,000 viewers.[20] The film's ardent reception made its leading actress, Ahn So-young, an overnight star and boosted erotic film production. Over 60 percent of South Korean movies made in 1982 turned out to be erotic films, and the ero genre took up a major portion of South Korean film production for the rest of the eighties. The film was followed by no less than ten sequels into the late nineties.[21] The 3S policy may thus have created the necessary conditions for the rise of ero film, but this does not tell the whole story. Had it not been for *Madame Aema*'s success and South Korean audiences' unwearying passion

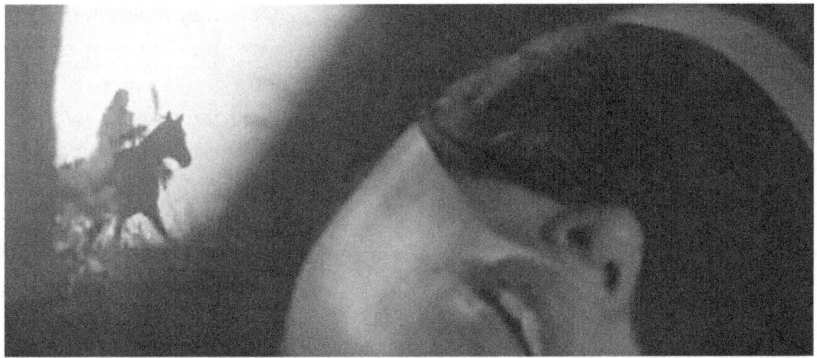

Fig. 10.1. Aema, whose name means "lover of stallions," fantasizes about horseback riding in bed. Courtesy of the Korean Film Archive.

for the erotic film genre, ero filmmaking would have either died out or have been limited to a few one-hit wonders. Moreover, there are reasons to believe that the ero film phenomenon did not quite advance the politically conservative agenda of the 3S policy. As one commentator noted, many South Koreans, especially college students, "threw rocks in protest against Chun Doo Hwan's oppressive policies during the day, and at night [they] giggled watching cheap erotic films that were in tune with Chun's policy of liberalization."[22] Indeed, even in its content, as we will observe further below, the ero film was often quite political, unlike the conventional prejudice against it. It was thus not the 3S policy alone that eroticized South Korean films of the eighties; rather, the ero film was born out of the complex imbrication of many factors such as Chungmuro's stagnation, television's rise, Chun's strategically liberal cultural policy, the appearance of cinematic eroticism, and South Korean cinemagoers' curiosity.

In the 1990s, the commercial appeal of cinematic eroticism extended further with the emergence of the ero video, which was not theatrically released but directly distributed to rental video shops.[23] As one of the most disruptive technologies in the industry, the VCR soon created a nationwide video rental system. Shot on cheaper 8mm or 16mm film, direct-to-video pornography was under no pressure to maintain mainstream legitimacy, and its contents were relatively free from government regulations. No social controversies arose from these videos, despite their presentation of nudity and sex as frequently and candidly as possible. Still, the ero video was not as explicit as today's hard-core pornography, as genitals were always hidden and sex acts simulated.

The ero film was, naturally enough, even less explicit and pornographic than its direct-to-video counterpart. Without a doubt, sexual spectacle was the raison d'être of these films, and what I call the "ero sequence," containing nudity, various sexual acts, and ecstatic facial expressions, was the constitutive iconographic feature of the ero film. Nevertheless, it is interesting to note how these sequences were generally neither frequent nor sexually spectacular in ero films.[24] More often than not, these films made ample use of censorship-aware visual strategies to avoid displaying the full nudity of a woman or man. These tactics included the practice of cutting away from a sex-act-related shot to a nondiegetic shot, in which the camera pans over the contents of a room (ceilings, walls, windows, fireplace, pictures, furniture, lighting equipment, and others) or a natural landscape (sky, mountain, water, snow, tree, rock, and vast field) during the sex scene. Besides, ero actors and actresses often cringed so much from exposing their bodies and simulating sex acts before the camera that the viewers could not help realizing how artificial and unspectacular the sequence was. Even the lighting during a sequence was often so low that it was difficult to figure out which body part was being displayed. Indeed, ironically but crucially, the ero sequence seemed to focus on concealing, rather than revealing, nudity and sex, and yet this concealment managed to give the ero film a more powerful erotic quality.

In spite of its subdued and at times even weird eroticism, the ero film of the 1980s played the role of legitimate quasi pornography for South Korean cinemagoers who had access to neither hard-core porn nor foreign soft-core except for a few theatrical releases. With the advent of the ero video in the 1990s, however, the pressure mounted on ero film producers to provide more cutting-edge and explicit content. The industry thus started replacing the discreet eroticism of previous ero films with more realistic sex scenes. Naturally, owing to competition from ero video, the production of mainstream minor-restricted films decreased. The last bona fide box office hit in the genre was *Seoul Rainbow* (*Sŏul mujigae*, 1989, dir. Kim Ho-sun). By 1987 the quantity of ero film production had dwindled to the extent that the genre occupied only 30 percent of total film production.[25] Adding to the decline of ero films, the bad name of ero videos eventually led to the disappearance of the "ero" label from mainstream South Korean films. Many filmmakers subsequently turned to nonerotic film genres such as the teenpic, the youth film, the romantic comedy, and the action film. Minor-restricted erotic films stayed afloat in the 1990s in the works of a few directors, such as Kwak Ji-kyoon, Park Chul-soo, Jang Sun-woo, Kim Ki-duk, and Im Sang-soo, who often chose eroticism to paradoxically emphasize political themes in their works.

We have so far sketched the development of South Korean cinematic eroticism from the 1950s to the 1990s within the domestic as well as international contexts. The eroticization of Chungmuro started in the late 1950s and gradually intensified through the 1960s in tandem with the rise of the pink film in Japan and the erotic soft-core movie globally. The 1970s brought the commercial success of the hostess film, which seamlessly evolved into the gigantic industry of the ero film in the 1980s. The genre then dwindled with the renaissance of South Korean cinema from the 1990s on. As seen from the vicissitudes of South Korean erotic film, genres and filmmaking trends cannot last without cinemagoers' positive responses. We will now move on to further probe the generic particularities of the ero film, especially in terms of its cultural politics, as a cinema of retreat that vacillated between progression and regression amid the political and cultural turmoil of 1980s South Korea.

The Cultural Politics of the Ero Film: Between Progression and Regression

Maria Mies has interestingly written, in reference to patriarchy, capitalism, and modernity, of a number of "dialectics of progress and retrogression." Through this phrase, Mies calls our attention to the retrogressive implications of much Euro-American socioeconomic development (progress) in the modern era. Among the hidden conditions of such progress, Mies argues, were the devaluation and exploitation of the labor of women through "housewifization" as well as the subjugation and deployment of the colonized in productive enterprises that were designed for the accumulation of capital at the imperial center.[26]

Mies's concept of a tension between progression and regression may be appropriated to discuss the ambivalence of the ero film toward the hegemonic ideologies of 1980s South Korea. Despite claims to the contrary, the ero film did not just conform to Chun Doo Hwan's regime or to the patriarchal scopophilic desire for half-naked women on the part of Korean men. Nor was the genre simply symptomatic of the influence of Hollywood and American popular culture in South Korea. Rather, as we will see in this section, many ero films appealed strongly to South Korean cinemagoers because of their imbrication with the era's countercultural forces including, but not limited to, minjung ideology and feminism. As I will try to show, the ero film in many ways incorporated countercultural ideas and turned them into its own film rhetoric of "counterdevelopmentalism," an umbrella term that conceptually covers doctrines as diverse as nationalism, Marxism, feminism, individualism, and more. Seen in this perspective, sex and eroticism were neither the sufficient condition for the emergence of the ero film nor the only draw for South Korean adult moviegoers in the seventies and eighties. Many ero films were equipped with proper narrative development, identifiable characters, and empathetic themes and messages. They were not just commercial eye candy but serious works that are liable to a reading for their political, economic, social, and cultural interventions into the debates of South Korea in the 1980s.

Apart from the overestimation of the role of the 3S policy, another myth surrounding the ero film is that, as a genre, it had a regressive impact on the development of South Korean cinema. This view has been advanced by, among others, 1980s first-generation feminist film critics, who were inspired by both American cine-feminist theories and Korean leftist minjung ideology. Feminist film scholars such as Joo Jinsook, Yu Gina, and Kang Sowŏn have variously denounced the ero film by using the canon of American antipornography feminism that includes the rubrics of "male fetishism," "visual pleasures of male voyeurs," and the "spectacles" of (half-naked) female bodies.[27] While Joo deems the genre's eroticism itself as harmful for the ethical integrity of national cinema, Yu questions the ways in which ero films sexually victimize women not only on the textual level, with images and narratives, but also in posters and marketing strategies that often treat women characters as "fallen beings" who have lost their virginity and chastity, the essential virtues of Korean women under a still prevalent Confucian ethics.[28] Kang also sees the genre as "similar to pornography, not because of its sexual explicitness, but because of its reception mechanism, function, and raison d'être."[29] All three commentators regard the ero film as, fundamentally, a sexploitative venture that ideologically enables the perpetuation of Korean men's sexual and political dominance over women.

Antipornography feminism, however, arguably relies on a Manichean vision that bisects gender into active male aggressor and spectator vis-à-vis passive female victim and spectacle. The view has been criticized within the American context. Alice Echols, for instance, has insightfully characterized 1970s and 1980s antiporn activists such as Susan Brownmiller, Andrea Dworkin, Robin Morgan, Diana Russell, and Kathleen Barry as "cultural feminists" who equate "women's liberation with the development and preservation of a female counterculture" against dominant male culture.[30] Taking a queer perspective, Echols has critiqued cultural feminism for mirroring normative gender essentialism and for falling for the reductionist view that pornography causes male sexual violence to women—"pornography is the theory, rape the practice" in Morgan's famous slogan.[31] In a similar spirit, Linda Williams has described the logic of antiporn feminism as a "feminist alliance with the patriarchs": "If phallic sexuality is contaminated by [patriarchal] power," writes Williams, "then female sexuality shall be defined as its opposite: as not-violent and not-perverse—a pure and natural pleasure uncontaminated by power."[32] Insofar as gender and pornography are socially constructed categories, Williams notes, porn is "not a monolith, either of apolitical pleasure or of unpleasurable power."[33] She hence proposes to subject it to a "historical and generic contextualization that would allow [the anticensorship feminists] to interpret the [sexually sensational] images."[34] As Williams stresses, "hard core [pornography] has changed ... it is a genre more like other genres than unlike them, and although it is still very patriarchal, it is not a patriarchal monolith."[35]

The critical interventions of Echols and Williams apply well to the Korean cine-feminist rejection of the ero film in the 1980s. Indeed, both the American and Korean opponents of the genre ground their arguments in a form of gender essentialism, and both disregard the fact that there were and are many women consumers of erotic and pornographic materials. Moreover, some of this pornography has actually evolved into female-friendly forms and contents. Women in ero films are often visually and diegetically complex entities. Despite their apparent roles as sexual seducers to male viewers with their half-naked bodies and ecstatically agape mouths, they are oftentimes not just the objects but also the subjects of the narratives and the gazes. This insight explains why it was common to find, among the ticket-purchasers of *Madame Aema* and other ero films, not only young men but also the middle-aged housewives who had traditionally held the keys to box-office success in the Korean film industry.[36] In short, in conventional ero film studies, these realms have been neglected: female spectatorship, female fetishism, female gaze of male nudity, and the queer possibilities of the aforementioned topics.

Further developing her critical stance, Joo Jinsook has categorically divided the South Korean cinema of the 1980s into the ero film and the minjung film, and she has evaluated the former to be politically regressive and the latter as progressive.[37] From such a perspective, an ero film like *Madame Aema* would be criticized for setting back the national cinema from the "progress" made by activist films such as *A Fine, Windy Day* (1980). Here again, the nudity and eroticism in ero films are presumed to be outgrowths of filmmakers' inartistic conformist choices made in compliance with the 3S policy.

Contrary to such assumptions, however, many ero filmmakers were not only critical of the developmentalism of the militarist state but were also invested in the artistic innovation of their medium. Many of their films were in fact recognized at a number of prestigious international film festivals. Lee Doo-yong's *Spinning the Tales of Cruelty toward Women* (1983) was invited to Cannes, for instance, and Hah Myung-joong's *Blazing Sun* (1984) was nominated for the competition section at the Berlin and Montreal film festivals. In addition, Im's *Surrogate Woman* (1985) and *Adada* (1987) were awarded with the best actress prizes at Venice and Montreal, respectively. These films, all ero costume dramas, variously portrayed Korean women who were oppressed by the patriarchal caste system in premodern Chosŏn Korea. The argument can be made that, far from being antithetical to minjung film, the female protagonists of ero film symbolically embodied the South Korean people who had been wronged by the system. In their own way, these films contributed to a poetic ethnography of South Koreans, welding pro-minjung messages with ero filmmaking artistry.

In another criticism of the ero film genre, Seung Hyun Park has attributed the "artistic and technological stagnancy" of 1980s Korean cinema to an erotic mannerism that was "low on plot and production values and high on nudity and eroticism."[38] In fact, however, it was through the ero film that important technical developments, including synchronous sound recording, were achieved. Until the early 1980s, it was common among local filmmakers to have sound nonsynchronously recorded so that the voices of actors were dubbed by either voice actors or the actors themselves during postproduction. This long-standing malady was finally overcome thanks to filmmakers such as Jung Jin-woo and Lee Doo-yong, who made their ero films, including Jung's *Parrot Cries with Its Body* (*Aengmusae mom ŭro urŏtta*, 1981) and Lee's *Spinning the Tales of Cruelty toward Women*, with synchronous sound recording.[39] The recording technology soon thereafter became standard in the industry.

Far from belonging to two exclusive categories, erotic and minjung film formulas were historically often blended in the works of the decade's most important auteur directors. For instance, Lee Jang-ho is today celebrated for pro-minjung films such as *A Fine, Windy Day*, but his debut film, *Heavenly Homecoming to Stars*, belonged to the ero genre and fore-

Fig. 10.2. The heroine of *Surrogate Woman*, who spends her days confined to a stuffy room, fans herself on a hot summer day. Courtesy of the Korean Film Archive.

shadowed his later erotic minjung films such as *Between the Knees* and *Ŏudong* (1985), which respectively projected anti-American and antiauthoritarian sensibilities. Such blending was also found in the works of other well-known directors such as Im Kwon-taek, Lee Doo-yong, Jung Ji-young, and Bae Chang-ho. The minjung-inspired ero films would easily include films such as *Madame Aema*, *The Flower at the Equator* (*Chŏkto ŭi kkot*, 1983, dir. Bae Chang-ho), *Between the Knees* (*Murŭp kwa murŭp sai*, 1984, dir. Lee Jang-ho), *Deep Blue Night* (*Kipko p'urŭn pam*, 1985, dir. Bae Chang-ho), *Mulberry* (*Ppong*, 1985, dir. Lee Doo-yong), *Ŏudong* (1985, dir. Lee Jang-ho), *Prostitution* (*Maech'un*, 1988, dir. You Jin-sun), and *Seoul Rainbow*.

Two of the most successful minjung ero films, Lee Jang-ho's *Between the Knees* and Bae Chang-ho's *Deep Blue Night*, endorse quite openly a nationalist theme along with the anti-American and anti-Western orientation of minjung ideology. These "nationalist ero films" (*minjokchuŭi ero yŏnghwa*) share the leftist nationalist concern for South Korea's semicolonial state under U.S. military occupation and its loss of national identity under rapid industrialization and Westernization.[40] Many other ero films deployed the progressive rhetoric of minjung ideology to critique the underbelly of South Korea's compressed modernization and industrialization process. In so doing, many of them also pursued female-friendly narratives by underlining Korean women's oppression and abuse by the Confucian patriarchal system and the modern, state-led developmentalist regime.

Nearly all South Korean erotic films project a dim view of male characters whose sole purpose in life seems to be winning in the competition for success and economic prosperity. We may label this critical function of the ero film, which partly derives from the anticapitalist stance of minjung discourse, "counterdevelopmentalism." It should be noted that this sort of ethos is often articulated in intersection with gendered representation. Problematizing an unethical, success-driven society, the ero film encourages viewers to question the meaning of success, economic wealth, and career. In this sense, many ero films respond to what Bruce Cumings has characterized as "the immense sacrifice . . . that the Korean people made to drag their country kicking and screaming into the twentieth-century rat race."[41] In *Madame Aema*, for instance, the titular protagonist suffers from a sexless relationship with her work-obsessed and cheating husband. In so doing, the film suggests that a happy family is founded on mutual effort and fidelity, and it reevaluates the meaning of the home and the private sphere by raising questions about the "contemporary Korean valuing of society, as a realm of selfless national endeavor, over the home, a place governed by . . . women."[42]

Another common theme of ero films, which in many ways plays on and expands a counterdevelopmentalist message, is that of a woman's revenge for the sacrifices she has been forced to endure. In its immense popularity, the theme is found in films as diverse as *Mist Whispers Like Women* (1982), *Slave of Love* (*Sarang ŭi noye*, 1982, dir. Ko Yŏngnam), *A Man with Color* (1985), *Ticket* (*T'ik'et*, 1986, dir. Im Kwon-taek), *The Wolf's Curiosity Stole Pigeons* (*Nŭktae ŭi hogisim i pidulgi rŭl humch'ŏtta*, 1988, dir. Song Yŏngsu), *Prostitution* (1988), *The Age of Success* (*Sŏnggong sidae*, 1988, dir. Jang Sun-woo), and *Water World* (*Mul ŭi nara*, 1989, dir. Yu Yŏngjin). In a feminist vein, these films also depict how women's labor played an important role in the process of modernization and industrialization of South Korea. As Cynthia Enloe has argued, developing economies in the 1970s and 1980s widely adopted the practice of "deliberately [hiring] women to produce goods cheaply" in "globally competitive industries such as the textile industry."[43] Ero film thus portrayed vengeful working-class women, factory girls, and hostesses who are abandoned by their ambitious boyfriends after helping them climb the social ladder. It was only in the mid-1970s, when a middle class had been successfully established and a majority of urban women could stay home from work, that the roles of mother and housewife supplanted that of factory worker as a culturally endorsed, normative ideal for women. The genre of ero film promptly followed suit, prominently featuring middle-class women who reacted to the frustration and alienation in their lives as housewives.

Alongside the housewifization of South Korean women, another societal issue that found representation in ero films was the expansion of the sex industry through the 1980s. As South Korea hosted the 1986 Asian Games and the 1988 Seoul Olympics, the number of foreign tourists surged, including patrons of the so-called *kisaeng kwan'gwang* (sex tourism, literally meaning courtesan tourism), which nationally had been one of the most profitable tourist draws between the 1960s and 1980s.[44] In her critique of the South Korean masculinist state and its culture, Jin-kyung Lee has discussed how working-class men and women in the country effectively served as sex and military laborers during the industrialization era as well as after.[45] Conceptualizing the "condemned," life-risking labor of sex and military workers as "necropolitical labor," Lee insightfully links the issue to the role of American militarism and to "the interplay between the United States' military engagement . . . in the Korean peninsula and in Southeast Asia and its economic supremacy in these regions."[46] The fraught, neocolonial nature of U.S.-Korean relations is indeed another theme that appeared in many ero films, including *Deep Blue Night, Between the Knees, Queen Bee* (*Yŏwangbŏl*, 1985, dir. Lee Won-se), *Into the Heat of the Night* (*Pam ŭi yŏlgi sok ŭro*, 1985, dir. Jang Gil-su), *America, America* (*Amerika, Amerika*, 1988, dir. Jang Gil-su), and *That Which Falls Has Wings* (*Ch'urak hanŭn kŏt ŭn nalgae ka itta*, 1989, dir. Jang Gil-su). In a rare instance, an ero film such as *X* (*Eksŭ*, 1983, dir. Hah Myung-joong) also portrayed the reality of *kisaeng kwan'gwang*.[47]

As a film genre, the ero movie thus illuminated, often through a gendered lens, social and political problems such as the moral corruption of ruling elites, the necropolitical nature of labor by sex and military workers, the exploitation of female housewifized labor, and the undue subjection of South Korea to the military and economic dominance of the United States. Along with an arguably progressive discursive function, however, the ero film was also characterized by a few regressive dimensions. Among these, erotic minjung or nationalist films often made an allegorical use of a woman's body, whose chastity was assumed as a symbol of Korean ethnic purity or the innocence of the ethnonational minjung. A female's suffering in such films thus often became an occasion for displaying South Korea's ethno-cultural peril under compressed modernization. In both *Deep Blue Night* and *Between the Knees*, for instance, the body of a South Korean woman sexually violated by non-Korean men serves as a national allegory for the loss of Korea's politico-cultural identity during the nation's process of modernization and Westernization.[48] And in historical costume dramas, the symbolic identification of women with the minjung and with commoners in premodern Korea problematically diluted the gendered violence of traditional patriarchy into a generic critique of class hierarchy within dynastic society. The androcentric reduction of Korean women to the minjung deserves criticism, for it appropriates a unitary category of Korean women as the national symbol of the oppressed and the subaltern, suppressing any consideration of women's diverse desires, thoughts, and concerns, as well as that of sexual violence frequently committed both on-screen and within the film industry.

In addition to a patriarchal bias, some ero films, especially those in the category of costume drama, exhibited a form of self-orientalizing tendency. As mentioned earlier, the 1980s were a pivotal era in Korean cinema's transformation into a globally visible national cinema, an era in which South Korean filmmakers such as Lee Doo-yong, Im Kwon-taek, and Hah Myung-joong emerged and delivered well-received performances at European film festivals. The international recognition of South Korean cinema, however, was often fueled by the exotic eroticism of costume dramas that represented premodern life in Korea as, in Jung-Bong Choi description, a "bewitching attraction [which was] part of the synchronic pleasure combining the cinematic spectacle with that of the national."[49] Ero costume dramas—such as *Spinning the Tales of Cruelty toward Women, Surrogate Woman, Blazing Sun, Ŏudong, Hanging Tree* (*Chanyŏmok*, 1984, dir. Jung Jin-woo), *Eunuch* (*Naesi*, 1986, dir. Lee Doo-yong), *Slaves* (*Sano*, 1987, dir. Um Jong-sun), *Karma* (*Ŏp*, 1988, dir. Lee Doo-yong), and *Sa Bangji* (*Sa Bangji*, 1988, dir. Song Kyung-shik)—often evoked a nativist vision of a mythical Korean past. In their projection of an essentialized traditional society and culture, these films were thus complicit in the distorting, orientalist construction of national imagery.

Ero film, therefore, at times regressed into the past and at other times retreated into an allegorical instrumentalization of women and their bodies. This retrogression into misogyny may have been caused by the oppo-

Fig. 10.3. Ŏudong's courtesan hat and folded skirt during her outing in this scene is one of the iconic fashion moments in Korean film history. Courtesy of the Korean Film Archive.

sition of the minjung as an overly public and polemical entity to the private, libidinal, and cultural dimensions of the masses, into which women's gendered interests are often classified to the effect of their trivialization and dismissal. For this reason, the minjung movement failed to "embrace a larger populace,"[50] which contributed to "deflat[ing] its revolutionary energy."[51]

Conclusion: Ero Film and Its Legacies

I have argued that, throughout its artistic experience, the ero film oscillated between progression and regression in terms of national and international cultural politics at the intersection of class, gender, and race. This oscillation has been disregarded by many Korean film critics who have read the ero film exclusively as a historical and aesthetic regression of national cinema. Such a critical view has hitherto overshadowed the genre's progressivist theme of counterdevelopmentalism, which it shares with the two major counterhegemonic discourses of the 1980s, the minjung ideology and contemporary feminism. The ero film is, however, only progressive and not revolutionary: as a form of popular culture, it offers "points of pertinence to the everyday life of the people" in contrast to "radical art forms that oppose or ignore the structures of domination."[52] The ero film also has its regressive facets, where it colludes with patriarchal nationalism as well as a tendency toward self-orientalization. In this sense, it is a cinema of retreat in its seesaw between progression and regression.

The mainstream production of adult movies greatly decreased in South Korea after the 1990s. Minor-restricted films were still made during the period, yet most of them were not erotic but increasingly violent and gory. The ero video market, too, began to shrink in the early 2000s with the downfall of video rental chains and had almost completely collapsed by 2005 with the rise of online downloading and streaming sites. A small resurgence of erotic film happened in the late 2000s, especially in the costume drama genre. This new-millennium boomlet yielded a few commercially successful films such as *Forbidden Quest* (*Ŭmnan sŏsaeng*, 2006, dir. Kim Dae-woo), *Portrait of a Beauty* (*Miindo*, 2008, dir. Jeon Yun-suŏ), *A Frozen Flower* (*Ssanghwajŏm*, 2008, dir. Yoo Ha), and *The Servant* (*Pangjajŏn*, 2010, dir. Kim Dae-woo). In the erotic modern drama genre, *Rules of Dating* (*Yŏnae ŭi mokchŏk*, 2005, dir. Han Jae-rim) was a mild hit, and director Jung Ji-woo returned to impressive erotic filmmaking with his *Eungyo* (*Ŭnkyo*, 2012) after his earlier sultry hit *Happy End* (*Haep'i endŭ*, 1999). However, the resurgence of erotic cinema has also been slowed by commercial and critical flops such as *The Treacherous* (*Kansin*, 2014, dir. Min Kyu-dong), *Scarlet Innocence* (*Madame Ppaengdŏk*, 2014, dir. Yim Pil-sung), and *Empire of Lust* (*Sunsu ŭi sidae*, 2014, dir. Ahn Sang-hoon).

As of 2017, the legacy of the ero film in South Korea is far from insignificant, and there are still a few gifted directors such as Im Sang-soo, Yoo Ha, Jung Ji-woo, Kim Dae-woo, and Min Kyu-dong who are interested in the topic of eroticism and its intersections with politics, aesthetics, and ethics. Although the label *ero* is no longer attached to mainstream Korean films, erotic filmmaking is not extinct but undergoing an evolution in twenty-first-century South Korea. Just as Rick Altman defines film genre not as "a transparent vessel of communication between sender and receiver" but as "a complex *situation*, a concatenated series of events regularly repeated according to a recognizable pattern,"[53] we may see the ero film as not only a communicative field but also a multifaceted situation in which the genre formula of the ero film, particularly the erotic sequence, has been restructured and reconstructed by its surrounding environs such as censorship, audience response, and the genre's relation with contiguous domestic and foreign genres.

As a singularly influential film genre, the ero film greeted a production boom in the 1980s when national and international filmmaking conditions—both trend and policy—converged with strong interest by cinemagoers. Despite its close affinity with minjung ideology and feminism, the ero film did not rebel against, but rather retreated from, state-led military developmentalism. In the end, the counterdevelopmentalism in the ero film was sometimes progressive and sometimes regressive. It not only retreated from the modern capitalist rat race and its unethical struggle for survival but also into a mobilization of the putative premodern ethnic purity and the national allegorization of Korean women. And yet, whether it was progressive or regressive, 1980s South Korean erotic film reflected a people's structure of feeling amid compressed modernization that is of undiminished historical and cultural importance for our consideration today.

NOTES

1. See, respectively, Yi Hyoin, "1980-yŏndae Han'guk yŏnghwa e taehayŏ," 27; Joo Jinsook et al., *Yŏsŏng yŏnghwain sajŏn*, 276; and Kim Mee Hyun, *Korean Cinema from Origins to Renaissance*, 272.
2. For minjung nationalism, see Namhee Lee, *The Making of Minjung*, and for contemporary feminist activism, see Louie, "Minjung Feminism," and Hye-Ryoung Lee's chapter in this book.
3. For feminist studies of melodrama, see Gledhill, *Home Is Where the Heart Is*, and Linda Williams, *Playing the Race Card*, and her essays "Film Bodies: Gender, Genre, and Excess," "Melodrama Revised," and "Something Else besides a Mother."
4. On the notion of a structure of feeling, see Raymond Williams, *Marxism and Literature*, 132.
5. The term was first used in Taisho Japan (1912–26), when it was one descriptor of the 1920s popular cultural trend known as *ero-guro-nansensu* (erotic-grotesque-nonsense). Since then, the term has been widely and variably used in Japan to refer to a quality that is erotic, sexual, obscene, and even perverse. The word was immediately adopted in Korea in a similar meaning, but it is today mostly associated with the ero films of the 1980s. For the terminological history of "ero" in modern Japan, see Silverberg, *Erotic Grotesque Nonsense*, and for its usage in modern Japanese film discourse, see Bordwell, *Ozu and the Poetics of Cinema*, esp. 151. For the Korean adoption of the term, see So Raesŏp, *Ero-Gŭro-Nŏnsensŭ*.
6. See Richie, "The Japanese Eroduction," in *A Lateral View*, 156–69.

7. According to Jasper Sharp, a Japanese sports newspaper (the *Naigai Times*) journalist, Murai Minoru, was the first one who called the eroduction films *pinku eiga*, recommending an opening of a Pink Ribbon Award for the genre vis-à-vis the Blue Ribbon Award, in which the best Japanese (mainstream) films were selected and awarded by film critics and journalists every year. See Sharp, *Behind the Pink Curtain*, 53.

8. For the history of Japanese erotic cinema, see also Standish, *Politics, Porn, and Protest*.

9. *Salò* is a film adaptation of the Marquis de Sade's novel *120 Days of Sodom*.

10. *In the Realm of the Senses* was in fact produced by a Frenchman, Anatole Dauman, who asked director Oshima to direct a sexual art film. Thus, the film's personnel was entirely Japanese, yet the film expressed in many ways the Euro-American spirit of revolt against repressive political authority. Besides, Japan's economic and cultural position in the 1960s and 1970s was relatively close to that of Western countries. On *In the Realm of the Senses* and Oshima Nagisa, see L. Williams, *Screening Sex*; Heath, *Questions of Cinema*; and Turim, *The Films of Oshima Nagisa*.

11. See L. Williams, *Screening Sex*, 155–80.

12. Ho Hyŏnch'an, *Han'guk yŏnghwa*, 246.

13. Watching the scene, it is said that some audiences left the theater, and some were even disgusted enough to vomit. *TV Report*, April 21, 2011.

14. See Kim Soo-yong, *Na ŭi sarang ssinema*, 66. The film was a remake of a Japanese pink film titled *Daydream* (1964, dir. Takechi Tetsuji).

15. Ibid., 65.

16. Ho Hyŏnch'an, *Han'guk yŏnghwa*, 252.

17. See Hunt, *The Invention of Pornography*. In her introduction, Hunt traces the etymological origin of "pornography" to a 1769 French article titled "Le Pornographe" and published by Rétif de la Bretonne.

18. In blending the class struggle with eroticism and sexuality, Kim directed woman-series films such as *Woman of Fire* (*Hwanyŏ*, 1971), *The Insect Woman* (*Ch'ungnyŏ*, 1972), *Ieodo* (*Iŏdo*, 1977), and *Water Woman* (*Sunyŏ*, 1979). Better known for *The March of Fools* (*Pabodŭl ŭi haengjin*, 1975), the representative youth film of the seventies, Ha also delved into the relations between political power and eroticism in his *The Pollen of Flowers* (*Hwabun*, 1972), *Fidelity* (*Sujŏl*, 1973), and *The Ascension of Han-ne* (*Han-ne ŭi sŭngch'ŏn*).

19. In a rare exception, Kim Ho-sun's *Winter Woman* (*Kyŏul yŏja*, 1977) featured a female college student, rather than a hostess, who gives up her virginity to comfort any unfortunate man around her. She does this after her high school sweetheart's suicide in frustration for her refusal to have sexual intercourse with him. The film broke the previous box-office record of *Heavenly Homecoming to Stars*, suggesting that South Koreans responded strongly to the film's representation of ordinary female sexuality.

20. In the 1980s, a film was usually first released in a theater in Seoul for a while and then the negative was moved to other local theaters in South Korea. The given record was counted by the Korean Film Council based on the number of cinemagoers for a certain film in Seoul. On the screening of *Madame Aema*, see Ho Hyŏn-ch'an, *Han'guk yŏnghwa*, 244–55, and Kang Sowŏn, "P'alsip-yŏndae han'guk yŏnghwa," 18.

21. Joo Jinsook et al., *Yŏsŏng yŏnghwain*, 287.

22. Sim San, "Aema puin ŭi abŏji–Lee Moon-woong," quoted from its English translation in Mee Hyun Kim, *Korean Cinema from Origins to Renaissance*, 278–79.

23. On the emergence of ero video in 1990s Korea, see Yi Kyodong, "Chŏtso puin ŭl wihan pyŏnmyŏng."

24. In her PhD dissertation on South Korean erotic films of the 1980s, Kang Sowŏn counts the number of sex scenes in them and concludes that there were initially less than three scenes per film in the early eighties, but they increased up to seven on average in the late eighties. See Kang Sowŏn, "1980-yŏndae Han'guk 'sŏngae yŏnghwa.'"

25. Joo Jinsook et al., Yŏsŏng yŏnghwain, 277.

26. See Mies, Patriarchy and Accumulation on a World Scale, 74–111.

27. See Mulvey, Visual and Other Pleasures. As I have argued elsewhere, this author's discussion of sexuality and spectatorship appears at times to polarize excessively between male voyeurism and fetishism, on the one hand, and female to-be-looked-at-ness on the other. Left out of this picture, I suggest, are phenomena such as female spectatorship, female fetishism, and queer possibilities. See Yun-Jong Lee, "Cinema of Retreat," 33–75.

28. Yu Gina, "Yŏsŏng mom ŭi changnŭ," 80–84.

29. Kang Sowŏn, "P'alsip-yŏndae Han'guk yŏnghwa," 57.

30. Echols, "Cultural Feminism," 35.

31. Morgan, "Theory and Practice," 139.

32. L. Williams, Hard Core, 22 and 20.

33. Ibid., 170.

34. Ibid., 28.

35. Ibid., 269.

36. Ho Hyŏnch'an, Han'guk yŏnghwa, 246.

37. Joo Jinsook et al., Yŏsŏng yŏnghwain, 263.

38. Seung-Hyun Park, "Korean Cinema after Liberation," 21.

39. Directors Jung and Lee proudly comment on the technological innovation of the DVD versions of Parrot Cries with Its Body and Spinning the Tales of Cruelty toward Women, respectively.

40. For a more detailed discussion, see Yun-Jong Lee, "Woman in Ethnocultural Peril."

41. Cumings, Korea's Place in the Sun, 388.

42. On the gendered aspects of the public-private distinction in South Korea, see Kendall, Under Construction, 10.

43. See Enloe, Globalization and Militarism, 34. Among other things, Enloe details the ways in which Park Chung Hee succeeded in turning countless South Korean young women into low-paid laborers by convincing rural parents that their daughters' stint at urban factories would give them good chances to marry well.

44. A kisaeng is a traditional Korean courtesan and artist-performer who is professionally trained to serve noblemen. Since foreign tourists from the West and Japan were much more affluent than ordinary South Korean customers during the Cold War, sex workers specialized for the tourists were deemed modern kisaengs, high-class call girls.

45. See Jin-kyung Lee, Service Economies.

46. Ibid., 1.

47. On the role of sex work and tourism in Korea's compressed modernization, see Pak Chŏngmi, "Palchŏn kwa seksŭ."

48. For a more detailed discussion of this theme, see Yun-Jong Lee, "Women in Ethnocultural Peril."

49. Jung-Bong Choi, "National Cinema: An Anachronistic Delirium?," 183.
50. Chungmoo Choi, "The Discourse of Decolonization and Popular Memory," 480.
51. Chungmoo Choi, "The *Minjung* Culture Movement and the Construction of Popular Culture in Korea," 117.
52. Fiske, *Understanding Popular Culture*, 127.
53. Altman, *Film/Genre*, 99 and 84.

REFERENCES

Altman, Rick. *Film/Genre*. London: BFI Publishing, 1999.
Bordwell, David. *Ozu and the Poetics of Cinema*. London: BFI Publishing, 1988.
Choi, Chungmoo. "The Discourse of Decolonization and Popular Memory: South Korea." In *The Politics of Culture in the Shadow of Capital*, edited by Lisa Lowe and David Lloyd, 461–84. Durham: Duke University Press, 1997.
Choi, Chungmoo. "The *Minjung* Culture Movement and the Construction of Popular Culture in Korea." In *South Korea's Minjung Movement*, edited by Kenneth M. Wells, 105–18.
Choi, Jung-Bong. "National Cinema: An Anachronistic Delirium?" *Journal of Korean Studies* 16, no. 2 (2011): 173–91.
Cumings, Bruce. *Korea's Place in the Sun: A Modern History*. New York: Norton, 2005.
Echols, Alice. "Cultural Feminism: Feminist Capitalism and the Anti-Pornography Movement." *Social Texts* 7 (Spring–Summer 1983): 34–53.
Enloe, Cynthia. *Globalization and Militarism: Feminists Make the Link*. 2007; New York: Rowman & Littlefield, 2016.
Fiske, John. *Understanding Popular Culture*. 1989; New York: Routledge, 2010.
Gateward, Frances, ed. *Seoul Searching: Culture and Identity in Contemporary Korean Cinema*. Albany: State University of New York Press, 2007.
Gledhill, Christine. *Home Is Where the Heart Is: Studies in Melodrama and the Woman's Film*. London: British Film Institute, 1987.
Gledhill, Christine, and Linda Williams, eds. *Reinventing Film Studies*. New York: Oxford University Press, 2000.
Hansen, Miriam Bratu. "The Mass Production of the Senses: Classical Cinema as Vernacular Modernism." In *Reinventing Film Studies*, edited by Christine Gledhill and Linda Williams, 332–50.
Heath, Stephen. *Questions of Cinema*. Bloomington: Indiana University Press, 1981.
Ho Hyŏnch'an. *Han'guk yŏnghwa paengnyŏn* [One hundred years of Korean cinema]. Munhak sasangsa, 2003.
Hunt, Lynn, ed. *The Invention of Pornography, 1500–1800: Obscenity and the Origins of Modernity*. New York: Zone Books, 1996.
Joo Jinsook et al. *Yŏsŏng yŏnghwain sajŏn* [Dictionary of women filmmakers]. Sodo, 2001.
Kang Sowŏn. "1980-yŏndae Han'guk 'sŏngae yŏnghwa' ŭi seksyuŏliti wa chendŏ chaehyŏn" [The representation of sexuality and gender in 1980s Korean adult films]. PhD diss., Chungang University, 2006.
Kang Sowŏn. "P'alsip-yŏndae han'guk yŏnghwa" [1980s Korean films]. In *Han'guk yŏnghwasa kongbu 1980–1997*, edited by Yu Gina, 9–79. Ichae, 2005.

Kaplan, E. Anne, ed. *Feminism and Film*. Oxford: Oxford University Press, 2000.
Kendall, Laurel. Introduction to *Under Construction: The Gendering of Modernity, Class, and Consumption in the Republic of Korea*, edited by Laurel Kendall, 1–24. Honolulu: University of Hawai'i Press, 2002.
Kim, Mee Hyun, ed. *Korean Cinema from Origins to Renaissance*. Communication Books, 2007.
Kim Soo-yong. *Na ŭi sarang ssinema: Kim Su-yong kamdok ŭi Han'guk yŏnghwa iyagi*. [My love cinema: Dir. Kim Su-yong's Korean film stories]. Cine 21, 2005.
Ko Kilsŏp et al. *Munhwa ikki: Ppira esŏ saibŏ munhwa kkaji* [Reading culture: From leaflets to cyberculture]. Hyŏnsil munhwa yŏn'gu, 1999.
Koo, Hagen. "The State, Minjung, and the Working Class in South Korea." In *State and Society in Contemporary Korea*, edited by Hagen Koo, 131–62. Ithaca: Cornell University Press, 1993.
Lederer, Laura, ed. *Take Back the Night: Women on Pornography*. New York: Morrow, 1980.
Lee, Jin-kyung. *Service Economies: Militarism, Sex Work, and Migrant Labor in South Korea*. Minneapolis: University of Minnesota Press, 2010.
Lee, Namhee. *The Making of Minjung: Democracy and the Politics of Representation in South Korea*. Ithaca: Cornell University Press, 2007.
Lee, Yun-Jong. "Cinema of Retreat: Examining South Korean Erotic Films of the 1980s." PhD diss., University of California, Irvine, 2012.
Lee, Yun-Jong. "Woman in Ethnocultural Peril: South Korean Nationalist Erotic Films of the 1980s." *Journal of Korean Studies* 21, no. 1 (2016): 101–35.
Louie, Miriam Ching Yoon. "Minjung Feminism: Korean Women's Movement for Gender and Class Liberation." In *Global Feminisms since 1945*, edited by Bonnie G. Smith, 119–38. New York: Routledge, 2000.
Mies, Maria. *Patriarchy and Accumulation on a World Scale: Women in the International Division of Labour*. London: Zed Books, 1998.
Morgan, Robin. "Theory and Practice: Pornography and Rape." In *Take Back the Night: Women on Pornography*, edited by Laura Lederer, 134–40.
Mulvey, Laura. *Visual and Other Pleasures*. 1989; New York: Palgrave Macmillan, 2009.
Pak Chŏngmi. "Palchŏn kwa seksŭ: Han'guk chŏngbu ŭi sŏng maemae kwan'gwang chŏngch'aek, 1955–1988-yŏn" [Development and sex: Korean government's sex trade and tourism policy]. *Korean Journal of Sociology* 48, no. 1 (2014): 235–64.
Park, Seung Hyun. "Korean Cinema after Liberation: Production, Industry, and Regulatory Trends." In *Seoul Searching: Culture and Identity in Contemporary Korean Cinema*, edited by Frances Gateward, 15–35.
Richie, Donald. *A Lateral View: Essays on Culture and Style in Contemporary Japan*. Berkeley: Stone Bridge Press, 1987.
Sharp, Jasper. *Behind the Pink Curtain: The Complete History of Japanese Sex Cinema*. London: FAB Press, 2008.
Silverberg, Miriam. *Erotic Grotesque Nonsense: The Mass Culture of Japanese Modern Times*. Berkeley: University of California Press, 2006.
Sim San. "*Aema puin ŭi abŏji*–Lee Moon-woong." *Cine 21*, no. 296, April 3, 2001, 3–10.
So Raesŏp. *Ero-gŭro-nŏnsensŭ: Kŭndaejŏk chagŭk ŭi t'ansaeng* [Ero, guro, nonsense: The birth of modern sensations]. Salim, 2005.

Standish, Isolde. *Politics, Porn, and Protest: Japanese Avant-Garde Cinema in the 1960s and 1970s*. New York: Continuum, 2011.
Turim, Maureen. *The Films of Oshima Nagisa: Images of a Japanese Iconoclast*. Berkeley: University of California Press, 1998.
Wells, Kenneth M., ed. *South Korea's Minjung Movement: The Culture and Politics of Dissidence*. Honolulu: University of Hawai'i Press, 1995.
Williams, Linda. "Discipline and Fun: *Psycho* and Postmodern Cinema." In *Reinventing Film Studies*, edited by Gledhill and Williams, 351–78.
Williams, Linda. "Film Bodies: Gender, Genre, and Excess." *Film Quarterly* 44, no. 4 (1991): 2–13.
Williams, Linda. *Hard Core: Power, Pleasure, and the "Frenzy of the Visible."* 1989; Berkeley: University of California Press, 1999.
Williams, Linda. "Melodrama Revised." In *Refiguring American Film Genres: History and Theory*, edited by Nick Browne, 42–88. Berkeley: University of California Press, 1998.
Williams, Linda. *Playing the Race Card: Melodramas of Black and White from Uncle Tom to O. J. Simpson*. Princeton: Princeton University Press, 2002.
Williams, Linda, ed. *Porn Studies*. Durham: Duke University Press, 2004.
Williams, Linda. *Screening Sex*. Durham: Duke University Press, 2008.
Williams, Linda. "Something Else Besides a Mother: *Stella Dallas* and the Maternal Melodrama." In *Feminism and Film*, edited by E. Ann Kaplan, 479–504.
Williams, Linda Ruth. *The Erotic Thriller in Contemporary Cinema*. Bloomington: Indiana University Press, 2005.
Williams, Raymond. *Marxism and Literature*. New York: Oxford University Press, 1977.
Yi Hyoin. "1980-yŏndae Han'guk yŏnghwa e taehayŏ" [On 1980s Korean films]. *Yŏnghwa ŏno* 4 (Winter 1989): 26–42.
Yi Kyodong. "Chŏtso puin ŭl wihan pyŏnmyŏng: Ero video wa chŏngch'i kyŏngjehak" [Apology for Madam Milk Cow: The political economy of ero video]. In *Munhwa ikki: Ppira esŏ saibŏ munhwa kkaji*, edited by Ko Kilsŏp et al., 478–87. Hyŏnsil munhwa yŏn'gu, 1999.
Yu Gina, ed. *Han'guk yŏnghwasa kongbu 1980–1997* [A study of Korean film history 1980–1997]. Ichae, 2005.
Yu Gina. "*Yŏsŏng mom ŭi changnŭ: Kŭndaehwa ŭi sangch'ŏ*" [Women's bodies and the genre: The wounds of modernization]. In *Han'guk yŏnghwa seksyuŏliti rŭl mannada* [Korean cinema meets sexuality], edited by Yu Gina, 77–98. Saengkak ŭi namu, 2004.

11

Reciprocal Assets

Science Fiction and Democratization in 1980s South Korea

Sunyoung Park

In one of the central scenes of Kim Chunbŏm's graphic novel *Metal Brain 109* (*Kigye chŏnsa 109*; 1989), the human-brained cyborg Cher is seen standing proud and waving the flag of the Cyborg Liberation Front.[1] The Front has at this point effectively been defeated, surrounded as it is by the better-equipped Human Army. The time is the early twenty-first century, and the context is that of the cyborg population's uprising against its bondage to human masters. Relationships have deteriorated since the so-called Science Revolution War of the 2010s, in which cyborg soldiers were an indispensable tool in the triumph of pro-science humans against a more traditionalist human faction. Under the leadership of Demos, a human who was raised by cyborgs, the cyborgs have for years vindicated their rights by fighting a war of resistance. They have managed to occupy a large energy complex, which has in the meantime become a sanctuary and the main hub of cyborg forces. Today, however, all that is coming to an end. Demos has been apparently shot and killed, and the complex is under siege. Defiantly, Cher vows to fight through the end: "The Cyborg Liberation Front will fight to defend our base until the last one of us falls."[2] She is then shot by MX-16, who is the head of the Human Army and, in a related plot, her ex-husband. The vile execution provokes the cyborgs who, in response, engage in a desperate riot against the humans.

Like many other products of the golden age of Korean *manhwa* (comics), *Metal Brain 109* (hereafter *Metal Brain*) took much of its inspiration

Fig. 11.1. The female cyborg Cher leading the Cyborg Liberation Front in Kim Chunbŏm's *Metal Brain 109*. Courtesy of Korean Manhwa Contents Agency (KOMACON).

from some easily identifiable Hollywood sources. The theme of class struggle between cyborgs and humans, for instance, was reminiscent of Ridley Scott's *Blade Runner* (1982). Also, Cher's character in the story closely resembled that of Sarah Connor in James Cameron's *The Terminator* (1984), and the image of Demos was drawn in the likeness of Arnold Schwarzenegger in that movie. The illustrator, Kim Chunbŏm, even paid explicit homage to early 1980s cyberpunk films by borrowing their names for some of the restaurants and cafés in the backgrounds of his scenes. As a recent interview confirms, Kim was himself a fan of those Hollywood blockbusters, and he counted on a like-minded reaction from his young audience to secure the commercial success of the graphic novel.[3]

Merely pointing to its filmic sources, however, is a way of missing an equally important but less obvious set of references that lies behind *Metal Brain*. In fact, an episode tragically similar to the cyborg uprising had actually taken place in the city of Kwangju, South Korea, in May 1980, when the Korean government used lethal force to quash one of the popular demonstrations that would eventually lead to democratization in 1987. Appearing in 1989, *Metal Brain* contained several unmistakable references to the Kwangju massacre. The sacrificial heroine Cher was therein celebrated as "the Flower of the Liberation Front," recalling how Chŏn Okchu, a television broadcaster, had come to be known as "the Flower of May 18" for her rousing but unheeded pleas to soldiers in Kwangju. The episode of a prison riot by the cyborgs, elsewhere in *Metal Brain*, fictionally reproduced events that were known of the infamous Samchŏng Reeducation Camp (Samchŏng kyoyuktae), a concentration camp facility that operated between August 1980 and January 1981 and became the emblem of the abuses of Chun Doo Hwan's regime. Finally, the self-immolation of a cyborg who climbs a TV tower, along with the subsequent funeral, was reminiscent of the many public suicides by protesters in the 1980s, which were also typically followed by mass funeral marches in remembrance of the deceased. At a time of extreme tensions in South Korea's political life, it turns out, *Metal Brain* made use of Hollywood's fantastic tropes to give allegorical representation to the era's very real struggle for democratization.

The link between democratization and popular culture in 1980s Korea, a link that is exemplified here by *Metal Brain*, is today still an unexplored topic within the academic study of Korean culture. There are a few reasons for this. One is that the cultural referent of the minjung democratization movement in Korea has historically been realist literature, which seems to share little with the science fictional vagaries of popular cultural products such as *Metal Brain*. Another reason is that the very mention of popular culture in 1980s Korea may strike one as odd, as it is widely believed that science fiction, mystery, and other "lighter" genres began to flourish in the country only during the more liberal and democratic decade of the 1990s.

In setting out to connect science fiction and democratization in 1980s Korea, the present chapter aims to put pressure on both of the above ideas. If a realist aesthetic is today rightly seen as the core of minjung culture, it is also important to notice the ways in which writers of other literary genres, including science fiction, managed to convey the era's activist spirit. Moreover, if science fiction indeed enjoyed its explosion only during the 1990s, it would be a mistake to neglect the ways in which that success was grounded in the achievements of the previous decade. This chapter is composed of two main sections. The first section will lay out some of the characteristics of minjung culture in 1980s Korea, in a synoptic attempt that is not definitive but functional in presenting the dialectic of the chapter. The second section will then provide an introduction and commentary to one of the most significant literary works of 1980s Korea: Bok Geo-il's 1987 alternate history novel *In Search of an Epitaph* (*Pimyŏng ŭl ch'ajasŏ*; henceforth *Epitaph*).[4] Based on this work's analysis, a brief conclusion will reiterate the main suggestion of the chapter: that against odds, the cultural form of science fiction and the political process of democratization in many ways aided each other in 1980s Korea. Whereas science fiction often promoted the values of democratization, the democratization movement in its turn gave a form of political legitimation to the writing of science fiction. Vis-à-vis each other the two could be seen, in effect, as reciprocal assets.

Minjung Politics, Culture, and Speculative Fiction

The provincial city of Kwangju is where the South Korean process of democratization had its turning point in early 1980. On May 18 of that year, students, workers, and local citizens staged a demonstration in protest of Chun Doo Hwan's coup d'état following the 1979 assassination of President Pak Chung Hee. They were met with brutal force by the army, whose attack on the crowd eventually left more than a hundred dead and thousands more injured.[5] The military regime subsequently sought to erase the bloody memory of the massacre by silencing the media and blaring its propaganda machine. A vast movement of remembrance and information, however, was kept alive through the underground circulation of survivors' testimonials and in the video footage that international journalists were able to smuggle out of the country. The discrepancy between reality and the official version of events deepened South Koreans' mistrust for their government and, in effect, put into question the entire system that had sustained three decades of military dictatorship—from the suppression of labor movements to the censorship of national culture, the outsize usage of martial law, and the American political patronage of the regime.[6] The contradiction between the official glorification of South Korea as a model developing nation and the everyday experience of despotic rule, a contradiction that was epitomized by the savagery in Kwangju, demanded that the system be made to collapse and that history be rewritten with a new subject at its center.

Accompanying the social movements and street protests of early 1980s Korea was a vast coalition of intellectuals, academics, journalists, and students who in many ways provided legitimation and a cultural foundation to the upheaval. What were the ideological ingredients and inspirations of minjung culture? By most accounts, the predominant, in many ways foundational, intellectual event of the early 1980s was the rediscovery of Marxist theories and, in an extension of Marxism aimed at its local application, the introduction of new theoretical formations such as dependency theory and world-systems analysis.[7] The texts bearing these theories were illegal and were mostly circulated through a well-connected underground network of bookstores in university areas.[8] With their inspiration, minjung intellectuals came to the influential conceptualization of 1980s South Korea as a fundamentally polarized and antagonistic society in which the interests of common citizens were at odds with those of the government and the ruling elites. If orthodox leftist theories had typically posited classes as engaged in a struggle for resources and capital, the outlook from 1980s Korea rather identified the stakes of social conflict with each group's claim to represent the true heritage and spirit of the Korean nation. A distinctive characteristic of minjung political ethos was indeed the commingling of the theme of class with that of the nation, a local formation that was evident in the idea of the people—the minjung—as the historical depositories of Korean culture and values.[9]

The minjung's claim to the nation manifested itself prominently in a new form of patriotism that openly shunned countries such as the ex-colonial master Japan, with which Pak Chung Hee's regime had reestablished diplomatic relations in 1965, and especially the United States, whose influence on South Korea was with some grounds deemed to be imperialistic in nature. In addition to having decreed the division of North and South Korea in 1945, U.S. authorities were seen as responsible for failing to prevent the massacre at Kwangju, as troops in the operation were under U.S.-Korea joint command.[10] The consequent rejection of American influence came hand in hand with intellectuals' warming to North Korea and to its official doctrine of Korean self-reliance (*chuch'e sasang*).[11] The thawing of relations with North Korea thus became a prominent cause in the movement as a necessary accomplishment of Korea's decolonization process.

Yet another distinctive feature of 1980s activist culture was the widespread sense of the need for a fundamental retelling and rewriting of Korea's modern history. At a time when founding values were a site of contestation, much of the effort of minjung cultural politics was indeed directed at constructing an alternative, counterhegemonic historical narrative of the Korean nation.[12] Contesting the official narrative according to which the year 1945 had marked a clear transition from colonial subjection to liberation, the revisionist historical outlook suggested a lineage between the colonial administration of imperial Japan and the South Korean government under U.S. tutelage. Historians pointed out the continuity in the ranks and personnel of many local administrations before and after liberation, suggesting that the supposed institutional divide may have been more cosmetic than substantial.[13] In this and other research, 1980s historians espoused a form of counterhegemonic historiographical practice that systematically gave priority to civil society over and above the state as the agent of history making. Their work had the effect, among others, of pluralizing national history. No longer a monolinear teleological narrative, Korean history became then a site of dispute and a bundle of narratives competing for truth claims.

Emerging from early-1980s debates was thus a countercultural and revisionist outlook on Korean history and society, a society that came then to be seen as polarized between the minjung and the privileged elites whose rule was secured via collaboration with a neoimperialist foreign power. While it was primarily historians and social scientists who took up the task of developing a coherent theory that was based on this outlook, an important cultural and, perhaps, affective role was also played in the process by novelists, poets, film directors, and other sorts of creative artists. Literature, in particular, was a formidable vehicle of ideological transmission and a natural site for the minjung's reappropriation of national history. Arguably the most celebrated literary work of the decade, Cho Chŏngnae's *The Taebaek Mountains* (*T'aebaek sanmaek*; 1989), narrated the epic story of South Korean natives who became partisans and sided with the North Korean regime during the Korean War. The novel's empathetic depiction of its protagonists broke a taboo of Cold War cultural politics in South Korea. In its attention to detail and the ample documentation of historical events, Cho's ten-volume work set the new standard for the era's positivistic and often reportage-like literary works.[14] In this and other works from the democratization era, works whose genre soon came to be known through the label of "Korean realism," the principle of verisimilitude was an evaluative criterion whose significance was as much political as it was aesthetic. The cultural task of retelling Korean history was simply not practicable at a time when the press was censored and official historiography mostly existed as a cultural extension of the regime. In the precarious political balance of 1980s Korea, the task of reporting facts often fell on the shoulders of writers of fiction, who took enormous risks in doing so.[15]

There is no doubt that, in its historical urgency, realist literature played a paradigmatic role in the cultural landscape of 1980s South Korea. Among other things, the label of "Korean realism" provided contemporary readers with a link to the celebrated tradition of early century realist novels. It was precisely because of its importance, however, that the cultural hegemony of realist fiction in the 1980s also had the consequence of overshadowing other noteworthy cultural formations. This was arguably the case with the vast creative territory that is known as "speculative" fiction and includes science fiction and fantasy as well as, with different parameters, horror, mystery, and more. For one thing, the amount of critical interest that was drawn to realist and modernist fiction in Korea quite inevitably drained academic resources from the study of speculative fiction. Moreover, the predilection for verisimilitude that is at the heart of the realist outlook was detrimental to the fortunes of genres that are by definition irrealist or antirealist. Even aside from the political urgency of the times, Georg Lukács's influential endorsement of realism provided a compelling theoretical basis for minjung critics' rejection of abstract or fantastic texts for their alleged contribution to maintaining a capitalist illusion for the masses, thereby delaying their awakening to class consciousness.[16] The irony is, of course, that in implementing an ideologically motivated vigilance over cultural production, the promoters of minjung realism may have been in unintended agreement with government censors. Both forces, each in their own way, contributed to suppressing allegedly "idle" cultural forms such as science fiction, fantasy, and horror. Activist intellectuals may have found speculative fiction to be not subversive enough in the urgent circumstances of a nation in revolt. The regime's censors, for their part, may have at least glimpsed an insubordinate element in the sort of literature and film that did not explicitly conform to the government's policies.[17]

In spite of an adverse critical environment, however, works in science fiction and other speculative genres were written and even enjoyed noteworthy success in 1980s Korea. It is possible to say, concerning science fiction, that the subversive and liberational energy released through democratization contributed to the overall increased production in the genre during the late 1980s. Particularly after the civil democratic victory, science fiction authors thrived and generated works such as Bok Geo-il's *Epitaph*, Sin Ilsuk's feminist romance *Born in 1999* (*1999-yŏnsaeng*; 1988), Kim Chunbŏm's *Metal Brain* (1989), and Sin Kihwal's postapocalyptic *manhwa* satire *The Chronicles of the Nuclear Bugs* (*Haekch'ung i nat'anatta*; 1985–87; reprinted in book form in 1989). Partly owing to the technological challenges of special effects, the science fiction boom in domestic film production did not arrive until the early 2000s, yet as early as in 1996, director Kang Jae-kyu's *Ginko Bed* (*Ŭnhaeng namu ch'imdae*) marked the advent of a locally produced sci-fi fantasy blockbuster.[18] The artistic achievement as well as the commercial success of these works paved the way for the current popularity of science fiction literature, film, and comics in South Korea.

Against the background of the current critical discourses, and in consideration of its several understudied aspects, it is important for us today to carry out a contextualized study of science fiction (as well as other popular genres) in the politically heated environment of 1980s South Korea. What impact did the democratization movement have on the development of science fiction in the decade? And what discursive function, if any, did science fictional works perform in democratizing Korean society? By raising these questions, I am proposing that we engage in a historically nuanced reading of Korean science fiction, instead of approaching it as merely a derivative of transnational cultural trends or as a passive reflection of accelerating technological modernity. There is no question that, especially during the 1980s, American SF cultural products enjoyed vast representation and success in South Korea. And it seems clear that the continued industrial development of Korean society throughout the 1980s, as well as the propagation of personal computers from the mid-1980s on, significantly contributed to the increase of interest in science fiction among the local public. Global influences and technological advancement alone, however, do not provide a sufficient explanation for the formal and thematic specificities of 1980s science fictional works, nor do they account for their discursive roles in the local context. For a more satisfactory account, we need to take a closer look at specific texts and their significance within their own social and cultural milieu.

In the following section, I will begin to probe the social and political significance of science fiction in 1980s Korea by analyzing one of the genre's most important texts: Bok Geo-il's *Epitaph*. As I will suggest, Bok's work can be read as part of a vein of science fiction that, short of being alien to the project of democratization, in many ways was ideologically (though not stylistically) continuous with it. I will go as far as to propose the label of "minjung science fiction" for what I believe to be a distinct science fictional trend of the decade of the 1980s. Labels, of course, are just that: signposts that we place there to signify certain territories. If it can be agreed that such a territorial demarcation is not entirely arbitrary, however, we will have achieved the result of beginning our scholarly engagement with science fiction as a critical genre in 1980s South Korea.

Fig. 11.2. The cover of Bok Geo-il's *In Search of an Epitaph* (1987). Courtesy of Munhak kwa chisŏngsa.

Back to the Colonial Present: Bok Geo-il's *In Search of an Epitaph*

In Search of an Epitaph was the first novel to be published by the then thirty-nine-year-old writer Bok Geo-il. It was the work that launched Bok's long and prolific career as a science fiction writer. He then went on to publish *A Wanderer of History* (*Yŏksa sok ŭi nagŭne*; 1988–90), the story of a twenty-first-century time traveler in sixteenth-century Korea, and *Under the Blue Moon* (*P'aran tal arae*; 1992), a futuristic tale of a rivalry between the two Koreas on their respective Moon bases.[19] Bok had come to literature and creative writing relatively late in his life, after an early career as a middle manager in the financial and commercial sectors. In his recollection, he was first exposed to Western science fiction while growing up next to a U.S. military base, and he continued to read and collect science fiction novels in English while pursuing his business career.[20]

The alternate-historical geopolitical premise of *Epitaph*—that Korea was still under Japanese colonial domination in the 1980s—quite directly took its narrative inspiration from Philip K. Dick's classic *The Man in the High Castle*, a novel that indeed sported a closely related novum in the imagination of the United States under Japanese and German domination in the 1960s.[21] Bok's novel, however, also had important local precedents in Choi In-hun's alternate history novels *The Voice of the Governor-General* (*Ch'ongdok ŭi sori*; 1967–76) and *The Typhoon* (*T'aep'ung*; 1973), both of which involved a postcolonial setting. The former work featured a series of radio-broadcast monologues by a fictional Japanese governor-general, who went underground in independent Korea in order to conspire for the country's recolonization.[22] The latter instead reimagined the last years of the Pacific War and its aftermaths, and it projected a utopian vision in which Korea and the East Asian region were radically decolonized and free from outside imperial influences.[23] While Bok explicitly acknowledged his inspiration from Dick's novel, he never quite expounded on his relation to Choi's novels and never showed any indication of his awareness of these local precedents. It is possible that Bok had not read Choi's works, as they were regarded as rather minor within Choi's mostly modernist production. Regardless, it is interesting how the narrative genre of alternate history, with its potential for counterfactual historical exploration, provided an especially congenial form for Korean authors who were interested in postcolonial themes.

The perhaps most notable fact about *Epitaph*'s reception history is the immediate success that the novel enjoyed among a reading public that, by all appearances, was not in the 1980s particularly attuned to science fiction and the speculative genres. One possible reason for this success was the recent popularity of imported Hollywood time-travel movies such as *The Terminator* (1984) and *Back to the Future* (1985). As the pages that follow will make clear, however, another important explanation lies in the thematic composition of *Epitaph* as a novel written at the climax of the process of democratization in South Korea. In its deep-reaching reflection on history, its rewriting, and the processes of its appropriation, along with its related musings on the very existence of historical reality, Bok's novel struck many chords among a public that was just then waking up to the mission of reinterpreting Korea's historical experience through a narrative that placed the Korean people at its center.

As the novel's subtitle, "Kyŏngsŏng, Shōwa 62," suggests, the plot of

Epitaph takes its departure from the fictional time-space of colonial Seoul (Kyŏngsŏng) in 1987. We are in the sixty-second year of the reign of Emperor Hirohito ("Shōwa" in his regal name) over Japan and its vast colonial empire. A brief preface, extrafictionally penned by Bok Geo-il himself, lays out the novel's fictive premise and its novum: counter to historical fact, Prince Itō Hirubumi, former resident-general of Korea, was not killed by Korean independence fighter An Chunggŭn in the city of Harbin in 1909. Having survived the assassination attempt, Itō went on to become governor-general of Korea upon the 1910 establishment of Japan's colonial rule over the peninsula, and in that position he pursued a policy of complete integration of the Korean Peninsula into the Japanese empire. The policy has proven successful, and the Koreans are reported to have become "completely assimilated" by the 1940s. Japan, in this alternative version of history, has gone through World War II unscathed thanks to its maintenance of political neutrality under the leadership of Prime Minister Tōjō Hideki. With its far-flung territory encompassing Korea, Manchuria, Taiwan, and the Marshall Islands in the Pacific, Japan has become a powerful empire in its own right, sitting next in the world only to the American and Soviet superpowers. In this reimagined postwar world order, it is Poland, not Korea, that is divided into two countries. A unified, never divided Korea is instead a prosperous colony of the Japanese empire and is about to host the 1988 Olympic Games—not unlike the real Seoul in which Bok lived.

As a record of the year Shōwa 62, *Epitaph* is composed of twelve chapters that are progressively named after the months of the calendar. "January" opens by introducing readers to the novel's ethnic Korean protagonist, Kinoshita Hideyo, as he goes through his morning routine of shaving, washing, and watering the house plants. A graduate of Kyŏngsŏng Imperial University, Hideyo is a thirty-nine-year-old middle manager at Handō (Peninsula) Metal Inc., a medium-sized company that produces aluminum. His white-collar office job allows him to live comfortably in a middle-class apartment with his Korean wife Setsuko and his teenage daughter Keiko. Hideyo is well off but not quite wealthy, as we learn from his morning musings that he cannot yet afford a car, which, as in real 1980s Korea, was then becoming the status symbol of bourgeois living.

A well-adjusted citizen and functionary within Japan's industrial complex, Hideyo lives the modest, unpretentious life of a Korean minority but, the reader soon realizes, he does not know Korean. As Bok reveals in the beginning and at various places throughout the novel, Japan's colonial authority has for decades pursued the systematic erasure of Korean culture and its memory on the peninsula. Hideyo is thus now oblivious to the fact that Korea had its own centuries-old political, cultural, and linguistic autonomy. He is surprised to read of the former existence of a "Korean government" in a banned book (89). He also listens with fascination to his uncle's tale about Pak Hyŏkkŏse, the mythical founder of the ancient Korean kingdom of Silla (128), and he barely recognizes the *han'gŭl* alphabet when he spots its "strange characters" (*natsŏn kŭlcha*) in a book of Korean poetry at a used bookstore (134).

Having set up the scenery of a quiet, unremarkable life, *Epitaph* proceeds to relate the series of events and circumstances that will eventually turn its protagonist into a murderer and a fugitive. Hideyo, we learn in "January," is also a poet and an avid reader. Having cultivated a passion for Japanese classical poetry since his youth, he is now about to publish his first collection of poems on themes related to Buddhism and naturalist philosophy. Hideyo's readings are disparate, mostly centered on religion and spirituality, and they appear to have the function of satisfying his uncommon intellectual curiosity. One day, however, Mr. Tanaka Shuji, a Japanese senior colleague and a fellow lover of books, cautiously hands Hideyo a hand-copied manuscript of a novel titled *Tokyo, Winter, Shōwa 61*. The work, Mr. Tanaka explains, has been banned by the authorities and should be handled with utmost secrecy. He himself received the manuscript from a good friend at Tokyo Imperial University. The novel's author appears to be someone whose name is "Takano Tatsukichi," a pseudonym that combines the (fictional) names of a well-known labor activist and a more obscure convicted member of the anti-imperialist resistance movement (69). Hideyo immediately recognizes in Mr. Tanaka a likely member of the resistance, and upon reading the manuscript he understands the reasons for its ban. In vivid, extremely realistic detail, *Tokyo* fancifully relates a "history" that is radically alternative to the one Hideyo knows. Contrary to fact, Itō Hirobumi did not survive the attempt on his life in 1909. A consequence of this was that Japan suffered a devastating loss in World War II, and that event, in turn, had the effect of Korea's gaining its independence from Japan in 1945. The counterhistorical imagination of an independent Korea makes a strong impression on Hideyo, who, for the first time in the novel, questions his second-class status as a minority within the Japanese empire.

After the introduction of the manuscript, *Epitaph* goes on to chronicle Hideyo's mounting interest in exploring the actual history of Japan, the empire, and Korea as part of it. His first encounter is with another banned book by (fictional) Japanese historian Sano Hisaichi, titled *Essays in His-*

tory (*Toksa sup'il*). The book, a worn-out copy of which was picked up at a Tokyo bookstore by Hideyo's brother-in-law, reveals to Hideyo that Korea once was a sovereign nation with its own culture and language, not unlike China and Vietnam today. The eye-opening discovery makes Hideyo want to know more. In a Kyŏngsŏng second-hand bookstore, he finds a book of classical Korean poetry that has been annotated by a Japanese scholar. Out of his desire to hear the Korean poems recited, he seeks out an old Buddhist monk who lives in a remote temple in the mountains. The monk presents Hideyo with yet another banned book: a volume of the poems of Han Yongun, a renowned Buddhist monk and a nationalist intellectual of early twentieth-century Korea.

With his innocence and historical consciousness profoundly upset, Hideyo finds himself unable to resume his quiet life of the everyday. He volunteers for an overseas trip to the Tokyo branch of his company with the intention of looking for books related to Korea (331). Once there, he searches through bookstores and libraries for more evidence of Korea's quasi-forgotten past. His travels eventually take him to the library at Kyoto University where, in the fictional world of *Epitaph*, most Korean books have been stored away by the authorities in pursuit of their policy of cultural erasure. He decides to appropriate some Korean dictionaries, history books, and poetry books, which he tries to smuggle back into Korea. Once at the airport, however, his plan is discovered and he is arrested by the police. Hideyo's situation is serious, and the political circumstances only compound the gravity of his arrest. As we learn in "July," a new military regime has recently been installed in Kyoto, the consequence of a coup d'état by the imperial army against a new, more democratic government. Hideyo is imprisoned and put under torture. He is pressed to commit to "ideological conversion" (*chŏnhyang*) via the practice of recantation of his past mistakes along with a promise to correct them (424). Eventually, a brutal indoctrination session with a converted former "thought criminal" (*sasangbŏm*) sees Hideyo forced to "convert" and pledge his renewed loyalty to the emperor. Once released on probation, Hideyo discovers that his supervised status as a "thought offender" is now threatening to undermine his employment at Handō Metal. His job is saved only thanks to the timely intervention of an American colleague named Michael Braunel. As a functionary of a U.S.-based multinational that partners with Handō, Braunel commands enough power to protect his Korean friend from abuse within the company's hierarchy.

The misery of his colonial condition, however, follows Hideyo home. He soon discovers that his wife Setsuko is having an extramarital affair with Major Aoki, who is the husband of one of her friends as well as the official with whom she has lobbied for Hideyo's release. Hideyo has no choice but to accept the situation. After all, he too has had an intense crush for Shimazu Tokie, a junior Japanese colleague who loved poetry and who eventually married an American colleague named Anderson. In a display of goodwill, Hideyo organizes a birthday party in honor of Setsuko, with Mayor Aoki and his wife among the invitees. The night goes well until Hideyo catches a drunken Aoki attempting to rape his daughter Keiko in the bathroom. At this climax of *Epitaph*'s plot, an enraged Hideyo strangles Aoki to death with a fishing line. It is an act of blind revenge that definitively ends Hideyo's quiet existence as a citizen (albeit a minority) of imperial Japan. The next morning, Hideyo sneaks out to catch a flight to Shanghai, China. His plan is to join the Provisional Government of Korea, of whose existence he had learned by reading a special issue of the American magazine *Newsworld* on the theme of colonialism. The novel closes on its protagonist's mulling over his own condition. "I am not a fugitive," Hideyo reflects. "I am an exile who sets out to find a land where he can live as himself" (509).[24]

As the alternate history of profoundly dystopian circumstances, *Epitaph*'s initial, most immediate effect is that of comforting readers through a form of negative eulogy of actual reality. In *Epitaph*, as in Dick's *The Man in the High Castle*, the imagination of a world dominated by the Axis powers functions in many ways to elicit the reader's relief at the fact that actual history did not turn out that way. At the same time, however, *Epitaph* also establishes several allusive links between its own dark imagination and the contemporary reality of 1980s South Korea. Notably reflected in the novel were actual current circumstances like the government's surveillance and censorship of print and mass media, the use of torture and extrajudicial killing by the police (246–47, 391–92), and the practice by citizens of tuning out official channels of information in favor of alternative underground sources.[25] The coup d'état at the heart of *Epitaph*, for instance, would easily remind Korean readers of President Chun Doo Hwan's military coup in 1979, when the then major general seized power in the immediate aftermath of the assassination of president Pak Chung Hee. And Hideyo's fear of the "poisonous" and "pathological" effect of his craving for truth, as well as his sense of alienation from others, would be a familiar emotion for Koreans used to life under dictatorship (92, 167, and 224).

The social reality of colonial Korea represented in *Epitaph* was thus so banal and so intimate to contemporary readers that the novel could be readily appreciated by them for its questioning of the status quo. In this way, the alternate-historical device in Bok's novel functions to effect a double estrangement that makes its critique of the status quo all the more effective. Readers would be initially relieved at the counterfactual nature of Hideyo's world, only to discover, with an enhanced sense of horror, that Hideyo's reality had been closely modeled after their own. In telling the history of a world that is by assumption not ours, Bok at once evaded the threat of censorship and, in a deft use of speculative fiction, he gave more power to his commentary on contemporary affairs.

Although the term "alternate history," translated into *taech'e yŏksa* in Korean, was virtually unknown in late-1980s Korean discourses, the idea of dystopian history in a science fictional key was vividly represented in many cultural imports of the decade. The editorial introduction of *Epitaph*, therefore, chose to describe the novel as a piece of "fictive history" (*kasang ŭi yŏksa*), and it drew a comparison between it and the speculative works of Jonathan Swift and George Orwell.[26] Interestingly, Orwell's *Animal Farm* and *Nineteen Eighty-Four* were then two "anticommunist" best sellers that were endorsed by the authorities.[27] It thus seems that, in *Epitaph*, the classic anticommunist themes of surveillance and state control, which had been staples of South Korea's officialdom, were appropriated and turned around in a critique of official culture itself. *Epitaph*'s ironic power lies, in part, in how it took the paranoias of everyday life in South Korea and cast them as dystopian features of life under a Japanese colonial regime.

In its other major borrowing from *The Man in the High Castle*, *Epitaph* too features a "book within the book" through the novel *Tokyo, Winter, Shōwa 61*. In Dick's novel, the plot of *The Grasshopper Lies Heavy* described a world that is in major ways like the actual world (the Allies have won World War II) but is also not quite our world (Pearl Harbor does not happen, for example, and Hitler survives the war to stand trial). The effect was that of conveying a sense of the contingency of history, which was a theme that Dick had imported from his reading of the *I Ching*, the ancient Chinese divination book. Similarly, in *Epitaph*, the world depicted in *Tokyo* resembles ours in the fact that Japan lost World War II and, as a consequence, Korea gained its independence in 1945. There are also important differences, however, in the counterhistorical theme of Japan's territorial losses—with Hokkaido going to the Soviet Union, Okinawa to the United States, and Manchuria to Taiwan rather than China. Inspired by Dick, Bok also played with the idea of alternate history having its own alternate history. The effect is a kaleidoscopic rendering of the many possibilities that are intrinsic to the historical process, but not only that. There is also, in both authors, the idea of speculative fiction offering a backdoor passage into a reality that, while not real, *could be* real. As the readers of *Epitaph* encounter *Tokyo*, they cannot help feeling a sort of metaphysical vertigo. Are we imagining the reality in *Epitaph*, or is it the world of *Epitaph* that is imagining us? Are we all implicit characters of *Tokyo*? Does it matter whether *Epitaph* contains *Tokyo* or, vice versa, it is *Tokyo* that contains *Epitaph*?

If *Epitaph* shared with *The Man in the High Castle* a pervasive sense of the contingency of the historical process, Bok's novel also took those concerns further in a reflection on the constructed, narrative, and ultimately political nature of history. At the heart of *Epitaph*'s plot, Hideyo's awakening to his colonial condition happens through the progressive discovery of books whose versions of history contradict the one he has been taught by the regime. The constructedness of history is consistently highlighted, in *Epitaph*, as a major theme and a source of reflections that again exceed the fictional space of the novel. Scattered throughout the text are numerous quotations and epigraphs, variably credited to actual and fictional figures, which repeatedly comment on the possibilities for the concealment, manipulation, and creation of history: "All the history that has ever been written is political in its nature" (Sano Hisaichi; 110); "The great masses of the people will more easily fall victim to a big lie than to a small one" (Adolf Hitler; 221); "History is never written; it is always rewritten" (Takano Tatsukichi; 508). At a topical moment of the novel, a famous quote from Orwell's *1984* is given emphasis: "Who controls the past controls the future; who controls the present controls the past" (138). Such recognition of the constructedness of an established master historical narrative inevitably leads to a plural interpretation of the historical past. Musing upon his increasing disillusionment with the official version of reality, Hideyo comes to endorse a perspectival and ultimately relativistic view of truth in history: "There is no need to distinguish realists from idealists," he ponders, since "one can never just see reality as it is. We can only see things after acquiring a certain perspective" (317). History, according to Hideyo, is never innocent. The future, freed from its confinement to a preestablished teleological path, becomes an open space of possibilities along with the past itself.

As was the case with its critique of the military regime, *Epitaph*'s reflections on the constructedness of history were also constitutive of a highly resonant theme within the political environment of 1980s democratization culture. Those reflections went to the heart of the then widely felt necessity of rewriting the historical past as a way of reclaiming the present and shaping its future orientation. When Hideyo finally confirms that Korea's history has been systematically erased by the Japanese regime, his reaction is at once incredulous and triumphant: "I am not dreaming now. . . . this means that all the history that I have learned for the last thirty-nine years, at least that of the Korean nation, is false" (137). His words here echo the sentiments of many readers of *Epitaph*, who would typically undergo their own historical awakening after either reading banned books or being shown grainy video recordings of the brutal state violence in Kwangju in 1980, in what was then sort of a ritual of initiation into the decade's counterculture.

In its chronicle of Hideyo's struggles as an imperial subject, *Epitaph* is also, and perhaps primarily, a Korean nationalist commentary on coloniality, the meaning of empire, and their consequences for history. More specifically, in the novel, Bok used the fiction of Japan's continued possession of Korea as a vehicle for reflection upon Korea's two actual colonial or near-colonial experiences in the course of the twentieth century: the country's subjection to Japan between 1910 and 1945 and its division and dependency on the United States from 1948 onwards. The plot of *Epitaph* is indeed inextricable from the emerging countercultural debates, in the 1980s, about South Korea's unofficial subjection to America. The figures of Michael Braunel and Anderson are subtly emblematic of friends who, because of their overbearing power, cannot also help being a sort of superior. Braunel likes Hideyo, with whom he has successfully collaborated on a company project, and he does not hesitate to use his influence with the Japanese to protect him. At the same time, however, Anderson is the man who symbolically takes Shimadzu Tokie away from Hideyo. The theme of the protagonist's sexual humiliation, to which we will return shortly, is deployed in *Epitaph* as an unmistakable conduit for a geopolitical reflection on South Korea's semicolonial condition.

If *Epitaph* indirectly hints at Korea's contemporary dependency on the United States, its plot also offers a straightforward re-evocation of the country's past colonial experience under Japan. References to the 1910–45 colonial era are ubiquitous in the novel, and they include themes such as the racial discrimination against ethnic Korean citizens, the state-sponsored erasure of national language and culture, and the practice of confession and forced ideological conversion that was imposed back then upon Korean nationalist intellectuals. The fictional life story of Hideyo, in its move from compliance to rebellion, recalls closely the central character of one of the most celebrated novels from the colonial period, Yŏm Sangsŏp's *On the Eve of the Uprising* (*Mansejŏn*; 1924).[28] In that story too, as in *Epitaph*, the protagonist is an intellectual who starts out being well integrated under Japanese rule. And like Hideyo, Yŏm's Inhwa too is gradually awakened to the painful reality of Korea's subjection to Japan. Both Hideyo and Inhwa literally *discover* their colonial condition in ways that profoundly change them, and both are married to Korean women but have each at one point been attracted to a younger and more modern Japanese woman. Overall, in *Epitaph*, the recovery of the memory of the colonial period is yet another important element of commonality between Bok's narrative universe and the activist culture of 1980s Korea. The reappropriation of the colonial experience was central to 1980s cultural politics. Bok's novel gave fantastic expression to this fact by pretty much superimposing the colonial period over the contemporary reality of 1980s South Korea.

As an extended reflection on the nation and the colonial condition, *Epitaph* gave narrative form to some of the major nationalist themes that were debated in 1980s Korea. Some of these themes appear dated today, and some rely on ideological underpinnings that were discarded in later eras. Such is the case with the book's casting of Korean women as a symbolic trope of the colonized nation rather than as subjects with their own individual agency. Major Aoki's violation of Setsuko marks the culmination of Hideyo's colonial humiliation, and Hideyo's slaying of the imperial official makes his wife again "pure like a [virgin] girl" (496). It is notable that Setsuko consents to the affair, in *Epitaph*'s plot, in order to save Hideyo from jail. The behavior is forced upon her, and there is no hint that hers may have been a deliberate choice. The seeming function of women, in Bok/Hideyo's patriarchal universe, is as possessions that are systematically stolen by foreign men, be it Major Aoki or Anderson. Setsuko thus becomes symbolic of the Korean nation, her comeliness is akin to the natural beauty of the homeland, and the "violation" of Korean women transpires as an emotionally overwrought representation of the colonization of Korea. In its staging of this patriarchal melodrama, *Epitaph* was fully participant in a contemporary discourse that mixed national pride with the perceived necessity of controlling women and supervising their sexual choices. At a time when women's movements were on the rise, patriarchal tropes such as these became more common and more intensely felt among the mostly male leadership of the democratization movement.[29]

Still, on a more positive note, the many themes in *Epitaph* converge to yield a fictional rendering of what are certainly some of *the* most important debates of 1980s South Korea. It would not be exaggerated to regard the novel as the fantastic epitome of the ethos and political sensibility of the decade's democratization movement. From its recuperation of the colonial memory, to its reflection on history as political narrative, and on to the embedding of contemporary events in an alternate historical dystopia, *Epitaph* gave impressive speculative representation to some of the most pressing concerns of contemporary South Korean politics. At a time when change was afoot and possibilities were open for Korea, Bok's novel had the contingency of history as its fundamental metaphysical theme. It did not stop there, however, because in Bok's hands, Dick's theme of contingency craftily morphed into that of the *flexibility* of the historical process: the vaguely Foucauldian realization that history is constructed and always political, and the consequent awareness, which was everywhere in 1980s Korea, that a people could reappropriate its past and, with it, take possession of the destiny of the nation. In this respect, *Epitaph*'s fictional premises could be revealed to be not so "fantastic" in 1980s Korea. The novel's success, which was unexpected and turned its author into an overnight literary sensation, amounted to an implicit recognition that *Epitaph*, and in general science fiction, could speak quite directly to the political concerns that had been up to then more commonly addressed by realist literature.

Conclusion: Science Fiction and Democratization in South Korea

Throughout the 1980s, many South Koreans engaged in the historical task of remapping their present and rewriting their past from the perspective of the minjung, the common citizens and grassroots activists whose interests lay far from those of the military regime and its alleged American and Japanese sponsors. The ensuing cultural and political confrontation over the future of Korea meant that this decade marked a watershed in Korean cultural history and, in the process, left the country deeply divided between progressive and conservative political sides. As we have observed in the previous section, one of the works that embraced the progressive cause belonged to the traditionally little regarded genre of science fiction. In Bok Geo-il's *Epitaph*, the nationalist, anti-imperialist, and antimilitarist ideals of the minjung movement transpired through a poignant illustration of coloniality in the everyday life of an alternative, fantastic, but historically all-too-possible colonial Korea of the 1980s.

There were other works of science fiction that endorsed the ethos and values of democratization. In the fictional comic book universe of Kim

Chunbŏm's *Metal Brain*, for example, a sharpened class perspective was evident in the action-oriented depiction of the cyborg revolt that we described in the opening. In another comic series, *The Chronicles of the Nuclear Bugs* by Sin Kihwal, a spectral, postapocalyptic landscape forms the background to a world in which humans have become extinct following a nuclear war, in an evident critique of the Cold War's arms race and the consequent installment of U.S. nuclear missiles in South Korea.[30] Each in its own way, works such as these illustrate the productive intersection that intervened between popular culture and the democratization movement in the heated social and political atmosphere of 1980s South Korea. We may coin the term "minjung SF," or the science fiction of democratization, to lend recognition to this small but important niche of 1980s South Korean popular culture. Its existence attests to the vitality and variety of cultural ferment that accompanied and followed the civil democratic victory of 1987. It may have been only a minor part of the activist culture that was then on the rise. It was also, however, a moment of cultural subversion and an influential precedent for the authors of fantasy and science fiction of the 1990s as well as of later decades in South Korea.

If science fictional works contributed to popularizing some of the ideals of the democratization movement, it is important to note that a reverse effect also occurred: the authors of science fiction, too, benefited from partaking in the activist zeitgeist of the decade. In many cases, the political content of science fictional stories helped them gain justification in the eyes of their readers. This legitimation was especially important in a country where speculative and irrealist fiction had been traditionally regarded with a measure of distrust if not derision. Introducing Bok Geo-il's alternate history in the activist cultural climate, for instance, the publisher of *Escape* cautiously justified the choice of a "fictional" (*kasang*) history by highlighting "its satirical representation of our reality with penetrating critical insights" as well as its ultimate "realism" in spite of what was coyly described as "an ingenious plot."[31] In retrospect, it is doubtful that a work such as *Metal Brain* would have been republished four times had it not been for its vital connection with the experience of democratization and its depiction of class conflict within several action scenes. Indeed, in a historical perspective, the political legitimacy of late-1980s science fictional works encouraged the public's appreciation of the genre in following decades, even as many continued (and continue) to regard the genre as commercial and even juvenile.

The reciprocal relationship between democratization culture and science fiction that is highlighted in this chapter also runs counter to two popular assumptions, one cross-cultural and the other historical. First of all, it contests the frequent view of Korean science fictional works as mere derivatives of foreign cultural products. The late-1980s resurgence of science fiction in South Korea was no doubt aided, in part, by the blockbuster success of Hollywood SF films and the continued TV broadcasting of Japanese SF animations. Still, as we have seen above, our understanding of this cultural phenomenon also benefits from a thorough contextualization within local history. It would be impossible to properly assess the significance of a work such as *Epitaph* without referencing as we did the historical specificities of South Korea's democratization movement. Second, the critical recovery of these works, and with them the very genre of minjung SF, also has the effect of complicating a currently widespread narrative of Korean cultural history, a narrative according to which a sharp discontinuity marked the transition between the two decades of the 1980s and the 1990s in South Korean culture. Few people would dispute the fact that the dominant cultural aesthetic of the 1980s was that of minjung realism, which advocated the representation of the life experiences of middle- and working-class Koreans in a plain, communicative, and often reportage-like writing style.[32] Understood as such, the culture of the 1980s is commonly seen as antagonistic to that of the 1990s, which is often characterized as "postmodern" and "postideological," and which was overall friendlier to genre fiction and popular culture.[33] While such an account does indeed correspond with the general tenor of the two decades, its dichotomous nature has also contributed to the misleading perception of the 1980s as having little relevance to Korea's cultural present. In fact, as is attested by *Epitaph*, *Metal Brain*, and other cultural products of the era, the 1980s saw the emergence of important trends that came to maturation only in the following decade and beyond.

In 1980s South Korea, popular genres such as mystery, horror, fantasy, and science fiction could all serve as a convenient vehicle for allegorical or metaphorical critique of the status quo. Until 1987, these genres were suppressed, in different ways, by both the regime and an activist culture centered on realism. The cultural prosperity of the 1990s, however, was in no small measure made possible by the 1980s channeling of political energy into popular culture. In retrospect, we may say that the liberational energy released through the democratization movement eventually overflowed its own epistemological and aesthetic frameworks in the postdemocratization era. This critical vein of Korean science fiction is well alive today in the works of writers such as Djuna, Jeong Soyeon, Kim Boyoung, and Pak Min-gyu, as well as filmmakers like Bong Joon-ho, Jang Joon-hwan, and

Chang Yunjŏng.³⁴ In their unsettling, subversive imaginations—in which the proletariat and the precariat frequently appear in the form of aliens and zombies and a postapocalyptic dystopia turns into a familiar stage for class struggle—as well as in their implied desires for another time and reality, the legacy of the 1980s democratization movement lives on.

NOTES

I would like to thank the Daesan Foundation and the Advancing Scholarship in the Humanities and Social Sciences grant program at the University of Southern California for their generous sponsorship for this research.

1. Kim Chunbŏm's *Kigye chŏnsa 109*, whose title literally translates into "Mechanic Warrior 109," was first serialized in the comic magazine *IQ Jump*. Kim, its graphic artist, produced the work based on No Chinsu's script. Upon the completion of serialization, the title was reprinted in four volumes by the magazine's publisher, Sŏul munhwasa, between 1992 and 1993 and again in 1998 with new cover pictures by fellow comic artist Pak Mujik. In 2002, it was reprinted in three volumes by Kŭrimi Press under the English title of *Metal Brain 109*. According to Kim, the English title was his original choice, but the publisher had him replace it with a Korean one, https://twitter.com/road2012/status/44715884228526080. In 2008–9, *Kigye chŏnsa 109* was serialized online in all-color webtoon format on Naver. I have referenced the 1998 and webtoon versions for this study. See Pak Sŏkhwan's review of the graphic novel in "Saibogŭ ŭi kyegŭp t'ujaeng." The review was originally serialized in the *Manhwa Encyclopedia* of Naver and is now available on the author's blog website.

2. Kim Chunbŏm, *Kigye chŏnsa 109*, 4:156.

3. See Kim Chunbŏm's interview, "20-yŏn mane toraon 'Kigye chŏnsa': Ije put'ŏga chinjja 'sijak'ida: manhwaga Kim Chunbŏm" (The return of *Metal Brain* after 20 years: Now is the true beginning—Kim Chunbŏm the comic artist). *Minjok 21*, November 1, 2008. http://www.minjog21.com/news/articleView.html?idxno=3482

4. Bok Geo-il, *Pimyŏng ŭl ch'ajasŏ*.

5. See the statistics on the homepage of the May 18 Memorial Foundation website, https://518.org/ease/menu.es?mid=a10304010000

6. See Kyung Moon Hwang, "Afterword: Kwangju: The Historical Watershed."

7. For the Marxist influences in 1980s South Korea, see Namhee Lee, *The Making of Minjung*, 164.

8. Quoting the representatives of well-known dissident publishers, a 1991 newspaper article reports that 80 to 90 percent of social science books were censored during the 1980s. Nonetheless, these banned books sold extremely well on the underground market in university areas. Ch'oe Hyŏngmin. "Pirok 80-yŏndae."

9. See the interdisciplinary analyses of minjung discourse in Wells, ed., *South Korea's Minjung Movement*. Particularly useful are Kang Man'gil's reflection on minjung historiography in "Contemporary Nationalist Movements and the Minjung," 35, and Choi Hyun-moo's account of the nationalist—as opposed to proletarian—character of the minjung literary movement in "Contemporary Korean Literature: From Victimization to Minjung Nationalism," 172.

10. See Cumings, *Korea's Place in the Sun*, 377–78.
11. See Namhee Lee, *The Making of Minjung*, 109–44.
12. The effort to rewrite modern Korean history was led by the multivolume collection titled *Haebang chŏnhusa ŭi insik*, whose first two and most important volumes were published in 1979 and 1985.
13. Aside from *Haebang chŏnhusa ŭi insik*, other well-known revisionary history books from the period include Han'guk minjungsa yŏn'guhoe, *Han'guk minjungsa yŏn'gu* (1987), and Pak Segil, *Tasi ssŭnŭn Han'guk hyŏndaesa* (1988).
14. Cho Chŏngnae, *T'aebaek sanmaek*. For a useful commentary on the reception of the novel in South Korea, see Paek Sŭngjong, *Kŭmsŏ, sidae rŭl ikta*. The documentary quality of Cho's novel was preserved and foregrounded in Im Kwon-taek's cinematic adaptation of the title in 1994. See Kyung Hyun Kim's discussion of the film's status in Korean cinema history in "Is This How the War Is Remembered?"
15. Cho Chŏngnae received death threats soon after the publication of the first volume in 1986, and he was sued in 1994 by right-wing groups for his alleged sympathy for communism, a charge from which he was acquitted only in 2005. See his interview in "T'aebaek sanmaek munhakkwan." See also Youngju Ryu's account of Hwang Sok-yong's activist literary practice and his political persecution in *Writers of the Winter Republic*, 136–75.
16. See Lukács, "Realism in the Balance."
17. For the censorship of science fiction in animation, see Hŏ Inuk, *Han'guk aenimaeisyŏn yŏnghwasa*, 106. As Hŏ's account suggests, the suppression of science fiction for its "nonsensical" (*hŏmu maengnang*) imagination was not a matter of the period's censorship policy but rather that of its arbitrary interpretation by censoring authorities.
18. See Hyunseon Lee, "The South Korean Blockbuster and a Divided Nation," 261.
19. Bok Geo-il, *Yŏksa sok ŭi nagŭne* and *P'aran tal arae*. The author serialized the first novel in the *Joongang Kyŏngje Sinmun* (*Joongang Economic Daily*) from 1988 through 1990. The second novel was instead first published electronically on HITEL, then a major Korean telecommunication network, between May and September 1992. Bok is today also known as a conservative social commentator.
20. This and other information come from my personal interview with the writer in Seoul on July 18, 2016.
21. *The Man in the High Castle* (1962) was not widely known to 1980s Koreans, as its full Korean translation did not become available until 2001. Bok recollects having read the work upon its appearance in the English original. Other inspirations that were cited by Bok himself, in *Epitaph*'s preface, include Ward Moore's *Bring the Jubilee* (1953), Keith Robert's *Pavane* (1968), and Harry Harrison's *Tunnel through the Deeps* (1972). None of the works were available in Korean translation in the late 1980s.
22. Choi In-hun, *Ch'ongdok ŭi sori*. Its first three episodes were published in 1967 and 1968, around the time of South Korea's restoration of diplomatic ties with Japan in 1964. The novel was completed in 1976 with the publication of its last episode.
23. Choi In-hun, *T'aep'ung*. The novel was originally serialized in the *Joongang Ilbo* between January 1 and October 13, 1973.
24. In leaving for his exile, Hideyo is in effect setting out to search for his Korean national identity. In one possible interpretation of the novel's title, the protagonist searches for the name that will be inscribed on his gravestone. Will it be Kinoshita

Hideyo, his Japanese name, or Park Young-se, his Korean name? See Dongshik Kim, "Postcoloniality and Imagining the Post-human." Another possible reading of the titular epitaph is as a reference to the historical case of the stele of Kwanggaet'o, which was a document of the Koguryŏ dynasty whose inscription was falsified by the Japanese government, during the colonial era, in order to assert Japan's entitlement over Korea. Lee Simyŏng's 2009 *Lost Memories*, a 2002 time-travel blockbuster loosely based on the novel, highlights this point by locating its time machine within this stele. For a comparative study of the novel and the film with a focus on the latter, see Kim Myŏngsŏk, "SF yŏnghwa *2009 Lost Memories*."

25. Torture by the authorities finds ample representation in *Epitaph*, and the chilling description of techniques such as "water drinking" (*mul mŏngnŭnda*) and "electric roasting" (*chŏn'gi jjimjil handa*) resonated with daily newspaper reports in 1980s Korea. In addition, Bok's novel fictionally mentions the mysterious death of Ueda Shigeru, a student protestor, during police investigation (246–47). This episode is particularly reminiscent of Pak Chongch'ŏl's controversial death under police custody, which happened on January 14, 1987, two months before the publication of the novel. Pak's death and the subsequent cover-up attempt by the police infuriated the public and eventually contributed to the political triumph of the democratization movement on June 10, 1987.

26. Bok Geo-il, *Pimyŏng*, v. Both *kasang yŏksa* and *taech'e yŏksa* have been used in Korea as a translation of "alternate history," but the latter has been gaining increasingly more currency and is exclusively used in recent critical discourse on the subject.

27. Orwell's works were translated into Korean as early as 1960. See *Tongmul nongjang/1984* [*Animal Farm* and *Nineteen Eighty-Four*], trans. Chŏng Pyŏngjo, vol. 79 of *Segye munhak chŏnjip* [World literature series] (Ŭllyu munhwasa, 1960). *Nineteen Eighty-Four* was translated at least twice more by the 1980s: by Kim Pyŏngik (1968; Munye ch'ulp'ansa, 1975) and by Kim Iryŏp (Chihye, 1984).

28. Yŏm Sangsŏp, "On the Eve of the Uprising."

29. For a penetrating critique of patriarchal nationalism in *Epitaph*, see Kwŏn Myŏng'a, "Kuksa sidae ŭi minjok iyagi." The trope of women as a symbol of the nation only became stronger in Bok's *A Wanderer in History*, another alternate history in which a twentieth-century male time traveler organizes a popular democratic revolution in sixteenth-century dynastic Korea. See Bok, *Yŏksa sok ŭi nagŭne*.

30. Sin Kihwal, *Haekch'ung i nat'anatta*. This graphic novel consists of five episodes, which were first serialized in the journal *Sidae chŏngsin* (Zeitgeist; 1985–97).

31. Bok, *Pimyŏng*, v.

32. For the minjung realist aesthetic in 1980s Korean film and literature, see Hyun-Moo Choi, "Contemporary Korean Literature"; Eungjun Min, Junsook Jo, and Han Ju Kwak, "Korean National Cinema in the 1980s"; and Sunyoung Park, "The Colonial Origins of Korean Realism and Its Contemporary Manifestation."

33. See, for instance, Hwang Chongyŏn et al., *90-yŏndae munhak ot'ŏk'e pol kŏssin'ga*. For more cautious explorations of nineties literature as both continuous and innovative of its eighties precedent, see *Chakka wa pip'yŏng, Pip'yŏng, 90-yŏndae munhak ŭl mutta*.

34. Examples include, but are not limited to, Djuna, *T'aep'yŏngyang hoengdan t'ŭkkŭp*; Jeong Soyeon, *Yŏpchip ŭi Yŏnghŭi ssi*; Kim Boyoung, *Chinhwa sinhwa*; Pak Min-gyu, *Chigu yŏngung chŏnsŏl*; Bong Joon-ho, *Sŏlguk yŏlch'a*; Jang Joon-hwan, *Chigu rŭl chik'yŏra*; and Chang Yunjŏng, *Kŭ ihu . . . mianhaeyo*.

REFERENCES

2009 Losŭt'ŭ memorijŭ [2009 lost memories]. Dir. Lee Si-Myung. Indecom Cinema and CJ Entertainment, 2002.
Barr, Marleen S. *Feminist Fabulation: Space/Postmodern Fiction.* Iowa City: Iowa University Press, 1992.
Bok Geo-il. *Kukchaehwa sidae ŭi minjogŏ* [The national language in an age of globalization]. Munhak kwa chisŏng, 1998.
Bok Geo-il. *P'aran tal arae* [Under the blue moon]. Munhak kwa chisŏngsa, 1992.
Bok Geo-il. *Pimyŏng ŭl ch'ajasŏ* [In search of an epitaph]. Munhak kwa chisŏngsa, 1987.
Bok Geo-il. *Yŏksa sok ŭi nagŭne* [A wanderer in history]. 3 vols. Munhak kwa chisŏngsa, 1991.
Chakka wa pip'yŏng, ed. *Pip'yŏng, 90-yŏndae munhak ŭl mutta* [Critical inquiry into the 90s literature]. Yŏrŭm ŏndŏk, 2005.
Chigu rŭl chik'yŏra [Save the green planet]. Dir. Jang Joon-hwan. Sydus and CJ Entertainment, 2003.
Cho Chŏngnae. *T'aebaek sanmaek* [The T'aebaek mountains]. 10 vols. Han'gilsa, 1989.
Ch'oe Hyŏngmin. "Pirok 80-yŏndae munhwagye siryŏn 28: 5-kong ŭi kŭmsŏ kaengyu inyŏm sŏjŏk sunan sidae: Minjung iran mal issŭmyŏn chadong kŭmsŏ" [Secret records of 1980s cultural repression 28: The age of prohibition for ideological books in the 5th republic—automatic bans for books with minjung in their title]. *Joongang Ilbo.* December 20, 1991.
Choi, Hyun-Moo. "Contemporary Korean Literature: From Victimization to *Minjung* Nationalism." In *South Korea's Minjung Movement*, edited by Kenneth Wells, 167–78.
Choi In-hun. *Ch'ongdok ŭi sori* [The voice of the governor-general]. Vol. 9 of *Ch'oe Inhun chŏnjip.* Munhak kwa chisŏngsa, 2009.
Choi In-hun. *T'aep'ung* [Typhoon]. Vol. 5 of *Ch'oe Inhun chŏnjip.* Munhak kwa chisŏngsa, 2009.
Cumings, Bruce. *Korea's Place in the Sun: A Modern History.* New York: W. W. Norton, 1997.
Dick, Philip K. *The Man in the High Castle.* In *Four Novels of the 1960s*, edited by Jonathan Lethem, 1–230. New York: Library of America, 2007.
Djuna. *T'aep'yŏngyang hoengdan t'ŭkkŭp* [The pacific express]. Munhak kwa chisŏngsa, 2002.
Foucault, Michel. *The Archeology of Knowledge and the Discourse on Language.* Translated by A. M. Sheridan Smith. New York: Pantheon Books, 1972.
Han'guk minjungsa yŏn'guhoe. *Han'guk minjungsa yŏn'gu* [History of the Korean people]. P'ulbit, 1987.
Hŏ Inuk. *Han'guk aenimaeisyŏn yŏnghwasa* [History of Korean animation]. Sinhan midiŏ, 2002.
Hwang Chongyŏn et al. *90-yŏndae munhak otŏk'e pol kŏssin'ga* [How to read '90s literature]. Minŭmsa, 1999.
Hwang, Kyung Moon. "Afterword: Kwangju: The Historical Watershed." In *Contentious Kwangju: The May 18 Uprising in Korea's Past and Present*, edited by Gi-Wook Shin and Kyung Moon Hwang, 133–42. New York: Rowman and Littlefield, 2003.
Jeong Soyeon. *Yŏpchip ŭi Yŏnghŭi ssi* [My neighbor Yŏnghŭi]. Ch'angbi, 2015.

Kang, Man'gil. "Contemporary Nationalist Movements and the Minjung." Translated by Roger Duncan. In *South Korea's Minjung Movement*, edited by Wells, 31–38.
Kim Boyoung. *Chinhwa sinhwa* [Myth of evolution]. Haengbokhan ch'aek ikki, 2010.
Kim Chunbŏm. *Kigye chŏnsa 109* [Metal brain 109]. Sŏul munhwasa, 1998.
Kim, Dongshik. "Postcoloniality and Imagining the Post-human: Bok Geo-il's *In Search of an Epitaph* and Djuna's *The Pacific Continental Express*." *Korean Literature Now* 20 (Summer 2013). Accessed July 31, 2015. http://koreanliteraturenow.com/features/postcoloniality-and-imagining-post-human-bok-geo-ils-search-epitaph-and-djunas-pacific
Kim, Kyung Hyun. "Is This How the War Is Remembered? Deceptive Sex and the Remasculinized Nation in *The Taebaek Mountains*." In *Im Kwon-Taek: The Making of a Korean National Cinema*, edited by David E. James and Kyung Hyun Kim, 197–222. Detroit: Wayne State University Press, 2002.
Kim Myŏngsŏk. "SF yŏnghwa *2009 Lost Memories* wa sosŏl *Pimyŏng ŭl ch'ajasŏ* ŭi sŏsa pigyo" [A comparative analysis of *2009 Lost Memories* and *In Search of an Epitaph*]. *Munhak kwa yŏngsang* 4, no. 1 (2003): 71–102.
Kŭ ihu . . . mianhaeyo [Afterwards . . . I am sorry]. Dir. Chang Yunjŏng. In *Iutchip jombi* [The neighbor zombie]. Dir. Chang Yunjŏng, Hong Yŏnggŭn, O Yŏngdu, and Ryu Hoon. DVD. Kino Mangosteen, 2010.
Kwŏn Myŏng'a. "Kuksa sidae ŭi minjok iyagi" [A national narrative in an age of national history]. *Silch'ŏn munhak* 68 (2002): 35–57.
Lee, Hyunseon. "The South Korean Blockbuster and a Divided Nation." *International Journal of Korean History* 21, no. 1 (2016): 259–64.
Lee, Namhee. *The Making of Minjung: Democracy and the Politics of Representation in South Korea*. Ithaca: Cornell University Press, 2007.
Lukács, Georg. "Realism in the Balance." In *Aesthetics and Politics: The Key Texts of the Classic Debate within German Marxism*, by Ernst Bloch et al., translated and edited by Ronald Tayler, 28–59. New York: Verso, 1977.
May 18 Memorial Foundation, "History." Accessed July 31, 2015. http://eng.518.org/sub.php?PID=0201
Min, Eungjun, Junsook Jo, and Han Ju Kwak, "Korean National Cinema in the 1980s: Enlightenment, Political Struggle, Social Realism, and Defeatism." In *Korean Film: History, Resistance, and Democratic Imagination*, 57–84. Westport, CT: Praeger, 2003.
Paek Sŭngjong. *Kŭmsŏ, sidae rŭl ikta* [Reading banned books and their times]. Sanch'ŏrŏm, 2002.
Pak Hyŏnch'ae and Cho Hŭiyŏn, eds. *Han'guk sahoe kusŏngch'e nonjaeng* [Debates on Korean social formation]. Vol. 1. Chuksan, 1989.
Pak Segil. *Tasi ssŭnŭn Han'guk hyŏndaesa* [New history of modern Korea]. Tolbegae, 1988.
Pak Sŏkhwan. "Saibogŭ ŭi kyegŭp t'ujaeng: *Kigye chŏnsa 109*, Kim Chunbŏm" [Cyborgs' class struggle: Kim Chunbŏm's *Metal Brain*]. *Han'guk manhwa chŏngjŏn* [Canonical works of Korean *manhwa*]. Accessed July 31, 2015. http://navercast.naver.com/contents.nhn?rid=196&contents_id=16652&category_type=series
Pak Soran. "20-yŏn man e toraon 'Kigye chŏnsa,' ije put'ŏ ka chinjja 'sijak' ida: Manhwaga Kim Chunbŏm" [The return of *The Metal Brain* after 20 years: Now is the true beginning—Kim Chunbŏm the comic artist]. *Minjok* 21, no. 92, November 1, 2008.

Park Min-gyu. *Chigu yŏngung chŏnsŏl* [Tales of the League of Justice of America]. Munhak tongne, 2003.
Park Min-gyu. "Road Kill." Translated by Esther Song. *Azalea: Journal of Korean Literature & Culture* 6 (2013): 135–55.
Park, Sunyoung. "The Colonial Origins of Korean Realism and Its Contemporary Manifestation." In "Aesthetics and Political Economy," edited by Tani E. Barlow. Special issue, *Positions: East Asia Cultures Critique* 14, no. 1 (2006): 165–92.
Ryu, Youngju. *Writers of the Winter Republic: Literature and Resistance in Park Chung Hee's Korea*. Honolulu: University of Hawaii Press, 2015.
Shin, Haerin. "Beyond Representation and Simulation: Surviving the Age of Mediation and Its Failure in Kim Young-ha's Quiz Show." *Journal of Korean Studies* 20, no. 2 (2015): 261–89.
Sin Kihwal. *Haekch'ung i nat'anatta* [Records of nuclear bugs]. 1989; Kilch'akki, 2013.
Sŏlguk yŏlch'a [Snowpiercer]. Dir. Bong Joon-ho. Moho Films and Opus Pictures, 2013.
Song Kŏnho, ed. *Haebang chŏnhusa ŭi insik* [Understanding pre- and postliberation history]. 6 vols. Han'gilsa, 1989.
"*T'aebaek sanmaek* munhakkwan yŏn chakka Cho Chŏngnae." [Novelist Cho Chŏngnae opens the museum of *The Taebaek Mountains*]. *Yŏnhap News*, November 24, 2008.
Wells, Kenneth, ed. *South Korea's Minjung Movement: The Culture and Politics of Dissidence*. Honolulu: University of Hawaii Press, 1995.
Yŏm, Sangsŏp. "On the Eve of the Uprising." In *On the Eve of the Uprising and Other Stories from Colonial Korea*, translated by Sunyoung Park and Jefferson Gatrall, 1–112. Ithaca: Cornell University Press, 2012.

Afterword

Differently Politicizing Literature from the Authoritarian Era—The State, Antistate Leftist Nationalism, and Aesthetics

Jin-kyung Lee

By way of an afterword, this last chapter attempts to (re)think the particular relations between politics and aesthetics during the decades of military dictatorship, spanning from the 1960s to the late 1980s. The cultural scene of 1980s South Korea under Chun Doo Hwan and Roh Tae Woo was largely both a continuation and an intensification of what had gone on during the Park Chung Hee era, albeit with some significant differences and changes, as the preceding chapters have pointed out. I will thus address the relations between the field of political economy, involving the state, capitalism, and the dissidents, on the one hand, and the role of what I am calling the "antistate leftist nationalist" literature and aesthetics, on the other, during the authoritarian era including the 1980s.[1] I first examine the postcolonial South Korean state's successful monopoly, under Syngman Rhee, of the definition of the political as the exclusive linkage between the state and the ethnonation (*minjok*). I then argue that the rise of leftist nationalism, in formulating its resistance vis-à-vis the authoritarian state, helped to redefine the political, homologically and oppositionally, as the relinking between the masses and the ethnonation—that is, *minjung*. I conclude the chapter by exploring how we might differently politicize our interpretation of South Korea's literary and cultural productions from the 1960s–1980s authoritarian era through deployment of dissensual politico-aesthetics, a concept I am borrowing from Jacques Rancière's work.

I rely on Rancière's theorization of the political and the aesthetic to reconsider the institution of literature during the three decades of authoritarian rule. In refuting the notion widely accepted both in the West and in modern Korea that politics and aesthetics are discrete and distinct entities, which, as such, requires us to "know whether or not they ought to be set in relation,"[2] Rancière provides a conceptual framework in which politics is a contingent notion: it is a deconstructive and anarchical operation that comes into being when there is a disruption of the existing juridical order that determines and distinguishes the perceptible from the imperceptible, the sensible from the insensible, the visible from the invisible, and the audible from the inaudible. Then, for Rancière, politics is actually another word for the more ancient meaning of aesthetics: perception by senses. For Rancière, like dissensual politics, dissensual aesthetics signifies a resistive reconfiguration or rearrangement of the sensible "by confronting the established framework of perception, thought, and action with the inadmissible."[3] Moving away from the dominant notion of politics, both in the West and increasingly in South Korea, which is premised upon identitarianism and the reification of various groups as "proletariat," "women," or "minorities," or upon a certain kind of message or orientation such as "conservative" or "progressive," Rancière conceives of politics as a "polemical universal" that operates necessarily in a contingent manner, in short, in spaces of dispute.[4]

Here Angela Davis's more concrete critique of identitarian politics can help us think through Rancière's abstract and "fundamentalist" critique of analytical categories such as class, gender, race, and sexual orientation. Davis suggests a complex and flexible strategy of mobilizing various identity-based groups around specific issues, thus forcing them to cross—and thus to constantly deconstruct and reconfigure—the existing boundaries of identities. For Davis, the category of "U.S. women of color" should not be conceived of as a "coalition" made up of discrete racial groups but rather as a "political formation" that collaborates on a particular issue or a set of problems on a contingent basis. She writes: "A woman of color formation might decide to work around the immigration issue. This political commitment is not based upon the specific histories of racialized communities or its constituent members, but rather constructs an agenda agreed upon by all who are a part of it. In my opinion, the most exciting potential of women of color formations resides in the possibility of politicizing this identity—*basing the identity on politics rather than the politics on identity.*"[5] This notion of "political formation," also deployed by other theorists, is not necessarily contradictory to the groupings of class, gender, race, and sexual orientation, which came to be ossified as the basis for identity politics in the U.S. and Western contexts; rather, it is complementary in a deconstructive manner to these major analytical categories and social groups. To begin with, we can think of these above-mentioned "groupings," as well as the state and the leftist nationalist dissident movements, *as* political formations: for example, as the state formation, class formation, racial/ethnic formation, gender formation, and sexuality formation. The concept of formation, more fluid and processual, allows us to further complicate our understanding of the ever-changing historicity of the state, capital, and their institutions and strategies, as well as their relations to the equally fast-shifting groupings, suppressions, emergences, and convergences of people/populations, issues/situations, and resistive ideas/movements.

In thinking about the interpenetration of politics and aesthetics in postcolonial South Korea, I will begin, in the first section, by examining the central categories of ideology and analysis that were available for and deployed by both the governing elites and their dissident counterparts, that is, the categories of the state, the ethnonation, and class. During the authoritarian decades, these categories/formations suppressed or obscured other less-politicized-then, to-be-more-politicized-later categories/formations such as (neo)empire, (global) race/ethnicity, gender, and sexuality. The most historically significant concepts/entities of postcolonial South Korea—the state (firmly entrenched since the premodern era and resisted by the colonized during the colonial era), the ethnonation (a modern category that came into being as subversive vis-à-vis the colonial state), and class (a Western import during the colonial era that was both coupled with and decoupled with the future sovereign state)—were thus epistemes, or categories of perception and cognition, that were made possible and maintained by the ruling structures and the dominant ideologies, including oppositional and subversive ones like Marxism. In the second section, I will argue that the ideological/epistemological/aesthetic category of class, mobilized by the dissident movements, came to deconstruct the state and the ethnonation during the industrializing era under the consecutive military dictatorships between the sixties and the eighties. It is fair to say that during the authoritarian era, whose dissident politics is the main topic of this chapter, it was more the traditional conceptual categories—that is, the state, the ethnonation, and class—rather than the notion of "formation," that were operative. I will argue in the third and last section of the chapter that reading differently the canon and the more marginalized literature and popular culture will help us see more clearly the complex formations of governance and resistance that lie beyond these categories. Based on these insights, I will close by considering the ways in which other categories such as gender, race/ethnicity, and sexual orientation have become perceptible, thus toppling the state, the ethnonation, and class as the unrivaled and unchallenged modes of political identification, governmentality, mobilization, and politicization in the postdemocratization era since the mid 1990s, and I will reflect on how we might further deconstruct these emergent categories and formations.

Before moving on, it is worth noting that the Korean language does not have an equivalent of "the political" or "politicization" in the way I am using those terms here. The word *chŏngch'i*, usually translated as "politics," means politics in the sense of governance or government. The English words/concepts of "the political" and "politicization" often imply progressive and subversive problematization of existing politics or political issues. In the Korean-language context, one would have to employ an altogether different word, such as *chinbo* (progressivism) or *chŏhang* (resistance), to connote such political problematization or resistance. In the rest of the chapter, the political will thus be conceptualized on two levels: first, as a polemical universal notion that disrupts the existing order, as Rancière would have it, and second, as a particular notion that corresponds to what the political came to mean in the specific chronotope of South Korean authoritarianism.

Rethinking the "Political": The State and/as the Ethnonation

In the context of the very recent liberation from Japan and the immediate onset of neocoloniality vis-à-vis the United States, it was not difficult for the ethnonational (*minjok*) to continue to occupy the important core dimension of the political. How to define the ethnonational became a metapolitical task for the contending elites, politicians, and intellectuals, both the dissidents and those aligned with the government. In the aftermath of the Korean War, the Syngman Rhee regime was successful in forging an exclusive linkage between the state and the ethnonational, laying the crucial foundation for the succeeding authoritarian regimes in the following decades. The state came to claim the ethnonational in two important ways: it established itself as the vanguard of anticolonial (specifically anti-Japanese) nationalism, and it made anticommunism one of its signature doctrines. Thus, the ethnonationalist state defined the sphere of the (concrete) political in terms of empire (Japan) versus ethnonation (formerly colonized Korea) and communism versus anticommunism, excluding other potentially dissensual elements from the realm of the political.

The subsequent military dictatorships of Park Chung Hee and Chun Doo Hwan continued to monopolize the ethnonational for the state to maximum effect, now by further fusing the ethnonational with economic development. Anticommunism could be recuperated into the state's emphasis on the economic development, which, it was argued, would ensure the defeat of communism (*sŭnggong*). In contrast to the earlier era under Syngman Rhee, in Park's state-contrived convergence among ethnonation, development, and anticommunism, the economic was made visible and legible; it was politicized as a dissensual dimension, and yet it was simultaneously and instantaneously reabsorbed into the existing confines of the political, meaning the ethnonationalist state, and thus "(re)de-politicized" in effect. Chun Doo Hwan, a further militarized successor to Park, maintained the policy of prioritizing economic development, above all as a means to sustain his even more violently repressive regime. The authoritarian governments' militarization of all spheres of life, always strongly associated with the ethnonation, only lent further support to the state's monopoly of ethnonationalism. Militarist ethnonationalism unconsciously harked back to the colonial period while consciously resisting the same, helping to further suppress heterogeneous dissensual elements that could reconfigure the field of the political.

Defined within the framework of post-anticolonial nationalism, the political under the authoritarian developmentalist state, both Park's and Chun's, displaced the ongoing transnationalizing and neocolonizing capitalization process. The South Korean state was in fact functioning as a racial state[6] in the midst of a fast-globalizing and highly stratifying capitalism where it brokered its own racialized proletariat to its neocolonial masters. In an era during which the South Korean proletariat was to serve as soldiers in Vietnam, as military sex workers for U.S. troops, as miners and nurses in West Germany, as sex workers and day laborers in Japan, as construction workers in the Middle East, and as cheap immigrant labor in the Americas, the potentially dissensual elements of this trans/national context, such as class, race, gender, and their intersections, remained excluded from the sphere of the political. These "demographic" sectors, these as yet politically imperceptible collectives, operated as categories of economic mobilization and exploitation for the ethnonationalist state of South Korea and for the transnational capital of Korea, the United States, Japan, and others. The ethnonationalist and developmentalist state absorbed these other potential political categories, or, rather, it obscured and obliterated the far more complex formations of the labor force and demographic populations. These formations were necessarily intersectional among and across these categories (of ethnicity/race, class, gender), and they were necessarily trans/national. These formations were made imperceptible.

During the three decades when the conflation between the state and the ethnonation became even more effective under the imperative of economic development, this (con)fusion dictated the terms of the debate and resistance: the dissent vis-à-vis the military dictatorship could only be conceptualized and structured at the ethnonational level and as an antigovernment movement. I will discuss this homological constraint in more detail in the next section.

The Antistate Leftist Dissidents and the Homological Relinking of the Ethnonation

As the 1970s dissident movement became more and more centered on the issues of labor and economic justice,[7] it brought about a gradual resuscitation of Marxist thought, which had gone underground in the peremptory anticommunization process under Rhee in the post–Korean War era. The dissident left was successful in delinking the ethnonation from the state by deploying class as a dissensual principle, but the repoliticization of class was to take place neatly and necessarily within the boundary of the ethnonation. It was in the late 1970s and in the early '80s that the dissident movement began to reconfigure more explicitly the proletariat or the masses (*minjung*) as the main historical subjects of the ethnonation, taking the place of the authoritarian state, big business, and the neoimperial formations that colluded with them. In this way, the more heterogeneously disruptive potential of class, both as a complex lived experience and as an analytical category, was curtailed by the ways in which the proletarian class was, again, joined to the ethnonation in a totalizing and identitarian manner. As Park's authoritarian state of the 1970s and Chun's new military regime in the 1980s set the conditions of contestation and the terms of engagement through their overriding emphasis on state-led developmentalism, the dissident movement was already being molded into an antigovernment but pro-ethnonationalist opposition. It turned, that is, into an ethnonationalist leftist movement that, as such, excluded the possibilities of deploying class as a subnational, supranational, or transnational concept and reality. The ethnonationalized proletarian class, now occupying the privileged position of the very definition of the political, lost its potential to deconstruct the complex intersections of the ethnonation, the state, globalization, and neocolonial transnational capitalism. Other concepts and categories such as gender, sexuality, and race that necessarily occur in intersecting articulations with class and the ethnonation became further obscured and elided. As many have pointed out, in the dissident circles under the Park and Chun regimes the political thus came to be reified as a particular demographic sector: as a male, high-skilled, ethnonational/ist worker.[8]

In a manner similar to the ways in which the antistate leftist nationalist dissident faction interjected class into the field of the political in an attempt to reconfigure it, in the last two decades of South Korea's transitioning into a liberal democracy and an immigrant subempire, other demographic and analytical categories such as gender, sexual orientation, race, and employment status ("temporary employee" being a critical emergent demographic and economic category) have been mobilized to redefine the political. As a result, what constitutes the political has become more complex, moving away from the axis of ethnonation and class to a set of multiple axes. However, these categories have also tended to become reified and transformed into more identity-based groups, including the working class, women, ethnic minorities, sexual minorities, and part-time workers in South Korea (as they have in the United States). While these analytical concepts or demographic sectors can still perform a dissensual role, their easy reification into identitarian groups still limits their potential for more radical intervention.

The Literary-Ideological Divide and Canon Formation during the Authoritarian Era

In this last section, I will discuss briefly how we might think beyond the division and opposition between two schools of literature and literary criticism under the authoritarian regimes. The leftist nationalist literature camp, *minjok* (and later *minjung*) *munhak*, emerged as a dominant formation in the early 1970s and remained powerful as the cultural representative, ally, and leader for the ongoing dissident movement until the 1990s. Its rise and dominance also reproduced the split of the literary establishment into the two factions of engaged literature versus pure literature, a division whose history dates back to the colonial period. Both the so-called engaged literature and pure literature camps operated with the presumption of the political as a particular set of predetermined issues, most importantly, the exclusive linkage between class and nation. For the engaged-literature camp, this particular notion of the political tended to perform a prescriptive and even censoring role: it regulated, and ultimately limited, the very boundary of what was representable, "sayable," "audible," and "visible," while having once opened up and expanded the very same. This continuing dominance resulted in diminishing the very circumference of how and what to conceive as political. The "political literature" of this era thus produced a depoliticizing effect, even as it intensely politicized its prioritized cause. Likewise, the pure literature camp made the assumption that art and aesthetics should be suprapolitical or apolitical, and it, too, was thinking of the political as a concrete set of issues rather than as a contingent principle necessarily enmeshed within an epistemological order. When the pure literature camp distanced itself from the set of "political" issues and the perspectives endorsed by leftist nationalists, this rejection or defiance helped shape their production, allowing pure literature practitioners to engage with a different set of issues or to engage with the same from an alternative point of view. We can, then, reconceive pure literature as having had a differently politicizing function, though as yet unrecognized and uninterpreted as such, rather than thinking of it as apolitical or depoliticized.

Below I cite only a handful of exemplary cases to make my point here. These are just some representative instances that I happen to be familiar with, but my hope is that the methodological principle can be applied more widely to the existing canon as a whole. The literary works by Kim Tong-ni, O Yŏng-su, and Hwang Sun-wŏn from the 1950s through the '60s were interpreted and evaluated, throughout the authoritarian decades, largely in relation to the ossified notion of class and in relation to the pure literature camp's implicit alliance with the conservative state. In today's postauthoritarian age, however, it might be possible in our reinterpretations of these works to recuperate the other axes of formations through which South Korean society was then being reconstituted.

During the authoritarian decades and through the 1990s, when feminism and feminist literary criticism began to take root gradually in post–student movement South Korea, women writers were pejoratively referred to as "lady writers," or *yŏryu chakka*. Today, however, they can be reinterpreted through the now-politicized lens of gender/gender formation, crossing with class along with other forces of social formation. Women writers such as Im Ok-in, Kang Sin-jae, Chŏng Han-suk, Son So-hŭi, and many others whose works have been canonized and yet simultaneously demeaned by the depoliticizing masculinist literary criticism, can be reinterpreted and recanonized. For example, women writers from the 1950s had their own take on the camptown phenomenon in the post–Korean War era, in contrast to the masculinist leftist nationalist representations of camptowns that since the mid-1960s have come to dominate the South Korean intellectual imagination, coinciding with the emergence of the leftist nationalist literature movement (*minjok munhak undong*).

Yi Mun-yol—that is, Yi Mun-yol of the 1970s and '80s and not of more recent years[9]—is both exceptional and representative of the writers who did not belong to the leftist nationalist literary mainstream: exceptional in that his works became canonized, and representative in that they belong to the "heretical" nonmainstream that is still considered important and major. In this respect, Yi Mun-yol's anthology of short stories, *Kuro Arirang* (Arirang of the Kuro Industrial Complex), offers us alternatively playful and heterogeneous representations of the working class, without following the doxa of the leftist nationalist literary establishment and its particular modes of championing the causes of minjung.

In an opposite spirit, we can also reconsider the cases of Lim Chul-Woo and Yun Chŏng-mo, whose works in many ways epitomize the literary-political mission of the 1980s while evincing symptomatically the ideological blindness of the decade's political and cultural articulations. Lim Chul-Woo's works, which memorialize and sacralize the Kwangju massacre under the harshly repressive military regime of Chun Doo Hwan, can be reread as involving a violent subordination and erasure of working-class women and women activists of the era, as Lim's works are staunchly masculinist and even misogynistic. Likewise, Yun Chŏng-mo's works are celebrated for boldly exposing the continuity between the colonial and neocolonial domination by the Japanese and U.S. empires and making the hitherto unexplored linkage between the imperial sexual exploitation of Korean women and anti-neocolonial resistive leftist ethnonationalism. Despite her works' overt feminist orientation, however, I would argue that their allegorization of women's sexual imperialization in effect subordinated the working class's racialized and gendered sexuality to the "higher" causes of the masculinist antistate leftist ethnonation, conceived as an anti-neocolonial resistance in global imperial contexts. While I am in agreement with the existing assessment of her ideologically innovative contribution, the canonization of her works arguably overlooks the simplifying tendencies of Yun's work. It seems to me that the level of complexity in her works' conceptualization of (South) Korea's neocolonial history remains low: her literature merges the "popular" narrative form and its simplicity with "serious" political topoi. The literary establishment's consecration of Yun's works could function as a reminder for us of how a political agenda based upon leftist nationalist intellectual dominance tended to obscure other kinds of more complicated social, economic, and political formations.

Conclusion: Differently Politicizing Culture

The legacy of this division in literary and critical fields is still felt very powerfully in many ways in the production, dissemination, and canonization of literary output in present-day South Korea. In our (re)thinking through and (re)writing of both the leftist nationalist and the "pure" literature of an earlier era, we can productively tease out how other less prioritized and nonprioritized categories and formations, such as gender, sexuality, and ethnicity/race, operated in the representations of the histories of that era through their necessary intersections with the state, the ethnonation, and class. In this respect, the eleven chapters in this volume expand the contours of our inquiry into the heterogeneity of 1980s culture and fill in significant lacunae, all the while serving as examples of how we might also reexamine the cultures of the authoritarian era as a whole.[10]

The opening essays by Namhee Lee and Kyung Moon Hwang reassess recent South Korean historiography, premised upon the persistent ideological divide, and they show how the progressive camp's keen sense of historicity continues to function as a disruptive dissensual principle in the intensifying rightist domination of contemporary Korea. The next two essays by Jae-Yong Kim and Ruth Barraclough, in Part II, enable us to see the transnational connections, both intellectual and grassroots resistance, between South Korean dissidents and their counterparts around the world, such as the Third World nonalignment movement of Asia, Africa, and Latin America in the 1980s and student activism in places like the Philippines, Taiwan, Indonesia, and Sri Lanka. Also in Part II, Sohl Lee's essay on the minjung art's transnational connections astutely deconstructs a series of binarisms, which tended to sustain the perception of South Korea as isolated, dominated, and peripheral vis-à-vis North Korea, Japan, and the United States. Her chapter helps us, in our efforts to revise our understanding of the '80s as a fraught temporal cultural front, to reconfigure and redraw more complex lines of alliances, hegemony, and subversions. In Part III, Jung-Hwan Cheon and Chang Nam Kim deal with the newly emergent labor culture of the 1980s, respectively workers' literary clubs and activist songs, enlightening us on how working-class subjects played a formative role in the ongoing cultural resistance of the decade. Their essays accomplish a great deal to disrupt and deconstruct our notions about the working class and its relations to the elite-led dissident movements. Part IV offers us two chapters, by Hye-Ryoung Lee and Kyunghee Eo, on how we might reconceptualize the representation of women as well as women's creative agency both on the literary and the popular cultural front. It is particularly interesting, as Eo's essay shows, that popular culture tended to be more subversive than so-called "high" literature in its representations of women and race/ethnicity. This leads us to the various popular cultural themes in the final section of the volume, with chapters by Yun-Jong Lee and Sunyoung Park, respectively, on the erotic films of the 1980s and the science fiction literature of the era. Linking up with the themes that I treated here, it is clear that the dominance of "high" literature in the sphere of cultural resistance during the authoritarian era was the proximate cause of the marginalization of "popular" culture. With the contemporary rise of K-pop and *hallyu* (the Korean wave), the popular cultural production of the earlier decades has received more scholarly attention in recent years. This current research into the history of popular culture and its consumption is a very much needed reexamination of the social-economic-cultural formations of the working class. *Minjung munhak*, or the leftist ethnonationalist literature movement, was an elite-led populist culture movement that included an effort to encourage more participation on the part of working-class subjects themselves. Popular culture, enjoyed and consumed by the working class of the authoritarian era, was none other than sounds and images, unheard and unseen, for the most part, by the elite dissidents. The essays in this volume contribute to our alternative and more complicated understanding of both "popular" and "populist" culture and aesthetics.[11]

Wendy Brown speaks of the "invisibility and inarticulateness of class" in the U.S. context, where elision of capital and thus erasure of class take place via identity politics.[12] In postdevelopment South Korea, class is also, in similar and yet significantly different ways, being obfuscated, as we also simultaneously see the emergence of identity politics, centering on women, (im)migrants, and the LGBT population. It is not just in the field of South Korean popular cultural productions that the invisibilized and yet more strongly entrenched structures and grammars of U.S. mass culture exercise their influence. In the arena of politics, both governance/governmentality and resistance/opposition debates are increasingly modeling themselves, both consciously and unwittingly, after the identity-based multiculturalism of the United States.

The internal geopolitical terrain of South Korea is an extremely complex one in this era of multiple and overlapping "post-ness" that encompasses both the residual and the emergent: post–student movement, post-authoritarian, post–Cold War. If the New Right is a contemporary revenant of the earlier conservative thought, then we would want to ask where the intellectual left itself is evolving in rethinking the constantly changing and ever more complex political formations of South Korea.

NOTES

1. Although the term "antigovernment" has been used in South Korea to refer to the dissident movements, my usage of the term "antistate" indicates a broader and theoretical sense of opposition, directed at the state, that might be applicable to cases outside of South Korea.
2. Rancière, *Aesthetics and Its Discontents*, 25.
3. Rancière, *The Politics of Aesthetics*, 85.
4. Ibid., 51.
5. Angela Davis, cited in Lowe, *Immigrant Acts*, 74–75, emphasis added.
6. Omi and Winant, *Racial Formation in the United States*, 77–91. See also Jin-kyung Lee, *Service Economies*.
7. As Choi Jang Jip eloquently argues, when the emphasis of the dictatorial states shifted from engagement with the traditionally defined political to economic developmentalism as the new "political" (the shift from the Syngman Rhee regime to the Park Chung Hee regime), the dissident movement was also obliged to change its orientation from professing liberal democratic desires and protesting against their repression (in the period leading up to the April 19 Revolution and the first half of the 1960s under Park) to labor and unionizing movements as the main focus of antigovernment activism in the second half of the 1960s and throughout the 1970s. Choi, "Political Cleavages in South Korea."
8. See Namhee Lee, *The Making of Minjung*, and Hagen Koo, *Korean Workers*.
9. See Namhee Lee's chapter in this volume, where she discusses Yi Mun-yol's *Sŏnt'aek* (Choice) from 1996 in the context of the ensuing controversy over its antifeminist and misogynist content.
10. Please see Kim Yŏngch'an's insightful essay, "1960-yŏndae chŏngch'isŏng ŭl 'tasi' saenggak handa" (Rethinking the political in the literature of the 1960s), where he explores the possibility of "rediscovering" different meanings of "politics" in 1960s literature. His readings of Kim Sŭng-ok, Choi In-hun, and Yi Chŏng-jun successfully tease out "other" political possibilities of the so-called modernist literature, urging us to "reread" literary works of the earlier era, as I have argued in this chapter.
11. Please see Stuart Hall for a valuable polysemic redefinition of the "popular": "Notes on Deconstructing the Popular."
12. See Brown, *States of Injury*, 61.

REFERENCES

Brown, Wendy. *States of Injury: Power and Freedom in Late Modernity*. Princeton: Princeton University Press, 1995.
Choi, Jang Jip. "Political Cleavages in South Korea." In *State and Society in Contemporary Korea*, edited by Hagen Koo, 13–50. Ithaca: Cornell University Press, 1995.
Hall, Stuart. "Notes on Deconstructing the Popular." In *Popular Culture: A Reader*, 64–71. London: Sage, 2005.
Kim, Yŏngch'an. "1960-yŏndae chŏngch'isŏng ŭl 'tasi' saenggak handa" (Rethinking the political in the literature of the 1960s). *Sanghŏ hakpo: The Journal of Modern Literature* 40 (February 2014): 185–211.
Koo, Hagen. *Korean Workers: The Culture and Politics of Class Formation*. Ithaca: Cornell University Press, 2001.
Lee, Jin-kyung. *Service Economies: Militarism, Sex Work, and Migrant Labor in South Korea*. Minneapolis: University of Minnesota Press, 2010.
Lee, Namhee. *The Making of Minjung: Democracy and the Politics of Representation in South Korea*. Ithaca: Cornell University Press, 2007.
Lowe, Lisa. *Immigrant Acts: On Asian American Cultural Politics*. Durham: Duke University Press, 1996.
Omi, Michael, and Howard Winant. *Racial Formation in the United States*. London: Routledge, 1994.
Rancière, Jacques. *Aesthetics and Its Discontents*. Translated by Steven Corcoran. Cambridge: Polity, 2009.
Rancière, Jacques. *The Politics of Aesthetics*. Translated by Gabriel Rockhill. New York: Continuum, 2004.

Contributors

Ruth Barraclough is associate professor in Pacific and Asian history at the Australian National University, where she teaches modern Korean history and literature. She is the author of *Factory Girl Literature: Sexuality, Violence and Representation in Industrializing Korea* (University of California Press, 2012) and coeditor of *Red Love across the Pacific* (Palgrave Macmillan, 2015) and *Gender and Labour in Korea and Japan: Sexing Class* (Routledge, 2009).

Jung-Hwan Cheon is professor of Korean language and literature at Sungkyunkwan University in Seoul. He is the author of *Reading Books in Modern Times: The Birth of Readers and Modern Korean Literature* (Kŭndae ŭi ch'aek ikki: Tokcha ŭi t'ansaeng kwa kŭndae munhak; P'urŭn yŏksa, 2003) as well as other monographs. He is also coauthor of *A Reflection on 1960: Intellectuals and Cultural Politics in Pak Chung Hee's Era* (1960-yŏn ŭl mudda: Pak Chung Hee sidae ŭi munhwa chŏngch'i wa chisŏng; Chŏnnyŏn ŭi sangsang, 2012). Among his previous publications in English are "The Development of Mass Intellectuality: Reading Circles and Socialist Culture in 1920s Korea" (*East Asian History*, 2014) and "Bend It Like a Man of Chosun: Sports Nationalism and Colonial Modernity of 1936," in *The Korean Popular Culture Reader*, edited by Kyung Hyun Kim and Youngmin Choe (Duke University Press, 2014).

Kyunghee Eo is a PhD candidate in English and gender studies at the University of Southern California. Her interests lie at the intersections of gender, sexuality, postcoloniality, and subimperialism across the transpacific world. Her dissertation, "Politics of Purity: A Queer Transpacific Genealogy of Korean Girlhood," focuses on literary and visual representations of girls in Korean, Japanese, and U.S. cultural productions. She has contributed translations to two forthcoming anthologies, *Remembering*

Queer Korea (Duke University Press, 2018) and *Readymade Bodhisattva: The Kaya Anthology of South Korean Science Fiction* (Kaya Press, 2019).

Kyung Moon Hwang is professor of history and East Asian languages and cultures at the University of Southern California. He is the author of *Rationalizing Korea: The Rise of the Modern State, 1894–1945* (University of California Press, 2015), *A History of Korea: An Episodic Narrative* (Palgrave Macmillan, 2016 [2010]), and *Beyond Birth: Social Status in the Emergence of Modern Korea* (Harvard University Asia Center, 2004). He is also coeditor of *Contentious Kwangju: The May 18 Uprising in Korea's Past and Present* (Rowman & Littlefield, 2003).

Chang Nam Kim is professor of media and communication studies at Sungkonghoe University in Seoul. He is the author of *K-Pop: Roots and Blossoming of Korean Popular Music* (Hollym, 2012). His books in Korean include *Understanding Popular Culture* (Taejung munhwa ŭi ihae; Hanul ak'ademi, 2014 [2009]) and *Popular Music, Music Activism, and Youth Culture* (Taejung munhak, norae undong, kŭrigo chŏngnyŏn munhwa; Hanul ak'ademi, 2004). He is also the founder and committee chair of the Korean Popular Music Award (since 2004).

Jae-Yong Kim is professor of modern Korean literature and world literature at Wonkwang University in Seoul. His publications in English include "From Eurocentric World Literature to Global World Literature" (*Journal of World Literature*, 2016). Among his works in Korean are the monographs *Asian Literature as World Literature* (Segye munhak ŭrosŏ ŭi Asia munhak; Kŭlnurim, 2012) and *North Korean Literature in the Division System* (Pundan kujo wa Pukhan munhak; Somyŏng ch'ulp'an, 2000). He is also coauthor of *History of Modern Korean Literature* (Han'guk kŭndae minjok munhaksa; Han'gilsa, 1993) and coeditor of *Rat Fire: Korean Stories from the Japanese Empire* (Cornell East Asia Series, 2013).

Hye-Ryoung Lee is associate professor at the Academy of East Asian Studies at Sungkyunkwan University in Seoul. She is the author of *Narratives of Sexuality in Modern Korean Novels* (Han'guk kŭndae sosŏl kwa seksyuŏlit'i ŭi sŏsahak; Somyŏng ch'ulp'an, 2007) and coeditor of several volumes, including *A Time under the Tree of Heaven: Reading Yŏm Sangsŏp* (Chŏsuha ŭi sigan: Yŏm Sangsŏp ŭl ikta; Somyŏng ch'ulp'an, 2014); *Empire of Censorship: The Control of Culture and Its Reproduction* (Ken'etsu no teikoku: Bunka no tōsei to saiseisan; Shin'yōsha, 2014); and *Interview: Shifting Terrains of Korean Humanities* (Int'ŏbyu: Han'guk inmunhak ŭi chigak pyŏndong; Kŭrinbi, 2011).

Jin-kyung Lee is associate professor of Korean and comparative literature at the University of California, San Diego. She is the author of *Service Economies: Militarism, Sex Work, and Migrant Labor in South Korea* (University of Minnesota Press, 2010) as well as coeditor of *Rat Fire: Korean Stories from the Japanese Empire* (Cornell East Asia Series, 2013) and *Modern Korea at a Crossroads between Empire and Nation* (Kŭndae Han'guk, cheguk kwa minjok ŭi kyoch'aro; Ch'aek kwa hamkke, 2011). She is also coeditor of a special issue of the *Review of Korean Studies*, "Korean Literature, Literary Studies, and Disciplinary Crossings: A Transpacific Comparative Examination" (December 2013).

Namhee Lee is associate professor of modern Korean history at the University of California, Los Angeles. Her publications include *The Making of Minjung: Democracy and the Politics of Representation in South Korea* (Cornell University Press, 2007) and *The South Korean Democratization Movement: A Sourcebook* (coedited with Kim Won, Academy of Korean Studies, 2016). She is currently working on a book about social memory of the 1980s in the context of globalization, neoliberalism, and the persistence of the Cold War in Korea.

Sohl Lee is assistant professor of modern and contemporary East Asian art in the Department of Art History and Criticism at Stony Brook University. Her articles have appeared in a variety of journals, including *Art Journal*, *InVisible Culture*, the *Journal of Korean Studies*, and *Yishu: Journal for Contemporary Chinese Art*. She is also coeditor of a special issue on ecology and contemporary art in East Asia for the *Journal of Contemporary Chinese Art*. She is currently working on a book project entitled "The Democratic Avant-Garde: Minjung Art and South Korean Revolution."

Yun-Jong Lee is assistant professor at the Institute of Northeast Asian Humanities and Social Sciences at Wonkwang University in Iksan. She received her PhD with a dissertation on South Korean erotic films of the 1980s from the Department of East Asian Languages and Literatures at the University of California, Irvine in 2012. She has authored "Woman in Ethno-Cultural Peril: South Korean Nationalist Erotic Films of the 1980s"

(*Journal of Korean Studies*, 2016) and has also published in Korean-language journals on a wide range of topics, including Korean film, cinematic genres, women and gender, capitalism, and popular culture.

Sunyoung Park is associate professor of East Asian languages and cultures and gender studies at the University of Southern California. She is the author of *The Proletarian Wave: Literature and Leftist Culture in Colonial Korea, 1910–1945* (Harvard University Asia Center, 2015) and the editor and translator of *On the Eve of the Uprising and Other Stories from Colonial Korea* (Cornell East Asian Series, 2010). She is currently working on a monograph on science fiction and the politics of modernization in South Korea, and she is coeditor of a forthcoming collection of fiction entitled *Readymade Bodhisattva: The Kaya Anthology of South Korean Science Fiction* (Kaya Press, 2019).

Index

Achebe, Chinua, 200
Across the Pacific: Contemporary Korean and Korean American Art (exhibition; Queens, NY; 1993), 121
activists (*undonggwŏn*): censorship by, 253, 282; and economic development, 224, 280, 286n7; elite, 285; and ethnonation, 280–81; intellectual, 1, 2, 24, 34–35, 50, 51; masculinist, 282–83; and middle class, 97; and music, 8, 149, 150–51, 154, 163, 164n2, 284; vs. popular culture, 9, 151–52; pro-North (*chongbuk chwap'a, chusap'a*), 18, 20–21, 34, 39n12; and Third World, 107; women, 7, 8–9, 169, 170–77, 180–81, 186, 188; and workers, 143, 280, 281, 284–85. *See also* students
Adada (film; Im Kwon-taek), 234
Adorno, Theodor, 152, 156–57
Africa, 66, 68, 69, 80, 91; literature of, 75, 77, 82, 105–10, 121n2, 122n3
African Americans, 9, 90–92, 99n15, 211; literature of, 201–2; male, 197–98, 205, 206–7, 215. *See also* black women
African National Congress (ANC), 91
Afro-Asian Latin American Writers' Association (AALA), 107. *See also* JAALA
Afro-Asian Writers' Workshop (Tokyo; 1961), 121n2
Age of Success (film; *Sŏnggong sidae*; Jang Sun-woo), 236
Ah, Park Chung Hee (Kim Chŏngnyŏm), 40n42
Ahn Junghyo, 198, 202, 215

Ahn So-young, 228
al-Afghānī, Jamāl al-Dīn, 69
alternate history (*taech'e yŏksa*), 261, 270n26. *See also In Search of an Epitaph; Man in the High Castle, The*
Alternative Textbook: Modern and Contemporary Korean History (*Han'guk kŭnhyŏndaesa: Taean kyogwasŏ*), 35–36, 37, 52
Althusser, Louis, 39n6
Altman, Rick, 240
America, America (film; *Amerika, Amerika*; Jang Gil-su), 237
Amnesty International, 94
An Chŏnghyo, 79
An Chunggŭn, 257
An Hamgwang, 66
An Pyŏngjik, 34
An Pyŏnguk, 49–50
Anderson, Perry, 25
Animal Farm (Orwell), 261
anticommunism, 19–22, 36, 261, 269n15, 280; and ethnonation, 278–79; in leftist vs. rightist historiography, 49, 50, 53–57, 59; and *minjung* art, 107, 114; and North Korea, 20–21; and U.S., 71, 72, 78; and women's movement, 174; and workers, 93, 131
Appadurai, Arjun, 90, 97
Are You Still Dreaming? (*Kŭdae ajikto kkum kkugo innŭn'ga*; Pak Wansŏ), 179
"Are You Still Dreaming of Revolution?" (*Tangsin ŭn ajikto hyŏngmyŏng ŭl kkumkkunŭn'ga*; Sin Chiho), 34

Arirang of the Kuro Industrial Complex (*Kuro Arirang*; Yi Mun-yol), 283
art, *minjung*, 103–24; and anticommunism, 107, 114; as art at the political site (*hyŏnjang misul*), 116; audience for, 105; in Canada, 112; censorship of, 104; and center vs. periphery, 119; collective production of, 115–16, 117–18, 120; decline of, 121; in demonstrations, 104, 109, 114; and globalization, 7, 120; and intellectuals, 105, 106–7, 109, 119; and international art, 105–10, 121n2, 122n3; and Japan, 7, 105–10, 117, 119, 284; and Mexican art, 119; and *minjung* song, 149; and *modŏnisŭt'ŭ* (modernist) art, 107; and neoliberalism, 104, 120; in North Korea, 7, 114–20, 123n30; in protest banners, 104, 109, 110–11, 115–19, 121; public (*kŏlgae kŭrim*), 115–19, 123n25; reproduction of, 117–19; state endorsement of, 120–21; and transnationalism, 104, 106, 108, 119, 284; and U.S., 7, 110–14, 117, 119, 284
Artists Space (art gallery; New York), 110–14
ASIA (journal), 80, 81
Asian, African and Latin American Literary Forum, 82
Asian and African Writers' Congress (AAWC), 75, 77
Asian Games (1986), 237
Asian Women at Work (Australia), 93
"Asphalt" (*Asŭp'alt'ŭ*; Hyŏn Kiyŏng), 72
"August Diary" (8-wŏl ŭi ilgi; Kim Taesuk), 178
Australia, 85, 87, 88–89, 93–94; indigenous people of, 91, 97–98; Paul Robeson in, 90–92
Australian Student Christian Movement (ASCM), 85, 93–94
authoritarianism, 22, 31, 35–37; vs. democratization, 17, 25; and economic development, 26, 36; and ethnonationalism, 10, 278; in leftist historiography, 48; and literature, 284; and *minjung* art, 114; and NSL, 19, 117, 123n27; and political categories, 275–78. *See also* censorship; Chun Doo Hwan; Park Chung Hee

Back to the Future (film), 256
Badiou, Alain, 19
Bae Chang-ho, 235
Bahc Mo, 112, 113, 123n20
Balkan Peninsula, 68
Bandung Conference (1955), 74
Barraclough, Ruth, 7, 178, 284; political exposure tour of, 85, 89, 95, 96–98
Belgium, 92
Bennett, Tony, 164
Berlin Conference (1884), 68, 69
Berlin Wall, fall of, 117
Bertolucci, Bernardo, 225
Between the Knees (film; *Murŭp kwa murŭp sai*; Lee Jang-ho), 235, 237, 238
Black Arts movement, 201
Black Panthers, 200
Black Woman (film; *Hŭngnyŏ*; Kang Taesŏn), 197, 198, 208–14, 215
"Black Woman" (*Hŭginnyŏ*; Pae Inch'ŏl), 196
black women, 9, 195–217; and class, 206, 208, 211, 216; and colonialism, 196, 198; and feminism, 198, 202, 215; in film, 208–14; lesbian, 197, 198, 206–8, 214, 216; and nationalism, 215; sexuality of, 198, 206, 207–8; urban, 211
Blade Runner (film; Scott), 248
Blazing Sun (film; Hah Myung-joong), 234, 238
Blyden, Edward Wilmut, 69
Body Heat (film; Kasdan), 226
Bok Geo-il, 10, 32, 33, 250, 253, 254, 266, 270n29
Bolshevism, 23–24
Bong Joon-ho, 267
Born in 1999 (*1999-yŏnsaeng*; Sin Ilsuk), 253
Bridle (*Koppi*; Yun Chŏngmo), 179
Britain, 68, 70
Brown, Wendy, 285
Buddhism, 115, 258, 259
Burma, 98; bombing in (1983), 57
Bush, George W., 25

Index | 295

Cambridge Companion to Pop and Rock, 155
"Camel's Eye" (Nakt'a nunkkal; Hwang Sok-young), 78
camptown narratives (*kijich'on munhak*), 9, 205–8, 215, 216, 283
Canada, 112
Capital (Marx), 19, 39n6
capitalism, 24–25, 275, 279, 281; critiques of, 69, 79; and democracy, 107, 173; and ero film, 224, 231, 236, 241; and globalization, 87; industrial, 68, 79; left vs. right on, 6, 54, 57, 59, 104; and mainstream music, 156–58; and neoliberalism, 20, 23; in textbooks, 35; and Vietnam War, 203, 204; and women's movement, 174, 177, 185
Carstens, Debbie, 93, 97
Castells, Manuel, 25
Castro, Fidel, 73
Catholic Church, 86, 92
censorship: and cassette tapes, 156; and democratization, 151–52; of ero film, 10, 226–27, 228, 230, 241; and historiography, 252; and Kwangju Uprising, 2, 11n5, 250; by leftists, 253, 282; of *minjung* art, 104, 116–17; of music, 8, 151, 155, 160, 161, 162–63; of science fiction, 260–61, 267, 269n17; of social sciences, 268n8; and women's literature, 189n22; and workers' literary clubs, 134, 142
Center for Free Enterprise, 33
Césaire, Aimé, 200, 201
Ceylon, 87. *See also* Sri Lanka
Ch'a Pŏmsŏk, 198, 199, 208–9
Ch'ae Kwangsŏk, 138
chaebol conglomerates, 58
Cheju Island uprisings, 72
Chi Chuhyŭng, 57, 58
Chigujŏk segye munhak (Global world literature; journal), 82
Chilsu and Mansu (film; *Ch'ilsu wa Mansu*; Pak Kwangsu), 4
China, 22, 67, 77, 120, 200, 226
chipch'ejak (collective production), 117–18
Cho Chŏngnae, 4, 72, 252, 269nn14–15
Cho Haejoang, 180–81

Cho Kapche, 27, 28–29, 30, 34
Cho Yŏngnae, 138
Cho Yongp'il, 158
Choe Byŏngsu, 110–12, 115, 121
Ch'oe Hongjae, 35
Ch'oe Minhŭi, 178
Ch'oe Wŏnsik, 200
Ch'ohondo (Memorial painting; Kim Bong-jun), 123n15
Choi In-hun, 256, 286n10
Choi Jang Jip, 49, 286n7
Choi Jung-Bong, 238
Choice (*Sŏnt'aek*; Yi Mun-yol), 32, 286n9
Cho-Joong-Dong (newspapers), 28, 33
Chŏn Chaeho, 28
Chŏn Okchu, 249
Chŏn T'aeil, 96, 131
Chŏng Han-a, 216
Chŏng Hŭisŏng, 143
Chŏng Hwajin, 178
Chŏng Inhwa, 132
Chŏng T'aech'un, 162–63
Chŏng Yŏng-man, 124n31
Chosŏn period, 2
Chosun Ilbo (*Korea Daily*), 27, 28, 31, 33, 34
Christianity, 7, 67, 85–100
Christofferson, Michael Scott, 24
Chronicles of the Nuclear Bugs (*manhwa*; *Haekch'ung i nat'anatta*; Sin Kihwal), 253, 266
Chun Doo Hwan, 275, 279, 280, 281; demonstrations against, 2–3, 85, 104, 249; end of regime of, 88, 112, 171; and *Epitaph*, 260; and ero film, 228, 229, 231; and Kwangju, 2, 48, 250, 283; in leftist vs. rightist historiography, 47–49, 52–54, 56, 57
Chungmuro film district, 223, 224, 227–29, 231
"Circle" (Tongŭrami; Ch'oe Minhŭi), 178
civil rights movement, U.S., 23, 93, 201
class: and black women, 206, 208, 211, 216; and capitalism, 25; in comics, 248, 266; and education, 146n2; and ero film, 238; and ethnonationalism, 10,

class (*continued*)
279, 280, 281; and European Enlightenment, 146n2; and identity politics, 276–78, 285; and industrialization, 86; in leftist vs. rightist historiography, 37, 55, 56, 57; and literature, 139, 142, 179, 186, 187, 253, 268, 282–83, 284; and *minjung* culture, 251, 252; and politics and aesthetics, 277–78; and race, 199; and the state, 280–81; and women, 170, 172, 174, 176–77, 179, 186, 187, 206, 208, 211, 216, 282–83; and workers' literary clubs, 131, 135, 137, 141, 144. *See also* intellectuals; middle class; workers

Cleaver, Eldridge, 200

Cold War, 19–22; end of, 18, 117, 121, 142; hot wars in, 20; in leftist vs. rightist historiography, 36, 49, 54, 55, 56; and literature, 77, 196; and *minjung* art, 107; and North Korea, 6, 252; political travel in, 7, 86–87, 89, 90, 91; and South Korean science fiction, 266; and Third World, 75, 77, 80; U.S. in, 31, 72–73, 107; U.S.S.R. in, 74; and women's movement, 174

"Collection of Maxims from Jupiter" (*Moksŏng chamŏnjip*; Bok Geo-il), 32, 33

comics (*manhwa*), 247–48, 265–66

commercialism: of ero film, 224, 225, 229, 232; and *minjung* song, 157–58; and science fiction, 254; of women's literature, 187

communism, 19, 142. *See also* anticommunism

Communist Party, Australian, 89

"Confession" (*Kobaek*; Sin Chiho), 34

Congress of the Peoples of the East (Baku, Azerbaijan; 1920), 74

conservatives, 5, 6; electoral losses of, 21–22; literature of, 32, 33; newspapers of, 27–28. *See also* New Right

constitutions, South Korean, 3, 48, 49

cosmopolitanism from below, 7, 90, 97, 98

counterdevelopmentalism, 232, 236, 240, 241

Creation and Criticism (Ch'angjak kwa pip'yŏng; activist collective and journal), 77, 142, 173, 190n24

"Crisis of Intellectual Literature and a Plan for a New National Literature" (Chisigin munhak ŭi wigi wa saeroun minjok munhak ŭi kusang; Kim Myŏngin), 139

Critical Biography of Chŏn T'aeil. See Life and Death of a Young Worker: The Critical Biography of Chŏn T'aeil

"Critique of the Current Theoretical Development of Korean Women's Liberation" (Han'guk yŏsŏng haebang iron ŭi chŏn'gae e taehan pip'anjŏk kŏmt'o), 174

Cuba, 73

Cultural Revolution (China), 22

culture: of democratization, 11, 129, 142–43, 152; and feminism, 180, 232–33; hegemonic, 151, 152, 153, 154, 156; and identity, 158–59; labor, 5, 8, 129–65; and subcultures, 152–54, 158; youth (*chŏngnyŏn munhwa*), 86, 158, 160. *See also minjung* culture; popular culture

Cumings, Bruce, 55, 236

Czechoslovakia, 89–90, 99n9

Darwish, Mahmoud, 202

Davis, Angela, 202, 276

Dawn (*Hyop'ung*; Yŏm Sangsŏp), 71

Dawn of Labor (*Nodong ŭi saebyŏk*; Pak Nohae), 4, 138

"Days and Dreams" (Nat kwa kkum; Kang Sŏk-kyŏng), 197, 198, 205–8, 215, 216

"Daytime Moon" (Nattal; Kang Sŏk-kyŏng), 183

De Christiana expeditione apud Sinas (On the Christian expedition to China; Ricci), 67

Deep Blue Night (film; *Kipko p'urŭn pam*; Bae Chang-ho), 235, 237, 238

democracy (*minju*), 24, 103, 108; capitalist, 107, 173; liberal, 52, 54, 57, 201

Democratic Party (U.S.), 23

democratization, 2–3; and 386 generation, 30; in Asia, 98, 99; and censorship, 151–52; conservative opposition to, 6, 17, 19,

22, 25, 27–28, 31; criticism of, 25, 27–28; culture of, 11, 129, 142–43, 152; and domestic violence, 184–86; and *Epitaph*, 256, 262–63; establishment of (1987), 46–47, 53, 54, 55, 59; as failure, 48–51, 59; historiography of, 4–5, 48, 49–53, 58–59; and industrialization, 47, 48; and intellectuals, 5, 142–43; and international exchange, 7–8, 48, 88, 119; and music, 149–50, 155, 161–62; vs. neoliberalism, 35; and science fiction, 10, 249, 254, 265–68; and subcultures, 152; teleology of, 52, 53, 57, 59; and women, 5, 9, 174, 177, 178, 180, 184–86; and workers, 129, 130–31, 134, 137, 140
demonstrations: anti-Security Treaty (Japan), 106; against Chun Doo Hwan, 2–3, 85, 104, 249; and *minjung* art, 104, 109, 114, 115–19; against Park Geun Hye, 10–11; rightist view of, 56; Tiananmen (China, 1989), 98; violence in, 110–12, 114, 143
Dick, Philip A., 256, 261, 265
Dirlik, Arif, 22–23
discontinuity, regime of, 17–19, 27, 38, 267
Djuna, 267
DMZ (Demilitarized Zone), 20, 100n27, 117
Dobson, Tamara, 211
domestic violence, 9, 171, 183–86
Dong-A Ilbo (*East Asia Daily*), 28, 34
"Dream of the Future of the Earth" (Chigusŏng miraemong; Sin Ch'aeho), 69
Du Bois, W.E.B., 69
Dylan, Bob, 159

Eastern Europe, 22
Echols, Alice, 232–33
economic development: and 1997 crisis, 25, 36–37, 58, 144; and class, 86; and ero films, 224; and ethnonationalism, 279–80; and global economy, 58; leftist vs. rightist historiography of, 21, 36, 52, 53–58; and *minjung* movement, 36, 224, 280, 286n7; and nonalignment movement, 75; and Park Chung Hee, 26, 28, 31, 32, 37, 40n42, 286n7; and workers' literary clubs, 137
education, 112, 146n2, 154, 210; of women, 135, 139, 176; and workers' literary clubs, 8, 129–31, 133, 135, 137, 139, 144, 145
elections, 85; direct presidential, 1, 3, 49, 104, 112; gymnasium (ch'eyukkwan sŏn'gŏ), 48
Emmanuelle (film; Jaeckin), 226
Empire of Lust (film; *Lunsu ŭi sidae*; Ahn Sang-hoon), 240
Empty Dream (film; *Ch'unmong*; Yu Hyun-mok), 226
Engels, Friedrich, 174
Enloe, Cynthia, 236
"Episode from Bygone Days, An" (Chŏmun nal ŭi saphwa; Pak Wansŏ), 9, 183–86
Epitaph. See *In Search of an Epitaph*
ethnonation (*minjok*), 2, 6, 24, 103, 275, 277–82, 284; and homosexuality, 204, 214; and women, 9, 10, 228, 279, 280
Eunuch (film; *Naesi*; Lee Doo-yong), 238
Eunuch (film; *Naesi*; Shin Sang-ok), 226
Eurocentrism, 74, 78, 79, 82
Europe, 22, 67–70, 87, 92, 146n2. *See also* West, the; *particular countries*
Everlasting Empire (*Yŏngwŏnhan cheguk*; Yi In-hwa), 31

Factory Girl Literature (Barraclough), 96
Factory Lights (*Kongjang ŭi pulbit*; Sŏk Chŏngnam), 135, 136, 156
Fanon, Frantz, 200, 201
Fatal Attraction (film; Lyne), 226
Father (*Abŏji*; Kim Chŏnghyŏn), 32
Feldman, Allen, 27
feminism: antipornography, 232–33; and black women, 198, 202, 215; in camptown narratives, 206, 207; and counter-developmentalism, 232; cultural, 180, 232–33; and ero film, 223–24, 236, 240, 241; fantasies of, 198; intersectional, 5, 9, 12n12, 169–217, 188n5; liberal middle-class, 176; and literature, 187, 282–83; Marxist, 173, 178; and *minjung* move-

feminism (*continued*)
ment, 3, 114, 169, 196, 264; and student exchanges, 85; Western, 174, 181, 185, 196–97. *See also* women

15 Years of Minjung Art, 1980–1994 (exhibition; National Museum of Contemporary Art; 1993), 120–21, 124n36

film: black women in, 208–14; blaxploitation, 211, 214; and comics, 248; Hollywood, 211, 226, 231, 256, 267; and home video, 225, 226, 229–30; hostess (*hosŭtisŭ yŏnghwa*), 9, 209, 210, 227, 228, 231; international, 224–26, 241; literature in, 188n4, 269n14; and *minjung* song, 149; *minjung* vs. ero, 233–34; science fiction, 254, 267–68; and technology, 234, 253–54; women's (*yŏsŏng yŏnghwa*), 224; youth (*chŏngch'un yŏnghwa*), 227, 242n18

film, erotic (*ero yŏnghwa*), 9–10, 223–44, 285; and adult video (AV), 225, 229–30, 240; black women in, 197, 198, 208–14, 215; censorship of, 10, 226–27, 228, 230, 241; and costume drama genre, 228, 234, 238, 240; at film festivals, 234, 238; history of, 226–31; and industrialization, 224, 227, 236; and international film, 224–26; legacy of, 240–41; and *minjung* movement, 232, 233–34, 235, 236, 239, 240, 241; nationalist (*minjokchuŭi*), 235–36, 238; *pinku eiga* (Japanese pink), 225, 231, 242n7; progression and regression in, 223–24, 231–39; *roman poruno* (fictional pornography), 225; and technology, 234; and Western films, 225–28

film industry: Japanese, 225; and *minjung* movement, 223–24; and television, 226, 227, 229

Fine, Windy Day, A (film; Lee Jang-ho), 234

Fitzpatrick, Sheila, 90

Flower at the Equator (film; *Chŏkto ŭi kkot*; Bae Chang-ho), 235

For Marx (Althusser), 39n6

Foster, Hal, 113

France, 35, 39n1, 70, 92, 226; 1968 protests in, 23, 89, 98, 225; revisionist history of, 22–23, 24; in Russo-Japanese War, 68

Frankfurt School, 157

Freire, Paulo, 137

French Revolution, 22–23, 24

Frith, Simon, 157

Furet, François, 22, 24

García Márquez, Gabriel, 73

gender, 60n17, 98, 281; and ethnonationalism, 10, 279, 280; and feminist literature, 282–83, 284; and identity politics, 170, 276–78. *See also* women

Germany, 23, 24, 38, 68, 70, 181, 256

Gilman, Sander L., 208

Ginko Bed (film; *Ŭnhaeng namu ch'imdae*; Kang Jae-kyu), 254

globalization (*segyehwa*), 5, 19, 279, 281; capitalist model of, 87; in leftist vs. rightist historiography, 56, 58; and literature, 80–82; and *minjung* art, 7, 120; and multiculturalism, 216; and New Right, 35, 36–37

"God Being Beaten" (Mae mannŭn hananim; Ko Chŏnghŭi), 183

Goethe, Johann Wolfgang von, 68, 80

Gong Ji-young, 169, 171

Great Labor Struggle (1987), 57, 140, 178

Greater East Asia Co-Prosperity Sphere, 106

Grier, Pam, 197, 211, 214

Ha Gil-jong, 227

Habermas, Jürgen, 38–39

Hackett, Robin, 208

Hah Myung-joong, 234, 237, 238

Half a Failure (*Chŏlban ŭi silp'ae*; Yi Kyŏngja), 179

Han Dae-Soo, 160

Han Sŏrya, 74

Han Wansang, 137

Hanging Tree (film; *Chanyŏmok*; Jung Jin-woo), 238

Hartfield, John, 113

Haryū Ichirō, 106, 107, 108, 122nn3–4

"Hat" (Moja; Han Sŏrya), 74

Heavenly Homecoming to Stars (film; Pyŏldŭl ŭi kohyang; Lee Jang-ho), 227, 234–35, 242n19
Hirohito, Emperor, 257
Historian's Dispute (1980s; Germany), 24, 38
historiography, 4–6, 46–60, 284; and censorship, 252; contingency in, 262, 265; of democratization, 4–5, 48, 49–53, 58–59; of economic development, 21, 36, 52, 53–58; English-language, 51; and *Epitaph*, 256, 262–63, 265; geopolitical, 53–58; of Korea, 251–52; leftist, 37, 47–51, 52, 55, 56, 57–58; and mass media, 27–33; on *minjung* movement, 50, 51, 59; "monumental," 38; neoliberal, 37, 50, 51, 55, 57, 59; political, 47–53; revisionist, 38, 269n13; of revolutions, 18, 24; rightist, 37, 39, 52–53, 56–58; social memory in, 6, 17–41
History of Modern Korean Literature (*Han'guk kŭndae minjok munhaksa*), 80
History of South Korea: Steps toward the Making of a Country, 1948–1987 (Yi Yŏnghun), 53–54
History of the National Liberation Movement (public art; *kŏlgae kŭrim*), 115–20; North Korean reproduction of, 117–19, 120
Hoggart, Richard, 131, 146n2
homosexuality: and cultural feminism, 233; and ethnonation, 204, 214; female, 197, 198, 206–8, 213–14, 216; and identity politics, 276–78, 281, 285
Hong Chinp'yo, 34, 35
Hong Sungdam, 117
Hong Yun'gi, 28
Horkheimer, Max, 152
How to Change the World with Minjung Culture (*Minshū no bunka ga sekai o kaeru tame ni*), 77
Hwang Sok-young, 78, 117
Hwang Sun-wŏn, 282
Hyŏn Kiyŏng, 71–72
hyŏnjang misul (art at the political site), 116

I Want to Be in Your Arms Again (film; Kŭdae kasŭm e tasi han pŏn; Kim Sagyŏm), 208–9, 211–12
identity: and class, 170, 276–78, 285; countercultural, 153; cultural, 158–59; feminist, 169; and gender, 170, 276–78; and history, 38–39; politics of, 120, 170, 276–78, 281, 285; and rise of capitalism, 25; and social memory, 26
Im Hwa, 66
Im Kwon-taek, 235, 236, 238, 269n14
Im Sang-soo, 231, 234, 240
IMF crisis (1997), 25, 36–37, 58, 144
imperialism: American, 6, 70–73, 140, 173, 251, 252, 263, 266, 278, 283; and English language, 96; and erasure of Korean culture, 257–58, 259, 263; and ethnonationalism, 278, 279; and intellectuals, 6, 263–64; Japanese, 72, 80, 122n3, 201, 252, 256–59, 263, 264, 270n24, 278, 279; and Korean science fiction, 263, 266; and nationalism, 69, 151; and New Right, 37; in non-Western countries, 66–67; opposition to, 7, 65, 67, 69, 70, 79–82, 151; and race, 201, 204, 213; sexual, 283; South Korean, 78–79, 215; Soviet, 6; Western, 66, 69, 87, 196; and women, 196, 197, 198
Imperialism: The Great Tragedy of the Twentieth Century (*Isip-segi tae ch'amgŭk chegukchuŭi*; Pyŏn Yŏngman), 69
Imperialism, the Highest Stage of Capitalism (Lenin), 66–67
In Search of an Epitaph (*Pimyŏng ŭl ch'ajasŏ*; Bok Geo-il), 10, 250, 253–67, 269n21
In the Realm of the Senses (film; L'empire des Sens, Ai No Corrida; Oshima Nagisa), 225, 242n10
Inagaki Saburo, 109
Inch'ŏn Workers' Literary Club, 133, 143
India, 67, 87
individualism, 37, 108, 145, 232
Indonesia, 75, 85, 87, 88, 284
industrial missions (*sanŏpsŏnkyo*), 86, 92–93, 97

industrialization: capitalist, 68, 79; and church missions, 92–93; and class, 86, 277; and democratization, 47, 48; and ero films, 224, 227, 236; European, 68, 69; and Korean women, 203–4; and political tours, 96; rightist historiography on, 53, 54, 56; and rural migrants, 227; and science fiction, 254; and women workers, 55, 236–37
informatization (*chŏngbohwa*), 35
Insooni, 209–10, 211, 212, 216
intellectuals: activist, 1, 2, 34–35, 50, 51; at center vs. periphery, 113; and democratization, 5, 142–43; and ethnonationalism, 278; First World, 113; and imperialism, 6, 263–64; Japanese, 35, 105, 106–9, 122n7; leftist, 105, 106–9, 119, 122n7, 122n8, 283–84, 286; in leftist historiography, 50, 51; and literature, 138–40, 144, 179, 186, 187, 253; and *minjung* art, 105, 106–7, 109, 119; and *minjung* culture, 150, 250; and modernity, 7, 65, 68–69, 70, 79–82; and North Korea, 72–73; on popular culture, 152; rightist, 4, 18; and sexual revolution, 225; and Third World, 7, 69, 107, 113, 198, 199–202, 204–5, 214; and U.S. dominance, 71–72; and U.S.S.R., 74; and victimhood, 78–79; women, 171, 179; and women, 170, 174, 176, 179, 186, 187, 199–202, 204–5, 214; and workers, 129, 130, 131, 138–40, 143, 146n2, 285; and workers' literary clubs, 134–37, 144–45. See also historiography
international relations: and democratization, 7–8, 48, 88, 119; and film, 224–26, 241; and labor movement, 66, 74; and *minjung* art, 105–10, 121n2, 122n3; and racism, 201; and science fiction, 254, 267; and students, 85–100; and travel restrictions, 105–6, 119; and women's movement, 174, 197. See also Third World; *particular countries*
International Youth Festival (Pyongyang; 1989), 7
Interpreting the French Revolution (*Penser la Révolution française*; Furet), 24

Into the Heat of the Night (film; *Pam ŭi yŏlgi sok ŭro*; Jang Gil-su), 237
Irish, oppression of, 201
Itō Hirubumi, 257, 258

JAALA (Japan, Afro-Asian, Latin American Artists' Association), 105–10, 121n2, 122n3
Jaeckin, Just, 226
Jang Gil-su, 237
Jang Sun-woo, 230–31, 236
Japan: colonial occupation by, 69, 73, 199, 256, 264, 283; defeat of, 71; exchange students in, 87; film in, 225, 226, 231, 242n7; and forced prostitution, 179; imperialism of, 72, 80, 122n3, 201, 252, 256–59, 263, 264, 270n24, 278, 279; intellectuals in, 35, 105, 106–9, 122n7; Korean liberation from, 36, 66; and Korean science fiction, 256, 257, 261, 263, 265, 267; Koreans living in, 107, 108, 122nn7–8; militarism of, 69, 106, 201; and *minjung* art, 7, 105–10, 117, 119, 284; and *minjung* culture, 251; music of, 165n19; and New Right, 35, 36; political dissent in, 106, 107–8; and Third World literature, 77, 200; U.S. relations with, 68, 120; wars of, 68, 69, 71
Japan Foundation, 122n3
Japanese language, 225, 241n5
Jeong In-yeob, 226
Jones, Grace, 197
Joo Jinsook, 232, 233
Joongang Ilbo (*Central Daily*), 28, 40n42, 112
Ju Dou (film; Zhang Yimou), 226
Juche. See *chuch'e sasang*
Juch'e sasang (North Korean self-reliance doctrine), 39n12, 72–73, 94, 196, 251; followers of (*chusap'a*), 18, 34
June Declaration (1987), 49
Jung Boksu, 112
Jung Jin-woo, 234, 238

Kang Chunman, 33
Kang Jae-kyu, 254
Kang Kyŏngdae, 143

Kang Sin-jae, 282
Kang Sŏk-kyŏng, 169, 181, 183, 197, 198, 205–6, 215
Kang Taesŏn, 197, 198, 208, 209, 214, 215
KAPF (Korea Artista Proleta Federatio), 66
Karma (film; *Ŏp*; Lee Doo-yong), 238
Kasdan, Lawrence, 226
Katsiaficas, George, 39n6
Kim Bongjun, 110, 114, 123n15
Kim Boyoung, 267
Kim Chaeik, 57
Kim Chinhong, 34
Kim Chinmyŏng, 31
Kim Chinsuk, 137, 138
Kim Chin-yop, 94
Kim Chŏnghwan, 138
Kim Chŏnghyŏn, 32
Kim Chŏngnyŏm, 28
Kim Chunbŏm, 247–48, 253, 265–66
Kim Dae Jung, 18, 19, 21, 40n32, 49, 50; in conservative literature, 32, 33; and New Right, 21–22, 36
Kim Hansu, 142
Kim Ho-sun, 227, 230, 242n19
Kim Hŭisuk, 178
Kim Hyŏngsik, 141
Kim Ilsung, 72
Kim Jae-Yong, 6–7, 284
Kim Jung-Heun, 105–6, 110
Kim Ki-young, 227, 242n18
Kim Minki, 156, 159, 160
Kim Myŏngin, 139, 202
Kim Namju, 143
Kim Sejin, 96, 100n27
Kim Yangsŏn, 178
Kim Yŏnghwan, 34
Kim Yŏngok, 187
Kim Yongtae, 114
Kim Young Sam, 25, 26, 27, 49, 50, 120, 143
Kkottaji (band), 163
Ko Chŏnghŭi, 180, 181, 183, 189n9
Ko Misuk, 18
Ko Yŏngnam, 236
kŏlgae kŭrim (banner painting), 115–19,
123n25; collective production of, 115–16, 117–18
Koo Hagen, 11
Korea Workers' Compensation and Welfare Service, 133
Korean Broadcasting System (KBS), 133
Korean Central Intelligence Agency (KCIA), 94, 96
Korean Confederation of Trade Unions (Minju Nochʻong), 93
Korean Democracy Foundation, 159
Korean Union of Women's Associations (Han'guk yŏsŏng tanchʻe yŏnhap), 3
Korean War, 114, 179, 252, 278; and DMZ, 20, 100n27, 117; and modernity, 70, 72, 74; and New Right, 21, 54
K-pop, 285
K-Pop Star (TV show), 216
KSCF (Korean Student Christian Federation; Hang'uk kidok haksaenghoe chʻong yŏnmaeng), 85, 88, 93–96
Kuro Solidarity Strike (1985), 3, 139, 141
Kuro Workers' Literary Club, 133, 134, 141, 143, 144
Kwak Ji-kyoon, 230
Kwangju Diary: Beyond Death and the Darkness of Age (*Chugŭm ŭl nŏmŏ, sidae ŭi ŏdum ŭl nŏmŏ*), 11n5
Kwangju Uprising (1980), 96, 108, 171; censorship of, 2, 11n5, 250; in leftist vs. rightist historiography, 47, 48, 49, 51, 55, 56; in literature, 139, 248–49, 263, 283; and New Right, 36; and U.S., 71–73, 79, 196, 201, 250; and workers' literary clubs, 131, 133, 137, 139
Kwon, Heonik, 20
Kwŏn Insuk, 3, 170, 185–86
Kyogwasŏ Porŏm association, 52

labor movement: culture of, 5, 8, 129–65; and demonstrations, 57, 140, 178; and economic development, 286n7; international, 66, 74, 91; and students, 86, 87, 96, 143, 169–70; and women, 169–70, 172, 176–79. See also workers; workers' literary clubs

Lady Chatterley's Lover (film; Jaeckin), 226
Lai Tai Han (children of Korean fathers and Vietnamese mothers), 79
Last Tango in Paris (film; Bertolucci), 225
Latin America, 80
Lavender, Stephen, 93
Leaving the Thick Footprints of Work Shoes (*Chagŏphwa kulgŭn chaguk ŭl jjgŭmyŏ*), 141
Lebanon, 106
Lee, Michelle, 216
Lee, Namhee, 1, 5–6, 51, 178, 196, 284
Lee Doo-yong, 234, 235, 238
Lee Jang-ho, 227, 234
Lee, Jin-kyung, 10, 202, 206, 207, 237
Lee Jonggu, 110
Lee Jong-uk, 202
Lee Kuan Yew, 88
Lee Sangkyung, 173
Lee Simyŏng, 270n24
Lee Won-se, 237
Lenin, Vladimir, 24, 66
Let Hanyŏl Live Again (banner; Choe Byŏngsu), 110–11, 115, 121
Letters from South Korea (T. K.), 98
Liberty Union (Chayujuŭi yŏndae), 34, 35
Life and Death of a Young Worker: The Critical Biography of Chŏn T'aeil (*Ŏnŭ chŏngnyŏn nodongja ŭi sam kwa chugŭm: Chŏn T'aeil p'yŏngjŏn*), 129, 135, 137, 138
Lim Chul-Woo, 283
Lim Oksang, 105, 110, 112, 114
Lim Sukyung, 7, 86, 94, 95, 117, 119, 123n27
Lippard, Lucy, 112, 113, 114, 119
literacy, 8, 130, 131, 135, 137, 144, 145
literature: African, 75, 77, 82, 105–10, 121n2, 122n3; African-American, 201–2; antiwar, 79; autobiography in, 12n11; from below, 131, 178; bourgeois, 142, 143; camptown prostitution, 9; and class, 139, 142, 179, 186, 187, 253, 268, 282–83, 284; Cold War in, 77, 196; conservative, 32, 33; engaged vs. pure, 139, 281–84; and feminism, 187, 282–83; film adaptations of, 188n4, 269n14; and globalization, 80–82; and intellectuals, 138–40, 144, 179, 186, 187, 253; of Kwangju Uprising, 139, 248–49, 263, 283; labor/workers' (*nodong/kŭlloja munhak*), 74, 129–46, 178; leftist nationalist (*minjung munhak*), 275, 281–84, 285; marginalized, 277; and *minjung* song, 149; modern Chinese, 66; as "monumental" history, 30; national (*kungmin munhak*; *minjok munhak*), 30, 65–67, 179, 196; nationalist (*minjokchuŭi*), 66; national-popular (*minjung munhak*), 66; non-Western global, 80–82; and the past, 29; and politics, 33, 275–76, 281–84; vs. popular culture, 285; proletarian, 66, 80; realist, 249, 252–53, 265, 267; speculative, 253, 285; Third World, 74–75, 77, 200–201; and Vietnam War, 9, 202–5, 215; women's (*yŏsŏng/yŏryu munhak*), 9, 170–71, 177–79, 186–87, 188n9, 282–83; women's liberation (*yŏsŏng haebang munhak*), 9, 169–91
Little Chicago (*Lit'ŭl Sik'ago*; Chŏng Han-a), 216
London Recruits, 91
Lonely Room (*Oettan pang*; Shin Kyung-sook), 135
Louie, Miriam Ching Yoon, 169
Louis, Joe, 195
Lover from Palestine, A (Darwish), 202
Lukács, Georg, 253
Lyne, Adrian, 226

Madame Aema (film; *Aema Puin*; Jeong In-yeob), 226, 228, 229, 233, 235, 236
Making of Minjung, The (Namhee Lee), 51
Man in the High Castle, The (Dick), 256, 260, 261–62
Man with Color, A (film), 236
Manchuria, 74, 257, 261
Mandela, Nelson, 91
Man's Road, A (*In'gan ŭi kil*; Yi Inhwa), 30, 32
Mansudae Art Studio (North Korea), 115
March First Movement (1919), 50
Mariátegui, José Carlos, 69

Martí, José, 69
Marxism, 2, 19, 22, 39n6, 251, 277, 280; and counterdevelopmentalism, 232; in leftist vs. rightist historiography, 34, 53, 54, 56, 59, 60n5; in translation, 96; and women's movement, 173, 174, 178; and workers' literary clubs, 131
Medal and Yoke (*Hunjang kwa kulle*; Yi Wŏn'gyu), 79
media: conservative, 6, 27–28; and discontinuity, 18; mainstream, 151, 153, 161, 163; new, 5; newspapers, 21, 27–28, 33, 34, 40n42, 112; and Park Chung Hee syndrome, 27–33; television, 179, 216, 226, 227, 229, 267; U.S., 197; and women's movement, 171–72, 180
memoirs, 135, 141, 142, 144, 178
Metal Brain 109 (*manhwa*; *Kigye chŏnsa 109*; Kim Chunbŏm), 247–49, 253, 265–66, 267, 268n1
Mexican mural art, 119
middle class: housewifization of, 237; in leftist vs. rightist historiography, 51, 55, 56; and literature, 139; and political travel, 87, 97; and sexual revolution, 225; and Third World women, 200, 203, 208, 216; and U.S. popular culture, 197; and women's movement, 176–77, 185
Mies, Maria, 231
militarism: American, 237; and antiwar literature, 79; and ero films, 224, 234; and ethnonationalism, 279; and industrialization, 224; Japanese, 69, 106, 201
Miller, Owen, 37
Min Jeongki, 105
Min Joong Art: A New Cultural Movement from Korea (exhibition; Artists Space, New York; 1988), 110–14
Min Joong Art: New Movement of Political Art from Korea (exhibition; Toronto and Brooklyn; 1987), 112
minjok. See ethnonation
Minjok Hakkyo (the National School), 117
minjung (the people, the masses): development of term for, 1–2; vs. *simin*, 2, 18;

vs. socialist (*sahoejuŭi*), 100n28; vs. *taejung*, 151
Minjung Cultural Movement (Minjung munhwa undong hyŏbŭihoe), 11n3
Minjung Culture and the Third World (*Minjung munhwa wa che-3 segye*), 77
Minmihyŏp (Minjok misul hyŏpŭihoe; Association of Korean People's Art), 104, 107, 123n26
Minor Injury (art gallery; Brooklyn, New York), 112
Mist Whispers Like Women (film), 236
modernity: alternative, 65–83; anti-imperialist, 7, 65, 67, 70, 79–82, 151; colonial/imperialist, 66, 67–70, 74, 77; and discrediting of revolutions, 22–23; and Korean War, 70, 72, 74; progression and regression in, 231; and science fiction, 254; Western, 67–70, 106; and women, 169, 176, 196
modernization: and ero film, 10, 236, 238, 241; in leftist vs. rightist historiography, 37, 54, 56; and *minjung*, 104
modŏnisŭt'ŭ (modernist) art, 107
Moktong district (Seoul), 3
mook (magazine-book), 180, 186, 190n24
Moon, Katharine, 205
Moon, Seungsook, 55
Morrison, Toni, 202
Most Beautiful Wandering, A (Gong Ji-young), 169
"Mother and the Zelkova Tree" (Nŭt'inamu wa ŏmŏni; Mun Sunt'ae), 216
"Mrs. Yuli" (Yulidaek; Yu Sich'un), 178
Mulberry (film; *Ppong*; Lee Doo-yong), 235
multiculturalism, 110, 120, 216, 285
Mulvey, Laura, 209
Mun Chino, 163
Mun Ikhwan, 117
Mun Kyuhyŏn, 119
Mun Pusik, 73
Mun Sunt'ae, 216
Munsa (Literature and society; journal), 142

music: censorship of, 8, 151, 155, 160, 161, 162–63; and democratization, 149–50, 155, 161–62; folk, 153, 159, 160–61, 165n20; gospel, 159; independent (*indi*), 154, 163–64; Japanese, 165n19; mainstream, 149, 156–58; popular (*taejung ŭmak*), 8, 150–58, 163; punk, 153, 161; reggae, 161; rock, 154, 158, 161, 165n22; standardization of, 156–57; and technology, 159, 160–61; traditional Korean, 159, 161; *trotto* (*t'ŭrotŭ*), 159, 161, 165n19; Western, 151, 153, 158, 161, 165n20; and youth culture, 158

music, *minjung* (*minjung kayo*), 8, 149–65, 284; audience for, 155, 158–59, 162; decline of, 153, 156; ideology in, 149, 151, 155; lyrics of, 149, 154, 159, 161; and music industry, 155, 156–58; musical quality of, 155, 159–61; and popular music, 150–55; production and distribution of, 157–58, 161–62; as subculture, 152–54; and technology, 155–56

"My Country" (Choguk; Sin Tongyŏp), 78

National Association of Workers' Literary Clubs (Chŏn'guk nodongja munhakhoe yŏnhap), 133
National Labor Council, 141
National Security Law (NSL), 19, 117, 123n27
National Union of Students (Chŏndaehyŏp), 94
nationalism: and anti-Americanism, 196; anti-imperialist, 69, 79, 151; and counterdevelopmentalism, 232; in *Epitaph*, 263, 265; and ero films, 223–24, 235–36, 240, 241; and ethnonationalsm, 2, 6, 9, 10, 24, 103, 204, 214, 228, 275, 277–82, 284; leftist, 275, 277, 286n1; *minjung*, 199–202, 223–24, 251; and New Right, 36, 52; and nuclear weapons, 32; official state, 66; and Park Chung Hee, 28, 30; patriarchal, 238, 270n29; and race, 213, 215; and Third World, 75, 199–202, 204, 214, 215; and women, 179, 187, 199–202, 204, 215, 241; and worker's literature, 140

nationalism, European, 69
nationalism, Japanese, 106
négritude movement, 201
neoliberalism, 18, 82; and capitalism, 20, 23; in historiography, 37, 50, 51, 55, 57, 59; and *minjung* art, 104, 120; of New Right, 22, 35, 36–37; and race, 198, 216; triumphalist, 6, 22, 23, 36, 37; and workers, 130, 145
New Daily (Internet newspaper), 34
New Right, 286; and anticommunism, 21–22; historiography of, 52–54, 56–57; and neoliberalism, 22, 35, 36–37; and Park Chung Hee, 25, 37, 52; triumphalism of, 18, 19, 21–23, 34–37, 52–53; in West Germany, 24
New Right Textbook Forum, 35
New York, 117, 120
New Zealand, 85
newspapers, 27–28, 31, 33, 34, 40n42, 112
Nietzsche, Friedrich, 29, 38
"Night and the Cradle" (Pam ŭi yoram; Kang Sŏk-kyŏng), 206
night schools (*nodong yahak*), 133, 135, 137
Nikkatsu studio, 225
9 1/2 Weeks (film; Lyne), 226
Nineteen Eighty-Four (Orwell), 261
No Chinsu, 268n1
Nolte, Ernest, 24
Nora, Pierre, 17
Norae (*Song*; magazine), 151
Nordpolitik policy, 55
North Korea, 99, 284; and anticommunism, 20–21; and Australia, 94; Black Panthers in, 200; and Cold War, 6, 252; division from, 36, 103; history of, 82n13; and intellectuals, 72–73; and leftists, 20, 55; *minjung* art in, 7, 114–19, 123n30; and *minjung* culture, 251; and New Right, 21, 25, 34, 36, 37, 52–55; reunification with, 35, 36, 50, 53, 94, 96, 114–15, 131, 140, 159, 173; self-reliance doctrine (*chuch'e sasang*) of, 18, 34, 39n12, 72–73, 94, 196, 251; and student exchanges, 86, 87, 88; sympathizers with partisans (*ppalch'isan*) of, 72; and U.S., 73; and

U.S.S.R., 74; World Festival of Youth and Students in, 7, 88–89, 94, 118

O Yun, 105, 110, 112, 119
Okakura Tenshin, 106
Olympics (Seoul; 1988), 54, 56, 119, 123n27, 237, 257
On the Eve of the Uprising (*Mansejŏn*; Yŏm Sangsŏp), 263–64
orientalism, 79, 202, 238, 240
Origins of Family, Private Property, and the State, The (Engels), 174
Orwell, George, 261, 262, 270n27
Oshima Nagisa, 225, 242n10
Other Cold War, The (Heonik Kwon), 20
Ŏudong (film; Lee Jang-ho), 235, 238, 239

Pacific War. *See* World War II
Pae Inch'ŏl, 195
Paek Musan, 144
Paekcha, 163
"Pagoda" (T'ap; Hwang Sok-young), 78
Paik Nak-chung, 198, 200, 201, 202, 204, 214
Pak Chongch'ŏl, 2, 49, 270n25
Pak Haeun, 142
Pak Kwangsu, 4
Pak Nohae, 4, 138, 139, 144, 178, 190n42
Pak Wansŏ, 9, 171, 179, 180, 181, 183
Palestine, 106, 202, 205
Palmer, Samuel, 75
pan-Asianism, 69, 106
Pang Hyŏnsŏk, 178
Park, Carey, 117, 118
Park Buldong, 112
Park Chung Hee, 1, 11, 251, 275; assassination of, 2, 250; and dissidents, 280, 281; and economic development, 28, 31, 32, 37, 40n42, 286n7; and ethnonationalism, 279; and film industry, 227; in leftist vs. rightist historiography, 48, 50, 52; and nationalism, 28, 30; and New Right, 37, 39, 52; and science fiction, 32, 260; and U.S., 31, 32, 71; and Vietnam War, 78; and women workers, 243n43
Park Chung Hee syndrome, 6, 25–33, 34
Park Chung Hee (Cho Kapche), 28

Park Geun Hye, 10–11, 26
Park Il-Joon, 210
Park Jong-ho, 226
Park Kwanhyŏn, 133
Park Seung Hyun, 234
Parrot Cries with Its Body (film; *Aengmusae mom ŭro urŏtta*; Jung Jin-woo), 234, 243n39
partisans (*ppalch'isan*), 72, 252
Pasolini, Pier Paolo, 225
patriarchy: and black women, 198, 215; and capitalism, 174; and Confucianism, 32; and domestic violence, 186; and ero film, 231, 233, 234, 236, 238, 240; and nationalism, 238, 270n29; and Third World, 197, 202; and women's literature, 180, 181, 182
Pax Americana, 70–73
p'Bitek, Okot, 202
Pedagogy of the Oppressed (Freire), 137
Philippines, 70, 71, 98, 284; art from, 106, 108; people's revolution in, 56; student exchanges with, 85, 88
Phillips, Jean, 97–98, 100n30
Poland, 257
political tourism, 87, 90, 91, 96–98
politics: and aesthetics, 275–86; and class, 276–78, 285; vs. cultural themes, 4–5; and ero film, 229, 231, 240; and ethnonation, 281; and history, 262, 265; of identity, 120, 170, 276–78, 281, 285; Korean terms for, 278; and literature, 33, 275–76, 281–84; and popular culture, 267, 277, 283; and sexual revolution, 224–25; and student exchanges, 88
Polizen (web magazine), 34
popular culture: vs. activist culture, 9, 151–52; and black women, 215; and ero film, 231, 240; and hegemonic culture, 152, 154; vs. high literature, 285; homogenization of, 157; and *minjung* culture, 9, 143, 150, 152, 249, 267; and politics, 267, 277, 283; and race, 210; and science fiction, 254, 266; and social memory, 5–6, 17; U.S., 197, 231, 254
Popular Education in South Korea (*Han'guk minjung kyoyungnon*; Han Wansang), 137

positivism, 53, 54, 252
Power of the Twenties, The (exhibition; 1985), 104, 114
Prague Spring, 89–90
Proletarian Nights (Rancière), 131, 146n2
prostitution: and black soldiers, 206–7; camptown, 9, 205–8; in ero film, 227, 228, 235, 236; and ethnonationalism, 279; military, 9, 179, 198, 205–8; sex tourism (*kisaeng kwan'gwang*), 237, 243n44; in Vietnam, 204
Prostitution (film; *Maech'un*; You Jinsun), 235, 236
Protestant churches, 86, 93
Puchŏn Literary Club, 140–41
Pyŏn Yŏngman, 69, 70–71
Pyongyang Times, 114, 115, 118
Pyongyang World Festival of Youth and Students, 177

Queen Bee (film; *Yŏwangbŏl*; Lee Won-se), 237

race: and class, 199, 281, 284; and ethnonationalism, 10, 279, 280, 281, 284; and identity politics, 276–78; and imperialism, 201, 204, 213; and nationalism, 213, 215; and neoliberalism, 198, 216; people of mixed, 79, 198, 199, 201, 205, 210, 216; and popular culture, 285; and sexuality, 212–13
racism: against Amerasian children, 210, 216; and imperialism, 201, 204, 263; Korean, 199–202, 215; and Third World alliance, 214–15; U.S., 23, 90, 205
Rancière, Jacques, 122n7, 131, 146n2, 275–76, 278
Rastafarian movement, 153
Reagan, Ronald, 54
Reality and Utterance (Hyŏnsil kwa parŏn; art collective), 113
Red Sorghum (film; Zhang Yimou), 226
revolutions: discrediting of, 22–25; historiography of, 18, 24; political and sexual, 224–25
Rhee, Syngman, 37, 39, 50, 72, 275, 280, 286n7; and ethnonationalism, 278, 279

Robeson, Paul, 90–92, 99n15
Roh Moo Hyun, 18, 19, 40n32, 50; and New Right, 21–22, 36
Roh Tae Woo, 1, 3, 49, 50, 54–55, 85, 112, 275
Room in the Woods, A (*Sup sok ŭi pang*; Kang Sŏk-kyŏng), 169, 206
Rose of Sharon Has Blossomed (*Mugunghwa kkoch'i p'iŏssŭmnida*; Kim Chinmyŏng), 31
Rüsen, Jörn, 38
Russia, 68, 73. *See also* Soviet Union
Russian Revolution (1917), 23–24
Russo-Japanese War (1904), 68, 69
Ryōma Goes His Way (Shiba Ryōtarō), 30, 41n54

Sa Bangji (film; *Sa Bangji*; Song Kyungshik), 238
"Sacred Life, A" (Kŏrukhan saengae; Hyŏn Kiyŏng), 72
Sakamoto Ryōma, 30
Salò, or 120 Days of Sodom (film; Pasolini), 225
Salt Flower Tree (*Sogŭm kkot namu*; Kim Chinsuk), 137
Samchŏng Re-education Camp (Samchŏng kyoyuktae), 2, 48, 249
samjŏ hohwang (three lows), 56
Sapphic primitivism, 208
Sarkozy, Nicolas, 23
"Sawing the Blanket" (Ibul ŭl kkoemaemyŏnsŏ; Pak Nohae), 190n42
Schwarzenegger, Arnold, 248
science fiction, 247–70; censorship of, 260–61, 267, 269n17; and democratization, 10, 249, 254, 265–68; in film, 254, 267–68; and Japan, 256, 257, 261, 263, 265, 267; *minjung*, 254, 265–68, 266, 267; and Park Chung Hee, 32, 260; political legitimacy of, 266–67; Western, 254–56, 265, 266
SCMs (Student Christian Movements), 86, 87–88, 96, 98
Scott, Ridley, 248
Seeger, Pete, 159
Seekers of Song (Norae rŭl ch'annŭn

saramdŭl; musical collective), 151–52, 160, 162, 164n5
Senghor, Léopold Sédar, 200, 201
Seo Taiji, 153–54, 163
Seoul Rainbow (film; *Sŏul mujigae*; Kim Ho-sun), 230, 235
sexuality: and black men, 205; of black women, 198, 206, 207–8; and identity politics, 276–78, 281, 285; Japanese terms for, 225, 241n5; and male voyeurism, 243n27; and politics, 281, 283, 284; and primitivism, 208, 211; and race, 212–13; revolution in, 224–25; of women, 197, 198, 206–8, 213–14, 216, 233. *See also* film, erotic; homosexuality; prostitution
Shadow of Arms (*Mugi ŭi kŭnŭl*; Hwang Sok-young), 79
Shiba Ryōtarō, 30, 41n54
Shin Eun-mi, 21, 39n11
Shin Kyung-sook, 135, 187
Shin nihon bungaku (New Japanese literature; journal), 107
Shout of a Little Stone (*Ŏnŭ tolmaengi ŭi oech'im*; Yu Tong'u), 129, 134–35
Sidae chŏngsin (*Geist*; journal), 34
Silch'ŏn munhak (Letters in action; journal), 80
Sim Ching'yŏng, 187
Sim Sangjŏng, 133
simin (citizen), 1–2, 18
Sin Ch'aeho, 1, 68, 69, 74, 201
Sin Chiho, 34, 35, 40n32
Sin Ilsuk, 253
Sin Kihwal, 253, 266
Sin Kyŏngnim, 83n18
Sin Tongyŏp, 78
Singapore, 75, 88
Sino-Japanese War (1894), 68
Slave of Love (film; *Sarang ŭi noye*; Ko Yŏngnam), 236
Slaves (film; *Sano*; Um Jong-sun), 238
Slotkin, Richard, 26
Sŏ Yusŏk, 159
social composition debate (*sahoe kusŏngch'e nonjaeng*), 50, 173

"Social Function of African Literature" (Lee Jong-uk), 202
social memory, 17–41; and New Right, 18–19; official and popular, 5–6, 17; and Park Chung Hee syndrome, 25–27; of sixties, 23
socialism, 22, 100n28, 121, 131; "actually existing," 23; international, 72, 73, 74, 75; and national literature, 65–67
socialist realism, 142
Society of Women's Historical Studies (Yŏsŏngsa yŏn'guhoe), 173–74
Sŏk Chŏngnam, 135, 136
solidarity: cosmopolitan, 99; horizontal, 7, 87, 90
Son Pyŏnghwi, 163
Son So-hŭi, 282
Song Changsup, 105
Song Kyŏngdong, 143
Song Kyung-shik, 238
Song of Lawino (poem; p'Bitek), 202
Song Yŏngsu, 236
Sōren (pro-North Korea *zainichi* group), 105
Soviet Union (U.S.S.R.), 6, 24, 79, 80, 90; collapse of, 23, 36, 50–51, 77; in *Epitaph*, 257, 261; and national literature, 66–67; and PRC, 77; and Third World, 67, 73–78; World Festival of Youth and Students in, 89
Sparrow, Jeff, 91
Spinning the Tales of Cruelty toward Women (film; Lee Doo-yong), 234, 238, 243n39
Spit on My Grave (*Nae mudŏm e ch'im ŭl paet'ŏra*; Cho Kapche), 28–29
Sri Lanka, 85, 87, 88, 284
Stalin, Joseph, 89
"Status and Trend of Minjung Songs in Korean Music Culture" (Han'guk norae munhwa sok esŏŭi minjung kayo ŭi wisang kwa hŭrŭm; Yi Yŏngmi), 152–53, 154
Story of O (film; Jaeckin), 226
students: April 19 (1960) uprising of, 71; and ero film, 229; female college (*hakch'ul*), 169–70; international

students (*continued*)
exchanges of, 7, 85–100; and labor movement, 86, 87, 143, 169–70; in leftist historiography, 50, 51; and *minjung* culture, 250; and *minjung* song, 149, 158, 160, 161; and night schools, 133; and sexual revolution, 225; violence against, 184, 185; and women's movement, 132, 139, 170, 171, 173, 174, 176, 177, 180; and workers' literary clubs, 8, 131, 137, 145
Sung Neungkyung, 112
Sung Wan-kyung, 113, 114, 119, 121, 123n20
Sunshine Policy, 21, 32
Surrogate Woman (film; Im Sang-soo), 234, 235, 238

Taebaek Mountains (*T'aebaek sanmaek*; Cho Chŏngnae), 4, 72, 252, 269n14
Taehwa (Dialogue; magazine), 134
Taft, William Howard, 70
Tagore, Rabindranath, 69, 80, 200
Taiwan, 75, 85, 88, 98, 257, 261, 284
tansaekhwa (South Korean monochrome paintings), 122n6
technology, 5; cassette, 155, 156, 164n13; CD, 156; and film, 234, 253–54; and music, 155–56, 159, 160–61; and science fiction, 254
television, 179, 216, 226, 227, 229, 267
Terminator, The (film; Cameron), 248, 256
textbook controversy, 6, 18, 35–36, 37, 38, 52
Thailand, 106, 108
That Which Falls Has Wings (film; *Ch'urak hanŭn kŏt ŭn nalgae ka itta*; Jang Gil-su), 237
theater, 4, 12n8, 149. See also *Tropical Fish*
Theory of Third World Literature, A (*Che-3 segye munhangnon*), 77
Third World: art from, 106; and Cold War, 75, 77, 80; and feminism, 197; and intellectuals, 7, 69, 107, 113, 198, 199–202, 204–5, 214; literature of, 7, 74–75, 77, 200–201; *minjung* alliance with, 9, 195–98; national liberation movements in, 75, 77; and nationalism, 75, 199–202, 204, 214, 215; nonalignment movement in, 74–75, 284; nostalgia for, 202–5; transnational alliance with, 6, 75, 196, 197, 204, 215, 284; and U.S.S.R., 67, 73–78; women of, 9, 196, 199–205, 208, 214, 215–16
"Third World and *Minjung* Literature, The" (Paik Nak-chung), 200–201
"Third World and Us" (JAALA's exhibitions), 106, 110
Three Monsters of the World (*Segye sam koemul*; Pyŏn Yŏngman), 69
3S policy, 228, 229, 232, 234
386 generation, 21, 30, 39n13, 51, 60n8, 188n4
Tiananmen Square demonstrations (1989), 98
Ticket (film; *T'ik'et*; Im Kwon-taek), 236
TK (Taegu-Kyŏngsang) military group, 48, 49
Tokyo Metropolitan Museum of Art, 105, 106, 109
Tonghak Uprisings (1894), 50
torture, 259, 260, 270n25
transnationalism, 5, 65–124; of *minjung* art, 7, 104, 106, 108, 110–14, 117, 119, 284; and political tourism, 86, 97; and Third World alliance, 6, 75, 196, 197, 204, 215, 284; and workers, 198, 280–81
travel, political, 85–100; in Cold War, 7, 86–87, 89, 90, 91; in "free world," 90–92; and middle class, 87, 97; restrictions on, 105–6, 119
Treaty of Versailles (1919), 71, 73
Tropical Fish (play; *Yŏldaeŏ*; Ch'a Pŏmsŏk), 198, 199–200, 203, 216; film adaptation of, 208–9, 211
Tto hana ŭi munhwa (*Another Culture*; feminist group and journal), 171, 174–76, 179–83, 186
Turŏng (art collective), 123n25
2009 Lost Memories (film; Lee Simyŏng), 270n24
Typhoon (*T'aep'ung*; Choi In-hun), 256

Uganda, 202, 205
Um Hyuk, 112, 113

Index | 309

Under the Blue Moon (*P'aran tal arae*; Bok Geo-il), 255
Understanding the Third World (*Che-3 segye ŭi ihae*; Palmer), 75, 76
United States (U.S.): anticommunism in, 71, 72, 78; black soldiers of, 197–98; civil rights movement in, 23, 93, 201; in Cold War, 31, 72–73, 107; and Cuba, 73; discrediting 1968 in, 23; identity politics in, 281; imperialism of, 6, 70–73, 140, 173, 251, 252, 263, 266, 278, 283; and Japan, 68, 120; and Kwangju Uprising, 71–73, 79, 196, 201, 250; in leftist vs. rightist historiography, 54, 55, 56–57, 58, 60n5; military occupation by, 9, 179, 197–98, 205–8, 236; and *minjung* art, 7, 110–14, 117, 119, 284; and North Korea, 73; opposition to, 196, 205, 235; and Park Chung Hee, 31, 32, 71, 251; popular culture in, 197, 231, 254; racism in, 23, 90, 205; in Russo-Japanese War, 68; and science fiction, 254, 256, 257, 261, 263, 265, 266; and South Korean prostitution, 179, 237, 279; South Korean relations with, 3, 21, 70–73, 86; and Third World, 75; and Vietnam War, 71, 78–79, 225; worker missions in, 93; and worker's literature, 140
Uniting Church in Australia, 86, 93, 94, 97
Urban Industrial Missions (UIM; South Korea), 86, 93, 97
Uses of Literacy, The (Hoggart), 131, 146n2

Vietnam, 200; women in, 79, 198, 202–3, 204, 215
Vietnam War, 20, 89; in literature, 9, 198, 202–5, 215; profits from, 203, 204; protests against, 107, 225; South Korean troops in, 54, 202–5, 279; subimperialism in, 78–79, 215; U.S. in, 71, 78–79, 225
Voice of the Governor-General (*Ch'ongdok ŭi sori*; Choi In-hun), 256
Voltaire, 68

Walker, Alice, 202
Wanderer of History (*Yŏksa sok ŭi nagŭne*; Bok Geo-il), 255, 270n29

"war of position," 27
Warsaw Pact, 89
Washington Naval Conference (1922), 71
Water World (film; *Mul ŭi nara*; Yu Yŏngjin), 236
WEC (Women's Equality Council; Yŏsŏng p'yŏnguhoe), 171–73
West, the: feminism in, 174, 181, 185, 196–97; film in, 225–28; imperialism of, 66, 69, 87, 196; modernity of, 67–70, 106; music of, 151, 153, 158, 161, 165n20; science fiction in, 254–56, 265, 266; and Third-World intellectuals, 69. *See also* Europe; *particular countries*
White Badge (*Hayan chŏnjaeng*; An Chŏnghyo), 79, 202–3, 204, 216
Whitney Biennial, 120
Wild Fire Night School (Tŭlbul yahak), 133
Williams, Linda, 225, 233
Williams, Raymond, 224
Wilson, Woodrow, 71
Winter Woman (film; *Kyŏul yŏja*; Kim Ho-sun), 242n19
Wolf's Curiosity Stole Pigeons (film; *Nŭktae ŭi hogisim i pidulgi rŭl humch'ŏtta*; Song Yŏngsu), 236
Woman in the Wall (film; *Pyŏk sok ŭi yŏja*; Park Jong-ho), 226
women: as activists, 7, 8–9, 169, 170–77, 180, 181, 186, 188; as allegories, 264, 283; and class, 170, 172, 174, 176–77, 179, 186, 187, 206, 208, 211, 216, 282–83; and democratization, 5, 9, 174, 177, 178, 180, 184–86; education of, 135, 139, 176; in ero films, 223, 233, 239; and ethnonation, 9, 10, 228, 279, 280; as factory girls (*kongsuni*), 137; films for (*yŏsŏng yŏnghwa*), 224; housewifization of, 231, 237; and identity politics, 281, 285; and imperialism, 196, 197, 198; and industrialization, 55, 203–4, 236–37; and intellectuals, 170, 174, 176, 179, 186, 187, 199–202, 204–5, 214; as intellectuals, 171, 179; and labor movement, 169–70, 172, 176–79; literature of, 9, 169–91, 282–83; as marriage migrants, 79, 198; mixed-

women (*continued*)
  race (*honhyŏl*), 198; and modernity, 169, 176, 196; and nationalism, 179, 187, 199–202, 204, 215, 241; and primitivism, 208, 211; sexuality of, 197, 198, 206–8, 213–14, 216, 233; Third World, 9, 196, 199–205, 208, 214, 215–16; Vietnamese, 79, 198, 202–3, 204, 215; violence against, 9, 185–86; as workers, 55, 169, 170, 236–37, 243n43; in workers' literary clubs, 135, 137, 140–41; as writers, 282–83. *See also* black women; prostitution
Women Workers' Congress (Yŏsŏng nodongja hoeŭi), 178
Women's Grand Cultural Festival (1984), 171
"Women's Liberation Literature" (April 1987 issue of *Tto hana ŭi munhwa*), 181–83
women's movement, 171–77; and capitalism, 174, 177, 185; German, 181; international, 174, 197; and Marxism, 173, 174, 178; and media, 171–72, 180; and middle class, 176–77, 185; and *minjung* movement, 176, 177–79; and students, 132, 139, 170, 171, 173, 174, 176, 177, 180; and workers, 170–71, 172, 174, 177, 178
women's studies, 171, 173, 174, 176, 189n23, 196–97
Wŏn Tongsŏk, 107, 123n15
workers: and activists, 143, 280, 281, 284–85; and anticommunism, 93, 131; culture of, 129–65; and democratization, 3, 5, 129, 130–31, 134, 137, 140; and ero film, 236–37; and ethnonationalism, 279, 280; and industrial missions, 86, 92–93, 97; and intellectuals, 129, 130, 131, 138–40, 143, 146n2, 285; leftists on, 51, 55, 283; literature of, 74, 129–46, 178; memoirs of, 135, 141, 142, 144; migrant, 10, 227, 279, 285; and *minjung* song, 8, 150, 153, 158, 161; model (*mobŏm kŭlloja*), 132; poetry of, 129, 138, 140–44; and sexual revolution, 225; students as, 169, 170; temporary, 281; transnational, 91, 198, 280–81; violence against, 185; women, 55, 169, 170, 236–37,

243n43; and women's literature, 179, 186; and women's movement, 170–71, 172, 174, 177, 178. *See also* labor movement
Workers' Cultural Festival (Kŭlloja Munhwa Yesulche), 133
workers' literary clubs, 129–46, 178, 284; class in, 131, 135, 137, 141, 144; decline of, 142–44, 145; examples of, 140–41; government-sponsored, 133, 135; growth of, 130–31; history of, 134–42; and Kwangju Uprising, 131, 133, 137, 139; and students, 8, 131, 137, 145; types of, 132–34
World Conference of the International Women's Year (Mexico City; 1975), 197
World Festival of Youth and Students, 88–90, 91, 117, 119, 123n27; delegates to, 93–94; as North Korean propaganda, 88–89, 94, 118
"World Literature" (Tagore), 80
World War I, 23, 80
World War II, 71, 93, 257, 258, 261
Wright, Richard, 200
WSCF (World Student Christian Federation), 87–90
WSCF Asia-Pacific, 88

X (film; *Eksŭ*; Hah Myung-joong), 237
X, Malcolm, 200

YADM (Youth Association for the Democratic Movement; Minjuhwa undong chŏngyŏn yŏnhap), 171
Yang Pyŏngjip, 159
Yellow (*Hwangsaeggin*; Yi Sangmun), 79, 204
Yeong-ja's Heydays (film; *Yŏng-ja ŭi chŏnsŏng sidae*; Kim Ho-sun), 227
Yi Chisang, 163
Yi Hanyŏl, 3, 110–12, 122n10
Yi Hyesuk, 183
Yi In-hwa, 30–31, 32
Yi Kyŏngja, 179, 183
Yi Mun-yol, 31, 32, 33, 283, 286n9
Yi Myŏngho, 178, 179
Yi Sangmun, 79, 204, 215

Yi Siyŏng, 143
Yi Wŏn'gyu, 79
Yi Yŏnghun, 34, 37, 53–54
Yi Yŏngmi, 152–53, 154
YMCA (Young Men's Christian Association), 87, 88–89, 95
Yŏm Sangsŏp, 74, 263
Yomiuri Independent (annual no-jury exhibition), 108
Yŏn Yŏngsŏk, 163
Yoon Soo-Il, 210
Yoon Yŏng-mo, 93, 97
Yŏsŏng (*Women*; journal), 173, 174
Yŏsŏng kwa sahoe (*Women and society*; journal), 189n19
Yŏsŏng p'yŏngu (journal), 172
Yŏsŏng ŭi chŏnhwa (women's hotline), 171
Yŏsŏng undong kwa munhak (Women's movement and literature; journal), 177, 180, 186
Young Christian Workers (South Korea), 93

Your Mother the Korean Whore (*Emi irŭm ŭn Chosenppi yŏtta*; Yun Chŏngmo), 179
Your Name Is Woman (film; *Nŏ ŭi irŭm ŭn yŏja*; Lee Hyung-pyo), 226
Yu Gina, 232
Yu Hyun-mok, 226
Yu Kŭnil, 34
Yu Sich'un, 178
Yu Tong'u, 129, 134–35
Yu Yŏngjin, 236
Yun Chŏngmo, 179, 283–84
Yun Sangwŏn, 133
Yun Sinae, 158
Yusin period (1972–79), 26, 48, 51, 53, 57
YWCA (Young Women's Christian Association), 87

zainichi (Koreans living in Japan), 107, 108, 122nn7–8
Zenkyoto movement (Japan), 35
Zhang Yimou, 226
Žižek, Slavoj, 19–20